# THE HILLARY DOCTRINE

# THE
# HILLARY
# DOCTRINE

*Sex & American Foreign Policy*

Valerie M. Hudson & Patricia Leidl

COLUMBIA UNIVERSITY PRESS
NEW YORK

Columbia University Press
*Publishers Since 1893*
New York   Chichester, West Sussex
cup.columbia.edu
Copyright © 2015 Valerie M. Hudson and Patricia Leidl
All rights reserved

Parts of chapter 2 are abridged from Valerie M. Hudson, Bonnie Ballif-Spanvill,
Mary Caprioli, and Chad Emmett, *Sex and World Peace*
(New York: Columbia University Press, 2012).

Library of Congress Cataloging-in-Publication Data
Hudson, Valerie M., 1958-
The Hillary doctrine : sex and American foreign policy /
Valerie M. Hudson and Patricia Leidl.
pages cm
Includes bibliographical references and index.
ISBN 978-0-231-16492-4 (cloth : alk. paper) — ISBN 978-0-231-53910-4 (e-book)
1. United States—Foreign relations. 2. United States—Politics and government.
3. Clinton, Hillary Rodham—Political and social views. 4. Women's rights.
5. Women and democracy. 6. Women—Social conditions.
7. Women—Government policy. 8. Sex role—Government policy.
9. International relations—Social aspects.
I. Leidl, Patricia II. Title.

E183.7.H84 2015
327.73—dc23

2014038206

Columbia University Press books are printed on permanent
and durable acid-free paper.
This book is printed on paper with recycled content.
Printed in the United States of America
c 10 9 8 7 6 5 4 3 2 1

Jacket Design: Jordan Wannemacher
Jacket Image: ©AP Images

*I dedicate this book to my daughters and my sons;*
*attend to the coal mine, and the canaries will be fine.*
*(Jacob 2:31–35)*

**Valerie M. Hudson**

*In memory of my mother, Joan, and twin brother, Petey, who,*
*although no longer in this physical world, are with me every single day.*

**Patricia Leidl**

# CONTENTS

★ ★ ★

# FOREWORD

★ ★ ★

THE PREMISE THAT we are all harmed when women are pre-
cluded from making the world safer is a fundamental and profound idea. At first glance, the foreign policy link may not be
obvious, even though we are reminded at every turn that public policy
decisions affect our economic and physical security in ways both apparent and invisible. We buy T-shirts from Thailand and sell U.S. semicon-
ductors in South Korea. We worry about wounded veterans of lengthy
wars, desperate Central Americans who choose to send their children
north alone, and extremists detonating bombs in Boston.

But in this remarkably readable book, Valerie Hudson and Patricia
Leidl push us—all of us—to think through the fundamental template for
making decisions. In foreign policy parlance, if our leaders focus on so-
called *hard security* issues (such as threats from nuclear pariah states or
rogue fanatics) rather than on broader *human security* concerns, are we
left less safe and prosperous than we could be?

Or, to put these questions another way, the authors ask trenchantly
whether Secretary of State Hillary Clinton was serious—and, if so, was she
right—in setting out her doctrine that the subjugation of women around
the world is a threat to the security of the United States. Critics see this
idea merely as a rhetorical or cynical stance on the part of U.S. policy
makers, including Clinton herself—a posture that can be ignored in a
particular case if it would undermine "real" American national interests.

Further, some suggest that it isn't our business how other countries treat half their populations. Altruism aside, from the narrow perspective of our national interests, should Americans care?

The answer, based on a wealth of evidence and the careful analysis of these scholars, is simple: yes, if we are determined not to repeat twentieth-century wars and cataclysms.

As things stand, we haven't begun the new century very capably, despite enormous efforts. After more than a decade of fighting in Afghanistan, the United States is trying to disengage from the longest war in our history. Obviously, the *casus belli* was the 2001 terrorist attack launched on our homeland—although shortly after the invasion, policy makers and pundits began pointing out virtuously that a corollary benefit was the liberation of women from unimaginable oppression under Taliban rule. But Hudson and Leidl examine the idea that our engagement vis-à-vis Afghanistan would have been altered if we had hewed to a different method of evaluating national threats prior to 9/11.

No one claims that faithful action spurred by the Hillary Doctrine would resolve all conflicts. Clinton herself, often termed a hawk for the foreign policy decisions she has espoused, has never held out for some kind of peaceable kingdom. Instead, taking to its logical conclusion Clinton's proposal to make the treatment of women a yardstick in decision making, the authors suggest that the United States and the international community would have moved against the Taliban *sooner*. Stopping the egregious abuses of women would not have been an afterthought, nor an excuse for an invasion already planned.

What difference would that have made to Americans? Impossible to know, but—without minimizing the impact from military engagement anytime or anywhere—we can ponder whether that modified approach might have prevented the watershed tragedy of 9/11, which brought ensuing shocks within the global community and an incalculable cost to our population's well-being.

More fundamentally, and drawing on research from a variety of disciplines, the authors explore the idea that subjugating women deprives them not simply of their safety, but of *agency*—their ability to contribute to security. A country needs the option of using *soft power* (the traditionally feminine strengths of persuading and attracting) in addition to military force to exert its influence effectively. Hudson and Leidl make clear the direct link to enhanced stability in countries where women actively participate in public life. The landscapes surveyed are startlingly broad, ranging from discussions of developments in China, India, and Rwanda, among others, to the in-depth case studies of Afghanistan, Guatemala, and Saudi Arabia. (Here the term *case study* definitely isn't code for boring analysis; the stories of real people on those pages bring tears.)

For the policy maker, the academic or student, and also for the broader public searching for the "right" thing to do in Syria or another crisis area, a huge dilemma involves weighing the risks of action against those of inaction. Especially in the wake of the discredited intervention in Iraq—but balancing that against the world's historically recent failures to prevent massacres in Rwanda or Bosnia—we're conscious of the need for a moral frame of reference. This question has haunted me for more than twenty years because, as the American ambassador to neighboring Austria, I was implicated by impotence as the United States stood by and watched Serb military forces (and far less often, their opponents' forces) slaughtering civilians in Croatia and Bosnia.

The Dayton Agreement, heralded as a great success, but lacking even one woman among the negotiating teams, has been a political disaster. Scores of women I've interviewed have told me not only "this was not our war," but also that if women had been at Dayton, they would have insisted on essential on-the-ground changes, such as the guaranteed detention of local indicted war criminals, whose dangerous presence prevented refugees from returning home and kept the country divided.

And so I commend Professor Hudson and Ms. Leidl for offering evidence on why "not a single Arab Uprising country has become a better place for women," despite the courage of women who risked everything to champion democratic transitions. Tragically, I have observed that conflict creates a power vacuum into which men rush while women are carefully deliberating their roles, but this is complicated further by male bonding over the subjugation of women, which the authors show is a typical occurrence both during and after violent conflicts.

We need the most influential players in the world to effect a broad-scale shift of the security paradigm. Full disclosure: Hillary Clinton has been my friend for more than twenty years; thus, the work of these authors holds special interest for me. Incidental to its purpose, the book offers illuminating insight into the thinking of an individual who—considering only her previous professional positions and the clout of the world's sole remaining superpower—can be acknowledged by detractors and supporters alike as one of the most influential females who has ever lived.

But this volume is important for anyone who wants to think seriously about the shape and purpose of foreign policy. At the end of a war that began just over one hundred years ago, an American leader unleashed consternation by proposing fourteen principles for sustainable peace, insisting they would further U.S. interests. Scholars have continued to debate the implications, initially calling him utopian but more recently acknowledging his realism. Without stretching the analogy, it is fair to say that Secretary Clinton's declaration that women's subjugation threatens our national interests has similarly been dismissed by many as mere idealism—yet it stems from a pragmatic approach and deep experience. Understanding what Hudson and Leidl reveal about the varying applications of the Hillary Doctrine strikes me as the start of wisdom.

Ambassador Swanee Hunt
*Chair, The Institute for Inclusive Security*

# PREFACE

★ ★ ★

THIS BOOK WAS born of an unlikely friendship between two women whose disparate paths crossed in 2009. At the time, one was working as a journalist in Kabul, Afghanistan and one as a university professor in Provo, Utah. Pat Leidl emailed Valerie Hudson late that November and asked for a Skype interview about Afghanistan's sex ratios in connection with a policy analysis she was then writing for USAID. She had just finished Hudson's co-authored book *Bare Branches: The Security Implications of Asia's Surplus Male Population*, and felt she was witnessing the same linkage between sex ratios and violence play out in Central Asia that Hudson had observed in China and India.

In many ways we couldn't be more different, but we were both noticing the same thing: the insecurity of women was seriously undermining the security of the nation-states in which they lived. While Leidl was documenting this connection through careful fieldwork and interviews, Hudson was doing the same through collecting, scaling, and analyzing massive amounts of cross-national data. We felt that our voices could be stronger if we pooled our skills and experience, and so we did, beginning in 2010 with a co-authored piece appearing in *Foreign Policy*.

The idea for the present volume came as we realized Hillary Clinton was determined to serve as U.S. Secretary of State for only one four-year term. She was (and is) the world's most influential and eloquent exponent of the proposition that the situation of women and the destiny of nations are integrally linked. During her term as secretary, she pulled out all the stops to incorporate that vision within the foreign policy establishment of the most powerful state in the international system, the United States. No such alignment of the constellations had ever before taken place—and it would be over in the proverbial blink of an eye.

We became determined that this unique moment in U.S. history—in world history—not disappear quietly into the slipstream of time. We wanted to document this window of time in which women became, at least rhetorically, a "cornerstone" of U.S. foreign policy.[1] Surely there were important lessons to be learned from both the successes and the failures of such a serious effort to integrate women into the world of foreign and security policy, and to place their concerns on the agendas of top policy-making bodies.

It is important our readers understand from the outset that this book is not, in the first place, about Hillary Clinton herself. Rather, it is the story of an *idea*—the story of the Hillary Doctrine, as we term it. This doctrine puts forward the revolutionary proposition that "the subjugation of women is a direct threat to the common security of the world and to the national security of the [United States]."[2] *The Hillary Doctrine: Sex and American Foreign Policy* also details and assesses the intensive efforts within the United States to turn the ship of state in this direction of seeing and acting upon the importance of women to its national interests and foreign policy.

In order to effect a comprehensive examination of the Hillary Doctrine, we marshal three complementary streams of analysis: history, fieldwork, and policy analysis. These correspond to the three parts of the volume.

In part 1, we focus on the historical backdrop of the Hillary Doctrine. Using Hillary Clinton's own journey as a springboard, we trace the earliest efforts within the U.S. foreign policy establishment to be more inclusive of women and their concerns, starting with the Carter administration's signing of the Convention on the Elimination of All Forms of Discrimination Against Women (CEDAW). We examine key benchmarks, such as the Fourth World Conference on Women in 1995, where Hillary Clinton asserted that human rights are women's rights, and then the unanimous approval in 2000 by the U.N. Security Council of Resolution 1325 mandating inclusion of women in peace negotiations and post-conflict reconstruction. We survey how the George W. Bush Administration implemented its own vision of the Hillary Doctrine following the invasions of Afghanistan and Iraq in the wake of 9/11, and from there we move forward to explore what Hillary Clinton herself accomplished as U.S. secretary of state from 2009 to early 2013.

In part 2, we offer the reader a series of insights gleaned from experience in the field in order to determine whether the foundational premise of the Hillary Doctrine is correct. Is there in fact a direct connection between the relative security or insecurity of women in a given society and that society's level of stability, security, and resilience? We begin by surveying the existing literature and then going to ground to see for ourselves. This section of the volume contains two in-depth case studies, that of Guatemala and of Saudi Arabia and its neighbor Yemen. Through this more detailed and nuanced treatment, we are able to trace the causal processes leading from women's insecurity to national and even international insecurity. It is also through this analysis that we come to understand otherwise mysterious phenomena, such as why contestations over political power often involve the strategic targeting of women and girls.

In the final part of the book, part 3, we undertake a focused evaluation of attempts by the U.S. government to implement the Hillary Doctrine while Clinton was secretary of state during the first term of the Obama Administration. During her tenure, Clinton devised an impressive array of action plans, guidance, regulations, and programming, and assembled a dream team to oversee the coherence of the effort. If the Hillary Doctrine has merit, this should have been the ideal moment to observe it. What was the result? And what lessons can be learned from U.S. governmental efforts to implement the Hillary Doctrine?

In a sense, then, this book serves a dual purpose: as a retrospective, yes, but also as a *prospective* exercise. Though at the time of this writing the spotlight does not shine as brightly as before, the Hillary Doctrine isn't going anywhere—the evidence for its validity, as we shall see, is just too overwhelming. But many questions remain, important questions of how to transform entrenched mindsets not only abroad but also in Washington, DC, that view an emphasis on women in U.S. foreign policy as a distraction from more important matters of Realpolitik, or see gender

programming as a box-ticking exercise catalyzed by an unconstrained ideology of political correctness. Worse yet, however, are intentional efforts
to subvert carefully constructed implementation measures in the field.

There are also deep and important questions of how and under what
circumstances to communicate our commitment to the Hillary Doctrine
to both enemies and friends, to set appropriate timelines and benchmarks, and to weigh the broader responsibility of the international community of nations to ensure the rights and security of one half of the
world's population. If there is to be a renewed commitment to the Hillary
Doctrine in the future—and we anticipate there surely will be, sooner
or later—these questions must be squarely faced. We offer this volume
as an opening commentary in what we hope will be a larger and longer
conversation about sex and American foreign policy.

# ACKNOWLEDGMENTS

## ★ ★ ★

V ALERIE HUDSON IS grateful to many people and institutions that made this book possible. First up, I am grateful to our agent, Jason Yarn, and our editor, Anne Routon, for having faith that people would be interested in reading this book. Second, I wish to thank the David M. Kennedy Center for International Studies at Brigham Young University and the George H. W. Bush Chair at the Bush School of Government and Public Service at Texas A&M University for their much-needed and much-appreciated support of this project.

Next up are the many wonderful individuals who talked to me in person, over Skype, by e-mail, and on the telephone as my interviewees. I am grateful for the time you were willing to spend with me so that I could understand your perspective. This list includes several people who wished to remain anonymous, as well as Gloria Steinem, Robin Morgan, Melanne Verveer, Paula Dobriansky, Ryan Crocker, Donald Steinberg, Lauren Wolfe, Caren Grown, Carla Koppell, Anne-Marie Goetz, Dara Kay Cohen, Natalie Florea Hudson, Ritu Sharma, Kathleen Kuehnast, Steven Steiner, Charlotte Ponticelli, Jessica Neuwirth, Yasmeen Hassan, Sarah Taylor, Shelby Quast, Jen Klein, Mariam Mansury, Anita McBride, Charity Wallace, Jane Mosbacher Morris, Cybele Cochran, Tobie Whitman, Farah Council, Michelle Barsa, Sarah Chatellier, Patricia Guerrero, Rosa Brooks, Kristen Cordell, Swanee Hunt, Deborah Cavin, Andrew Natsios, K. P. Vijayalakhshmi, Lee Waldorf, Lauren Hersh, Sue Smalley,

Suzanne Griffin, Tcholpon Akhmatalieva, the Nobel Women's Initiative Conference Participants of May 2013, Samia Ahmed, Lena Ag, Rebecca Chiao, Soraya Chemaly, Christine Fair, the Institute for Inclusive Security, Joseph Vess, the WomanStats Project, Becca Nielsen, Jodie Evans, Louise Olsson, Zohra Rasekh, Palwasha Kakar, Peter Van Buren, Ann Jones, Matt Pottinger, Alexandra Tenny, Iris Bohnet, Sima Samar, Sanam Anderlini, Michele Flournoy, and Charles Brown. I have no doubt that I have forgotten someone, and I apologize if that is the case.

The following five individuals made this book possible, and I cannot adequately express my gratitude for their unwavering efforts in its (and my) behalf: Quinton Jones, Amber Hall, Taylor Richards, Eliza Campbell, and Jenny Russell. God bless you all.

I also wish to express my deep appreciation to my coauthor, Patricia Leidl, who was such a trooper through all the travels and travails of writing this book.

Finally, I wish to apologize to my family for being somewhat distracted by the writing of this book. I hope when you read it, you will feel that it was all in a good cause.

Patricia Leidl would like to extend her gratitude to the many friends who supported her while researching and writing this book. In particular I would like to thank Jason Yarn, who tirelessly worked to make the book a reality, and Anne Routon, who believes, like us, that violence against women critically undermines the very basis of what we know to be a civil and just society. I would also like to acknowledge Luis Hinojos for arranging and translating interviews in Ciudad Juarez. Although this material did not make it into our book, his insight and facility for pulling in contacts I would never normally have enjoyed access to was absolutely invaluable. Thanks also to journalists Sergio Rodriguez Gonzalez, Charles Bowden, and Molly Molloy. Being exposed to opposing viewpoints enables a journalist to approach subject matter with much more rigor. I'd also like to thank Ylva Mossing for setting up interviews and interpreting for me in Mexico City and Wendy Mendoza for risking her own safety to assist with my research in Guatemala City. To the many women human rights defenders who risked their lives to speak to me there I extend my humble gratitude: Iada Batres, Lucia Moran, Suzanne Moran and Estela Maldonado. I would also like to acknowledge the victims of violence and their families who shared with me painful recollections of loss and abuse. I hope that one day soon, justice will catch up with the perpetrators.

Special thanks also go to the many women and men working on USAID-funded development projects who spoke to me on the condition of anonymity. Your willingness to come forward was critical to telling the story of *The Hillary Doctrine*. I'd also like to thank my writing partner, Valerie M. Hudson, whose idea it was to write this book and whose unflagging encouragement enabled me to write more words than I ever thought possible.

Special mention goes to Katherine Monk, who provided me with a space in which to work, encouragement, and invaluable pointers about how to survive the writing process.

My most heartfelt admiration, however, is reserved for the many human rights defenders, forensic specialists, families of murdered and disappeared women, and the journalists—both female and male—who continue to work in the face of harassment, death threats, and unrelenting persecution.

Your courage and dedication continue to shine a light on the most pervasive human rights abuse of our time. There are too many of you to adumbrate here, but this book is dedicated to your work and the millions of women who have either lost their lives to—or are living with— violence and repression.

# THE HILLARY DOCTRINE

# PART I

★ ★ ★

## HISTORY AND EVOLUTION

# 1

# HOW SEX CAME TO MATTER IN U.S. FOREIGN POLICY

★ ★ ★

The United States has made empowering women and girls a corner stone of our foreign policy because women's equality is not just a moral issue, it's not just a humanitarian issue, it is not just a fairness issue. It is a security issue, it is a prosperity issue, and it is a peace issue. . . . Give women equal rights and entire nations are more stable and secure. Deny women equal rights and the instability of nations is almost certain. The subjugation of women is therefore a threat to the common security of our world and to the national security of our country.

—HILLARY CLINTON[1]

O N JANUARY 22, 2009, the entryway to "the Building" was jam-packed: More than one thousand people were sandwiched in there to see Hillary Rodham Clinton arrive on the job as U.S. secretary of state. The main floor and the overhead balcony were filled with people hoping to catch a glimpse of a true political star. As Clinton entered, enthusiastic applause erupted from the crowd, and she shook as many hands as she could on her way to the stairway, before ascending the first landing. The crowds trained their cameras and cell phones on her. The cheering and clapping reached a crescendo, and Clinton began to applaud as well. She offered a short speech to the assembled crowd, punctuated by yet more applause, urging the State Department's employees to "Be of good cheer, and be of strong heart! And do not grow weary as we attempt to do good on behalf of our country and the world. . . . Now, let's get to work!"[2]

Hillary Clinton was not the first female U.S. secretary of state, but she was the first to declare clearly that "the subjugation of women is a direct threat to the security of the United States."[3] This declaration has come to be known as the Hillary Doctrine, and it was formally incorporated into the first-ever Quadrennial Diplomacy and Development Review of U.S. foreign policy in 2010.[4] For the first time in its history, the United States of America has committed itself to the proposition that the empowerment of women and girls is a stabilizing force for peace in the world, and should thus be a cornerstone of American foreign policy.

Now that Clinton is out of government—for the time being at least—this might be an opportune time to reflect on the origins and development of the Hillary Doctrine, the challenges and controversy it engendered while she was secretary of state, and how the doctrine has affected both the United States and the nations with which it interacts.

These reflections will help us answer important questions, such as whether U.S. foreign policy should continue to include a focus on women and girls. Is the Hillary Doctrine truly in the U.S. national interest? Is it in the interests of those countries beset by war and instability? To what extent does the rhetoric of the Hillary Doctrine match the reality of U.S. government policy and programming? Will it indeed help bring about a more stable future for the nations of the world as Clinton has articulated time and time again?

In order to speak of the future, however, it is necessary first to examine the past. While this book is not primarily a historical account, in this chapter we set the stage by offering a timeline—which is by no means comprehensive—of just how and why sex came to matter to U.S. foreign policy. Thus, while this book is about a foreign policy doctrine most famously enunciated by Hillary Clinton, it is not primarily about Clinton herself except as that doctrine pertains to her own journey of awakening.

## SEX AND AMERICAN FOREIGN POLICY

Many regard international affairs as primarily a male realm, a subject that speaks principally to men about political, economic, and strategic interests largely defined by a male perspective. The fact that international affairs also affect women and that women might have something valuable to contribute is one of those issues that feminists assert everyone knows yet refuses to Know; that is, people might sense this is true but do not (or even will not) acknowledge that truth, let alone act upon it.

For example, although there was ample evidence that the Nazis perpetrated sexual crimes during World War II, the Nuremberg judges refused to acknowledge or prosecute the perpetrators—ostensibly to spare the victims the trauma of testifying and to refrain from exposing the broader audience to such shocking testimony.[5] It was not until fifty years later that researchers published the first accounts of these crimes—in addition to similar violations committed by the Red Army and even U.S. soldiers.[6]

In the Pacific theater, the situation was similar: Although atrocities against women were both widespread and horrific—the Rape of Nanjing, the fall of Hong Kong—the Tokyo War Crimes Tribunal omitted these crimes from its deliberations and instead classified them under the generic term of "inhumane treatment."[7] Indeed, the case of the "comfort women"—women from Korea, the Philippines, Indonesia, and other occupied lands whom Japanese combatants kidnapped, raped, and forced into sex slavery—was not even acknowledged by the Japanese government until the 1990s, and even now that government refuses to pay reparations to the survivors. These crimes only came to light because a particularly dedicated male Japanese scholar undertook a painstaking search of the relevant archives to document what many still consider to be merely a footnote to the main conflict.[8]

Everyone knew, but no one Knew.

★　★　★

Like these cases of almost eighty years ago, violence against women and girls—and how it relates to national and international security—continues to be hidden in plain sight to this day. When the media do pay attention, their accounts invariably evoke a mixture of terror and titillation and include nebulous exhortations for someone—the United Nations, countries, nongovernmental organizations, *someone*—to do something about these terrible crimes. Nevertheless, even though gender-based violence represents an assault against one half of the human population and, we argue, affects everyone, rarely have sovereign states tackled the issue with any seriousness—certainly not in the hard-nosed fashion that characterizes multilateral sanctions imposed on other behaviors such as nuclear proliferation or chemical weapons.

Similarly, when Americans think of U.S. foreign policy and its many challenges, they tend to consider it much akin to a large, geostrategic game of chess involving relations with China or the byzantine politics and endless conflicts that characterize the Middle East. Although Americans may apprehend at least on some level that part of the reason these countries have so many difficulties is their treatment of women, the United States government nevertheless remains reluctant to broach the topic during dialogues with these nations.

For example, some Americans know that sex-selective abortion in China has resulted in an estimated 50 million "missing girls," that Saudi women will not cast their first vote until 2015 (and then only in municipal elections), and that Pakistan has one of the largest literacy gaps between men and women in the world.[9] Nevertheless, even though many Americans may lament these clear violations of the rights of women and girls, they tend to think of them as idiosyncratic national attributes, such as average local temperature, irrelevant to and untouchable by U.S. foreign policy.

"Oh, it is just their culture," people say—although most Americans would likely never dream of dismissing genocide, for example, as an immutable way of life that is best not tampered with for fear of inflaming ethnic sensitivities. What Americans are only just beginning to understand—to Know—is that these so-called women's issues are in fact central to the security and stability of nations and, indeed, to us all.

This realization, we argue, dawned during the twilight years of the past century. It came about as a result of a confluence of factors, including academic research concerning the role of women in national economic development combined with news reports from the rape camps in the Balkans; the dedication and fearlessness of individual women and men who spoke out about what others had previously refused to hear, even at great personal cost to themselves; and the new technologies of the late twentieth century that amplified their voices in a manner previously impossible. But amplification needs an amplifier, and Hillary Clinton, to her everlasting credit, chose to play that role on the world stage.

## BEIJING: THE GAME CHANGER

In September 1995 on a sweltering day in Beijing, a petite woman in a light pink pantsuit and pearls mounted a stage. The event was the Fourth World Conference on Women. The woman was the then–first lady of the United States, Hillary Rodham Clinton. What she said on that day and at that place was nothing short of electrifying.[10] Kate Grant vividly recalls Clinton's performance:

> After her name was announced, she graciously greeted the dignitaries on the stage, and the large auditorium fell into a hushed nervous silence, with a few awkward coughs in the audience as Hillary Clinton took over the podium . . .
>
> After she thanked the hosts and participants, she gathered steam. While citing ways that women's lives across cultures and continents had similar challenges, she then proceeded to address a litany of abuses, framing them each not simply as "women's problems," but as profound violations of human rights.
>
> In the final moments of the speech, when she and her remarks became an unstoppable cadence to rally the world, she labeled domestic abuse, sex slavery and the lack of ability to plan and space children as the human rights abuses they are. She was dazzling. She was forceful. Most of all, she was brave. On display was the strength of an unwavering soul there to tell the world what she and the United States believed. In the capital of a brutal communist regime, known for too often turning a blind eye to female infanticide, forced abortions and other assaults on women's rights, Hillary Clinton stood there and proclaimed eleven earth shaking words: "Women's rights are human rights and human rights are women's rights." The normally staid crowd erupted in applause. That simple powerful phrase became the battle cry of a global movement.
>
> As Clinton left the stage, the American delegation, where I was seated, overflowed with exuberant pride. There were high-fives. There were tears. There were hugs. I looked out over the audience with delegates

representing virtually every nation on earth to hear a thunderous applause and many taking to their feet, a sea of women and men giving Hillary one big "you go, girl." . . . This was about taking on arguably evil forces that oppress half of humanity. This was American power at its best.[11]

Clinton's speech at Beijing was a watershed event for the United States and arguably for the entire world.[12] To this day, women and girls from Cape Town to Cambridge can quote Clinton's words verbatim.[13] Something in the global zeitgeist changed with that speech and with that conference; suddenly, foreign affairs no longer belonged only to the gray-haired diplomats and decorated military leaders but also now rightly concerned the empowerment of women both young and old.

Theresa Loar, senior coordinator of women's issues in the State Department at that time, noted, "I think the Beijing Conference had a huge effect in policy development. . . . That dialogue, all of that, was still around a year later in October of 1996 when the Taliban moved into the capital of Afghanistan and said that girls can't be educated, and women can't walk outside the home without being accompanied by a male. . . . I don't think our government would have responded the way we did if we had not had this conference ahead of time."[14]

Loar has a point, and the clearest way to see it is to contrast it with the Carter administration's response to the Soviet invasion of Afghanistan in December 1979. Gloria Steinem remembers attending a briefing of women's organizations in a State Department auditorium toward the end of Carter's tenure. Although the subject was an upcoming U.N. women's conference and Afghanistan wasn't mentioned, the Soviets had rolled into Kabul that very day.

Newspapers were full of articles about the mujahideen and their declaration of war against their own Soviet-supported government. Their leaders gave three reasons for why they wanted to drive the Soviets out: girls were permitted to go to school; girls and women could no longer be married off without their consent; and women were being invited to political meetings.

During the discussion that followed the meeting, Steinem stood up and posed an obvious question to her State Department hosts: Given what the mujahideen themselves had said that day, wasn't the

United States supporting the wrong side? Steinem remembers the question falling into that particular hush reserved for the ridiculous. She doesn't remember the exact answer, but the State Department made it clear that the United States opposed anything that the Soviets supported—the government spokesman made no mention that the United States was arming violent, antidemocratic, misogynist religious extremists.

It was clear that matters of war and peace were about Realpolitik and oil pipelines—and not about honoring the human rights of the female half of the human race. And so it happened that the mujahideen waged their brutal war with weapons supplied by the United States and, of course, Saudi Arabia—the birthplace of the doctrinaire interpretation of Islam known as Wahhabism. Together, they gave birth to the Taliban, al-Qaeda, and other affiliated terror networks that now reach far beyond the borders of Afghanistan.

Steinem says she has never stopped regretting that she didn't chain herself to the seats of that State Department auditorium in public protest.[15] After Beijing in 1995, however, the U.S. government would never again be able to condemn Steinem's question as ridiculous. (Whether the government would dismiss it as infeasible is a topic to which we will return in later chapters.)

Before we discuss why the mid-1990s brought about such a sea change, we must first step back and ask what brought Hillary Clinton to that moment in Beijing, for it is surely that occasion that led to the inception of the eponymous Hillary Doctrine fourteen years later. In a way, the journey of Hillary Clinton and the evolution of the Hillary Doctrine are intertwined.

## CLINTON'S ROAD TO BEIJING

When Hillary Clinton became first lady of the United States in 1993, she had already developed a strong and abiding interest in the situation of women and their children. Born in Chicago as the eldest child and only daughter of a staunch Republican father and a mother with a strong social conscience, Clinton excelled intellectually but also faced discrimination owing to her sex. Her experiences were typical of the United

States during the 1950s and 1960s; for example, in middle school, she set her sights on becoming an astronaut:

> So I wrote a letter to NASA and asked them what [I had to] do to be an astronaut. I told them something about myself and they wrote back and said, "We are not accepting girls as astronauts." Which was very infuriating. . . . I later realized that I couldn't have been an astronaut, anyway, because I have such terrible eyesight. That somewhat placated me.[16]

Although attracted to liberal views through the worldview of her mother and her Methodist pastor in Illinois, when Clinton went off to Wellesley College in 1965, she nevertheless campaigned first for Barry Goldwater but then Hubert Humphrey, and ultimately supported Eugene McCarthy. Her political views were clearly changing, and after a short stint on the Nelson Rockefeller campaign, she exited the Republican Party for good soon after the 1968 convention.

In 1969, Clinton attracted national press attention as the first student commencement speaker at Wellesley. Former Wellesley president Ruth Adams recalled, "She was liberal in her attitudes, but she definitely was not a radical. She was, as a number of her generation were, interested in effecting change, but from within rather than outside the system. They were not a group that wanted to go out and riot and burn things. They wanted to go to law school, get good degrees and change from within."[17]

And that is exactly what Clinton did: Yale Law School followed hard on the heels of Wellesley. Along the way another "astronaut moment" acutely reminded her that others might still attempt to limit her ambitions because of her gender. That moment cemented her choice of Yale over Harvard:

> An exploratory visit to Harvard quickly soured her. . . . A friend . . . who attended Harvard Law School introduced her to a distinguished older law professor. Her friend told the professor, "She's trying to decide whether to come here next year or attend our closest competitor."
>
> Hillary later recalled . . . "This tall, rather imposing professor . . . looked down at me and said, 'Well, first of all, we don't have any close competitors. Secondly, we don't need any more women.' "[18]

It was at Yale that Clinton began researching a project examining the legal implications of the mental development of children, which was the genesis of her career-long interest in child welfare issues. Working pro bono at the New Haven Legal Assistance Association, she specialized in child abuse cases, eventually working for the Children's Defense Fund and the Carnegie Council on Children and in 1974 writing her first scholarly article on the competence of children under the law.

Although Clinton worked on the Nixon impeachment hearings as a staff researcher and seemed poised for a career in Washington, D.C., she had by this time fallen in love with Bill Clinton, whom she met at Yale and who had moved back to his home state of Arkansas to run for Congress. She passed the Arkansas bar exam but not the one in Washington, D.C.—a sign, it seemed, that she should join Bill Clinton in Arkansas.

She married him in 1975. Clinton continued to work as a lawyer, writing several more articles about children's legal rights and also remaining politically active in the Democratic Party at the national, regional, and local levels.

After her husband's election as governor of Arkansas, Clinton became first lady of that state from 1979 to 1981 and then again from 1983 to 1992. She gave birth to their only child, Chelsea, in 1980. She remained actively involved in childhood education but expanded her public and political interest to include the status of women in her role as chair of the American Bar Association's Commission on Women in the Profession and in her appointment as the first female member of Walmart's board of directors. She also worked with the League of Women Voters and was instrumental in having the state government produce a *Handbook on Legal Rights for Arkansas Women*.

It was not until her husband was elected president of the United States in 1992, however, that we find Hillary Clinton increasingly emphasizing the pivotal and multifaceted role of women in society. It would be only the second time since the days of Eleanor Roosevelt, a personal heroine of Clinton's, that the White House had tackled the issue with any real seriousness. After the inauguration, Hillary Clinton staked out her own office in the West Wing, which was symbolic of the fact that she was to become undeniably the most powerful first lady in terms of policy influence that the United States has ever seen.

Though Clinton had not yet established herself as an international women's ambassador during these early years, the foreshadowing of that role was already apparent. Swanee Hunt, later appointed ambassador to Austria, recalls:

> My knowledge of Hillary begins in 1992 with the campaign. And in fact, that had to do with foreign policy and women because I put together an event, that was an all-day seminar, when [Hillary] was the wife of the candidate. She and Tipper Gore came, and [we] called it, "Serious Issues, Serious Women." . . . And then I was asked to be part of the transition and the role I was given was to look at how we could have women as a more important force in foreign policy. That was my specific job for the transition. . . . So what I spent my time doing was interviewing all kinds of people who were in the foreign policy establishment, asking them what could be done to integrate women.
>
> . . . After she became First Lady, she asked me if I would come and see her. And she said, look (in fact I think Suzanne Mubarak was with her and had just walked out of the room), and she said, "I have all these women leaders who are coming to see me. And often they come as the 'wives of,' so my husband is meeting with the men and I am asked to meet with the wife." And she said, "Tell me what I can do, help me come up with a strategy of what I can do for women around the world."[19]

Despite this growing consciousness that she could use her role to promote the rights of women worldwide, in those first two years Clinton's energies were focused primarily on domestic health care reform. Even with respect to that issue, much of her zeal can be attributed to the realization that women and children were too often completely unable to access health care—in talks, Clinton would mention the woman who could not obtain a cervical biopsy after an abnormal Pap smear; the mother who was too poor to immunize her child; the pregnant woman who could not afford anesthesia during delivery.

When talk of health care reform ground to a halt in 1994 and various perceived scandals threatened to derail the Democratic legislative agenda, Clinton realized that expending all of her influence in one policy area might not necessarily be the most strategic path. She refused to "return to first-lady purdah."[20] By then, she had already championed the Labor Department's 1994 "Working Women Count," the largest survey of working women ever undertaken in the United States to that point. She was beginning to broaden her horizon.

She was encouraged by the example of those who came before: Madeleine Albright, then–U.S. ambassador to the United Nations, and former U.S. representative Bella Abzug, to name but two. As 1994 drew to a close, Clinton began to consider how in her role as first lady she was developing networks that might be used to advance the cause of international development and peace through the improvement of the status of women and the often miserable conditions in which they lived. Albright had applied this same thinking to her own role as U.S. ambassador to the United Nations. During her tenure there, Albright initiated weekly meetings of women representatives at the United Nations, which, according to author Robin Morgan, inspired male colleagues to whisper that the women involved were "radical and terrible: that [they] must be plotting midnight vasectomies."[21]

Clinton's new definition of her role would build upon nascent U.S. efforts undertaken during previous administrations to engage with so-called women's issues. For example, the U.N. Decade for Women (1976–1985) represented a critical consciousness-raising exercise that trained the spotlight on the role of women in issues of international concern, such as economic development and trade. The Ford administration supported a national commission to prepare the U.S. observance of the U.N. Decade for Women, and Gerald Ford's successor, President Jimmy Carter, signed the Convention on the Elimination of All Forms of Discrimination Against Women (CEDAW) in 1980. This particular treaty, however, foundered on the shoals of apathy, suspicion, and conservative ideology and thus was not ratified by the U.S. Senate, a condition that persists to this day.

The Carter administration also established the Women in Development office of the U.S. Agency for International Development (USAID) in addition to the National Advisory Council on Women. Patricia Derian, as the first U.S. assistant secretary of state for human rights and humanitarian affairs, joined civil society actors such as the Coalition Against Trafficking in Women (CATW) in opposing "white slavery" (what we now call sex trafficking). She also supported the cause of women in Northern

Ireland who were advocating not only peace but also a role for women in the peace process, laying the groundwork for what would eventually take shape as U.N. Security Council Resolution 1325, mandating that role globally.[22]

Though Carter's successor, President Ronald Reagan, was no feminist, in 1985 Reagan's own daughter Maureen led the American delegation to the final U.N. Decade for Women conference in Nairobi. Even the George H. W. Bush administration championed "The Girls' and Women's Education Project" to be undertaken by USAID and successfully lobbied for the appointment of Catherine Bertini to become the first female head of the World Food Programme (WFP) and Barbara Hackman Franklin to become the first female U.S. secretary of commerce. Such appointments created lasting change: Bertini, for example, was able to change the ethos of WFP from "we do guy things; we do trucks, planes, and ships" to an emphasis on the role of women as integral to the food security of any nation.[23]

Although during this earlier period, support for women's issues often amounted to little more than lip service, the international women's human rights movement was gathering steam, and the U.S. government could no longer ignore it—even though, as Charlotte Ponticelli notes, she was only one of two people "doing women" in the entire bailiwick of foreign affairs during the Reagan and George H. W. Bush administrations.[24]

Furthermore, by 1992 when Bill Clinton was elected president, rape as an international humanitarian emergency and crime against humanity was looming large owing to the conflict between Serbs and Muslims in Bosnia-Herzegovina, in which mass rape was openly used as a tool of ethnic cleansing. Picking up the story from *Ms. Magazine*, publications such as *Time* and *Newsweek* ran cover stories vilifying perpetrators, while a new generation of women-focused nongovernmental organizations (NGOs), including Equality Now, the Women's Environment and Development Organization (WEDO), and others, kept the issue on the international policy agenda.

A critical development came in June 1993 at the U.N. World Conference on Human Rights in Vienna, when the international community for the very first time explicitly condemned human rights violations perpetrated against women, such as female genital cutting, female infanticide, and sex tourism. This unprecedented move signaled a real shift in international consciousness.

The U.S. delegation, which included Arvonne Fraser and Geraldine Ferraro, championed this new emphasis on women's rights. Indeed, NGOs such as the Global Campaign for Women's Human Rights and its spokeswoman, Charlotte Bunch, had been pressuring the administration to act. By the end of the conference, delegates declared that women's rights are "an inalienable, integral, and indivisible part of universal human rights."[25] Indeed, as historian Karen Garner relates, the Global Campaign for Women's Human Rights went even further, and

> convened a "Global Tribunal on Violations of Women's Human Rights" that took place at the NGO forum held just prior to the opening of the UN government conference. At the Tribunal, 33 women from 24 countries gave emotional and powerful testimony documenting widespread instances of domestic violence, female genital mutilation, torture, terrorism and war crimes specifically directed at women. . . . The public tribunal [was] presided over by a panel of international judges who connected these abuses to violations of existing international human rights treaties and attended by government delegates.[26]

In his summary to Congress on the human rights conference in Vienna, John Shattuck, the U.S. assistant secretary of state for human rights and humanitarian affairs, pronounced, "The Clinton Administration regards promoting the cause of women's rights as a key element of our overall human rights policy."[27]

Although Hillary Clinton was not yet in the public eye as spearheading these efforts, 1993 and 1994 were important years with respect to U.S. interest in international women's issues. One of the first acts of the new Clinton administration when it came to power in 1993 was to overturn the Reagan "global gag rule" that prohibited U.S. funding for overseas family planning organizations that offered referrals to safe abortion services. It was also the year when USAID first formally integrated gender into its programming. In 1994, Congress also passed the Violence Against Women Act, and in response, the Department of Justice created an Office on Violence Against Women.

During the Clinton administration, the State Department reinstated a section of its annual Human Rights Report examining the human rights of women: the Carter administration had initiated this particular innovation, which was promptly mothballed by the Reagan administration when it came to power in 1980. More importantly, in 1994 the Clinton administration established the Office of International Women's Issues (OIWI) and nested it within the portfolio of the under secretary of state for global affairs in the State Department. Even during this early period, it was clear that the Clinton administration was taking the rights of women seriously, including as a foreign policy issue.

As Hillary Clinton turned from domestic health care reform as her signature issue, new, more international vistas beckoned. Melanne Verveer, who was then First Lady Clinton's chief of staff, recalls how the Office of the First Lady was in constant communication with the newly created OIWI. In early 1995, the State Department decided in concert with the National Security Council that Hillary Clinton—and not Bill—would represent the United States at the U.N. World Summit for Social Development in Copenhagen in March of that year. It was to be the largest-ever gathering of heads of state. Luminaries such as Ambassador Madeleine Albright and activists from a variety of U.S. NGOs urged her on. During Clinton's remarks concerning the need to eradicate poverty and foster development, she spoke specifically of the role of women:

> Although women comprise 52 percent of the world population; although they are the primary caretakers for children and the aged; and are a significant presence in the workforce, they continue to be marginalized in many countries.
>
> Worldwide, more than two-thirds of the children who never attended school, or have dropped out, are girls. Of the one billion people who remain illiterate, two-thirds are women. And a disproportionate number of those living in absolute poverty, are women.
>
> Investing in the health and education of women and girls is essential to improving global prosperity, and I am glad that this Summit has endorsed the principle of equal rights and opportunities for women. In parts of Asia and South America we have seen education of girls help lift whole populations out of poverty. We have seen the education of women enhance their roles as mothers and increase their participation in civic life. So we must

do more to ensure equal rights for women, along with equal pay and equal access to health care and education.[28]

It was at that world summit and in honor of International Women's Day that Clinton announced a new, $12 million-per-year USAID-funded program to keep impoverished African, Asian, and Latin American girls in school.[29]

Clinton's strategic transition into the international arena was swiftly underscored when she embarked—sans the president—on a precedent-setting twelve-day trip to five Asian nations (Pakistan, India, Nepal, Sri Lanka, and Bangladesh) immediately after the summit. In Clinton's words, "this was my first serious exposure to the developing world."[30] With her fifteen-year-old daughter Chelsea at her side, Clinton began to hone her message during this trip:

> I think by talking about girls and women, you're talking about human rights. . . . I think there's an absolute correlation there. . . . I don't think girls and women get as much attention on a regular basis as some of the well-publicized other instances of human rights concerns, and I believe we have to emphasize as much as possible that the denial of education, the denial of basic health care, the denial of choices to girls is a human rights issue.[31]

This trip seems to have been a catalyst for Clinton to see these global issues as the extension of those she had been working on for so long domestically. In her own words:

> Reporters asked me soon after my speech why I hadn't addressed these issues sooner. I understood the question, though I had been working for twenty-five years on improving the status and dignity of women and children in America. In this region, where purdah and abandoned baby girls coexisted with women prime ministers, I could see the issue in higher relief—and so could the press. Health care reform, family leave, the Earned Income Tax Credit or lifting the global gag rule on abortion were all part of the same theme: empowering people to make the choices they decide are right for them and their families. Traveling halfway around the world helped make that clear.[32]

The 1995 South Asian journey also marked the beginning of Clinton's signature foreign policy style: meeting with non-elite women outside of the halls of power. While Melanne Verveer points out that Clinton had already met with women's groups on several overseas trips in 1994, during the South Asia excursion Clinton specifically planned her itinerary to accommodate face-to-face meetings with women from all walks of life. Verveer notes, "after the Social Development Summit and her first extensive solo trip to South Asia in 1995, she made this an element of her trips—one that would continue throughout much of her travels."[33] Indeed, Clinton notes that this style of trip caused consternation in some circles:

> The Secret Service was nervous about the trip and would have preferred that I restrict my travels to government compounds and isolated resorts. They were amusingly at odds with the State Department, which wanted to send me to hot spots around the world—places where ongoing conflict made security too difficult for visits by the President or Vice President. The point of my mission was to meet rural as well as urban women, to jettison the predictable itineraries and get into villages where most people lived. Advance teams and security experts planned each stop carefully, and I was painfully aware of how difficult and disruptive it was for our host countries and our embassies to accommodate such an unorthodox trip.[34]

Clinton visited "families, schools, a worker's union, government officials and even one of Mother Teresa's orphanages," in addition to small health clinics and large hospitals.[35] By convening with and recognizing women who hailed from a variety of socioeconomic strata, Clinton hoped to raise their profile within their own societies and legitimize them in the eyes of their governments.

Upon her return, Clinton sought to replicate her new, more holistic approach to women's issues within the government's policy-making apparatus. She helped to establish the President's Interagency Task Force on Women in August 1995, chaired by herself and Donna Shalala, and also the associated President's Interagency Council on Women (PICW), headed by Theresa Loar. The aim of these initiatives was to coordinate and facilitate the implementation of domestic and foreign policy that touched upon women's concerns.

The Fourth World Conference on Women, set for September 1995 in Beijing, was but one month away and would be the culmination of years of preparation by the global feminist community. After her debut at the world summit in Copenhagen, Clinton was determined to attend, though few remember that her unforgettable appearance almost didn't take place. Although she had been appointed honorary chair of the U.S. delegation in June, a number of critics—who not only included Republicans but also members of Clinton's own party—opposed having the first lady appear in the People's Republic of China. Among the latter was Nancy Pelosi, who objected to the fact that China had detained the American human rights activist Harry Wu, whom the government of China accused of being a spy.[36] Theresa Loar, who helped organize the U.S. effort at Beijing, said, "I did get a call from someone on the National Security Council who said to me, 'My job is to make sure Hillary Clinton doesn't go to China.' I am thinking, my job is to make sure it's a rip-roaring success—and guess who is going to succeed?"[37]

China ultimately deported Wu in late August, paving the way for Clinton's attendance. Clinton agreed to the condition, laid out by her own government, that she not meet with any Chinese government leaders while representing the United States there.

In preparation for the conference, the U.S. government pledged to implement (or at least attempt to implement) a list of commitments on behalf of women that would take advantage of existing foreign and domestic policy instruments. Chief among these was a determination to redouble efforts to persuade the U.S. Senate to ratify CEDAW, an objective that was predictably unsuccessful.

The conference attracted an unprecedented number of attendees. Estimates put the number of participants at the official government-sponsored conference at seventeen thousand, with more than another thirty thousand attending the associated NGO forum.[38] The rest was, as the old saw goes, history. Alyse Nelson, who attended the Beijing conference as a college student, suggests that something changed for Hillary Clinton that day: "What Mrs. Clinton so clearly realized in Beijing was that she had a voice and she had power. And she could use that voice to help those who had no power."[39] Melanne Verveer concurs: "history will document that she just never stopped from that

moment on. We traveled to some 80 countries, [and] she was a mission-
ary for the role of women."[40]

Hillary Clinton had arrived on the world stage as an outspoken ambassador for women and from that vantage point began to lay the foundation
of what would one day be called the Hillary Doctrine.

## THE ROAD TO 1325

In this abridged history of how women came to matter in U.S. foreign
policy, our next milestone is U.N. Security Council Resolution 1325
(UNSCR 1325) of October 31, 2000 concerning "Women, Peace and
Security," the name of the policy agenda that was the product of many
years of advocacy by the global feminist movement. Chief among the
commitments outlined in the declaration is that member states should
"ensure increased representation of women at all decision-making levels in national, regional, and international institutions and mechanisms
for the prevention, management, and resolution of conflict."[41] The roots
of this advocacy date back to the late 1970s, when women peace activists in Northern Ireland refused to acquiesce to their exclusion from
the peace negotiations. Civil society groups had taken up the cause of
inclusion and had made some progress with several of the missions at
the United Nations, especially those from Scandinavia. Further aspirations articulated in UNSCR 1325 included incorporating more women as
field operations personnel, including as military peacekeepers; assessing
peace proposals based in part on their impact on women and girls; and
prosecuting sex crimes in war without the possibility of granting amnesty.

This resolution represented yet another step forward for women—
a major one—for it defined them not as merely passive recipients of
aid or justice but also as *agents* integral to peace, stability, and security.
UNSCR 1325 represents a critical intellectual turning point concerning how women are perceived with respect to foreign policy. Prior to
the Clinton administration, women had been conceptualized primarily
as victims; during the Clinton administration, the concept of women as
beings with rights deserving of protection was advanced. However, one
more step was necessary, which UNSCR 1325 represents—that is seeing
women as important agents of security and peace.

It took quite some time to arrive at that vision. While policy makers had, over time, embraced the concept that the educational and economic empowerment of women and girls is key to the advancement of nations, at the turn of the twenty-first century, war and peace continued to be a male province. Linking women to "hard" national security affairs, culminating in UNSCR 1325, was the obvious next step after Beijing.[42] It is noteworthy that the first place where the linkage was drawn most explicitly, at least for the Clinton administration, was not with respect to conventionally acknowledged regions of gender inequality, such as Afghanistan or India, but rather post-Soviet Eastern Europe.

In 1993, the Clinton administration appointed Swanee Hunt as ambassador to Austria, where she served until 1997. During this time, the United States was also wrestling with how to manage the Bosnian conflict, which would leave more than 200,000 dead and hundreds of thousands displaced. Hunt had cultivated extensive personal networks in Europe, where she lived while her husband pursued his career as a symphony conductor. Like Clinton, she was convinced that the concerns of women were integral to the long-term stability and security of the world following the end of the Cold War. As Melanne Verveer explains, "If these new democracies [in Eastern Europe] were to be successful, women had to take their place at the table."[43] And Hillary Clinton herself stated in March 1997, "A democracy without the full participation of women is a contradiction in terms."[44]

Hunt soon began traveling to these new European democracies, as well as arranging for women representing these countries to meet in Vienna, a city whose historical neutrality offered a natural location. Despite many discussions of the issues directly affecting women and girls—such as sex trafficking—the Bosnian conflict was of special concern.

The widespread use of gender-based violence (primarily targeting Bosnian Muslim women) occurred on a scale not witnessed in Europe since World War II—nor had the media ever covered rape in war in such heartbreaking detail. *Newsweek*, *Time*, and the *New York Times* all carried leading stories after picking up the story from *Ms. Magazine*. In Bosnia, the world saw clearly that rape wasn't collateral; it was intentional and designed to break communities and clear territory. Commanders *ordered* their men to rape and severely punished those soldiers who refused to do so.[45]

The Serb military established rape camps where soldiers forcibly impregnated women of differing ethnic groups and religions. The aim was to shatter the cohesion of families and by extension the communities in which they lived by forcing their victims to bear the children of their worst enemies. There was—and is—no more effective tactic of war for clearing a contested territory than engaging in the mass sexual assault and torture of women and girls.[46]

The cruelty was unimaginable. No one, not even tiny girls, was spared. Sabrija Gerovic was a Bosnian Muslim woman with two children, four-year-old Samira and three-month-old Amira. Early in 1993, Serb soldiers forced Gerovic and her children into a truck and drove them to a house in Pilnica, where she found herself placed with many other Muslim women like herself. Her captors were Serb soldiers, "chetniks":

> In the next room were the women aged 15 to 19. "Every night they were taking the girls out."
>
> That night two men came into the room and took her daughter Samira [the four-year-old]. "She was gone for 24 hours, at midnight the next night a man came in and told me to come and take my child. I went into a room. It was empty and there was only a table."
>
> "They told me to take off my clothes and I was completely naked and there were seven of them. Then they all raped me. They had been drinking but only two were really drunk. One of them was biting at my breast." She pulls back the soiled cream lapels of her shabby navy toweling dressing gown and points to the purple puncture marks all around her left breast. "Here is where he bit me," she said.
>
> "There was a curtain across the room and when they had finished they said: 'Go and get your baby.' I went behind the curtain and Samira was naked, her head was blue and she had foam on her mouth. She had no pants and there was lots of blood streaming down her legs and I knew they had raped her."[47]

It became increasingly difficult to refuse to know that violence against women was part and parcel of what armed conflict meant—that it was well-planned and strategic. Indeed, the sexual assaults of women committed during the Bosnian war led the U.N. Tribunal on Bosnia in

June 1996 to indict Serbian military and paramilitary perpetrators of on charges of rape and to declare that rape was a war crime and would be prosecuted as such. It was the very first time in human history that sexual violence against women during war was viewed as anything other than a "natural" consequence and entitlement of soldiers who encountered civilians.[48] Two years later, the International Criminal Tribunal in Rwanda reinforced this legal understanding. Said presiding judge Navi Pillay, "From time immemorial, rape has been regarded as spoils of war. Now it will be considered a war crime."[49]

Feminist advocacy groups, such as Equality Now, were instrumental in making sure that the war crimes tribunals for Rwanda and the former Yugoslavia would prosecute sexual crimes of violence—fifty years after the silence at Nuremberg.

Soon after, the United States and the United Nations developed postconflict reconstruction programs for Rwanda and Bosnia and each contained a significant women's initiative dedicated to assisting and empowering women. This was unprecedented. The boundary between the realm of national security—coded male—and the world females inhabited was beginning to crumble.

Still, old mindsets were hard to shake. After Swanee Hunt began to hold international symposia on the Balkan situation, in 1994 she was also asked to host two rounds of formal negotiations between the warring parties. Hunt describes how even she herself—a strong feminist convinced of the importance of women's voices—was hit with an "aha moment" that made her realize to what extent she herself had been acculturated to overlook women when it came to foreign affairs, war, and peace:

> [There were] those negotiations I had hosted in Vienna for fourteen days and I didn't notice that there were no women until we got to the White House for the signing of the peace agreement.
>
> I looked in the auditorium and I thought, holy cow, it's all men! And I had had fourteen days that I could have said holy cow. In fact, I could have required as host that the delegations be one-third, or one-fourth, or one-half women. . . . I would have been [viewed as] this crazy lady in Vienna, but the point is that *I didn't even see it.* Because I was looking through the lens of security: I was looking through foreign policy. . . . There was no

model. . . . So when I realized it was all men, I thought well, maybe I'm just confused here. I've been meeting with a lot of Bosnian women, but maybe it's culturally inappropriate, like maybe you can't find women . . . maybe there aren't women who could have been on these negotiating teams. And come to find out Yugoslavia had the highest percentage of women PhDs of any country in Europe.[50]

Hunt's revelatory moment was only strengthened by subsequent experiences. In December 1997, President and Mrs. Clinton flew to Bosnia to cheer up peacekeeping troops, and Hunt, though no longer ambassador, accompanied them. She organized a meeting between Hillary Clinton and Bosnian women from all ethnic groups, while Bill Clinton met with the government leaders:

So I put together this meeting [with Bosnian women for the First Lady]. Meanwhile President Clinton is meeting with the newly elected hardliners because of Dayton. Dayton was such a horrible treaty [because] it ensured that only hardliners would be in the government. And so there are these two meetings happening concurrently. Afterwards, [the First Lady] is coming out, and I was in the meeting with her, she is so buoyed, she is so excited, she said this country is going to move forward, and it is extraordinary the sense of goodwill and ability to reconcile that the people of Bosnia have. And [the President] met her, and I don't know which of them actually spoke first, but he was holding his forehead in his hand and he was saying, "I wasn't able to budge them one iota." You would have thought they were in different countries! He said, "I don't think there's hope for this country. They are so solidified. They are so entrenched." And I went to . . . the press conference after that and it was Sandy Berger and Madeleine and they were all going up in front of the international press. And they were saying, "Well, ya know, it's gonna be a hard road, etc., etc." And I'm standing on the side and I'm saying, "Sandy, the First Lady just had this extraordinary meeting with these women; tell the press!" And he didn't. And this was one of those big lessons for me. How you can be so close to a step forward—like what if Sandy Berger *had* told that story? It would have been news; but he didn't. And neither did Madeleine. Because they weren't in the room. They didn't see it.[51]

When Hunt later visited the United Nations and asked why there weren't any women on any of the negotiating teams in Africa, she was told that, "the warlords don't want them because they're afraid they'll compromise."[52] But despite considerable pushback, the notion that women had to be at the table in order to bring about peace finally began to jell as a coherent policy agenda item. That the status of women and their concerns were pertinent to the "hard" issues of war and peace was gaining traction. When the U.S. government established the Vital Voices forum in 1997, few understood that the new initiative would subsequently play a critical role in pushing the agenda toward the international understanding that would eventually become UNSCR 1325.

It was Hunt's husband, Charles Ansbacher, who actually dreamed up Vital Voices. He suggested his wife hold a "big going-away party" on the eve of her last day as ambassador. The big party ended up morphing into a three-day event at the U.N.'s Vienna headquarters in July. Three hundred twenty women leaders and activists from thirty-six countries—primarily in Europe and the United States—were invited, with Hillary Clinton tapped as keynote speaker. The aim was to emphasize strategies and solutions, as opposed to a simple critique of the many human rights violations that women and girls face on a daily basis.

So successful was the gathering that participants realized this could not be a "one-off" event. The State Department then took over Vital Voices as a public-private partnership initiative, with conferences organized in many different parts of the world. As Alyse Nelson, then at OIWI, described, "Following that conference, our tiny office at the State Department was flooded with calls from women all over the globe who wanted us to organize a Vital Voices gathering in their region, too. . . . By the time I left the State Department in 2000, dozens of reporting cables were coming in each day from US embassies, highlighting women's issues around the world; whereas when I began, there had been months before even one cable was received."[53]

When the Clinton administration ended, Vital Voices became a 501(c)(3) organization, with Senator Hillary Clinton and Senator Kay Bailey Hutchinson named as honorary cochairs, representing both sides of the U.S. political aisle. Bipartisanship has been a consistent and distinguishing hallmark of the women, peace, and security agenda in the

United States. The State Department appointed Melanne Verveer as the first director of the Vital Voices board and eventually its CEO; she only stepped down when the Obama administration called her back into government service. As an organization, Vital Voices continues to this day to dedicate itself to training and equipping women from all sectors of society and from every nation to take their rightful place at the tables of power—whether in politics, law, the media, or in business.

Also sending her greetings to that historic first meeting of Vital Voices (she was at a NATO Summit in Madrid at the time) was Madeleine Albright, who in February 1997 had become the first female secretary of state in U.S. history and the highest-ranking woman ever in the U.S. executive branch. Her appointment was a clear signal that the bastions of American foreign and security policy were no longer an all-male preserve. A month after her appointment, Albright stated:

> Let me begin this morning with one very simple statement. Advancing the status of women is not only a moral imperative; it is being actively integrated into the foreign policy of the United States. It is our mission. It is the right thing to do, and, frankly, it is the smart thing to do.
>
> The reason is that as we approach the new century, we know that we cannot build the kind of future we want without the contribution of women. And we know that, around the world, women will only be able to contribute to their full potential if they have equal access, equal rights, equal protection and a fair chance at the levers of economic and political power.
>
> Towards these goals, we have made progress. I said once that if I had been born a generation or two earlier, and if I had wanted to make a definitive statement on American foreign policy, my only option would have been to enter society and then pour tea into an offending Ambassador's lap. . . .
>
> I am not among those who believe that if the world were run solely by women, war would disappear. The human capacity for folly and miscalculation is widely shared. But the history of this century tells us that democracy is a parent to peace. And common sense tells us that true democracy is not possible without the full participation of women.[54]

To shore up the connection between women and American foreign policy, the secretary of state was also asked to chair the President's

Interagency Council on Women (PICW), which also strengthened the hand of OIWI within the State Department. When Theresa Loar, who was then head of OIWI, insisted, for example, that the United States refuse to recognize the new Taliban-dominated government of Afghanistan until women's rights were restored, the administration not only gave her words serious consideration but actually agreed.

And it wasn't only government officials who adopted this attitude. Indeed, State Department officials told feminist activist Eleanor Smeal, who had been very active in revealing the plight of Afghan women under the Taliban, that in 1999–2000, the department "had received more mail from Americans on restoring women's rights in Afghanistan than on any other foreign policy issue."[55] Notice that this public awareness precedes the events of September 11, 2001, and, as we will see, would help set the stage for the American response to that attack.

In a sense, the stars had aligned. The U.S. government was finally acknowledging women as central to issues of war and peace. This convergence was largely owing to the high level at which these discussions were advanced. As Alyse Nelson put it:

> Mrs. Clinton and Secretary Albright emerged as a dynamic "tag team" on global women's issues. Secretary Albright would raise issues in bilateral meetings with world leaders, and the First Lady served as an effective, albeit unofficial, ambassador for women, chairing roundtable discussions with women leaders and visiting microcredit cooperatives and shelters for women fleeing violence around the globe. This was a radical shift for the United States. For the first time in history, the American government committed to making the advancement of women around the world a top foreign policy objective.[56]

The State Department was changing as well. In 1998, Theresa Loar reflected on that first year when for the first time, the United States had a female secretary of state:

> I can tell you that with Secretary Albright at the head of this department, her example sends very strong signals. When Assistant Secretaries go out to the region, they come and ask me [the head of OIWI] for a briefing; what

are the issues; who are the people I should be working with; what of your issues or your points can I be sure to incorporate in this trip?

This is not the way it was a few years back at the State Department. This is a sea change. This is a dramatic change in the one year that there has been a great emphasis on this, and it really has to do with example at the top, and it has to do with follow-through throughout the whole State Department.[57]

Apparently, other world leaders also began to take notice of these changes in U.S. emphasis. Noted Secretary Albright,

I went to my first meeting of the Gulf Cooperation Council (GCC), and the first meeting I said, you may notice that I don't look quite the way my predecessors have looked; and this time, you've all been very generous to me, and next time we get together, we'll talk about women's rights. And we did. . . . I have to tell you that as the representative of the United States and as a woman, I have been greeted in all countries with the highest respect. And I think that having a woman represent the most powerful country in the world is a message in itself that they react to.[58]

A related series of new developments marked the second term of the Clinton administration. Among them, in a fateful 1997 compromise to save USAID from a Republican campaign led by Jesse Helms to dismantle the institution, President Clinton agreed to "integrate" USAID into the State Department with the caveat that the former retain a nebulous form of semiautonomy. At the same time, the "peace dividend cuts" after the end of the Cold War decimated USAID. Former USAID administrator Andrew Natsios noted that during the 1970s, USAID was staffed with twelve thousand foreign service officers. Under Reagan, staff dropped to four thousand, and by 2001, there were only eleven hundred foreign service officers left, and twenty-six overseas USAID missions had been closed during that same time period. According to Natsios, USAID was left with only six engineers and sixteen agricultural experts.[59] Indeed, to meet the demands of the Afghanistan and Iraq interventions, USAID would have to rehire its own retirees—through for-profit contractors. This trend, moreover, only accelerated under the Clinton administration:

in a very real sense, USAID was being transformed from a development agency to what Beebe and Kaldor call "a contract management agency for the State Department."[60] This, in addition to the 1994 passage of the Government Results and Performance Act, was to have important consequences for U.S. foreign policy, a process we will discuss in chapter 5.

During President Clinton's second term, a growing awareness of the impact of sex trafficking and human trafficking on women began to inform the efforts of the administration. It was an issue that united—very uniquely—both the Left and the Right in U.S. politics. While reproductive rights and family planning led to harsh discord and legislative stalemate, sex trafficking was one "women's issue" that brought together both sides of the U.S. political aisle. Though feminist civil society groups had been raising the alarm for quite some time, a discussion between Hillary Clinton and Ukrainian women leaders at the 1997 Vital Voices conference helped catalyze government action. Comments Melanne Verveer, "When we got back home, the First Lady said, 'What is this? What is going on? We need to understand this!' And at that time, we were able to get resources through the CIA to State to do the first-ever assessment of what is this thing, human trafficking? . . . Trafficking was one of those issues [that] were it not for the role of Hillary Clinton in the White House, I don't know when the United States would have passed its law [the Victims of Trafficking and Violence Protection Act]."[61] This interest in trafficking inspired Clinton's team to plan a trip to Thailand in late 1996, where she heard firsthand from young girls who had been rescued after being trafficked into the brothels of Bangkok.

The Clinton administration charged PICW with the development of recommendations for antitrafficking legislation that the government then placed before Congress, resulting in the landmark Victims of Trafficking and Violence Protection Act of 2000. Chief among the provisions outlined in the new legislation was that the State Department formally assess nations according to what extent they were acting to prevent trafficking from or within their borders and whether they were offering the kinds of services necessary to protect victims and to ensure that traffickers were punished and their activities halted.

All in all, this greater understanding of the link between so-called women's issues and national security—revolving around issues such as the prosecution of rape as a war crime, the representation of women during peace negotiations, and the increased activity against human trafficking—ultimately laid the groundwork for U.S. government support for UNSCR 1325.

Various feminist organizations involved in the NGO Working Group on Women, Peace, and Security, with which the U.N. Development Fund for Women (UNIFEM) was later to join forces, had been advocating for a resolution to mark the "Beijing Plus 5" anniversary. Albright had been very supportive when she was U.S. ambassador to the United Nations. However, the drive for UNSCR 1325 was not spearheaded by the United States.[62] In 2000, the executive director of UNIFEM presented a copy of a draft resolution to Ambassador Anwarul Chowdhury of Bangladesh, the country that was then chairing the Security Council.[63] In March 2000, on International Women's Day, Chowdhury made the following remarks: "Members of the Security Council recognize that peace is inextricably linked with equality between men and women. They affirm that the equal access and full participation of women in power structures and their full involvement in all efforts for the prevention and resolution of conflicts are essential for the maintenance and promotion of peace and security."[64]

The government of Namibia then took up the presidency of the Security Council—which was fortuitous given the country's reputation for being very progressive on issues such as gender mainstreaming in U.N. peace-keeping operations. In October 2000, Namibia urged Security Council member states to discuss gender issues and to educate themselves about their importance. It then put forward a draft resolution for the council's consideration, which had originated with the NGO Working Group on Women, Peace, and Security. Using the "Arria formula"—whereby NGOs interact directly with member states on the Security Council—the working group brought in women from conflict zones around the world to speak directly to Security Council members about their experiences in wartime, an event that participants later described as visceral.[65]

The Security Council unanimously passed Resolution 1325 one day later. It is difficult to overstate the symbolic significance of UNSCR 1325. For the first time in history, humanity had declared that the male monopoly over issues of war and peace was unwarranted and unjustifiable. The potential ripple effects could not then be calculated, and, indeed, the full effects have yet to be fully understood. As political scientist Natalie Florea Hudson explains, "[I]f war is to end altogether, gendered identities and expectations may have to be reconstructed. The intricate interdependencies between gender and international security are significant, and any genuine shift in how gender roles are perceived by the Security Council has potentially profound consequences for the very nature of war itself."[66]

Indeed, with the election of George W. Bush, a Republican, in November 2000—an election that also saw former First Lady Hillary Clinton elected U.S. senator from New York—and ten months later the trauma of 9/11, one might assume U.S. foreign policy would resume a strict separation between "women" and "security." To the contrary, the shift created by Beijing and UNSCR 1325 was real. The Bush administration did not relinquish a focus on women even as it tackled the unprecedented foreign and security policy challenges of the first years of the new century.

## THE GEORGE W. BUSH ADMINISTRATION PICKS UP THE BATON IN ITS OWN WAY

George W. Bush's presidency did not start well in terms of perceived sensitivity to women's concerns. One of his first acts as president was to reinstitute the global gag rule and to defund the United Nations Population Fund (UNFPA) once more.[67] Feminists and other human rights activist were immediately disheartened, taking this as a sure sign that the new administration would be far less open to a feminist foreign policy agenda than its predecessor. While not overlooking the significance and symbolism of this first official act, in retrospect, the administration's record with regard to women and foreign policy—especially programming—was more significant than it has perhaps been given credit for. All of the initiatives and declarations that culminated in UNSCR 1325 had indeed altered the global discourse on women, war, peace, and security. These could not help but influence the Bush administration's approach to foreign policy.

When Bush's first secretary of state, Colin Powell, requested a review of the many offices and envoyships that the Clinton administration had established during its tenure, Paula Dobriansky, who was appointed under secretary of state for democracy and global affairs (and who served through both terms of the Bush administration), needed no encouragement to write a strong recommendation that OIWI be retained under her reporting line.

Indeed, Dobriansky believes that under the Bush administration, OIWI's voice was actually strengthened. Under the Clinton administration, the Office of the First Lady had been the primary champion of OIWI—not the State Department. Under the Bush administration, OIWI would have support from both sources.[68] In Dobriansky's view, OIWI's extraordinary access to the White House, coupled with the personal receptivity of both President and Mrs. Bush to the concerns of women and girls, transformed it into a force to contend with—despite its small budget, its lack of programming funds, and its equally tiny office on G Street (which Charlotte Ponticelli, OIWI's senior coordinator from 2002 to 2006, cheerfully notes was actually closer to the White House than the main State Department building).[69]

Ryan Crocker, who held several critical positions in the Bush administration, including U.S. ambassador to Iraq, attests that this personal receptivity by President and Mrs. Bush was real: "Those programs to benefit women had [Bush's] full support, no question."[70] Dobriansky also recounts how other assistant secretaries envied the access and influence that OIWI enjoyed with the president and first lady.[71] Ponticelli concurs: "There were constant meetings on the issue of women at the White House. . . . We were small, but we were not small potatoes; we were at the table and heavy hitters were going to bat for us."[72]

Nevertheless, while some in the Bush administration embraced what President and Mrs. Bush believed about the importance of women with respect to international security and stability, it is also true that many did not. The White House's intense interest in women's rights apparently existed side-by-side with a constant scramble by OIWI for attention and resources from the rest of the executive branch during the tenure of the Bush administration.

Ponticelli recalls, for example, attending her first planning and budgeting meeting with Deputy Secretary of State Richard Armitage. He asked her if the Future of Iraq Project office, tasked with coming up with a viable post-invasion road map for Iraq, had included OIWI in its discussions. She told him "No, sir, I'm sorry to say. We've made the approach to them, but we haven't really been involved in their discussions." Armitage then banged his fist on the table and said, "I'm not happy about this! I'm not happy about this at all!"

Later, Armitage called her by telephone and said, "I appreciate the job you did today. I want you to have a full whack at the ball. If you have a problem, let me know." The next day, Paula Dobriansky called Ponticelli and said, "It's all over the building that Armitage called you." Ponticelli was then invited to attend the meetings of the Future of Iraq Project and was given additional funding for more office space and to hire additional staff.[73]

This anecdote suggests that while top administrators were on board with the president's belief that the interests of Afghan and Iraqi women should be included in foreign policy discussions, many in the State Department didn't see the need to do so—unless higher-ups openly prodded them. The fact that Paul Bremer, head of the Coalition Provisional Authority (CPA) in Iraq, opposed quotas for women in the national legislature is illustrative of how uneven the emphasis on women could be. The Bush administration eventually overruled Bremer, but his original stance is quite telling. Indeed, as Swanee Hunt and her coauthor Cristina Posa put it, "The United States set a disastrous precedent even before the invasion of Iraq by creating a government-in-waiting led by an exile group almost entirely bereft of women. The CPA appointed only three women to the 25-member Iraqi Governing Council."[74]

Further complicating the picture was the perception by numerous commentators outside the government that the Bush administration was promulgating a form of "imperial feminism," a Frankenstein-like distortion of feminist values that would be mobilized to promote and justify militarism and empire. This was particularly acute with reference to the invasion of Afghanistan, given the Bush administration's inclusion of Afghan women in the rationale. When asked about Laura Bush's famous radio address (which we will discuss in a moment), Jessica Neuwirth, one of the founders of Equality Now, commented, "Of course Laura Bush felt like this [situation for women in Afghanistan] was terrible, but you just had to wonder, well, why didn't she think it was terrible a year ago?

Why didn't she talk about it a year ago? . . . [It] was so politically calculated, in my opinion, the timing, it was so obvious . . . it's a great cover
for invasion of Afghanistan."[75]

In an essay widely read at the time, Iris Marion Young went further,

> While the Bush administration initially justified the war as a defensive
> action necessary to protect Americans, its rhetoric quickly supplemented
> this legitimation with an appeal to the liberation of Afghan women. I sug-
> gest that some of the groundwork for this appeal may have been laid by
> feminist campaigns concerning the Taliban, which the Bush administration
> chose at that moment to exploit. . . . Appeal to women's rights was thus
> a cynical attempt to gain support for the war among the citizens of the
> United States and other liberal countries.[76]

Those who took this position usually also implied that the Bush administration's rhetoric was either completely insincere or was in the style
of old-fashioned imperialists of previous centuries—white men who
enjoyed the idea of saving helpless brown women from brutish brown
men and, of course, acquiring land and profit along the way.[77]

There is no doubt that the Bush administration's position was both
complex and at times contradictory: an entire book could be, and perhaps should be, written on the subject. Nevertheless, it was the unanimous consensus of those we interviewed who worked with President and
Mrs. Bush that they were sincere in their rhetorical promulgation of this
link, despite the fact that the military invasions of Afghanistan and Iraq
profoundly destabilized the security situation for women in both countries, and despite the fact that quite a number of administration personnel apparently disagreed that women should be viewed as important in
achieving national and international security.

It may be possible to see the Bush administration's stance as a predictable stage in the evolution of the then still nascent international understanding that the security of women and the security of states and of
the international system are inextricably intertwined. In a sense, the two
terms of the Bush administration fostered the development of something
akin to a "feminist hawk" position; that is, the idea that if the security
of women and the security of states are linked, then the use of force by

the international community to protect and liberate women from severe oppression might eventually have a salutary effect on national and international security.

If that proposition is carefully examined, it can be seen as one possible incarnation, if you will, of what would come to be known as the Hillary Doctrine. Remember that it was Hillary Clinton who, not ten years later as secretary of state, would say, "The subjugation of women is a direct threat to the security of the United States." The phrase, "direct threat to the security of the United States" has a very specific meaning within the security policy-making establishment—a meaning that implies possible use of force to address threats to a vital national interest.

Indeed, Senator Hillary Clinton of New York supported both the invasion of Afghanistan and the invasion of Iraq, and later on, Secretary of State Hillary Clinton urged the United States to participate actively in the world's first Responsibility to Protect (R2P) action in Libya. The Hillary Doctrine may give rise to many and varied interpretations, but it is clearly not by definition a pacifist doctrine. In one sense, then, the approach of the Bush administration was but one very aggressive interpretation of what would later come to be known as the Hillary Doctrine, and not a contradiction of it. Indeed, Iris Marion Young saw this as well, asking us to

[consider] the ease with which feminist rhetoric can be taken up by today's imperialist power and used for its own ends. It also helps account for the support of some feminists for the war against Afghanistan. Sometimes feminists may identify with the stance of the masculine protector in relation to vulnerable and victimized women. The protector/protected relation is no more egalitarian, however, when between women than between men and women. . . . What is wrong with this stance, if it has existed, is that it fails to consider the women as equals, and it does not have principled ways of distancing itself from paternalist militarism.[78]

In suggesting that the Bush approach may be located on the Hillary Doctrine spectrum, we are certainly not saying that the primary reason the Bush administration invaded Afghanistan (or Iraq, for that matter) was to protect and liberate women. We are also not suggesting that the invasions were the optimal course of action—particularly with respect to Iraq—or that they did not result in substantial harm to women. There is plenty to critique from a feminist (and human rights and international law) perspective with regard to both incursions. Nevertheless, what we contend is that George and Laura Bush genuinely believed that in addition to achieving other goals, U.S. military intervention in both Iraq and Afghanistan would protect and liberate women. They were also sincere in their belief that the improved security of women in these countries would, over time, improve national and international security.

Ritu Sharma of Women Thrive expresses this well: "The Bush approach to women was not an empowerment approach; it was about respecting and protecting women and keeping them safe."[79] This could explain why many feminist groups felt that the administration's position was deeply hypocritical. However, one could level the same charge against the larger U.S. conservative worldview at that time: Many Republicans believed that opposing abortion rights and the ratification of CEDAW while pro-actively fighting sex trafficking and maternal mortality and, at the same time, supporting the education and entrepreneurship of women and girls, constituted a coherently pro-woman political agenda. The deep philosophical differences between conservatives and progressives on issues such as abortion rights should be explicitly acknowledged but should also not obscure that there was a genuine bipartisan consensus at this time on a number of other policy initiatives, such as the Victims of Trafficking and Violence Protection Act, which were consistent with feminism.

In order to fully appreciate this unique convergence, we turn to one of the most famous speeches of the Bush administration, which was delivered not by the president, but by the first lady. It was President George W. Bush who was originally slated to give a radio address to the nation on November 17, 2001—a few days after the U.S.- and NATO-supported Northern Alliance rolled into Kabul—an address that would, for the first time, explicitly mention women as part of the rationale for U.S. military action.

According to Anita McBride, former second-term chief of staff for First Lady Laura Bush, after reading the text, President Bush said, "Laura should give it." Speech author Karen Hughes agreed.[80] The plight of Afghan women was not only on the minds of the president and first lady but had also captivated the imagination of many Americans. Anita McBride recalls that during a visit with her daughter at the University of Texas soon after the invasion, Laura Bush was approached by women in a local department store and asked, "How can we help these women in Afghanistan?" The OIWI ended up establishing a gift fund for the countless donations that poured in from all over the country in a broad-based and deeply affected reaction to the Taliban's treatment of women.[81]

The radio address, unprecedented for a first lady, is worth reading in full, for each word was carefully chosen, and as Laura Bush recalls, "At that moment, it was not that I found my voice. Instead, it was as if my voice found me."[82]

Good morning. I'm Laura Bush, and I'm delivering this week's radio address to kick off a world-wide effort to focus on the brutality against women and children by the al-Qaida terrorist network and the regime it supports in Afghanistan, the Taliban. That regime is now in retreat across much of the country, and the people of Afghanistan—especially women—are rejoicing. Afghan women know, through hard experience, what the rest of the world is discovering: The brutal oppression of women is a central goal of the terrorists. Long before the current war began, the Taliban and its terrorist allies were making the lives of children and women in Afghanistan miserable. Seventy percent of the Afghan people are malnourished. One in every four children won't live past the age of five because health care is not available. Women have been denied access to doctors when they're sick. Life under the Taliban is so hard and repressive, even small displays of joy are outlawed—children aren't allowed to fly kites; their mothers face beatings for laughing out loud. Women cannot work outside the home, or even leave their homes by themselves.

The severe repression and brutality against women in Afghanistan is not a matter of legitimate religious practice. Muslims around the world have condemned the brutal degradation of women and children by the Taliban regime. The poverty, poor health, and illiteracy that the terrorists and the Taliban have imposed on women in Afghanistan do not conform with the treatment of women in most of the Islamic world, where women make important contributions in their societies. Only the terrorists and the Taliban forbid education to women. Only the terrorists and the Taliban threaten to pull out women's fingernails for wearing nail polish. The plight of women and children in Afghanistan is a matter of deliberate human cruelty, carried out by those who seek to intimidate and control.

Civilized people throughout the world are speaking out in horror—not only because our hearts break for the women and children in Afghanistan, but also because in Afghanistan we see the world the terrorists would like to impose on the rest of us.

All of us have an obligation to speak out. We may come from different backgrounds and faiths—but parents the world over love our children. We respect our mothers, our sisters and daughters. Fighting brutality against women and children is not the expression of a specific culture; it is the acceptance of our common humanity—a commitment shared by people of good will on every continent. Because of our recent military gains in much of Afghanistan, women are no longer imprisoned in their homes. They can listen to music and teach their daughters without fear of punishment. Yet the terrorists who helped rule that country now plot and plan in many countries. And they must be stopped. The fight against terrorism is also a fight for the rights and dignity of women.

In America, next week brings Thanksgiving. After the events of the last few months, we'll be holding our families even closer. And we will be especially thankful for all the blessings of American life. I hope Americans will join our family in working to insure that dignity and opportunity will be secured for all the women and children of Afghanistan.

Have a wonderful holiday, and thank you for listening.[83]

Melanne Verveer, who was attending a Vital Voices meeting in Paris at the time, told Anita McBride that when she heard the address, she thought to herself that if Hillary Clinton had expressed the same sentiments, her words would have elicited a negative reaction in some parts of the world. Because Laura Bush is not necessarily identified with a feminist agenda, Verveer therefore believed she was likely in a better position to express support for Afghan women and girls while avoiding offense to conservative allies such as Saudi Arabia (who had, in fact, openly funded the Taliban right up until 9-11).[84]

In this atmosphere where everyone seemed to want to do something on behalf of Afghan women, the U.S.-Afghan Women's Council was created in January 2002 when the then-interim leader of Afghanistan,

Hamid Karzai, arrived in the United States for his first meeting with President Bush. It was Paula Dobriansky—along with her team at the Women's Issues Office (WIO) at State—who came up with the notion that the Council be a public private partnership—including corporations, educational institutions, and think tanks. It was an idea that senior White House aides subsequently endorsed. The President and First Lady were enthusiastic—they saw it as an opportunity to advance American interests while supporting the women and children of Afghanistan.

Paula Dobriansky recalls the luncheon in Washington, D.C., that set the wheels in motion. In attendance were Secretary of State Colin Powell and the interim Afghan foreign minister Abdullah Abdullah. Powell turned to Dobriansky and asked if she had anything to say, offering an opening to ask Abdullah if he would cochair the council. He agreed to her request. Dobriansky felt it was imperative to demonstrate Afghan male support for the council's work. Abdullah did not disappoint. He faithfully attended the twice-yearly formal convocations of the council's leadership (one of the meetings would be in Kabul and the other in Washington, D.C.) until he relinquished his position to his successor.[85]

The United States was also keen that women participate in the 2002 *loya jirga* ("grand assembly"), which would determine the complete governance structure for post-2001 Afghanistan—including a Ministry of Women's Affairs. Slightly more than 10 percent of the delegates were female. Paula Dobriansky recalls

> The big issue was, would women be at the table? And discussing what future governance framework would be put forward for Afghanistan. And that was an issue that I became very involved in, the head of the office became very involved in, the Secretary of State became involved in. . . . There were a number of factors [that explain this involvement]. First it was . . . the record of what had happened, the fact you had, during the time of the Taliban, women being denied education, women not being able to work, women who were brutalized, subjected to violence, all sorts of issues.
>
> So for the future of Afghanistan it was a natural issue. . . . [And also] there were many Afghan women who we also had met [who] made a very strong appeal while the conflict was ensuing and also had the forethought to put forward their own recommendations . . . It was definitely part of our position to really ensure that at that *loya jirga* there would be women. . . .

Women who were conservatives, women who were liberal, NGOs, as well as other governments, foreign governments, I mean there were a variety of people who came and said, look, you know, we need to have women represented at this meeting. . . . The administration definitely took a strong stance going into that *loya jirga* and made it very, very clear that women had to be represented and basically that in terms of that meeting having any credibility, it would not have any credibility if women were not represented.[86]

For Dobriansky, this was a uniquely important step in the evolution of the worldview that women actually mattered to a nation's future. Dobriansky opines, "I do see a critical turning point here, when you have a negotiation going on and a demand for women in that negotiation. That is different from issues about human rights and domestic violence, if you can see what I am saying. You ask the question about foreign policy and how did [the issue of women] become integrated. It became integrated into the *future* of a country [because women were at the table]."[87]

The issue of women's representation in the Afghan national legislature arose later, but was also a focus of the Bush administration. As the formalization of the Afghan government proceeded, the State Department held a series of meetings involving Afghan women, including the Ministry of Women's Affairs. The goal was to offer these women an opportunity to hear differing viewpoints concerning the contentious issue of quotas not only from U.S. NGOs, but also from women working within the governments of other Islamic countries, such as Pakistan, Jordan, and others.

Did they want quotas or didn't they? Dobriansky says, "We provided a lot of information, but didn't impose a decision." After Afghan women decided in favor of quotas, however, the Bush administration got behind it: "we definitely indicated our position and what we thought was very appropriate."

Asked about other issues, such as Afghanistan agreeing to sign CEDAW without reservations, Dobriansky says, "The Bush Administration . . . had leadership at the top, in terms of President Bush and Mrs. Bush, both, who had their arms around this issue, who both talked consistently about this issue and its importance in foreign policy. . . . They were personally involved. At the State Department, Secretary Powell and then later Secretary Rice, both also got very personally involved, very supportive, constantly."

That being said, setbacks and problems slowed progress. The Afghan government, for example, never accepted a proposed Afghan Women's Bill of Rights. Moreover, on many occasions, the administration's walk did not match the talk—that, or they simply dropped the ball. Ritu Sharma remembered when the first head of the Afghan Ministry of Women's Affairs visited the United States in 2002. She came away from meetings with U.S. officials with no more than a promise of a new roof and one hundred chairs for the building. Shocked, Sharma helped mobilize support from Congress to raise an additional $2 million for the ministry.[88]

More important, many rightly argued that outside of Kabul the level of violence against women never abated in the wake of the invasion, while within the capital, assassinations of high-profile women became a regular occurrence. Even more troubling, in order to inveigle the warlords to agree on a government structure, the Bush administration brought those who had committed atrocities against women into the fold and offered them full immunity for past crimes, which many Afghan women viewed (and still view) as a deep betrayal. Despite these failures, it is also true that the enrollment of girls in primary school soared, maternal mortality dropped by almost half, and, for the first time in years, women were sitting in the Afghan national legislature. These latter developments count as stunning progress compared to the previous decades of civil war and Taliban rule.

In such a mixed context of progress and failure, the United States saw a need for continuous programming. It is here where the U.S.-Afghan Women's Council became a major player. Now located at Georgetown University with a Foreign Service officer as executive director, the council remains active to this day. According to Dobriansky, "Afghan women set the agenda"; that is, they set the five overarching programming emphases of the council (education, health, economic empowerment, political/legal rights, and children).

The list of council projects is lengthy indeed: the Women's Teacher Training Institute, which brought women from rural provinces to Kabul to learn how to teach and then sent them back again; the donation of computer equipment by Microsoft and Dell to women's organizations in Afghanistan; the Laura Bush Afghan Women's Leaders Fund, which brought women leaders to the United States for training; the building of women's resource centers in Afghanistan and the CONNECT project to train women's legal NGOs in Afghan and international law concerning women; training for Afghan women judges; Project Artemis, bringing Afghan businesswomen to the United States to be trained at Thunderbird University; the training of women farmers and midwives; and many other initiatives. Private partners, such as Daimler Chrysler, as well as the public partners, such as USAID, also contributed.

Laura Bush's first trip to Afghanistan proved to be yet another milestone. Indeed, "I want to go to Afghanistan!" were the first words out of her mouth to Anita McBride soon after the latter was hired as Laura Bush's chief of staff. McBride countered, "Does the president know about this and support you?" "Yes."

Knowing that the U.S.-Afghan Women's Council traveled regularly to Kabul, McBride hit on the idea of surreptitiously folding the first lady's visit into their next trip. That visit, in March 2005, would be the first of three that Laura Bush would make to the country as first lady, cementing her resolve to "continue working with Afghan women for the rest of her life."[89] Bush has remained true to her word, and today the Bush Institute's Women's Initiative has as one of its three core activities the Afghan Women's Project. Laura Bush continues as an honorary adviser for the U.S.-Afghan Women's Council, and the Bush Institute, the council, the Bipartisan Congressional Women's Caucus on Afghanistan, and Vital Voices have all cooperated with respect to programming.[90]

When the United States invaded Iraq in 2003, the Bush administration deployed similar tactics to bring women to the table as they had in Afghanistan, including establishing a legislative quota. At first, as we have noted previously, the Coalition Provisional Authority under Paul Bremer proved a major stumbling block. Garner quotes an unnamed Iraqi woman stating,

> Initially many of us were hopeful. We did not like foreign soldiers on our streets, but we were happy Saddam was gone. Once the general chaos and looting settled down a bit, women were the first ones to get organized. Women lawyers and doctors started to offer free services to women.

> We started to discuss political issues and tried to lobby the American and British forces. But especially the Americans sent people to Iraq whose attitude was: "We don't do women." Bremer was one of them. Iraqi women managed to get a quota despite the Americans who opposed it.[91]

Iraqi writer Zainab Salbi shares that opinion: "[The Americans'] patriarchy and chauvinism was harder on Iraqi culture than Iraqis themselves."[92]

Charlotte Ponticelli also offers a revealing anecdote on this theme. As we have already noted, it took the direct intervention of Richard Armitage for OIWI to be included in the Future of Iraq Project discussions. Nevertheless, Ponticelli claims that she was rarely invited to other meetings she believed pertinent to women and that she was often forced to confront organizers directly, "You should be including OIWI!" It appears that direct pressure was required for reluctant government officials both in Washington, D.C., and in the field who did not comprehend that the administration's emphasis on women was not optional and that when such pressure was applied, wonders often ensued. The ad-hoc nature of the situation was telling. Ponticelli once received an e-mail from an aide to Paul Bremer who wrote, "If I gave you 15 minutes to tell me how you would spend $10 million on behalf of Iraqi women, could you send me an email in that 15 minutes?"

Shocked and with no time to clear any plans with anyone, Ponticelli drafted an e-mail, hit send, saw the e-mail bounce back because of a typing error, and resent it just within the fifteen-minute window she was given. She got the $10 million, and this became the foundation of the Iraqi Women's Democracy Initiative, the Bush administration's flagship women's initiative to train Iraqi women to navigate the political process.[93]

As important as this initiative was, its genesis bears all the hallmarks of vertical pressure applied from higher-ups in Washington, D.C., taking reluctant officials on the ground to task for failing to pay attention to women, with these reluctant officials in turn responding by throwing money at the problem as evidence they had done their due diligence—but only in order to make the issue go away. Fortunately, in this case the money appears to have gone to meaningful programming, but in chapter 5 we will examine cases where it did not.

According to Dobriansky, the Bush administration pushed to mainstream women and their concerns into every important government policy initiative. To do so, the Bush administration discontinued the President's Interagency Council on Women, but opted instead to make sure that gender experts were present at various new interagency groups established, for example, to combat trafficking.[94] Dobriansky feels that this strategy did not undermine the importance of women's issues; noting that members of the new Presidential Interagency Group on Trafficking were cabinet members—and not the midlevel officials who had typically attended PICW meetings previously. Dobriansky also points to the Middle East Partnership Initiative (MEPI), the President's Emergency Plan for AIDS Relief (PEPFAR), the Education in Africa Initiative, the President's Malaria Initiative (PMI), the Millennium Challenge Corporation (MCC), and many other Bush administration programs that explicitly included women and girls from their very inception. Ritu Sharma of the NGO Women Thrive explicates, for example, that the brand-new MCC's funding eligibility criteria for nations desiring bilateral aid required attention to gender issues from the very beginning—including an obligation to invite civil society women's organizations to collaborate on programming—and that the MCC had not only a gender policy but also a senior gender advisor on its staff.[95]

In addition to efforts specifically targeting women, Andrew Natsios, former head of USAID under the Bush administration from 2001 to 2006, brought up a largely overlooked point: "Bush doubled foreign aid. He, Truman, and Kennedy were the three most important presidents [in terms of] foreign aid reform and foreign aid spending. He had 23 foreign aid initiatives. . . . When I got to AID, the whole spending was like $10 billion. By the time I left, all foreign aid for all federal departments was up to $23 billion."[96] Granted, a sizeable proportion of this increased aid was targeted to Afghanistan and Iraq to support both invasions, but a significant proportion was spent on projects in other regions of the world.

The Bush administration also came out strongly in favor of U.N. Security Council Resolution 1820, which called on all parties to halt sexual violence in conflict, and during preliminary discussions in the Security Council also supported the eventual creation of UNWomen, which was to unite under one roof the disparate parts of the U.N. system tasked with addressing women's priorities. But the administration maintained a stony silence with respect to CEDAW. Jessica Neuwirth notes, "it was so embarrassing to be at the UN, because [the Bush Administration] would not allow mention of CEDAW in anything. Just the word was prohibited in anything . . . it was like they had an allergy to CEDAW."[97]

Running hot and cold represents a persistent theme with respect to the Bush administration's engagement with so-called women's issues, yet even so, the hot stuff was important. Bush's strong support of the Victims of Trafficking and Violence Protection Act and its antitrafficking stance, for example, led him to outlaw the buying of commercial sex by any federal employee, including contractors, even when off duty, through National Security Presidential Directive 22 in 2002. In 2003, the PROTECT Act was passed, which criminalized sex tourism by U.S. citizens abroad, and in 2005 the Uniform Code of Military Justice was revised to punish—with a dishonorable discharge and one year in prison—any service member who purchases a sex act. Also under Bush, Congress voted to deny funding to groups that advocate for the legalization of prostitution or support prostitution as a legitimate form of work for women.

There were both practical and strategic dimensions to gender programming under the Bush administration. Some of the programming was quite savvy. Natsios described one example:

> Simply increasing the education level of girl children through high school has a profound effect on family size, on income level, and agricultural production. . . . So we established a scholarship program because it would pay [girls'] school fees, it would pay for their books, it would make sure they stayed in [school], and it was done on a large scale, thousands of scholarships, to make sure girls got through high school.
>
> And we increased the education budget. When I started I think it was $150 million. [It was] $800 million by the time I left. A massive increase in education. In Afghanistan, there were no schools, basically, in large parts of the country because the place was in chaos from 1979 when the Soviets invaded to 2001. Well, the second mission director I sent, Patrick Fine, was an education officer in his younger career before he became a senior manager. And I said, Patrick, we gotta do something. All these

women, they're all illiterate. 85 percent illiteracy rates. I said, you're not gonna modernize Afghanistan with 85 percent illiteracy rates among the women. When we arrived, 6 percent of the 900,000 kids in school were women. Right now it's 35 percent and there are 8 million kids in school as opposed to 900,000 when we arrived. Patrick [also] started an accelerated program of literacy for grandmothers and mothers. And there are 300,000 women in that program. . . . So women who were 50, 60, sometimes in their 70s, were going back to school with their grandchildren or children. . . .

There were 50,000 teachers when we arrived. They hadn't been in a school in years. . . . And I said, we need to get all these women back in the classroom, particularly in grammar schools. They were mostly women. How do we do that? So we gave vouchers for food from the food programs of AID. You didn't get cash to be a teacher. You got a voucher—enough to feed your family for a month. That was your pay. For two years the principal way we got the 50,000 teachers back in the classroom was through [these] vouchers, [and] we've printed 67 million textbooks. All textbooks for all grades, for all subjects except religion, were printed by USAID. . . . I don't think those gains will be reversed. . . . It's been 12 years now. Kids who started in the first grade have now graduated.[98]

The inventory of international programs targeting women initiated under the Bush administration is substantial, whether one looks at the issue areas of education, microcredit, women's leadership training, or efforts to fight female genital cutting, trafficking, maternal mortality, and mother-to-child HIV transmission.[99] It is also worth remembering that the State Department's International Women of Courage Award was created under the Bush administration in 2007.

While a number of critics charge that George W. Bush waged a virtual war on women,[100] it is difficult not to conclude that both George and Laura Bush were personally and sincerely concerned for women and steadfast in their belief that nations could only flourish if women flourished. As President Bush put it in 2003, "No society can succeed and prosper while denying basic rights and opportunities to the women of their country."[101] Again, we may lament the hot-and-cold inconsistency and also particular policy stances taken, such as against abortion rights and against CEDAW, lament that the overall effect of any military invasion can only be the destabilization of women's lives, and condemn the fact that at critical junctures, women's interests were jettisoned when they conflicted with "larger" U.S. national interests. But uneven as the Bush legacy for women was, it was rooted in an understanding that the Hillary Doctrine would later make explicit.

Charity Wallace, former deputy chief of protocol in the Bush administration and now director of the Bush Institute's Women's Initiative, remembers discussing with George W. Bush whether to train Egyptian women as activists. He said to her, "Peace and democracy will come to the Middle East through women, not men. Get on that." Wallace took that to mean, "create programs to prepare women to do this,"[102] and that is what the Bush Institute has done.

Moreover, many of President and Laura Bush's closest advisers believed there was no doubt that women would continue to be a major focus of their efforts after the second term of the Bush administration ended. As Wallace puts it, "It is not rhetoric and never has been. They would not take it on if they were not going to follow through. They looked for results and not just rhetoric."[103] The Bush Institute's Women's Initiative has continued its dedicated programming on women's issues, including offering testing for cervical and breast cancer in Sub-Saharan Africa; participating in the first-ever African First Ladies Summit in 2013 to discuss issues of common concern to women throughout the region; creating the Women Freedom Advocates Program, which trains Egyptian and Burmese women to take a greater role in their country's future; and, of course, continuing the Afghan Women's Project.

Thus it may be said that while the Bush administration's foreign policy legacy for women is both mixed and controversial, how history will judge it is a complicated question. Remember how Gloria Steinem wished she had chained herself to her seat in 1979 when the Carter State Department remained silent on the subject of what our "allies," the mujahideen, thought about women? Twenty-three years later, the Bush administration expressed the same sentiments as Steinem, viewing "respect for women" as one of the "non-negotiable demands of human dignity" in Afghanistan and around the world.[104]

## THE HILLARY DOCTRINE

In a precedent-shattering series of events, Hillary Clinton was elected a senator from New York in November 2000 and took the oath of office in January 2001, a few days before her husband stepped down as president. She was reelected handily for a second term in 2006. In January 2007, she announced her intention to campaign for the presidency herself. During her stint in the Senate, Hillary Clinton made a name for herself as a get-it-done-without-grandstanding legislator.

Senator Clinton was firm in her support for the invasion of Afghanistan. It is also worth noting how she viewed the relationship between the events of September 11 and the treatment of women under the Taliban: the parallels with Laura Bush's radio address are unmistakable. On November 24, 2001 (a few days after Laura Bush's address), Clinton wrote an editorial for the *Washington Post*, which is well worth reading in its entirety,[105] in which she noted that, "President and Mrs. Bush have properly highlighted the mistreatment of Afghan women by the Taliban and insist that women play a role in Afghanistan's future." Addressing critics who would assert that America has no right to impose its values on Afghan society, Clinton countered with two major arguments. First, hearkening back to her remarks in 1995 at the Beijing conference, she stated that, "the argument that supporting the rights of women will insult the Muslim world is demeaning to women and to Muslims. Women's rights are human rights. They are not simply American, or western customs. They are universal values which we have a responsibility to promote throughout the world."

Clinton's second argument presages the Hillary Doctrine she would articulate a little over seven years later:

> [Promoting women's rights in Afghanistan] is not only the right thing to do; it is the smart thing to do. A post-Taliban Afghanistan where women's rights are respected is much less likely to harbor terrorists in the future. . . . There is an immoral link between the way women were treated by the oppressive Taliban in Afghanistan and the hateful actions of the

al-Qaeda terrorists. . . . Long before the Taliban was at war with the civilized world, they were at war with half their population. The mistreatment of women in Afghanistan was like an early warning signal of the kind of terrorism that culminated in the attacks of September 11. Similarly, the proper treatment of women in post-Taliban Afghanistan can be a harbinger of a more peaceful, prosperous and democratic future for that war-torn nation.

The similarities between this opinion piece and the radio address of Laura Bush are striking: they both clearly articulate a "feminist hawk" position.

While Clinton's views on Afghanistan were not controversial given a time when September 11 was still fresh in everyone's memory, it was her later vote in support of the Iraq War Resolution in October 2002 that really roiled feminists. Jodie Evans of Code Pink recalls how she and other members showed up at Clinton's Senate office in pink slips demanding to speak with her. Clinton's staff refused until the Code Pink group began loudly singing peace songs.

Finally, Clinton agreed. She heard them out and then told them that she was voting as a representative of the citizens of New York and that her vote would be in favor of the resolution. In retort, the Code Pink group took off their pink slips and threw them at her, symbolically firing her. To this day, Evans does not feel that she can regard Clinton as a feminist—for Evans's definition of feminism includes a renunciation of militarism, which she feels Clinton represents.[106]

As discussed earlier, whether the link between the security of women and the security of states and the international system justifies the use of military force is a contentious one. Are you a truer feminist if you are willing to articulate an international "Responsibility to Protect Women" by military intervention if necessary—or if you embrace nonviolence and work against militarism as being inimical to women and all that they care about?

Both sides walk the razor's edge: the former dances with the specter of morally foggy armed conflict that will surely bring tangible harm to women; the latter risks being condemned for choosing to be passive bystanders in the face of horrifying evil perpetrated against women and girls. We will return to this controversial question in chapter 7 when we discuss the future of the Hillary Doctrine, drawing in part upon the history we have outlined in this chapter.

By 2008, Senator Clinton was opposing the proposed surge in Iraq and cosponsored a bill to reduce the number of troops there, which the Bush administration vetoed. She also joined the Senate Women's Caucus on Burma and developed a keen interest in that country and its imprisoned champion, Aung Sang Suu Kyi. At the same time, critics note that she also refused to endorse a treaty that would prohibit arms transfers to countries involved in gross human rights violations. And like her husband before her, she did not support the Land Mine Treaty or the Rome Treaty establishing the International Criminal Court.[107] This mixture of views positioned Clinton as a U.S. foreign policy centrist.

It is also important to note that Clinton was an important champion of women in the domestic policy arena throughout her Senate career, supporting the Paycheck Fairness Act, raising awareness of teen date rape, and opposing cuts to survivors' benefit in Republican proposals to privatize Social Security.

When Hillary Clinton chose to run for the presidency in 2008, a new moment had arrived for the United States: It was the first time in U.S. history that a woman had a real shot at the presidency. Though at the beginning of that year, polls found that only 55 percent of the U.S. electorate felt the country was ready for a female president, Clinton quickly became the Democratic primary frontrunner.[108]

Nevertheless, she eventually lost the Democratic nomination to Barack Obama (and in the process was the object of incredibly sexist media coverage). Obama went on to defeat John McCain for the presidency, which was historic in its own right. Carl Bernstein offered an insightful commentary on Clinton's run:

> What we wanted from Hillary was the campaign Hillary Rodham might have run: a campaign in which the merits and abilities of a self-made woman could stand up to any man in the country; a campaign that would

highlight and emphasize success earned through achievement, not experiences gained through close proximity to a powerful spouse; a campaign in which a woman would forge her own path without help or hindrance from anyone else.[109]

The campaign indeed showed us a powerful, accomplished, experienced woman, with the potential to do much good for her country. Though she did not break that final glass ceiling in 2008, she cracked it to the point that Americans could realistically conceive of a future woman president. After the election, Obama broached the idea of Clinton becoming secretary of state. While initially hesitant, she finally accepted, and on December 1, 2008, Obama announced his intention to appoint her to that post.[110]

During his first week in office, Barack Obama repealed the global gag rule, which had been alternately repealed or reinstated over the past several presidencies, and the very first piece of legislation that he signed was the Lily Ledbetter Act—both moves offering striking evidence of how his administration's stance on issues that concerned women would differ from those of his predecessor.

Furthermore, quite a number of Obama's top appointments went to women, such as Susan Rice, who was tapped to be U.S. ambassador to the United Nations, Samantha Power, who was appointed to the National Security Council staff, and others recruited to positions in the domestic policy sphere, such as heads of the departments of Homeland Security, Health and Human Services, and Labor. The administration also passed other legislation important to women, such as a revision of the Violence Against Women Act. In addition, Obama announced the formation of the White House Council on Women and Girls in March 2009—a successor to the PICW of the Clinton administration.

Perhaps most important, Obama elevated the OIWI, which became the OGWI, the Office of Global Women's Issues, increasing its budget tenfold.[111] The natural choice to head the new office was Melanne Verveer, Hillary Clinton's former chief of staff and former director of Vital Voices. Obama also granted her the rank of ambassador and stipulated she would report directly to the secretary of state. Clinton had persuaded the administration to establish the office to ensure that U.S. foreign policy would provide the support and ensure the institutional memory necessary to emphasize the security and socioeconomic well-being of women well into the future.

An OGWI representative also joined the State Department's Policy Planning staff, its strategic think tank, and OGWI moved from that little office on G Street to the top floor of the main State Department building. In bureaucratic terms, there could be no clearer signal that the State Department was taking gender issues seriously.

Some had hoped that Clinton would reverse the Bush administration's decision to place USAID under the State Department (even though USAID still held quite a bit of autonomy). But Clinton was advocating a new smart power for the United States that would place as much or more emphasis on diplomacy and development as it did on defense, and she wanted the State Department to hold two of those three cards. In Clinton's eyes, Realpolitik for the United States in the twenty-first century had to mean more than a reliance on military instruments of power. Clinton sought and obtained a significant increase in funding—more than 7 percent—for the State Department and USAID to reflect this new understanding.

She also pioneered a new State Department emphasis on outreach using social media, with the department opening hundreds of Facebook accounts and Twitter feeds and backing the concept of the right to Internet freedom. Even with this emphasis on new information sources, Clinton maintained that personal relationships were the key to diplomacy and accordingly logged just under a million miles of travel to 112 countries (more countries than visited by any other secretary of state). Similar to her modus operandi as first lady, these visits almost always included meetings with civil society groups, especially women's organizations, in addition to those with government officials.

There is no doubt that Clinton's signature issue during her tenure as secretary of state was women's empowerment: The Hillary Doctrine is simple and direct in its assertion that "the subjugation of women is a direct threat to the security of the United States" and thus should be a major focus of U.S. foreign policy.[112] As Theresa Loar expressed in 2011, "I honestly think Hillary Clinton wakes up every day thinking about how to improve the lives of women and girls. And I don't know another world leader who is doing that."[113] Clinton initiated the first-ever Quadrennial Diplomacy and Development Review (QDDR), published in 2010, to outline a four-year plan for the State Department and USAID: women and girls are mentioned a total of 133 times in its 242 pages.

The QDDR asserts that American foreign policy will "focus our development efforts in six specific areas that build on our strengths: sustainable economic growth, food security, global health, climate change, democracy and governance, and humanitarian assistance. In each area, we will invest in women and girls at every turn, with the goal of empowering them."[114] This document lays out a rationale for supporting women that not only is rooted within a human rights discourse but also invokes realist principles:

> The protection and empowerment of women and girls is key to the foreign policy and security of the United States. As President Obama's National Security Strategy recognizes, "countries are more peaceful and prosperous when women are accorded full and equal rights and opportunity. When those rights and opportunities are denied, countries lag behind."
>
> And as Secretary Clinton has emphasized repeatedly and consistently, "women are critical to solving virtually every challenge we face as individual nations and as a community of nations . . . when women have equal rights, nations are more stable, peaceful, and secure." The status of the world's women is not simply an issue of morality—it is a matter of national security.
>
> To that end, women are at the center of our diplomacy and development efforts—not simply as beneficiaries, but also as agents of peace, reconciliation, development, growth, and stability.
>
> To foster and maximize the diplomatic and development outcomes we seek, we will integrate gender issues into policies and practices at State and USAID. We will ensure that gender is effectively addressed throughout all bureaus and missions, include gender in strategic planning and budget allocation, and develop indicators and evaluation systems to measure the impact of our programs and policies on women and girls.[115]

The programming associated with this new emphasis on women and girls was remarkable. Clinton's Feed the Future Initiative and Global Health Initiative prioritized programs for women. Clinton created the Secretary's International Fund for Women and Girls to channel private donations in this area. She partnered with the United Nations to disseminate 100 million cookstoves, aiming to mitigate the endless respiratory and eye infections that resulted from laboring over traditional hearths that usually burned dung or wood; Clinton made sure the State Department's budget figures highlighted how much money was devoted to programs for women and girls; and she put forward the Data 2X Initiative to improve the collection of statistics about the situation of women and girls to serve as benchmarks for policy evaluation.

Clinton also supported the creation of UNWomen and promoted U.N. Security Council resolutions that furthered the aims of UNSCR 1325, such as UNSCR 1820, 1888, 1889, and 1960,[116] which addressed several related issues, including reporting and accountability for sexual violence in war. She was also instrumental in pushing through the U.S. National Action Plan for Women, Peace, and Security detailing the actions to be implemented by the U.S. government in fulfillment of UNSCR 1325 and in issuing the first-ever secretarial policy directive on promoting gender equality.[117]

These governmental frameworks were comprehensive and cumulative. For example, in just one year—her last full year as secretary of state, 2012—the U.S. government put forth a Counter-Trafficking in Persons Strategy in February, a Policy on Gender Equality and Female Empowerment in March, an Implementation Plan for the National Action Plan on Women, Peace and Security in August, a Strategy to Prevent and Respond to Gender-based Violence Globally also in August, the Equal Futures Partnership in September, and a Vision for Ending Child Marriage and Meeting the Needs of Married Children in October.[118] In addition, it was while Clinton was secretary of state—though not at her behest—that Female Engagement Teams began to be used in Afghanistan, which we will discuss in chapter 5. Clinton established the U.S.-Pakistan Women's Council, which operates in a similar fashion to the U.S.-Afghan Women's Council, in order to support the women of that critical country.

The rhetorical front was promoted vigorously: Clinton's many speeches concerning the importance of women and girls to the security and stability of the international system fill hundreds of megabytes on a computer's hard drive. As secretary of state, Hillary Clinton was simply indefatigable in her support of women and girls. As she explained, "A lot of the work I do here in the State Department on women's or human-rights issues is not just because I care passionately—which I do—but because I see it as [a way] to increase security to fulfill American interests. These are foreign policy and national-security priorities for me."[119]

The larger American culture was also becoming more receptive to these ideas. The pioneering journalism of Nicholas Kristof and Sheryl WuDunn for the *New York Times*, culminating in the blockbuster book *Half the Sky* in 2009, opened the eyes of American citizens to issues they had never heard of before—such as obstetric fistula—and enlisted the visible and enthusiastic support of many Hollywood celebrities, such as Meg Ryan and Eva Mendes. It's no stretch to suggest that nearly every women's book club in the United States read *Half the Sky* when it came out. Jeffery Gettleman, also of the *New York Times*, must be credited with raising awareness of the mass rapes and horrific brutality that characterized the conflict in the Democratic Republic of the Congo.[120] The United States finally began to understand why Hillary Clinton, as secretary of state, persistently made the case for supporting the rights and security of women and girls. In a sense, the United States finally began to know why women were important to U.S. foreign policy.

Clinton also attempted to change attitudes within the State Department. During March 2012, she issued a Policy Guidance Advancing Gender Equality and Promoting the Status of Women and Girls.[121] This was an internal document that went out to every bureau and embassy, asking each to gather information and perform a gender analysis of the situation of women within their area of expertise. She also requested that the State Department examine how the integration of women and girls would improve overall political participation, peace and security, and economic advancement.

The integration of women would also be incorporated into the State Department's three-year strategic plans in the areas of planning/budgeting, programming, monitoring/evaluation, and management/training. A three-day course on gender integration was developed in order to incorporate it into the Foreign Service Institute training curriculum, and gender modules will soon be integrated into the institute's courses so that from day one of a Foreign Service officer's career, he or she will be well briefed on these issues.[122]

Clinton also creatively implemented a "women's track" to various annual, diplomatic, bilateral strategic meetings that took place with India, Pakistan, China, Indonesia, Australia, and other countries. This enabled Melanne Verveer to attend the meetings in her official capacity as head of OGWI, in effect forcing the other country to provide a counterpart to Verveer at the same level (or to create one if they didn't have such a counterpart). The aim was to provide an opening to discuss women's issues. Notably, most nations welcomed this initiative.[123] One OGWI staffer observed that the meeting with China offered the United States, for the very first time, access to the highest-ranking woman in the Chinese government, whom the U.S. Embassy staff in China had never before met. In addition, bilateral memoranda of understanding were also signed that pledged cooperation in specific areas pertaining to women. For example, a Memorandum of Understanding (MOU) with Brazil concluded by Clinton included a section promoting the participation of women in science, technology, engineering, and math.[124]

The Department of Defense was also not immune to the changes sweeping the U.S. government: A Women, Peace, and Security Working Group was formed in U.S. Africa Command (AFRICOM), and gender "points of contact" (specific individuals tasked with being the point person on these issues) were established in all commands and services, and also in the Office of the Secretary of Defense. All of these helped work on the National Action Plan for Women, Peace, and Security.[125] According to Rosa Brooks, former counselor to Under Secretary of State for Policy Michele Flournoy, the Department of Defense "hadn't thought of themselves as caring about gender, but Iraq and Afghanistan helped them see."[126]

During Clinton's tenure as secretary of state, a larger "Hillary effect" also began to unfold. Owing to her position and stature, new opportunities began to open up for women in other countries. This was not only because Clinton inspired so many women to engage the political and economic life within their own countries, but also because her visibility lent both power and protection to women.

One way to see the Hillary effect is to count how many female ambassadors to the United States were appointed while Clinton was secretary of state. One count puts the number at twenty-five, a historic first. "Hillary Clinton is so visible," said Amelia Matos Sumbana, who had just arrived in Washington, D.C., as ambassador from Mozambique. "She makes it easier for presidents to pick a woman [ambassador] for Washington."[127]

Even in the United States, "more than half of new recruits for the U.S. Foreign Service and 30 percent of the chiefs of mission are now women, according to the State Department."[128] For those countries wishing to engage with the State Department, appointing a woman to a powerful diplomatic post signals that a country is progressive and that the United States should take it seriously as a potential partner.

In addition, advocates for women can use Clinton as a yardstick by which to measure their own leaders in a very public fashion. Lena Ag of the Swedish feminist advocacy group Kvinna till Kvinna recounts,

> We used extensively [Hillary Clinton's] speeches and articles to . . . influence our own government. Carl Bildt, our foreign minister, he wasn't hostile to the Women, Peace, and Security agenda, but it wasn't on his radar at all. . . . So for us it was really a leverage to enter into a discussion with him. . . .
>
> We did some journalistic work, and looked at all his speeches, all his blogs, all his press releases, all his blogs, which were all open source, and [we] found he never talked about Women, Peace, and Security. . . .
>
> We published the results in *The Daily News* [Dagens Nyheter], the equivalent of the *New York Times* here, the most prestigious morning paper, and it generated some commotion, and people were talking about it. A year and a half later, we did it again to see if anything had changed, and we gave it to the top news show of the Swedish broadcasting company,

which is like the BBC in Great Britain, and it went viral, because we showed the same results, nothing had changed. . . . We heavily used Hillary Clinton as an example. . . .

After this, he interacted with us on Twitter; when he went to the Balkans, we tweeted him and asked if he had seen any women, are you meeting with any women, and he said that he had seen a few! After that, he has been kind of sensitive, and on International Women's Day, he published something on the government's webpage on Women, Peace, and Security, and now and then he mentions that he meets with women, such as in Afghanistan. . . . If Hillary Clinton talks about it, then the conservative Swedish government we have pays attention. . . . I'm very appreciative.[129]

Mariam Mansury of the Institute for Inclusive Security tells a poignant story of how Hillary Clinton directly used her influence on behalf of women:

At the London Conference in December 2010, there were no women in the Afghan Government's delegation. Secretary Clinton heard that we had brought a group of Afghan women leaders to London. She and her staff secured passes for them to hear her remarks at the conference plenary. And on stage, she specifically referenced the women as critical partners for peace, asking them to stand and be recognized.

As governments were scrambling to finalize the conference communique, her staff reached out to us again. The Secretary wanted the women's recommendations. We sent them over; the final version of the communique included an explicit commitment to ensure that Afghan women's rights would not become a bargaining chip with the Taliban. The Secretary had heard their voices and made sure they were not forgotten.

I was there and saw firsthand how much her commitment meant to the women with whom we work. They had found an ally who delivered when it mattered. From a policy perspective, it set a standard for both the Afghan government and international actors in negotiating with the Taliban. Policymakers began to emphasize their own commitment to the preservation of women's rights. Women were included as formal delegates to the Afghan development conference in Kabul the following July.[130]

While we might wonder why Clinton had not ensured women would be present at the London conference beforehand, this was an important moment for Afghan women, and Clinton was there for them.

Clinton also catalyzed the understanding that the problems women faced were not particular to certain countries or regions, but were truly transnational phenomena. Professor K. P. Vijayalakhshmi of Jawaharlal Nehru University in India explains, "Hillary Clinton helped activists in India. I think one of the things you're seeing is now there's no more shame about what happens in India because you're a poor country. It's not poverty; it's so much more, and it's beyond countries—it's about men and women all around the world. . . . Now when we go back and see those inequalities, we don't see that as a peculiar, India-only problem anymore. I think we are now realizing that women's bodies are the terrain upon which conflict, peace, and security are built across the world."[131]

Perhaps more importantly, Clinton's role allowed her to offer a protective cloak for women, even though some critics complained that "Clinton was devaluing the office of secretary of state by meeting with so many, well, women."[132]

In a speech at the 2012 Women in the World Summit, the actress Meryl Streep recalled her own experiences: "And all weekend long, women from all over the world said the same thing: I'm alive because she came to my village, put her arm around me, and had a photograph taken together. I'm alive because she went on our local TV and talked about my work, and now they're afraid to kill me. I'm alive because she came to my country and she talked to our leaders, because I heard her speak, because I read about her."[133]

Somaly Mam, who established one of the most effective shelters for trafficked women in Cambodia despite backstory issues, told of how her government only began respecting the work of her shelter after a visit by Clinton: "She protects our lives. . . . Our people never paid attention. Hillary has opened their eyes, so now they have no choice; by her work

she has saved many lives in Cambodia—our government is changing."[134]
Leymah Gbowee, Nobel Peace Prize laureate from Liberia, put it this
way: "The men know they can't mess with us because we know BIG
people now."[135]

Despite all of these accomplishments, Clinton's efforts, like those of
Laura Bush, have been tarred with the broader foreign policy agenda
of their respective presidential administrations. Critics condemn the
Obama administration for, among other things, escalating U.S. reliance
on drone strikes, bungling Libyan and Syrian regime change, expanding
the surveillance state, and being willing to enter into peace talks with
the Afghan Taliban. Hillary Clinton was not a bystander to these policies. She supported the 2009 troop surge in Afghanistan. Jodie Evans
of Code Pink remembers collecting the signatures of more than four
thousand Afghan women, pleading with President Obama to call off
the surge: "You have to listen to the women." Obama replied, "I do.
I listen to Hillary."[136]

Two years later, it was reportedly a coalition among Hillary Clinton,
Susan Rice, and Samantha Power that swayed the president toward
military action in support of the Responsibility to Protect operation in
Libya in 2011, even though Obama's secretary of defense and his vice
president opposed the intervention.[137] As one critic opined, "We'd like
to think that women in power would somehow be less pro-war, but in
the Obama administration at least it appears that the bellicosity is worst
among Hillary Clinton, Susan Rice and Samantha Power. All three are
liberal interventionists, and all three seem to believe that when the
United States exercises military force it has some profound, moral, life-
saving character to it. . . . They rode roughshod over the realists in the
administration."[138]

Some have even seen in the Hillary Doctrine echoes of the imperial
feminism they so criticized during the Bush administration. For example,
Mallika Dutt of the human rights organization suggests, "There were
moments with Hillary Clinton when I felt like we were getting too close
to a rescue narrative: 'Here's Hillary Clinton and here's the United States.
We are going to save the women of the world.' " She continues, "US foreign policy creates conditions for enormous amounts of violence against

women. It is ironic—I don't think [Clinton] would have been able to get much traction on women's issues if she hadn't been seen as being tough in these other spaces."[139]

Critics also note that it was under Hillary Clinton's watch that the rights of women in the Arab Uprising countries were curtailed. Perhaps most troublingly, in a 2012 *Washington Post* op-ed, Laura Bush felt compelled to plead with the Obama administration—and by extension Hillary Clinton—not to throw Afghan women "under the bus" as they sought an expeditious exit from that country:

> Last fall, I received a letter from an Afghan woman who wrote encouragingly of refugees who are now home, girls who attend school, women who are able to work and participate in public life, and farmers who have reclaimed their land. But she added, "Though many victories have been won for the Afghan people, I fear it is all at risk, and the return of the Taliban is an impending threat." The rippling consequences of such a return would be devastating.
>
> Many of the vital gains that Afghan women have achieved over the past decade were made because of the sacrifice and support of the United States and the broader NATO alliance. The United States and NATO deserve international gratitude for their role in helping to improve the lives of women in Afghanistan. But now, as the U.S. and NATO mission in Afghanistan changes, the world must remember the women of Afghanistan.
>
> In 2001, the world's eyes were opened to the horrors suffered by Afghanistan's women. Leaders from government, business and civil society around the globe, as well as private citizens, stepped forward to support these women, sending a powerful signal that progress is possible only if it includes all of a country's citizens.
>
> But if this progress is to last, these business and educational investments must be protected and expanded. And, every bit as important, the Afghan government cannot negotiate away women's rights. At their gathering, NATO officials have an opportunity to communicate that aid, investment and alliances are not guaranteed if women are simply to be treated as a bargaining chip.

Having already seen the terrible cost of denying the most basic of human freedoms, do we dare risk the consequences now of abandoning the women of Afghanistan?[140]

In interviews conducted at UNWomen in New York City, some even suggested that Hillary Clinton would have "blood on her hands" because she encouraged Afghan women to stand up, and now these would be targeted for assassination after the U.S. drawdown.[141] Even a former head of USAID, Andrew Natsios, reflected, "I think a lot of the stuff we do actually puts women at risk sometimes. I know in Afghanistan, I think when we leave they're going to start executing the women who have become leaders. We've trained all these women now, they are defending their rights, but they don't have guns."[142] And others have justifiably asked why the empowerment of Afghan women can be advocated publicly, but the empowerment of Saudi women, for example, cannot.[143]

Still others at UNWomen pointed out that the rhetoric emanating from Washington does not match the experiences women have engaging with U.S. State Department and USAID employees and contractors on the ground in their own countries and that gender programming requirements had become a thoughtless box-checking exercise that did not, in the end, help women. Others ask how Hillary Clinton could be a credible voice for women if her own country has not ratified CEDAW and if her own country espouses militaristic values that put women's lives in danger and set back the cause of women by fanning ethnic hatreds. The consensus at the UNWomen brown bag lunch that day in May 2013 was that Hillary Clinton was either a hawk, a hypocrite, a naif—or all three.

On February 1, 2013, Secretary Clinton stepped down from her post to make way for Senator John Kerry. Thus it is that the history outlined in this chapter must now give way to a more important discussion: Is it feasible for a state or even the international community to make women a cornerstone of foreign policy as Hillary Clinton has advocated? Is it in the U.S. national interest to do so, or are there contradictions between the national interest and women's interests that cannot be vouchsafed? For example, surely one litmus test of whether the Hillary Doctrine has been more than rhetoric is what the United States will do to safeguard

Afghan women as it draws down its troops in that country: What is being planned? More generally, what have we learned from the U.S. attempt to follow the Hillary Doctrine, and what is its future, especially now that Clinton is no longer secretary of state?

To set the state for that more policy-oriented discussion, however, we must first ask if there is in fact a relationship between the security of women and the security of the states in which they live, which is the subject of part 2 of this volume.

# PART II

★ ★ ★

## THEORY AND CASES

# 2

# SHOULD SEX MATTER IN U.S. FOREIGN POLICY?

★ ★ ★

Investing in the potential of women and girls is the smartest investment we can make. It is connected to every problem on anyone's mind around the world today. . . . There are people who say, well, women's issues is an important issue, but it doesn't rank up there with the Middle East or Iran's nuclear threat or Afghanistan or Pakistan. I could not disagree more. I think women are key to our being able to resolve all of those difficult conflicts, as well as provide for a better future.

—HILLARY CLINTON, 2010

How is it a national security threat to the United States for women to be at a low status or whatever term you want to use? How is that a threat to American national security interests? I don't see how you can make that argument . . . National security is what's the threat of attack on the United States, during the Cold War or now because of terrorism. I don't see how the two are connected.[1]

—ANDREW NATSIOS

I N THE STUNNING documentary *It's a Girl*, she is unforgettable—a gaunt, ramrod-straight Indian woman in a bright red sari. In a very matter-of-fact voice she explains to the film crew, "I felt we could keep it only if it was a male and kill it if it was a female child. I just strangled it soon after it was born. I would kill it and bury it. Since we were not having any male children. I killed eight girl children."[2] She then takes the cameraman to the low mounds where she had buried her daughters' bodies. More than anything, and long after the movie has ended, it is her lack of emotion and her candor that haunt the viewer.

Indeed, the viewer begins to wonder about the future of a nation that so despises its women that having two X chromosomes constitutes the most dreadful and intolerable of birth defects. Is this just a personal tragedy or is the fate of this woman's nation integrally tied to the fate of her dead daughters?

The foundational question is this: Do the situation, security, and status of women within a nation affect that nation's security, stability, and prosperity? If so, then the premise of the Hillary Doctrine is sound, and warrants a prominent place in U.S. foreign policy. In this chapter, we examine a variety of cases to determine whether the premise is in fact sound.

## WOMEN AND NATIONS

The international policy-making community is already well aware of the relationship between gender inequality and the health and prosperity of a nation: the research literature is replete with robust empirical findings that associate the education and empowerment of women and girls with everything from lowered rates of infectious diseases, malnutrition, infertility, mortality, and morbidity to improved national economic growth, less corruption, and higher gross domestic product per capita.[3]

The authors of the World Bank's 452-page *World Development Report 2012: Gender Equality and Development* conclude:

> Gender equality is smart economics: it can enhance economic efficiency and improve other development outcomes in three ways. First, removing barriers that prevent women from having the same access as men to education, economic opportunities, and productive inputs can generate broad productivity gains—gains all the more important in a more competitive and globalized world. Second, improving women's absolute and relative status feeds many other development outcomes, including those for their children. Third, leveling the playing field—where women and men have

equal chances to become socially and politically active, make decisions, and shape policies—is likely to lead over time to more representative, and more inclusive, institutions and policy choices and thus to a better development path.[4]

Indeed, the evidence is becoming overwhelming: Consider a 2011 Food and Agricultural Organization (FAO) report that demonstrates women farmers could achieve the same yields as men if they enjoyed access to the same resources. Although the "yield gap" between the sexes averages around 20 to 30 percent, the FAO research shows that this is largely attributable to the fact that women have access to far fewer resources than men. Providing equal resources to women would increase the agricultural output of developing countries by 2.5 to 4 percent according to the FAO. This would in turn reduce the number of undernourished people worldwide—925 million according to the FAO's latest estimates—by 12 to 17 percent. In other words, closing the gender gap in agricultural production could bring the number of undernourished people down by as much as 100 million to 150 million people.[5]

The above example reveals that it is now well-nigh impossible to discuss economic development or global health without mentioning the role that gender plays. As Caren Grown, senior gender advisor to the U.S. Agency for International Development (USAID), puts it, "We have a thirty-year evidentiary base now. I think the weight of the evidence demonstrates that the onus is on others to make the case that the gaps between males and females *don't* matter for development outcomes."[6]

Nevertheless, and as the opening quotations for this chapter demonstrate, when the subject is not development and health but national security and foreign policy, many still find it controversial to link the security of women to the overall security of the states in which they live. Grown notes, "In security and diplomacy and in foreign policy, it's not that the case can't be made, it's just hard to get the evidence."[7] That is why in 2009, Valerie Hudson and her colleagues made a first stab at the empirics in large-$N$ statistical testing using data compiled over a ten-year period in the database of the WomanStats Project.[8] The question was straightforward: Is violence against women associated with poorer outcomes on measures of national security and stability?

Hudson and her colleagues did not necessarily begin at square one.[9] A small but burgeoning empirical literature in feminist security studies was beginning to complement the more in-depth ethnographic case studies, process tracing, and poststructuralist discourse analysis that has more typically accompanied the theoretical work in this field.[10] Below is a short survey of just a few of these findings.

In a recent empirical analysis, M. Steven Fish argues against the proposition that Islamic societies per se are disproportionately involved in conflict or disproportionately suffer from authoritarian rule.[11] Rather, Fish uncovers two indicators that better explain the variance in levels of conflict throughout the Islamic world: the sex ratio and the literacy gap between males and females. Fish found that statistical models that included both these variables significantly track authoritarianism in Islamic countries. He hypothesizes that the oppression of females—one of the earliest social acts observed by children—lays the foundation for other types of oppression, including authoritarianism.

In the same vein, Mary Caprioli linked measures of domestic gender inequality—although these measures do not include levels of violence against women—to higher levels of state conflict and insecurity with statistically significant results. Furthermore, states with higher levels of social, economic, and political gender equality were found less likely to rely on military force to settle disputes.[12]

Caprioli and Mark Boyer also demonstrated that states exhibiting high levels of gender equality also display lower levels of violence when they do become involved in international crises and disputes.[13] Examining aggregate data over a fifty-year period (1954–1994), they found a statistically significant relationship between levels of violence during a crisis and the percentage of female leaders. Caprioli extended this analysis to include militarized interstate disputes, a broader category than international conflicts, and found a similar relationship: States with the highest levels of gender equality display lower levels of aggression during these conflicts and were less likely to use force first.[14] Virtually the same pattern was found with respect to intrastate incidents.[15]

And the relationship does not end there. Research undertaken by Caprioli and Peter Trumbore revealed that states characterized by norms of gender and ethnic inequality, as indicated through higher rates of human rights abuses, are more likely to become involved in militarized and violent interstate disputes and to be the aggressors and to use force first when involved in international disputes.[16] David Sobek and coauthors confirmed Caprioli and Trumbore's findings that domestic norms centered on equality and respect for human rights correspond to lower levels of involvement in international conflict.[17] In sum, this body of work demonstrates that the promotion of gender equality goes far beyond the issue of social justice and has important consequences for international security.

These results linking gender and conflict participation are echoed in studies of individual behavior. Rose McDermott and Jonathan Cowden examined sex differences within the context of a simulated crisis game.[18] In these experiments, all-female pairs proved significantly less likely than all-male pairs to spend money on weapons procurement or to go to war when confronted with a crisis.

During further research, McDermott and her coauthors found that when simulating a conflict situation, males are more likely to display overconfidence prior to gaming and are more likely to use unprovoked violence as a tactic.[19] Despite their constraints, these types of simulations permit the inclusion of sex-based psychological variables in theories concerning how gender differences might affect state security decision-making and its outcomes.[20]

Although they did not research nation-state behavior per se, Ronald Inglehart and Pippa Norris examined psychological attitudes toward women across cultures. They discovered that, contrary to popular impression, beliefs about democracy and other political values were not that different between, for example, Islamic and Judeo-Christian cultures. Nevertheless, beliefs concerning gender equality differ markedly, which the authors take as evidence that the conceptualization of culture, or the nation-state, or indeed civilization itself, must be redefined to include a gender perspective. Furthermore, they found that attitudes toward women were strongly associated with country-level indicators such as the percentage of women elected to the national legislature.[21]

These findings are encouraging: There is growing empirical evidence for the proposition that the security of women and the security of the states in which they live are linked. In a 2009 article for *International*

*Security*, Hudson and her colleagues hypothesized that additional, more comprehensive empirical testing would bolster this evidentiary base.[22] Noting that the existing research at that time did not examine a clear marker of women's insecurity—violence against women and girls—the authors used a multivariable index examining the physical security of women in 141 nations and then chose several indicators of state security, including the Global Peace Index (GPI), an index examining intrastate and interstate peacefulness. They also included several alternative hypotheses as statistical controls to explain a state's GPI score, such as the levels of state democracy, economic wealth, or its "civilization" as defined by political scientist Samuel Huntington.

What the research team found was that the best predictor of a state's peacefulness was not level of democracy, or wealth, or civilizational identity: The best predictor of a state's peacefulness was its level of violence against women. These findings cut across wealth, regime type, and region. The authors discovered, for example, that democracies with a high level of violence against women were more likely to score considerably worse on the GPI than those with low levels. While preliminary in nature, this empirical investigation has added to the growing evidentiary base revealing a link between the security of women and the security and stability of the states in which they live. (In our concluding chapter, we will discuss the need to add to that evidentiary base.)

Statistical testing is important, but statistical correlations merely point to the possibility of causation. Even controlling for factors such as democracy and wealth, there could still be other relationships or perturbing variables at work. These could include, for example, negative conditions such as war or famine, which worsen the situation of women. Women are often considered to be a "canary in the coal mine," their plight simply one more sign of whether the society is functional or not. Those skeptical of including women within the purview of U.S. foreign policy often ask the very same question that U.S.-based journalist Charles Bowden recently posed during an interview for this book: "Isn't focusing on women just putting a gas mask on the canary, when you really should be fixing the coal mine?"[23]

After almost two decades of intensive research, however, we now no longer see women as canaries. We believe it is possible to argue that women, or more precisely male-female relations, *are* the coal mine, and the canary that keels over in response does so in the form of explosive national instability. If that is the case, then U.S. foreign policy has only ever been in the business of putting gas masks on that canary and, until the advent of the Hillary Doctrine, hadn't even considered tackling the coal mine. Let's turn our gaze more broadly to examine those cases where it is clearly evident that dysfunctional male-female relations producing serious harm to women undermine the security of nations.

## BEGINNING TO SEE:
## THE BARE BRANCHES OF ASIA

Most graduate students of foreign and security policy during the past century sat through years of coursework with little indication that women even existed on planet Earth. It may have appeared natural and normal back then, but many women involved in security studies today can only recollect those days with complete amazement. The journey that the academic world undertook in order to see and make the invisible visible arguably parallels that of the U.S. government as outlined in chapter 1. One of the first areas of recognition that the situation of women affected national security concerned the sex ratios of Asia.

Sex ratios tell an interesting tale about our world: Standard demographic analysis has already confirmed that there is an abnormal deficit of females in Asia.[24] The preference for sons is not only confined to that part of the world however: Christian Armenia and its neighbor, the largely Muslim Azerbaijan, for example, also exhibit abnormal sex ratios. Nevertheless, the vast majority of the world's "missing women" are from the continent of Asia. Established ranges for normal sex ratios account for anticipated variations with respect to overall population sex ratios and for those associated with childhood and birth, and may be adjusted for country-specific circumstances such as, for example, maternal and infant mortality rates. Using these established normal sex ratio ranges combined with official census data, it is relatively straightforward to determine if there are fewer women in a country's population than could reasonably be expected.

Of course, there are perturbing variables here as well; for example, many of the Gulf states have abnormal sex ratios favoring males, but this is largely due to the high number of predominantly male guest workers that labor in the oil economy. Once these regional and national idiosyncrasies have been taken into account, it becomes evident that the deficit of females in Asia is a real phenomenon. Most of these disparities are the result of the prevalence of sex-selective abortion. This is because inexpensive and widely available ultrasound examinations have made it easier for parents to determine the sex of the baby fairly early on in the pregnancy. If they prefer a son, then securing an abortion is relatively easy.

To determine the scale of the deficit, some comparisons are in order. If we examine overall population sex ratios, for, say, Latin America, the ratio is 97.4 males per 100 females (using 2010 figures)—the corresponding figure for Asia is 104.3 males per 100 females. Perhaps that difference of a few points does not seem significant, but one must also keep in mind the sheer size of the populations of Asia: India and China alone comprise more than 40 percent of the world's population. Those few points of difference translate into millions and millions of women.

Indeed, because Asia has such an enormous share of the world's population, the overall sex ratio of the world is now 101.4 males per 100 females, despite the fact that the ratios for the rest of the world (excluding Oceania) range from 93.1 (Europe) to 99.7 (Africa).[25] It is stunning to realize that women no longer constitute half of humanity—and that the deficit is man-made.

Birth sex ratios in several Asian countries also lie outside the established norm of 105 to 107 boy babies born for every 100 girl babies. The Indian government's 2011 estimate of its birth sex ratio is approximately 109 boy babies born for every 100 girl babies, with some locales reporting ratios of an astounding 156 boys to 100 girls and higher.

The Chinese government states that its birth sex ratio is approximately 118 male babies per 100 female babies, while a number of Chinese scholars have gone on record as stating it is at least 121:100. Again, in some locations, the ratio is higher: The birth sex ratio of the island of Hainan has been as high as 135:100. Other countries of concern in Asia include Pakistan, Bangladesh, Nepal, Bhutan, Taiwan, Afghanistan, and Vietnam. (No data are available for North Korea.)[26]

Another indicator of gender imbalance is early childhood mortality. Boys typically have a higher early childhood mortality rate, which virtually cancels out their birth sex ratio numerical advantage by age five. The reasons behind this include sex-linked genetic mutations, such as hemophilia, as well as higher death rates for boys from common childhood diseases, such as dysentery. Nevertheless, in a number of the Asian nations just mentioned, including China, early childhood mortality rates for girls may actually be higher than those for boys.[27] Moreover, orphanages tend to be filled with healthy girl children, along with a few disabled boys. These indicators reflect a deep cultural preference for boys.

Other statistics also factor into the observed gender imbalance. In the West, for example, male suicides far outnumber female suicides. But in countries with deficits of women, female suicide rates are higher than those of males. In fact, Chinese women of childbearing age make up approximately 55 percent of all female suicides in the world.[28]

What forces drive the deficit of females in Asian nations such as China and India? How do we account for the disappearance of so many women from these populations—estimated conservatively at more than 90 million in seven Asian countries alone, and perhaps as high as 163 million or more?

While the one-child policy in China plays a significant role in driving the deficit in that country, the dynamics in India have their own unique characteristics. For example, in India, far from occurring only among the poor and illiterate, sex selection also appears to be most prevalent in regions that boast high levels of educational attainment and relative prosperity. In the 2011 census, India's population was estimated to be more than 1.2 billion, up from 967 million in 1997. What did not rise, however, but rather declined, was the proportion of females in the zero to six-year age range.

Although the natural sex ratio slightly favors boys at birth, sex ratios in India have been steadily rising, from 103 boys for every 100 girls younger than age seven in 1961, to 108 boys for every 100 girls in 2001, and, according to the latest numbers from the 2011 census, 109.4 boys for every 100 girls. In the area dubbed the "Bermuda triangle for girls" in north and northwest India, the 2011 census reveals that a number of districts are populated with almost 130 boys to every 100 girls. Needless to say, this has population analysts and authorities alike worried. Very worried.

And the problem, maintains François Farah, former chief of population and development for the United Nations Population Fund (UNFPA), can be attributed to what he terms an "unholy alliance" between a modern desire for smaller families, the availability and affordability of prenatal screening technology and abortion, and a strong preference for sons.

In India, a preference for sons is influenced by a plethora of social and economic factors that effectively relegate girls to the status of burden. Parents desire sons because they carry on the family name, inherit family property, and, in the absence of social welfare plans, are perceived as insurance against an impoverished old age. The high costs of providing a dowry means daughters are often viewed as *paraya dhan* (to be married and sent away)—another reason why females are singled out for abortion—or, in its absence, infanticide.

"The whole concept of equality has not sunk in along with modernization," said Farah. "Sex selection occurs when modernization moves ahead of an internalized sense of equity. . . . It is the ultimate manifestation of discrimination. It is particularly vicious. It doesn't affect your conscience because there is no evidence."

Furthermore, a shortage of females does not necessarily translate into improved prospects for those who remain. Indeed, the diminished pool of marriageable women has only increased demand for trafficked women for the purposes of both marriage and prostitution. In order to meet an insatiable demand for marriageable young women, parents—most notably the poor—will often force girls to forgo their education in order to wed and bear children.

Although existing laws ban sex-determination testing in India, in 2013 at least 60 million girls in that country are now "missing"—effectively falling into a demographic black hole from which, analysts fear, there will be no return.[29] In Punjab, the government claims that the numbers of missing girls will increase by 40 percent in the forthcoming generation. Furthermore, while legislation may be an important first step toward the elimination of the practice, the deeper problem of gender discrimination needs to be addressed alongside effective law enforcement.

By far one of the worst consequences, notes Ena Singh, assistant UNFPA representative for India, is an escalation of violence against women and girls. "There is already a problem with sexual violence in this country," she says. "That either increases or decreases depending on the number of girls in a given society. I ask you, could you send your young daughter out into the street happily if there were nothing but young men around?"

Evidence is also mounting that skewed sex ratios, combined with the long-established low status of Indian women, are beginning to have an effect on traditional concepts of the family. In rural Punjab, where the shortage of women is most pronounced, a desire to keep rural family holdings intact is now driving a trend toward polyandrous unions where one woman, often "purchased" from poorer regions or from lower castes, is forced to be "wife" not only to her husband, but also to brothers and even, according to some reports, her own father-in-law. Known as Draupadis—so named after the wife of the five Pandavas in the epic poem *Mahabharata*—these women inhabit the very lowest rungs of the family hierarchy and are subjected to ongoing sexual and physical abuse.

"Once these kinds of boundaries of shame break down," Singh said, "it is really hard to tell where this rubbish will stop. The levels of violence in these situations are unimaginable. If these kinds of practices become widespread, it will be very, very destabilizing for society."

In Haryana State, where sex ratio imbalances are among the highest, women have banded together to form *jagriti mandalis* (forums of awakening) aimed at promoting the rights of daughters. To counter the huge profits inherent in providing sex identification services and abortions, these groups are attempting to convince families and doctors of the broader social costs. In Himachel Pradesh, the state government recently revoked laws penalizing elected representatives that choose to have more than two children; while in Punjab, religious leaders have issued condemnations of couples that abort female fetuses.

It is, however, an uphill battle. Although governments are striving to control the use of ultrasound, and operators are now forbidden to divulge the sex of would-be offspring, in many regions implementation remains spotty to nonexistent. Reports have also surfaced of authorities targeting women, who are themselves victims of discrimination, instead of focusing their attention on the doctors and technicians who have the most to lose.

In many regions, women who fail to deliver boys are harassed by their in-laws or thrown out on the street. In a recent interview with an Indian nongovernmental organization (NGO), Dr. B. S. Dahiya, a former civil surgeon and Haryana State Appropriate Authority for the Pre Natal Determination Technique Act, charges that doctors, "have forgotten their ethics, and are organized in gangster-like Mafia and are making 2000 rupees [about $40] per day in commissions for ultrasonographers."

Singh, for one, concurs, for female birthrates are lowest among the most affluent. This points to a demand that shows no sign of abating—despite legislation and judicial sanction. "If you can afford to buy a car, a refrigerator and a microwave, then maybe you can afford to make sure you have a son as well." Wealthier families where the wife does not work outside the home are also more likely to opt for sex selection. "In these homes, women are valued more for their reproductive role, as mothers and sexual caretakers, than as productive citizens in their own right," says Singh. "They are more likely to be susceptible to family pressure for a son."

Experts also blame dwindling numbers of girls on the two-child norm heavily promoted throughout the country; in some states, government employment is linked to having a small family size. As we see in China, a strong push toward smaller family size leads to sex-selective abortion in cultures where females have traditionally been devalued. Says Farah, "It is promulgating the idea that the perfect family involves one girl and one boy." According to Farah, families are more likely to abort a female fetus if the first child is also a girl.[30]

Is the situation hopeless or is this a case of insufficient political will? Consider the following experience of the municipality of Shenzen in southern China. Alarmed at its rising birth sex ratio, which reached 118:100 in 2002, local officials instituted a strict crackdown on black market ultrasound clinics. Officials offered 200 yuan (US$32) for tips as to where these clinics could be found and then vigorously prosecuted the owners of the machines and the technicians using them. They also applied a minimum prison term. By 2004—that is, in just two years—the birth sex ratio had dropped to 108:100.[31]

These types of accounts support the thesis that the modern gender imbalances in Asia, as with historical gender imbalances elsewhere, are largely a man-made phenomenon. Girls are being culled from the population, whether through prenatal sex identification and female sex-selective abortion, or through relative neglect in early childhood (including abandonment), or through desperate life circumstances that might result in suicide. But what is "man-made" is susceptible to policy initiatives that disincentivize such behavior—or incentivize it.

China's one-child policy is a case in point, for it is a significant reason why China's birth sex ratio has increased so dramatically over the past thirty years. Originally deployed as a strategy to keep the lid on China's runaway population growth, the one-child policy was announced in 1978 and made law in 1981. Although it did indeed slow growth, planners did not factor in how powerful son preference was, nor could they have predicted the explosion in ultrasound technologies. When the one-child birth policy went into effect, the sex ratio at birth was 108.5:100, which is only slightly abnormal. It is now officially more than 119:100, with scholarly estimates ranging higher.

This alteration of the birth sex ratio has produced a startling result: At least 40.6 million women are now missing from the population of China (some estimates are as high as 50 million).[32] Furthermore, it is not older women who have gone missing, but younger women and girls: the younger the cohort, the greater the proportion and number of missing females. In 2013, China loosened its one-child policy as part of a larger policy to encourage more normal sex ratios, allowing couples where only one spouse was an only child to have two children. Previously, both spouses had to be only children in order to qualify.

Demographers are skeptical that this small tweaking of the one-child policy will produce its intended effect. But even if it does, China must cope with the severely abnormal sex ratios of those generations who have already been born. There is reason to believe that the culling of so many girls from China's population will not have a salutary effect on its national security.

## BARE BRANCHES AND RISING VIOLENCE

The excess sons of China represent the other side of the sex ratio coin from the missing daughters. For every daughter culled from the population, another son will become "surplus"—or in colloquial Chinese, a "bare branch" on the family tree. Our estimates are that by the year 2020, young adult bare branches (aged 15–34) will number approximately 22 million to 25 million in China alone, or 13 percent of total adult population of young males. As noted, the Chinese government estimates that the figure is actually closer to 40 million, while other Western researchers cite figures closer to 50 million.[33]

No society has ever had to cope with this number of bare branches before, and the percentage of surplus boys increases in lockstep according to the year in which they were born. That is, in 1986 there was a higher percentage of surplus sons in the birth population than in 1985, and in 1987 than 1986, and so on.

In projecting the effects of this unprecedented demographic shift, it is important first to understand which young men will become bare branches: it will be those who are unlikely to marry or to establish a family. Well-off young men with education, skills, money, looks, or some combination thereof will be the fortunate ones in the marriage sweepstakes. Young disadvantaged men, however—those who are poor, unskilled, and illiterate—are more likely to find themselves unable to marry and to have a family. These men occupy the lower rungs of the socioeconomic ladder and are already disenfranchised and alienated from established society: Their inability to form a family only deepens their sense of grievance with the existing social order.

Every society faces the critical task of transitioning those who have little stake in a social order based on law toward developing a meaningful personal stake in that society. It is typically young men who prefer a social order based on physical force, wherein they would possess a natural advantage. Almost every traditional society accomplishes the transition of its bachelor males into a more law-abiding path through marriage and the birth of children.

This is because marriage and child rearing has a significant impact on male aggression. For decades now, sociologists have noted that male criminal behavior drops significantly upon marriage or a serious commitment either to a relationship or to children. In societies where a majority of men are unable to undergo this passage, negative social repercussions will ensue—as in a number of Middle Eastern countries, China, and India.[34] By 2020, at least 13 percent—and perhaps as many as 15 percent—of young adult Chinese males will forfeit the transition owing to a lack of marriageable young women.

Social stability will likely take a serious hit as a result. Among the most critical repercussions will be a jump in crime rates: most notably violence, intimate and sexual violence against women, substance abuse, and the formation of gangs involved in all of the above antisocial behaviors.[35] Research is confirming these predictions; for example, using annual province-level data, Edlund and colleagues found that for every 1 percent alteration of the sex ratio in favor of males, there was a corresponding 3.7 percent increase in violent and property crime rates in China.[36] Other empirical studies have also revealed similar results in other nations such as India and Korea.[37] Violent crime rises in tandem with sex ratios; what affects women's security affects national security.

And crime is not the only trend that corresponds to sex ratios: protests and demonstrations are also increasing in size and frequency. Writing in the *Atlantic*, Alan Taylor notes, "According to research by the Chinese Academy of Governance, the number of protests in China doubled between 2006 and 2010, rising to 180,000 reported 'mass incidents.' "[38]

Why would alterations in sex ratios affect societal stability? According to Hudson and Den Boer, this is because unattached young adult males are many times more likely to engage in criminal or self-destructive behaviors than those who are in a relationship or married.[39] Furthermore, unattached young adult males tend to congregate in groups, and when they do, their behavior is even more antisocial than as individuals. These empirical findings are the same worldwide: Young adult males—especially unattached young adult males—monopolize violence in every human society.

Gangs made up of bare branches also coalesce into small armies—which in turn may expand into even larger forces more likely to challenge the authority of the government, be it local or national. One such example occurred in China during the mid-1800s. The Nien Rebellion was made up of insurgents who opposed the Qing dynasty, which also had to contend with yet another movement, the Taiping, which was active in the south.[40]

The Nien originally formed during 1851 in the Huai-pei region, as it was known at the time. Because of a series of natural and man-made disasters, families turned to female infanticide to such a degree that the sex ratio spiked to approximately 129 males for every 100 females. In the absence of work, young men—most of who were bare branches—began to join smuggling rings. Over time, the gangs merged, and as their forces grew, so did their ambitions.

A Nien county magistrate concluded that three categories of men were behind the unrest—bare branches, smugglers, and bandits—and that the overlap between the three groups was considerable. By 1862, the Nien controlled a territory of almost 6 million people. It took the imperial army until 1868 to crush the insurgency.[41]

Governments are only now beginning to recognize the growing threat posed by groups formed primarily of bare branches. Historical commentaries from China, India, and other nations make reference to these "surplus males" as a continuing source of instability.[42]

The problem for governments, however, is how to meet this internal threat. Most focus on lowering the number of bare branches by engaging in strategies such as encouraging outmigration, colonizing frontier areas, initiating large-scale public works projects, easing the immigration of women, and so forth. China has already deployed a number of these, including encouraging young males to emigrate to the Russian Far East and other countries, expanding the number of settlements in Xinjiang and Tibet, constructing the Three Gorges Dam and a series of immense canal projects, among other initiatives. Another tactic is to turn a blind eye to cross-border chattel markets—that is, trafficking—of women from North Korea, Laos, Vietnam, Myanmar, and other neighboring nations. Nevertheless, many argue that China has not yet come to grips with the likely future consequences of this real threat: The sheer number and proportion of bare branches in China (and India, Pakistan, Vietnam, Taiwan, and several other surrounding nations) continues to grow every year.

In their survey of the historical literature, Hudson and Den Boer also stumbled upon two other troubling trends. First, governments facing appreciable numbers of bare branches tend to become more autocratic in order to counter the ensuing instability. Second, in a number of cases, governments have felt compelled to conscript bare branches into the military in order to pacify them by providing a steady income, but then found it necessary to send these bloated militaries to fight in other

countries because of the risks posed by keeping armies too close to population centers and seats of power. Arming bare branches and training
them in military tactics only amplifies the threat. The end result? Prospects for both democracy and peace are diminished when large numbers
of bare branches flood a society unprepared to deal with such a demographic calamity.

As security analysts contemplate potential future conflicts in disputed
areas such as Jammu and Kashmir and the Taiwan Strait as well as the
spiraling crime rates and ethnic tensions in India, they should also keep
in mind that large numbers of bare branches will likely seriously undermine the logic of deterrence and restraint in affected countries over the
next several decades.

Abnormal sex ratios are certainly not a necessary precondition for all
conflicts or war (for example, in 1994 the sex ratio of Rwanda was normal); rather, the existence of a large surplus of young adult males may
aggravate the likelihood of instability and armed aggression.

When bare branch collectives rise to a level where they more directly
challenge government control, the government may well perceive this
as more menacing than traditional external threats. For example, the
historical record shows that when faced with serious numbers of bare
branches, in some cases monarchs have actually opted to initiate interstate war.[43] That these external conflicts wound up as intractable, long,
and bloody turned out to be the very reason these monarchs initiated
them in the first place: to send the unwanted bare branches away from
centers of national power and to ensure they never came back.

The Chinese government is not ignorant of this problem and has
launched a multipronged national campaign to normalize sex ratios.
Although in 2004 the government hoped to normalize birth sex ratios
by 2010—a failure, since the birth sex ratio is worse now than in 2004—
government intervention did manage to slow the demographic trend
toward more baby boys. In contrast, the Indian government has been far
less effective in combating this problem.

As we noted previously, in 2013 the Chinese government slightly
revised the one-child policy. Nevertheless, there are additional signs
that further change may be in the offing. For example, that same year a
government think-tank urged China's leaders to allow two children for

every family, saying the country had paid a "huge political and social cost" for the one-child policy.[44] Unfortunately for China (and other countries with seriously abnormal sex ratios), the proverbial horse has already left the barn: the sex ratios from 1980 to the present day cannot be undone. The sex ratio of China's young adults will be distorted for decades more to come.

Thus, Asia—and possibly the entire world—will live with the consequences of its contempt for daughters for decades to come. Case studies of the bare branches of China and India make plain the linkage between the security of women and the security of the states in which they live. By allowing this gross harm, China, India, and other lands, such as Vietnam, will surely encounter a whirlwind of instability and insecurity. In this case, "gendercide," as manifested in the unceremonious dispatch of girl fetuses, is not the consequence but the actual cause of a national security threat; not the canary, then, but the coal mine.

## EXTENDING OUR GAZE: MALE-FEMALE RELATIONS AND NATIONAL SECURITY

Sex-selective abortion and female infanticide are not the only cases where the link between violence against women and the stability of the societies in which they live can be observed. Conflict researchers, scholars, and economists are only now investigating many such intersections—such as between polygyny and the recruitment into terrorist/rebel groups, for example, or between arranged patrilocal marriage for underage girls and the rise of clan governance, which undermines the possibility of democratic rule.[45]

In this section, however, we want to delve deeper and confront the "why" question: Why are women so pivotal to a nation's security? Why is the character of male-female relations within a society so salient to national security? To begin, we first return to Hillary Clinton, who has often expressed an understanding of this critical nexus: "So the next time you hear someone say that the fate of women and girls is not a core national security issue, it's not one of those hard issues that really smart people deal with, remind them: The extremists understand the stakes of this struggle. They know that when women are liberated, so are entire societies. We must understand this too. And not only understand it, but act on it."[46]

We will investigate what Clinton is saying before we examine, in later chapters, how to act upon this knowledge. Clinton is asserting that how women are treated is not epiphenomenal to the security of a given society—it is integral.

For example, why is the Pakistani Taliban so terrified of the sight of a little girl attending school—so frightened that they would shoot a mere child in the face, as they did to Malala Yousafzai? Is it a mere coincidence that Saudi Arabia—a U.S. ally—is both one of the largest exporters and patrons of terrorists as well as the largest proselytizing force behind an interpretation of Islam that dictates a profoundly sub-ordinate status for women?

Something is going on here; something very deep, very old, and very ugly. As Clinton goes on to note, "Why extremists always focus on women remains a mystery to me. But they all seem to. It doesn't matter what country they're in or what religion they claim. They want to control women: They want to control how we dress; they want to control how we act; they even want to control the decisions we make about our own health and bodies."[47] To our modern minds it may seem a "mystery"—but in order to proceed we must first plumb its depths.

One way of approaching this is to go to ground and carefully trace the multi-faceted effects of open attacks on women, such as those character-ized by the conflict in the Democratic Republic of the Congo, where one U.N. force commander opined, "It is more dangerous to be a woman than to be a soldier."[48] If we can train our eyes to see that web of effects, answers to our "why" question may come into view. We begin this pro-cess-tracing with the fieldwork of Ann Jones, and then in chapter three, extend that exercise with our own fieldwork in Guatemala.

As Ann Jones writes in *War Is Not Over When It's Over*, the con-sequences of waging a war on women are dire—and not only for the women themselves:

> But shaming or provoking enemy men [through wholesale rape of women] is merely the beginning of a process meant to destroy the life of a whole community and/or "cleanse" an area. In eastern Congo, the process goes

like this: Husbands cast out raped wives to fend for themselves, with or without their children. Or raped wives with no visible injuries conceal the fact of rape from their husbands and try to carry on. In either case, women are afraid to venture out to gather firewood, or fetch water, or cultivate their fields. For a time, women band together to work the fields, until soldiers abduct a group en masse. Terrified, women begin to neglect their crops, or soldiers steal the produce, and families suffer malnourishment and hunger. With no surplus products to sell at market, women have no money. They can't pay school fees for their children. Girls are afraid to go to school; now boys drop out, too. Some men leave the village, shamed by a wife's rape. Some men leave to join a militia, voluntarily or by force. Some men never come back. Some outcast women leave, too, for cities or truck stops where they take up "survival sex," selling the only asset they have left, their already dirtied bodies.

The localized famine spreads. People weaken and grow ill, but there is no money to pay for a visit to the hospital, and the trip may be too dangerous to undertake. (Women have been raped on the way home from hospitals where they were treated for rape.) People begin to die of commonplace complaints like diarrhea, pneumonia, or malaria that they would have survived in better days. A study conducted by the IRC [International Rescue Committee] concluded that between August 1998 and April 2007, 5.4 million "excess deaths" occurred in the DRC, most of them from easily preventable and treatable diseases. Significantly, 2.1 million of those deaths occurred after the war formally ended in 2003.

So divisive is rape, and the shame and terror that attend it, that even in the best case a family may fall apart. The rare husband who stands by his raped wife finds that his brother's family no longer visits him, nor his uncle's either. The durability of extended family ties, the allegiance of kinfolk, the pleasant give-and-take of hospitality at the heart of Congolese life—all fade and fracture. Fragments of families pack up and move to places they believe to be more safe, leaving empty houses in the village, soon looted by soldiers. In this way the community falls apart. Those who leave are desperate, penniless, often ill with sexually transmitted infections. Those who stay are old, ill, infirm. Those who return find their property ransacked, and their friends and neighbors vanished. They move away again. In this way the people who have not already been removed to serve the soldiers are cleared off, leaving an open field for armies to go about the real business of war, which is, of course, business. In the Congo, that business is—as it has been since the first sales trip of Henry Morton Stanley—extracting natural resources and selling them. All of that is made possible by rape used as a tactic of war—millions dead and a way of life gone. And along the roads, begging and threatening, are gangs of boys: orphans of war and unwanted offspring of rape who aspire to be soldiers.[49]

In this passage lies a partial glimpse of what we seek. Although Jones is writing about the Democratic Republic of the Congo, her observations could encompass any number of locales—such as along the Burmese border, in Iraq or in the jungles of Colombia. What Jones has so eloquently laid out is the degree to which women weave the fabric of every human community. Even though one would never know it by reading the glorified "bromance" that passes for the historical record of humanity, women weave the web of life.

Even as woman makes temporal existence possible for herself, she also nurtures men, children, other women, and the children placed in her care. She does so according to gender roles usually assigned to her at birth. Water, food, heat, clothing, and rudimentary medical care are part of what she must do every day to keep everyone alive. And the very future of the community—its children—comes from her body. Through her efforts, she socializes them to develop a desire to remain part of the larger community.

If women are incapacitated or killed, the family and the community unravels just as surely as if a weaver had left her loom. And if the women leave, the men and the children will follow. One of the most effective tactics of war, therefore, is to explicitly target women.[50] Observed through this lens, it is clear that one cannot speak of national security without speaking of what is happening with women.

There is a deeper level to this realization we must also see. Jones also notes that those "in charge"—overwhelmingly men—are profoundly, and thus humiliatingly, dependent on those who are "not in charge," that is, women. The powerful are not indispensable, but the powerless are. In traditional societies, it is primarily women who till the soil, provide for a man's next meal, and ensure his very future through children, even though he too often deems the women in his life as inferior beings.

Indeed, a man knows that his very existence originates from what he may consider to be the deformed and unclean body of an inferior, a woman. Furthermore, his cherished customs and values and beliefs would simply evaporate if that inferior woman refuses to cooperate in socializing the young to accept his belief system or if she is persuaded by other ways and other beliefs. It is an awful psychological state to find oneself in—to *feel* oneself as powerful but simultaneously *know* one is powerless. It is a recipe for the deepest shame and humiliation and thus for the cruelest abuse based on the fear that the inferior will not forever accept that status.

Indeed, one can argue, that there lies at the very core of extremism an overwhelming imperative to contain and ultimately obliterate female agency. Men know that a woman who is left to her own devices and is free of fear is also more likely to reject his need of her, whether that need be for temporal sustenance, children, socialization of the young, or sex.

For the man whose ego is based on hypermasculine notions of total power, even a woman's sexual autonomy may threaten his very self. He may be the rapist, but she is to blame. He wants her, but he loathes that he wants her and he hates her even more for not wanting him. Furthermore, he hates that he desires a body so polluted, one that bleeds and leaks and is soft and not hard.

While women fear that men will kill them, men fear that women will humiliate them by repudiating their control, which casts into doubt their manhood. Even today, many courts consider humiliation a mitigating factor when men beat or murder women. This control can be subtle or overt, but it is woven into the daily lives of women. While in Côte d'Ivoire and Liberia, Ann Jones gave cameras to women and asked them to record the scenes of their daily lives:

> Wives were told every day to do things they didn't have the time or strength to do, let alone the inclination. Failure brought punishment. When the women began to bring in their photographs, I learned that men routinely beat their wives for their failure: to produce dinner on time, wash the clothes, sell tomatoes, stay at home, go to the field to work. The list was endless. Men also beat their wives for small acts of assertion; going to visit a

neighbor, answering back, being tired or "lazy." Men referred to wife beating as "education." Men said that educating a wife in proper conduct was a great and tiring responsibility. . . . This was another reason the women wanted education: to relieve men of the duty of beating them. Annie . . . said she enrolled in a literacy course for precisely that reason, but every day her husband ripped the latest exercise from her notebook and used it as toilet paper. Kebeh . . . said that when she disobeyed her husband's order to give up her literacy class, he got out his gun . . . and tried to kill her. Annie and Kebeh reached the same conclusion . . . "He doesn't want me to be educated," Annie said, "He'd rather hit me."

What emerged from these massed photos was a bigger picture, a broader definition of gender-based violence. For village women gender-based exploitation, enforced by violence, seemed to be life itself—a life that requires relentless forced hard labor *because they are women.* Here was the perfect political economy of misogyny: gender-based servitude. Women labored. Men profited. . . . For some women, it seemed, the difference between peace and war was not what was done to them, but which men did it.[51]

A deep pathology of resentment lurks beneath the surface of these "traditional customs," whose parallels can be found in so many societies around the world—even in the twenty-first century, and even in more developed nations and among more educated demographics. To despise women is to despise your own life; to attack women is to attack your own life. You can beat her, rape her, kill her, control her, but you will always need her. And that need means that in actuality, you are not powerful and she is not powerless. She is not, in the end, "yours." Charles Lindholm offered the following observation from the Swat Pukhtun of northern Pakistan:

Relations between husbands and wives tend to be warlike. Even in sex, tenderness is said to be absent. . . . The problem of sexual relationships is understandable given the ideology that all women are, in themselves, repulsive and inferior, and have the potential to shame men. The repulsiveness of women is linked to the conundrum they pose in the social structure as the foci of the contradiction between the necessity of exchanging women and the social ideal of the self-sufficient [patrilineal] family. Also linked is the prevalence of homosexuality among the men, who find a relationship with a boy less demanding and more pleasurable than with a woman. Yet, though women are despicable, men know they cannot survive without them. A woman can chase her husband from the house by simply refusing to cook for him. Women are powerful, despite the ideology of their inferiority. This ambiguity further stirs the disgust of the Pukhtun. . . . A woman not only exposes the contradictions of the patrilineal pose of splendid male isolation and domination, but she is also in herself a contradiction, embodying both weakness and strength.[52]

And thus it is that the most terrifying thought for any patriarchal society is a free woman, for she represents the demise of gender-based servitude and all parasitical lifestyles for men based on that servitude.

What our years of study and observation lead us to conclude, in agreement with the Hillary Doctrine, is that the character of relations between men and women in society is the originary template for all other relations within that society and between it and other societies. As Robin Morgan expressed, "whatever cruelties men visit upon one another they have first tested and refined on women."[53]

As the German philosopher Klaus Theweleit notes in *Male Fantasies*, a remarkable meditation inspired by the writings of the proto-Nazi Freikorps, fascism, like all forms of extremism, is predicated on a horror and ambivalence about the female body: one that underpins hatred of the Other. As with patriarchal ideologues the world over, Freikorps soldiers tended to characterize their own bodies as "hard, phallic and machine like," and the enemy—whether Russians, communists, or the German working class—as "a soft, dirty, feminine morass" that nevertheless threatened to subsume their authority.[54]

If true, this means that the character of male-female relations determines to what degree a society will encourage injustice, coercion, and violence or justice, democracy, and peaceful resolution of conflicts. The research cited earlier showing that the most powerful predictor of state peacefulness is not democracy or wealth or culture but rather the level of violence against women reflects this deeper reality.

As Susan Moller Okin wrote:

> The family is the first, and arguably the most influential, school of moral development. It is the first environment in which we experience how persons treat each other, and in which we have the potential to learn how to be just or unjust. If children see that sex difference is the occasion for obviously differential treatment, they are surely likely to be affected in their personal moral development. They are likely to learn injustice, by absorbing the message, if male, that they have some kind of "natural" enhanced entitlement and, if female, that they are *not* equals, and had better get used to being subordinated if not actually abused.[55]

The obsession of those whom Clinton characterizes as "extremists" with how women dress, their behavior, their education, and their horizons is undeniably fierce. The emotions behind the condemnation and hatred of all things female are visceral and touch chords of shame, humiliation, disgust, and fear, and are among the most powerful motivators in the human repertoire.

Such extremists will never be able to relinquish their obsession, for they know if women ever win their freedom, extremism will have lost the very foundation of its "power." As Robin Morgan puts in her classic work, *The Demon Lover*, "What cannot be totally erased must be controlled . . . much as he can conquer her, possess her, own her, kill her—*he cannot become her* . . . bound, hobbled, silenced, battered, raped raw, starved, exhibited, bought and sold and traded, pedestaled or guttered, derided, trivialized, dismissed, erased—*something there is in her that refuses it*," and so is unleashed the "fury at whatever cannot be controlled."[56]

There is a continuum here, one that runs from the coal mine to the state to the world. When a member of the Afghan Independent Human Rights Commission notes that in Afghanistan, "[i]t's like a civil war between men and women," we understand why the land is filled with violence.[57] This is no new equation; John Stuart Mill argued that the tyrant at home becomes the tyrant in the state and the tyrant at war with other nations. Home is the training ground for "bigger" games.[58]

What we have explored thus far vindicates the premise of the Hillary Doctrine: There is an underlying sexual politics to all extremism that is ignored at the risk of undertaking misplaced policy initiatives, such as emphasizing gas masks for canaries. Thus, the explosive societal instability, violence, and extremism that U.S. foreign policy makers typically focus on emanates from deeper sources that they do not—or will not—see.

## NATIONALISM'S MINION: VIOLENCE AGAINST WOMEN

*Patria o Muerte*: the Fatherland or Death. Whether from the Right or the Left, the direction is dizzyingly the same. . . . It is a male community. . . . Again and again, the erasure of women permeates the theory and practice of political change—and thus leaves the political structure inherently intact.[59]

On a spring day in 1994, nationalism came for Denise, a newly married young woman in Rwanda. She later described what happened:

They began to beat me on the legs with sticks. Then one of them raped me. He said, "you are lucky. Your god is still with you because we don't want to kill you. Now the Hutu have won. You Tutsi, we are going to exterminate you. You won't own anything." When he finished, he took me inside and put me on a bed. He held one leg of mine open and another one held the other leg. He called everyone who was outside and said, "you come and see how Tutsikazi are on the inside." Then he said, "You Tutsikazi, you think you are the only beautiful women in the world." Then he cut out the inside of my vagina. He took the flesh outside, took a small stick and put what he had cut on the top. He stuck the stick in the ground outside the door and was shouting, "Everyone who comes past here will see how Tutsikazi look." Then he came back inside and beat me again. Up to today, my legs are swollen. Then they left. I crawled out of the house bleeding. There was blood everywhere.[60]

While sex differences across animal species produce a dazzling diversity of male-female interaction, Richard Wrangham and Dale Peterson note that out of "4,000 mammals and 10 million or more other animal species," only two (humans and chimpanzees) live in "patrilineal, male-bonded communities wherein females routinely reduce risks of inbreeding by moving to neighboring groups . . . [creating] a system of intense, male-initiated territorial aggression, including lethal raiding into neighboring communities in search of vulnerable enemies to attack and kill. . . . The system of communities defended by related men is a human universal that crosses space and time."[61]

In contemporary terms, these male dominance hierarchies are the foundation of nationalism, which we will argue is highly colored by patriarchy. By nationalism, we refer not only to groupings based on ethnic ties, but all groupings created by male-bonded communities, where those are primarily of an ethnic, religious, racial, geographic, ideological, or other nature. Wrangham and Peterson write of this type of social system, "Patriarchy is worldwide and history-wide. . . . It serves the reproductive purposes of the men who maintain the system. Patriarchy comes from biology in the sense that it emerges from men's temperaments, out of their evolutionarily derived efforts to control women and at the same time have solidarity with fellow men in competition against outsiders. . . . Patriarchy has its ultimate origins in male violence."[62]

This violence is most tellingly directed against women, including those belonging to one's own group. Given that sexual dimorphism characterizes human beings, the system "works." That is, women accede to coercion because of "the one terrible threat that never goes away"—the need of females to be protected from killer males outside their closest social unit, who will injure or kill not only females but also the children that females guard.[63] As the criminologist Neil Boyd noted, "Men are bigger, stronger and faster. It is this, coupled with a tendency towards aggression, that has historically put women and girls at a tremendous disadvantage."[64]

The battering—and often death—that women suffer at the hands of the males they live with is the price paid for such "protection" and occurs "in species where females have few allies, or where males have bonds with each other."[65] It is also more likely to occur when women are economically dependent on male kin. As we will explore, from a woman's perspective, nationalism often takes on the characteristics of a "protection racket," where, as we have previously mentioned, "the difference between peace and war was not what was done to them, but which men did it."[66]

Indeed from an evolutionary perspective, it is astonishing to reflect that sex differences among humans trump the blood ties associated with natural selection for inclusive fitness. As anthropologist Barbara D. Miller notes, "Human gender hierarchies are one of the most persistent, pervasive, and pernicious forms of inequality in the world. Gender is used as the basis for systems of discrimination which can, even within the same household, provide that those designated 'male' receive more food and live longer, while those designated 'female' receive less food to the point that their survival is drastically impaired."[67]

The entrenchment of patrilineal, male-bonded groups breeds a collective identity that we here term nationalism, but of course predates nation-states and can be based on other characteristics besides nation-state affiliation, such as those linked to religion, race, ideology, geography, clan, and so forth. This patriarchal style, the hallmark of which is the targeting of in-group women for control and domination, will also inevitably lead to aggression against out-groups. Males in these male-bonded groups quickly discover that resources may be gained at little cost and risk through coalitional violence. Though they first learn this modus operandi through being socialized to use violence against women within their group to obtain resources and services, they extend the lessons learned to men and women from different groups.

How does this male bonding arise? In the first place, the form of exogamy practiced among humans and chimpanzees (where daughters leave the group to mate) mean that males of the group are kin. As a result, blood ties provide the necessary trust for male-bonded gangs to engage in such violence. Thus, the coercion of out-groups becomes relatively inexpensive, with a potentially great payoff.

Dominant males in coalition with their male kin are therefore able to adopt a parasitical lifestyle based on physical force that requires an initial "investment" of violence but, when exercised over the long haul, demands very little effort. Adopting a willingness to harm, kill, and enslave others, they thereby gain every resource that natural selection predisposes them to desire: food, women, territory, resources, status, political power, pride. The anthropologist-psychologist Barbara B. Smuts suggests, "The degree to which men dominate women and control their sexuality is inextricably intertwined with the degree to which some men dominate others."[68]

Contemporary human societies, of course, do not inhabit the evolutionary landscape of hundreds of thousands of years ago. We would be remiss, however, if we did not note that male coalitionary violence and resulting patriarchy are primal, and how that influence remains a powerful influence into today. While many male-bonded groups around the world are still based on blood ties between men, such as the tribes of Afghanistan, other groups may foster a brotherhood based on other commonalities, such as shared religious beliefs. However, all groups that have at their heart the male bond will share many behavioral characteristics, including violence against women and out-groups, characteristics that have been shaped by the legacy of evolution.

Bradley Thayer notes that humans are only about four hundred generations removed from this landscape.[69] Indeed, only eight generations have passed since the industrial revolution, and the past still bears heavily on human behavioral tendencies. Thus, the men among us have certain behavioral proclivities induced by the "strange path" our ancestors took. Wrangham and Peterson argue, "Men have a vastly long history of violence [which] implies that they have been temperamentally shaped to use violence effectively, and that they will therefore find it hard to stop. It is startling, perhaps, to recognize the absurdity of the system: one that works to benefit our genes rather than our conscious selves, and that inadvertently jeopardizes the fate of all our descendants."[70]

In other words, the foreign policy of human groups, including modern states, is more dangerous because of the human male evolutionary legacy:

Unfortunately, there appears something special about foreign policy in the hands of males. Among humans and chimpanzees at least, male coalitionary groups often go beyond defense [typical of monkey matriarchies] to include unprovoked aggression, which suggests that our own intercommunity conflicts might be less terrible if they were conducted on

behalf of women's rather than men's interests. Primate communities organized around male interests naturally tend to follow male strategies and,
thanks to sexual selection, tend to seek power with an almost unbounded
enthusiasm.[71]

Patriarchal nationalism and its attendant violence among human collectives are not inevitable, however; and this is not simply a politically
correct view—it is the view of evolutionary theorists. As Wrangham and
Peterson note, "Patriarchy is not inevitable. . . . Patriarchy emerged not
as a direct mapping of genes onto behavior, but out of the particular strategies that men [and women] invent for achieving their emotional goals.
And the strategies are highly flexible, as every different culture shows."[72]

Notably, several theorists believe that the rise of democracy is rooted
in the amelioration of patriarchal control over women. For example, a
number have posited that the social imposition of monogamy and a later
age of marriage for women (leading to a lessening of gender inequality)
were necessary, though not sufficient, conditions for the rise of democracy and capitalism in the West.[73] Breaking key elements of male dominance over women—such as polygamy, patrilocality, early- to mid-teen
marriage for females—may have been the first critical steps toward eventually breaking the political power of such violence-prone, parasitical,
patrilineal kin groups. Although in the initial stages the rise of democracy did not facilitate the acquisition of political power for women, these
scholars assert that without an adjustment in the fundamental character
of male-female relations, democracy may never have been a historical
possibility for humans. And as norms of democracy arose, the stage was
finally set for women to achieve at least a modicum of political power.

If these theorists are correct, then we have another explanation for
why levels of violence against women should be more predictive of state
security and peacefulness than levels of procedural democracy. In other
words, in states where democracy arose from within through the amelioration of gender inequality, we should find greater state security; but
where democracy was imposed or veneered over systems where male-
female relations did not undergo fundamental transformation and are
still the product of male-bonded nationalism as we have defined it here,
state security and peacefulness are less likely to be much better than

when the state was more autocratic—and in many cases worse, as witnessed by the unrest that has followed in the wake of the Arab uprisings and the fall of the communist bloc.

Just as a proclivity toward international peace in democratic societies is based, in part, "on tolerance and a respect for the rights of opponents," scholars might also contemplate how norms of gender-based violence might lead to an inflammatory impact on domestic and international behavior.[74] For example, studies have shown that if domestic violence is a routine means of family conflict resolution, then that society is also more likely to rely on violence and to be involved in militarism and war than those societies characterized by lower levels of family abuse.[75] There is a continuum of violence that runs from the household level to the national level.

A vicious circle may result, whereby state violence may in turn lead to higher levels of gender-based violence.[76] Indeed, more equal gender relations actually hinder the ability of societies to mobilize for aggression, for such mobilization may explicitly include the demonization of all things female, especially the women of the "other side," as we saw in our example from Rwanda.[77] The persistence of patriarchal violence and control provides a natural wellspring for the continuing social diffusion of the idea that aggression is functional in the cause of nationalism.

Thus it is no coincidence, for example, that in the early days of the civil wars that followed in the wake of Yugoslavia's collapse, Serb and Croat nationalists specifically targeted women's groups while, at the same time, promoting a vision of the ideal home where men ruled the family and women did as they were told or faced violent consequences. As in Nazi Germany, the Serb and Croat states were pronatalist, enjoining women to stay home, be obedient, and produce many babies—preferably male— who would then go on to defend the nascent nation state.[78] That the term *wombfare* is a neologism in modern international affairs testifies that this phenomenon is still with us and is understood for its true character.[79]

Thus we find that nationalism is both strongly gendered and powerfully predisposed to the use of violence. Nationalism and misogyny are joined at the hip, and, as we have seen, it is males who almost exclusively define group membership, based on male bonds of kinship or other affinity. As feminist theorist V. Spike Peterson has noted, "Gender relations are a crucial, not peripheral, dimension of the dynamics of group identities and intergroup conflicts," thus helping to explain inherent nationalist antipathy toward feminist goals.[80] Given the links between violent patriarchy and nationalism, any potential reform of the social distribution of power between men and women will invariably be viewed as a threat to nationalist efforts to protect or unify the community, leading to predictable and emotional debates about "woman's place" in an idealized society.[81]

Legitimized by gendered structural and cultural violence, patriarchal nationalism offers a persuasive justification for advancing state interests through the use of force. The Hillary Doctrine clearly understands this linkage better than most conceptual frameworks for identifying U.S. national interests: "[The subjugation of women is] a threat to the common security of our world, because the suffering and denial of the rights of women and the instability of nations go hand in hand."[82]

Seen in this light, it is clear that without a real effort to bring about gender equality, we can expect neither a meaningful decrease in societal violence nor a sustainable peace among and within nations.[83] Furthermore, nationalism's most faithful minion will always be heightened levels of gender-based violence and a rollback of women's rights, as the women of the Arab Uprising have learned.

## THE FIRST THING FROM THEIR LIPS

The photos from 2011 were riveting: women massing in public spaces to show their support for the overthrow of the sclerotic regimes of Egypt, Tunisia, Libya, Yemen, and other nations. And in nearly every case, these movements successfully toppled the old dictators from power. But then the photos—and the news—changed. Women assaulted, harassed, beaten, raped in those same public squares where they had so recently stood side-by-side with their brothers in the quest for freedom—and by those same brothers:

> She saw them running towards her as she approached Cairo's Tahrir Square and within seconds she was surrounded.

What followed for Yasmine El-Baramawy was the most terrifying 70 minutes of her life—a prolonged, brutal rape and sexual assault by dozens of men, while a crowd looked on. And did nothing.

"I felt hands all over my body, as they tore at my clothes like savage animals and tried to pull down my trousers," recalls the 30-year-old musician and composer. . . . More than 100 thugs also beat her with sticks and slashed at her with knives. "[It started when] about 15 men rushed from the crowd and trapped me by linking hands in a circle," she explains.

"It happened quickly and in such a way that I later realized it was well rehearsed. I was cornered, trapped and stripped from the waist up before I had time to recover from the shock. I managed to run, but tripped and fell on my face." They were on her again in an instant. Despite her statuesque 5 ft 9 in frame, Yasmine could do nothing to stop them. The daughter of a businessman and a chemist, Yasmine is a strong, intelligent and confident young woman, who has always felt able to take care of herself. But the numbers were overwhelming.

More sets of hands than it was possible to count clawed at her, grabbing her breasts and groping inside her underwear. "It was as if I was in a washing machine, being pushed and pulled and grabbed," she says. "I didn't know what was happening to me or when it would end. I thought that I would faint or die, but I still tried to fight back."

She was dragged several hundred yards as the mob feverishly tore at her clothes. Some tried to cut them off while she desperately clung to her trousers. "When they couldn't get the jeans off, they slit them at the back with a knife. I was bleeding from my face and nose, but that didn't stop them."

Surprisingly, her attackers were not feral kids or teenagers, but grown men "aged in their 20s to 40s." Some were well dressed and respectable. Dozens of people had stood by watching her ordeal in the square—but none intervened.[84]

El-Baramawy described her sense that, quite apart from the sexualized violence, there was something more going on: "At the height of the attack, I looked up and saw 30 individuals on a fence. All of them had smiling faces, and they were recording me with their cellphones. They saw a naked woman, covered in sewage, who was being assaulted and beaten, and I don't know what was funny about that. This is a question that I'm still thinking about, I can't stop my mind from thinking about it."[85]

That something more was a determination to put El-Baramawy—that is, women—in their place, rape being perhaps the most visceral and direct means of doing so, by terrorizing and humiliating them at the same time. We have already explored how male-bonded groups that seek power over others are obsessed with dominating women. Therefore, in a perverse way we understand that when they force woman into her place for the sake of the male bond, they will then offer each other utter impunity for such violent and brutal acts. Hannagan and Arrow have studied this phenomenon in the military, but it applies equally well outside of that institution.

When military socialization is designed to forge men into male-bonded groups, women are commonly viewed as a threat to group cohesion. Cross-cultural studies have documented an extremely common cultural pattern in which women's influence on men's hunting and war is seen as harmful. Taboos against women using weapons associated with these male activities effectively exclude women from the ranks of warriors.[86] "If this view of women as harmful intruders is normative for a group, sexual assault of military women may be used to protect the male-bonded unit. Assault may include gang rape, which both punishes women who are violating gender norms and binds the men in a collective deviant act."[87]

As competing male-bonded nationalist groups struggle for power, they inevitably will seek to roll back any advances for women, even long-standing ones, in order to promote the male bond that they hope will ensure their legitimacy in the eyes of the men of the society. After the fall of Egyptian president Hosni Mubarak, for example, the Morsi government made it a priority to axe the small quota for women in the legislature that Mubarak has introduced in 2010—even though it did not drop the quota for farmers or other groups. Indeed, in a stunningly hypocritical move, the Muslim Brotherhood claimed the quota violated the constitution of Egypt, which outlaws gender-based discrimination!

Soon after, the Morsi government stated that it supported the re-legalization of female circumcision, also outlawed under Mubarak, and that it would seek to overturn laws granting women greater rights to divorce abusive husbands, nicknamed "Suzanne's law" after Mubarak's own wife, who had championed the change. The Morsi regime also summarily sacked women who worked for the government. Dress codes for women became more restrictive, and the new government—which had plenty of pressing economic and political problems to think about— began discussing the possibility of lowering the legal age of marriage for girls from eighteen to nine.

Thus the Brotherhood is quite literally exactly what it purports to be: a fraternity of males who first and foremost bond with each other over the fact that they are not women, who will seek to forge unity among each other and other males by means of the effort to return women to their "rightful place," offering each other absolute impunity even when their violence escalates to the level of brutality El-Baramawy experienced. The exploitation and abuse of women is not only justified and naturalized but also becomes an important mechanism through which to consolidate this fraternity of men—with men becoming the in-group and women the out-group.

Without the subordination of women and the establishment of universal male privilege, these male bands would more easily fall apart over status differences. However, under nationalism, even a man with the lowest status among the males in the group enjoys a higher status as a man than any woman associated with the group. At a minimum, the group can offer him this guaranteed measure of power.

That is why those male onlookers were smiling and taking cell phone photos of El-Baramawy as she was being raped, beaten, and smeared with excrement—in effect telling all women that they are filth—nothing of any value next to maleness. El-Baramawy was making a crucial observation when she said, "They saw a naked woman, covered in sewage, who was being assaulted and beaten, and I don't know what was funny about that. This is a question that I'm still thinking about, I can't stop my mind from thinking about it."[88] What she was seeing right before her eyes is usually not so clearly visible: *She was seeing men create their in-group and their national identity by violating her female body.*

The male bonding bought with her degradation was deeply satisfying to participants and onlookers alike; it reaffirmed their sense of belonging to the group that was naturally superior and made them smile. By making her, and by extension her sex, the hated out-group against which male group violence could be used with complete impunity, the new "nation" of Egypt was to be born. Violence against women is, indeed, nationalism's most faithful and most horrible minion.

The presence of women in a place such as Tahrir Square is thus an offense and affront to those who wish to consolidate power among men. These women must be forced from the square through the most humiliating tactics of male-on-female violence—sexual violation. In the kind of repressed homoerotic atmosphere in which hypermasculinity is acted out, gang rape is the ultimate form of male bonding; at once an annihilation of the weak but nonetheless threatening feminine, and a proxy for actual physical bonding between men. It is also a form of reward for battles well fought, as in Syria and Iraq where Islamist clerics have effectively given jihadist fighters carte blanche to violate en masse any non-Sunni Muslim women and girls who have the misfortune to fall into their hands.[89] And in this game of one-upmanship in male bonding, any extreme measure showing full control over another body, such as mutilation or cannibalism, will strike fear into the hearts of potential rivals even as it elicits veneration and esteem.

Regression for women is also under way in other Arab Uprising nations, though without the stunning escalation in gender-based violence seen in Egypt and Syria.[90] So, for example, in Libya, the very first legal change the head of the brand new interim government proposed after the ouster of Muammar Gadhafi was the re-legalization of polygamy. In February 2013, that proposal became law.[91]

Iranian women could have warned Arab women that this would happen. Shirin Ebadi, Nobel Peace Prize laureate from Iran, recalled, "In Iran, before the new constitution was written [after the overthrow of the Shah], the Revolutionary Council decreed men could marry four wives. We women wondered if we had had a revolution so men could have four wives."[92] In a speech at the Wilson Center, Ebadi continued this theme, according to those present at this event:

> "The best way to prevent what happened to women in the aftermath of the Iran revolution is to call for women's rights during the struggle. Don't wait for the victory. Choose your allies. Dictate these conditions before the alliance. . . . Look at Iran; do not repeat our mistakes."

When Ebadi saw images of the protestors in Syria, Yemen, and Tunisia, she saw them demanding democracy, "Did anyone say we are against polygamy? That we want divorce rights? That we are human beings and need equal rights? You are making the same mistake Iranian women made. We thought we could demand women's rights after the revolution. We all know now that it is too late."[93]

The similarities across time, space, and culture are striking and are worth further analysis. We have already discussed how the facilitation of male bonding, and thus group identification and nationalism, may be fairly easily accomplished through the unifying experience of jointly participating in acts that oppress women. We also note that power-seeking groups find it very useful to encourage men to experience for themselves the rush derived from committing gender-based violence with impunity, for this group-sanctioned impunity helps establish a cohesive group of fighters ready and willing to use force against all out-groups. But there is more to it—and it is invisible even to the men who exuberantly participate in putting women in their "rightful place."

## THE SECRET OF NATIONALISM

An important clue that more is at work than the pursuit of male bonding through female oppression can be found in this poignant anecdote from the failed Iranian "Green" Revolution of 2009. Many of the male dissidents began to appear in women's headscarves, the *rusari*, in their photos and public appearances. While the backstory on this was complex, one dissident stated something remarkable. He said, "We Iranian men are late doing this. . . . If we did this when *rusari* was forced on those among our sisters who did not wish to wear it 30 years ago, we would have perhaps not been here today."[94]

The man who said this put his finger on an even deeper truth about nationalism, one that commends the Hillary Doctrine not only to the women of the world, but to every man as well. Men who approve or even simply acquiesce to the domination of women in their society are approving and acquiescing to something more. What such male-bonded groups do not recognize until much later—if at all—is that if their leaders allow or encourage men to attack and degrade women with impunity, *they will do the same to men.*

This is the great and hidden truth of nationalism as we define it here: *A social order based on the subordination of women will always subjugate all but the most powerful men.* The tactics used to repress women will also be used on other, less powerful, men; by bonding over the subordination of women, men wind up binding themselves.

One would think, then, that at some point men would realize that the only revolution capable of leading to true freedom would be one in which women were simultaneously empowered to progress forward from their subordinate status.

This almost never occurs; in all of our years of study, it is almost impossible to find cases where male revolutionaries recognized or acted upon this truth. (The Marxist revolutions in Russia and China come close, but the aim of these was the imposition of totalitarian rule, not the achievement of liberty or democracy, and women were never accorded real power in either country. The same holds true for other supposedly women-friendly Marxist or Maoist movements such as the Kurdistan Workers' Party [PKK] and the Shining Path.)

Further, we would argue that the surest route to democracy proceeds along a track that parallels consistent advances—even if those advances are initially small—in women's rights and status, as observed in the case of the United States. The corollary is that if the export of democracy is a foreign policy goal, this cannot be meaningfully attempted without the simultaneous establishment of universal norms of women's rights such as those enshrined in the Convention on the Elimination of All Forms of Discrimination Against Women (CEDAW).

## THE DOUBLE-EDGED SWORD

Despite this twisted relationship with women, nationalists invariably encourage their female compatriots, comrades, or 'sisters' to stand with them, at least while the contest for power is not yet settled. During the power struggle, nationalists may even promise women a role in the postrevolutionary order—only to impose even greater restrictions than existed previously. Once again, Egypt is the most telling recent example:

While in power, the Muslim Brotherhood announced it was "not opposed to having women in government, but that it must come *after* the establishment and creation of a new Egyptian government."[95]

As mentioned before, with depressing predictability the interim Brotherhood government immediately jettisoned the quota for women and then allowed only six women out of one hundred delegates into the constitutional assembly—most of the six delegates being from the Muslim Brotherhood's own ranks.

As Moushira Kattab, former minister of family and population for Egypt, described it, before the military stepped in during summer 2013, the Muslim Brotherhood remorselessly rolled back women's rights: "Women were utterly marginalized . . . they were excluded; the representation of women in parliament was miserable, less than two percent; in the cabinet it went down from four ministers down to one minister. . . . I s[aw] women forced to cover behind black. First they were asked to cover their heads, then they started to cover up and the debate became whether to show one eye or two eyes."[96]

Ironically, the counterrevolution that toppled the Morsi regime and brought the military back to power is seen by Kattab and other Egyptian feminists as restoring hope that democracy may yet come to Egypt. For example, Kattab, when asked about the military's overthrow of Morsi, commented, "I will not say this is a military coup; this is democracy in action for a country still in a revolution. . . . So now the people call it a correction of the revolution . . . to restore Egypt on the right path to democracy. . . . Women have new hope now."[97] In the context of our discussion of the connection between freedom and the status of women in this chapter, Kattab surely has a point—there cannot be anything that could justifiably be called democracy in the context of such striking regression for women. However, the post-Morsi government has not been any more inclusive: only five of fifty seats have been reserved for "women and youth" (effectively classifying all women as protoadults) on the committee that will draft a new constitution, and the "expert group" that is the real power behind the drafting of the document does not include any women at all.[98]

Egypt is not the only Arab Uprising country where the anticipated spring has turned into a winter for women. Madiha al-Naas, of the NGO

Women Are Coming, said that in Libya, "The situation for women has become disastrous. . . . There are plans to oust Libyan women, marginalize them and dwarf their role. This is unfortunate because women's aspirations to improve their tragic situation were great under the former regime. . . . Women were looking forward to greater opportunities, but instead they are losing the ones they had before."[99]

To somewhat lesser extent this is also true of Tunisia, where Amal Karami notes, "There are attempts to destroy the achievements women have made over the decades." And in Algeria, Nafissa Larache, president of the Algerian Association of Women in Communication, concurs, saying, "Contrary to what we hoped would come from the Arab Spring, we've even lost the few rights we previously had."[100]

This paradox—where nationalists court women to attract their support during the struggle only to betray them afterward—reveals just how nationalist groups view women: as a double-edged sword. Nationalists need women's support: not only do women provide much-needed legitimacy—especially as putative mothers of the nation—but they also offer temporal support in the form of food, shelter, clothing, sex, and care. The involvement of women is also increasingly necessary to attract the kind of international backing that allowed the likes of the Muslim Brotherhood and Libyan and Syrian rebels to acquire and consolidate power.

This appearance of supporting the rights of women can be reassuring to the governments of the United States, Britain, and France, which must justify expensive interventions to increasingly skeptical and war-weary electorates. Revolutions attract considerable press, but eventually the band moves on; the international media turn elsewhere, and the repression of women and minorities becomes the order of the day. Once reporters and news crews have pulled up and left, reactionary forces are free to put women back into their "place."

In the face of nationalist struggles, women are thus left in a double bind. If they support the revolutionaries, they must surely anticipate that they are helping to bring about their own disenfranchisement and higher levels of gender-based violence. If women refuse to offer support, then nationalist rebels may simply kidnap them and force them to serve—that is, cook food, haul water and fuel, and provide sex at the point of a gun, thereby establishing higher levels of gender-based violence. Hope may spring eternal, but in a nationalist context women's hope is all too likely to be sadly misplaced.

## PUSHING THE ENVELOPE

We have argued that democratization cannot be meaningfully attempted without the simultaneous advancement of women's human rights, including the right to physical security. There is more to be said on this subject as we contemplate the connection between the governance of a society, on the one hand, and its economic system on the other. Too often, scholars have overlooked how this association ties in with the character of male-female relations within the society.[101]

As we have shown, societies established on a foundation of female subordination simultaneously promote the normalization of violence as a means of dispute resolution. Individual men who participate in group-sanctioned, violent coercion of women are more likely to become fighters willing to use force to obtain political ends—while also creating a template of victory that looks a lot like pillage.

After all, female subordination is itself a form of pillage, and men socialized in such societies learn very early on the advantages of ensuring its continuation. If a nationalist male-bonded group is successful in seizing control, this template of pillage will inevitably set the stage for a type of parasitical governance based on the extortion and redistribution of rents (goods and services obtained without recompense), mirroring the character of male-female relations within that type of society. The hand-in-hand character of these two phenomena, the subordination of women and the establishment of rent-based parasitical governance, must not be overlooked.

This is because the subjugation of women not only means the suborning of meaningful democracy; it also undermines any attempt to establish an economic system in which all people enjoy an equitable share of the nation's wealth, including those men who do not occupy the upper echelons of the pyramid of power.

When we observe cultural attitudes dictating that women must not be allowed to claim any part of a nationalism that is deeply gendered as male, such as we see in Egypt, this is a clear hallmark that a parasitical type of governance system is in place. Parasitical governance systems cannot thrive where rents are not collected. But the template for this is found in male-female relations: originary rents are collected first and foremost from women in the form of uncompensated domestic, sexual, and maternal service. In these societies, rentier governance is learned at the level of the household.

But while the nation or group is marketed to all men as the male cosa nostra—the male rent collection system, if you will—in reality it is the cosa nostra only of the most powerful men, as our unnamed Iranian dissident finally understood. In a sense, then, while we see that those who wish to destroy communities for the purpose of pillage target women as the weavers of all human societies, it is also true that those who wish to consolidate political power as a form of pillage also target women.

These types of parasitical systems not only are unstable, fragile, and prone to explosive violence, but also their ascendance portends increasing peril for women over time.[102] We have remarked how the subordination of women in the context of complete impunity in the first place offers a template for violent domination as a means to an end, whether economic or political. As the system shudders and shakes from its inherent instability and intergroup conflicts increase, the expression of that violent domination in the quest for power and resources leads to ever more extreme gender-based violence and subordination, worsening it and making women even more of a target.

In this malevolent spiral even existing taboos against certain forms of violence are violated. This includes forms of aggression that almost defy belief as they push to the very limits of sadism itself. Indeed, Leatherman argues that "taboo violation is central to the culture of patriarchy itself"; that is, pushing to the final frontier, exploring virgin lands, unlocking secrets, boldly going where no man has gone before, going in without invitation, and the like constitutes the male eroticization of the forbidden, for "[d]oing something that is prohibited and getting away with it demonstrates one's power much more fully than doing something acceptable."[103]

Leatherman goes on to note the association between sexual violence and the global political economy of war and rebellion. Echoing Carolyn Nordstrom's identification of the "shadow sovereigns of war" as behind much of the escalation of violence in conflict zones, Leatherman instructs us to ask whether these shadows would profit, economically or politically, from the emptying of a territory. If emptying a territory is advantageous, then sexual violence will ensue, for it is the surest means of accomplishing that aim. Thus, we should expect to see greater and more egregious sexual violence in wars of partition, wars of natural resource control, and wars of predatory economics where pillage is the template for victory. As Leatherman noted, "The bodies of women, girls, and sometimes men may be the last lootable goods."[104]

The manner of this sexual violence is also telling. In the contexts we have described in this chapter, the winner is the group that has pushed the furthest with regard to terrifying sexual violence, thereby showing its dominance among competing hypermasculine groups, as in the horrifying story told by Denise at the beginning of this section. Gang rape is used as a form of male bonding; indeed, any extreme measure showing full control over another body, such as mutilation, cannibalism, breaking the incest taboo, and so forth, will be esteemed in this game of one-upmanship.

As Ann Jones asserts, for women war isn't over when it's over.[105] The breaking of these societal norms in wartime inevitably shifts the boundary of acceptable behavior when so-called peace has returned. As Leatherman observes, rates of sexual violence tend to remain high during peacetime after conflicts in which rape had been deployed as a weapon of war—as in the Democratic Republic of the Congo, Liberia, and South Africa.

Perhaps nowhere, however, is this dynamic of patriarchal nationalism and rentierism more evident than in the nations of Central America. In this region, the imprimatur of rapacious militarism mixed with the unfettered pillage of corporatism can be clearly observed. In chapter 3, we travel to Guatemala, where Mayan women—and indeed all women in the society—are still paying the price for Guatemalan nationalism.

# 3

# GUATEMALA

★ ★ ★

## A Case Study

WHEN DARKNESS FALLS in Guatemala, the fear that slumbers all day suddenly awakes. As twilight stretches across this lush country of 15 million, merchants, housewives, professionals, schoolchildren, and workers all make haste: closing shops, paying their bills, and hurriedly doing their grocery shopping before heading back to the relative safety of their own homes. The end of the short tropical dusk signals the beginning of darkness. In Guatemala, few people want to be caught outside when death comes calling.

For today, Guatemala is facing an ongoing crisis. Since the signing of the 1996 peace accords that signaled an end to the genocidal 36-year civil war, the country has been plagued by a violent crime rate that is among the highest in the world along with its gang-infested neighbors El Salvador and Honduras, both of which abut Guatemala's southern border.

All three were once embroiled in the region's "Dirty War," which ostensibly pitted the United States against Cuba and the former USSR in a proxy conflict that claimed the lives of more than 200,000 indigenous peoples, human rights workers, intellectuals, and guerrillas in Guatemala; an estimated 75,000 in El Salvador; and hundreds in Honduras, a country that was nominally at peace during this same period.[1] These statistics do not include *los desaparecidos* (the disappeared), who number in the tens of thousands, and the displaced, who number in the millions.

But as the trope goes, the war may have ended but the killing is far from over. By mid-2012, Guatemala had become one of the most murderous countries in the world, with a death rate of 39 per 100,000— eight times that of the United States.[2] It is also home to one of the highest femicide rates in the world—part of an escalating crisis that has gripped the nation since 2000. Although exact definitions vary, unlike homicide, femicide refers specifically to the killing of women by men for no other reason than the victim is female. It usually involves sexual violence, mutilation, "overkill," and is motivated by hatred and misogyny. Murders stemming from domestic violence fall into this category, as do a significant number of the non-domestic killings of women now taking place throughout Central America.

Since 2012, the femicide rate has on average leaped 20 percent per year: Between 2000 and 2008, for example, Guatemala was home to the highest female murder rate in the entire region at 4,159 from 2000–2008, according to the Procuraduría de Derechos Humanos (the Office of Human Rights in Baja California). An estimated 2,900 were murdered between 2008 and 2011—an average of sixty girls and women per month, according to the agency. In 2012, the Instituto Nacional de Ciencias Forenses de Guatemala (INACIF; National Institute of Forensic Sciences) reported that more than 600 women were slaughtered, and 2013 proved to be the most murderous year for women thus far with 759 deaths, according to the INACIF.[3] These are alarmingly high numbers for a comparatively small nation of 15 million people.[4]

Murder is not Guatemala's only problem. According to the CIA's *World Factbook*, nearly one half of the country's children under the age of five are chronically undernourished—one of the highest malnutrition rates in the world.[5] The country also has among the lowest tax rates, which means little money is available to fund schools, build roads, or otherwise undertake any of the other improvements necessary to nudge its population out of poverty.

Guatemala is just another example of how the syndrome of predatory rent-taking by the powerful can destroy a country's future—its children. High child mortality and morbidity are primary manifestations of the type of malignant male-bonded nationalism we discussed in chapter 2. Moreover, Guatemala's level of violence against women exceeds even that of Ciudad Juárez, Mexico, during the height of *its* femicide.[6]

As is typical of femicides in neighboring countries, most victims are found dumped in empty lots and ditches around cities, towns, villages, and indigenous settlements scattered throughout the troubled country—many of the victims had been raped, decapitated, and dismembered. Their bodies also bear signs of sadistic torture: gouged eyeballs, severed genitals, and, in a number of particularly gruesome cases, the skin completely peeled away from their faces.

Their killers do so, according to reports, not only to impede identification but also to extract the maximum amount of suffering from victims and families alike. Irma Chacon, coordinator of the Sobrevivientes, an acclaimed Guatemala City–based women's shelter, comments, "The dismemberment and torture we are seeing represents a desire to annihilate women, to erase their identities, destroy their femininity and to engender fear so great that women and girls are afraid to leave their homes."[7]

While this is not dissimilar to what is happening in other Central American nations, including the United States' next-door neighbor Mexico, Guatemala took a detour into genocide that the former did not. Thus the case of Guatemala allows us to examine more closely the role that violence against women plays in the horrifying logic of the extermination of an entire people: the link between gendercide and genocide.

## BITTER LEGACY

Guatemala City lies within a central plateau surrounded by a volcanic chain that makes up the Pacific leg of the Ring of Fire. Ravines crisscross the city, which is home to an estimated 5 million residents. Many of these *arroyos* are so cluttered with makeshift shanties that one cannot detect a single inch of soil or grass—only a welter of multicolored dwellings. Only at high noon and during the summer does the sun reach those unfortunate enough to reside in the valley floors where greasy water filled with sewage and litter pools in the stifling dark.

The poor reside here, quite literally on top of each other. During the rainy season, water cascades down the cliffs, washing unstable homes down the steep sides and into the thickly inhabited ravines where flooding, mudslides, and drowning are common. Earthquakes regularly shake these informal settlements, adding to the death toll.

Just outside of the city, however, lie a growing number of gated communities. Huge mansions crouch behind heavily guarded perimeters. Wide lawns of emerald grass and gardens filled with flowering shrubs and exotic songbirds lap up against these dwellings, which are home to Guatemala's tiny but well-heeled elite.

As with many Latin American countries, the lion's share of property, resources, and political power are overwhelmingly concentrated in the top 20 percent of the population, who account for 51 percent of the country's consumption.[8] Known collectively as criollos, these are the ruling classes of Spanish and European descent whose fair skin distinguishes them from the estimated 40.5 percent of the population whose distinct copper-hued skin and finely arched noses classify them as indigenous. The other 39.5 percent of the population are ladino (mestizo in other usage), of mixed European and indigenous ancestry.[9] Thus it is that in Guatemala, the color of a person's skin and even their height distinguishes the in-group from the disadvantaged and despised out-group.

It is here in Guatemala City that women's remains first began to show up in numbers that made local women's rights activists sit up with a collective start. Although Guatemala has long harbored a reputation as a dangerous place for women, the gendered nature of the killings had been more or less subsumed by the generalized mayhem consuming the country. At the turn of the twenty-first century, that all changed. Suddenly, the country was engulfed in a riptide of femicidal terror that left few families untouched. Bodies began to show up—stuffed into trash cans or abandoned in forsaken dumps and parking lots. Many of the victims were mutilated and bore distinct signs of rape and torture.

To those who survived the earlier genocide, however, the killings were oddly familiar. In order to understand Guatemala's femicide, then, it is first necessary to examine its origins within the context of the country's 36-year civil war—a war that was not only waged against communist rebels but also against the Maya, and more particularly against Mayan women.

Sixty-eight-year-old Alba Estela Maldonado is a tiny woman—well under five feet. Her long dark graying hair is pulled back into a simple bun, and her large eyes are expressive, warm, and sparkle with a keen intelligence. Maldonado is retired now, but she once she commanded the entire central region of Guatemala for the Unidad Revolucionaria Nacional Guatemalteca—most commonly known as the URNG. She fought on the side of the guerrillas against the dictatorships of Generals Romeo Lucas García (1978–1982), José Efrain Ríos Montt (1982–1983), and Óscar Humberto Mejía Victores (1983–1986).

Commandante Lola, as she was then known, was a force to be reckoned with not only in Guatemala's male-dominated guerrilla movement but also in the post-1996 Guatemalan Congress, where she helped draft the country's first femicide law, which came into effect in 2008.

She is also a repository of memory and views Guatemala's descent into femicidal anarchy as no more than a continuation of a genocidal conflict waged almost entirely against the nation's indigenous peoples, human rights workers, and the progressive intelligentsia. Women represented a significant proportion of those targeted, 40 percent, unprecedented given that an overwhelming majority were noncombatants.[10]

"The direct line is very clear," she explains, noting that government soldiers and right-wing paramilitary squads raped and murdered an estimated 100,000 women, primarily Maya, during the Guatemalan civil war.[11] "When it came to insurgent women, they [the military] would inflict additional violence upon them. They would rape even women who were pregnant, they would hammer sticks into their vaginas—there was extreme violence to women. The army would take over the entire community, separate the women from the group, rape them, open up their stomachs and take out the fetus.

"They would hang the fetuses on the trees. If any women survived this kind of treatment, the army would put the women in the churches and schools and set fire to them.

"The horror was so extreme it is almost impossible to narrate."[12]

## CONQUEST AND FEMICIDE

Like other Central American nations, Guatemala's passage through the Spanish conquest and into the modern age was tumultuous—one that was characterized by extreme cruelty, repression, and the wholesale enslavement of its indigenous population.

And, like other Latin American countries, Guatemala was never to shake off its status as a client state—first of the Aztecs, and then of Spain, and most recently of the United States, which since the 1940s onward cast its eyes south to the fertile and resource-rich countries of Central America and the "southern cone."

The roots of Guatemala's femicide, however, are buried in its post-Conquest past: the wholesale die-off of Amerindian peoples as a result of European diseases, violence, slavery, and sexual predation. For while Hernán Cortés was busy conquering what is now modern-day Mexico, he dispatched his protégé Pedro de Alvarado to oversee the conquest of the Mayan K'iche, who had refused to continue paying tribute once they realized that the Spaniards had vanquished the Mayans' Aztec nemesis. By the standards of his time, Alvarado cut a striking figure—tall, fair-haired, with piercing blue eyes. According to historians, his zeal for adventure was only outstripped by his cruelty and avarice.

In February 1524, Alvarado and his men successfully routed the K'iche at the battle of El Pinal—thereby ending the last hope of large-scale native resistance in Central America. With the mighty K'iche laid low and their capital city of Utatlán reduced to a smoldering heap, Alvarado leisurely picked off the remaining kingdoms one by one and was subsequently appointed governor of Guatemala, a post he occupied for the next seventeen years.[13]

Thus, the close of 1532 marked the end of Mayan autonomy and the beginning of the finca system—Guatemala's answer to the hacienda system in Mexico—which effectively finished off what war, wholesale rape, and pestilence had already started. During this time, Hispanic overlords were busily forcing Mayan peasants to labor on cacao and coffee plantations. Although in theory the *encomienda* was a series of laws designed to encourage indigenous peoples to exchange their labor for Spanish language and religious training, in practice those who were granted this privilege—former soldiers, landowners, conquistadors, and the like—treated their charges as little more than slave labor.

Thousands perished from overwork and starvation. The Dominican friar, historian, and social reformer Bartolomé de Las Casas was among those who protested the abuses meted out by the Spanish under the colonial system.[14] Among these was what in French is known as droit de seigneur: the right of a feudal lord to deflower serf brides on their wedding night – or indeed, force sex on any woman or child of his choosing. An import from the Old World, it was a practice that fundamentally altered Guatemalan society: first, by reducing formerly autonomous indigenous women to sexual objects that could be as violently plundered as the land itself; and second, by giving rise to the ladinos, the mixed-race offspring of these forced couplings. Although ladinos occupied a higher stratum of the social and economic totem pole than the despised Maya, they nonetheless shared a common ancestry—thereby engendering a form of self-hatred that could only find expression in racism and the destruction of the Mayan feminine. In essence, it naturalized the intertwining of genocide and gynocide.

"During the war the same attitudes that prevailed through the hacienda system extended into the modern age," said Lucia Moran, director of Women Transforming the World, an NGO dedicated to assisting victims of Guatemala's femicide. She continued, "It was very easy to ignite the right of soldiers to rape women. It was also used to humiliate anyone who tried to stand up for the people . . . they were effectively telling everyone 'not only do we have own your territory but we own your women.' It as a form of sexual enslavement, but even now little is spoken about the specific crimes against women."[15]

Nobel Peace Prize laureate Rigoberta Menchú Tum described it thus: "When the Spaniards arrived five hundred years ago, they raped our ancestors, our grandmothers, our mothers, to breed a race of *mestizos*. The result is the violence and cruelty that we are still living with today. The Spaniards used a vile method to create a mixed race, a race of children who doubted their own identity."[16]

Creating a new national identity through the wholesale violation and rape of women caused a wound that still festers and has inflamed the current spate of femicidal violence. The conflation of racism with misogyny taught generations of men that their identity and their bond are formed through the exploitation of women's bodies. It has been their schoolmaster in the curriculum of male impunity for any crimes perpetrated against their sisters.

It was also this period (1760 to 1940) that signaled the beginning of the era of the oligarchs. These were criollos, families of direct Spanish and European descent, who concentrated wealth, land, and power within their own spheres of influence, subordinating the indigenous Maya as had their rapist-fathers the conquistadores before them. The massive inequality, racism, and increasing unrest that prevailed would eventually lay the groundwork for the decades of instability, civil war, and repression to come.

## THE WHITE TERROR

In 1821, Guatemala obtained its independence from Spain. Mayan leaders who tried to help form the new government were killed, and elite families gained control. Nevertheless, it was not until 1954 that Guatemala began its descent into La Violencia, as the long civil war is known. It was during that same year that the Central Intelligence Agency (CIA) backed the overthrow of General Captain Jacobo Árbenz Guzmán, who was elected president in 1951. Árbenz had continued the land reform polices instituted by his predecessor, writer and teacher Juan José Arévalo Bermejo (1945–1951). Arévalo was the first democratically elected president in Guatemala to complete his term of office. Arévalo's "Christian Socialist" policies, which were inspired by the New Deal of President Franklin D. Roosevelt, were nevertheless roundly condemned as communist by criollo and ladino landowners among the upper classes, who feared that his reforms would loosen their grip on power.

Upon his election, Arévalo's protégé Árbenz went on to adopt a major land reform policy that redistributed uncultivated lands owned by large estates—most notably those belonging to the U.S.-based United Fruit Company (which later became Chiquita Brands International; then-CIA Director Allen Dulles had been a board member)—to landless peasants, primarily indigenous Mayans. The idea was to increase the production of crops and provide impoverished laborers with a much-needed income. Árbenz's popular program of land reform, credit, and literacy was largely successful: the gap between the poor and the wealthy slowly began to close.

The United States, however, was unhappy—always the case whenever a Latin American government so much as hinted at land reform. On the pretext that the socialist government represented a communist threat, the CIA backed an invasion, which was launched from neighboring Honduras. In 1954, Árbenz was quickly toppled and replaced by Carlos Castillo Armas, a leader whom the U.S. considered more friendly to its interests.

Many historians and analysts have since charged that the United States ordered the coup to protect the interests of the aforementioned United Fruit Company, which was facing the prospect of losing vast tracts of land owing to agrarian reform.[17] Then–vice president Richard Nixon actually flew to Guatemala to thank the junta for its actions. Castillo quickly reversed the policies of his predecessor and ruled until one of his own personal guards assassinated him in 1957.

Next to assume power was General Miguel Ydígoras Fuentes, and historians date the beginning of the Guatemalan civil war to 1960 under this intensely pro-U.S. leader. Ydigoras authorized the training of five thousand anti-Castro Cubans in Guatemala. He also provided airstrips in the Petén (the densely forested area of northern Guatemala) for what later became the U.S.-sponsored but disastrous Bay of Pigs invasion in 1961. In 1963, the Guatemalan Air Force engineered Castillo's ouster under the leadership of his defense minister, Colonel Enrique Peralta Azurdia.

In 1966, Julio César Méndez Montenegro was elected president under the umbrella of the Revolutionary Party, a center-left party. It was during his watch that the United States began to fund right-wing Guatemalan paramilitary organizations, such as the Hand (Mano, also referred to as the White Hand) and the Anticommunist Secret Army (Ejército Secreto Anticomunista)—both forerunners of the infamous death squads, or *esquadrones des muertes*, that would play such a prominent role in the genocide to come.

Coups and rigged elections followed for more than a decade. Widespread discontent after the 1976 earthquake (the 7.5 magnitude temblor killed more than twenty-three thousand people and injured thousands more) contributed to popular unrest, which in turn triggered a military crackdown that evoked one of the blackest periods in an already murky history—the Mayan genocide.

In 1999, the U.N.-sponsored Commission for Historical Clarification documented much of what took place during those years. Its authors found that both the army and related paramilitary groups undertook massacres in 626 villages and were responsible for 93 percent of documented killings and human rights violations.[18] Of the murdered, 83 percent were Maya.[19] The suppression of the countryside had a distinctly racial and ethnic cast.[20]

In 1979, and in response to growing international pressure, then U.S. president Jimmy Carter suspended all military aid to Guatemala, citing the widespread and systematic abuse of human rights. Despite this indirect public acknowledgment of U.S. complicity in mass murder, the administration continued to quietly provide funding for military intelligence.[21] After he took office in 1981, Ronald Reagan immediately lifted the ban, effectively permitting the genocide to continue under new management.

## "DIRTY WARS":
## GUATEMALA THEN AND NOW

In 1982, the government was again overthrown, but this time by the infamous Efraín Ríos Montt, who was made president of the military junta. A priest belonging to a U.S.-based Pentecostal denomination, Ríos Montt pursued the guerrillas and their Mayan supporters in a genocidal campaign so vicious it could have been the handiwork of Pedro de Alvarado himself.[22]

According to the United Nations, more than 90 percent of the human rights violations of the conflict took place between 1978 and 1984 during the dictatorships of Lucas García and Ríos Montt, with the latter responsible for the lion's share of atrocities.[23]

At the height of Ríos Montt's rule, more than three thousand Guatemalans were murdered and disappeared every month. Given the small population of Guatemala at this time, Ríos Montt was easily the most brutal dictator in Latin America's recent history—surpassing even Augusto Pinochet in Chile, Hugo Banzer in Bolivia, and Jorge Rafael Videla in Argentina.[24]

Now-declassified CIA documents reveal that the U.S. government was fully cognizant of its ally's genocidal intent.[25] But on December 5, 1982, Ronald Reagan famously declared Ríos Montt to be "a man of great personal integrity . . . totally dedicated to democracy," and claimed that the Guatemalan strongman was getting "a bum rap" from human rights organizations for his military's campaign against leftist guerrillas.[26]

The very next day, a platoon of Guatemala's elite U.S.-trained Kaibiles (special forces) entered the village of Las Dos Erres and killed 162 of its inhabitants, 67 of who were children.

> Soldiers grabbed babies and toddlers by their legs, swung them in the air, and smashed their heads against a wall. Older children and adults were forced to kneel at the edge of a well, where a single blow from a sledge-hammer sent them plummeting over the edge. The platoon then raped a selection of women and girls it had saved for last, pummeling their stomachs in order to force the pregnant among them to miscarry. They tossed the women into the well and filled it with dirt, burying an unlucky few alive. The only traces of the bodies later visitors would find were blood on the walls and placentas and umbilical cords on the ground.[27]

On the morning of December 8, as the Kaibiles were preparing to leave, another fifteen villagers arrived in the hamlet. With the well already stuffed with bodies, the Kaibiles took the newcomers to a location half an hour away, then shot all but two of them. The two surviving teenage girls probably wished they had been dispatched alongside family members. The Kaibiles kept them for a few extra days, raping them repeatedly, and finally strangling them once they were no longer useful.[28]

Maldonado recalls going into many other Mayan villages after what had become routine military sweeps: "I remember entering Cholula with my comrades. The military had just left and the river was clogged with female bodies. After they had done raping them, they [the military] made them all stand in line at the edge of a bridge and they killed them one by one over the bridge with hammers. It was very, very systematic."[29] Soldiers also imprisoned women at military bases, raped them, and forced them to work as cooks and laundresses.[30]

## WOMEN AND CULTURAL IDENTITY

So why did Ríos Montt, his predecessors, successors, and his fanatical compadres in arms focus their aggression on women? The key to the destruction of the out-group involved targeting women, because they are (correctly) perceived to be the gatekeepers of cultural identity. "The role of women in indigenous culture is very special," Maldonado explained. "They conserve and promote the identity, the tradition and the cosmological view of the community."[31]

Moreover, contrary to popular belief, a significant proportion of the women killed were also elders. The objective was to destroy the Mayan culture, to gut its traditions and obliterate the wisdom and the link that goes from one generation to another. "In the indigenous tradition they [the female elders] are the ones who give advice, resolve disputes, have the last word," Maldonado said, adding, "only now are we beginning to speak of this."[32]

As we have shown, while history books recount the story of conflicts largely in terms of battles won and territory taken, the unseen and unspoken history of the war on women reveals a different and perhaps much more important set of tactical engagements. These not only determine the success of the campaign but also establish the foundation for the new normal once the conflict has ended—rampant gender-based violence.

In its celebrated 1998 report *Nunca Más*, the Proyecto Interdiocesano de Recuperación de la Memoria Histórica (REHMI; Interdiocesan Project Recovery of Historical Memory) reported acts of sexual violence constituted a form of victory for the army. Eliminating Mayan women was inextricably linked with extirpating the guerrillas, according to the report's authors. Thus, and as we have seen, do male-bonded nationalist groups eventually find it strategically useful to justify extreme acts of violence against women.

Furthermore, the report's authors maintained that the wholesale assault and butchery of women succeeded in ensuring the breakup of the family and the overall weakening of the community. It guaranteed that survivors spent the rest of their lives crippled with chronic medical problems, psychological damage, life-threatening and venereal diseases, forced pregnancy, infertility, stigmatization and/or rejection by family members and communities.

Guatemala is a traditional "honor and shame" society still influenced by its colonial past and retrogressive attitudes toward rape survivors. As is usual with such societies, rape victims are perceived as polluted, broken, dishonored, or sullied. Many still believe that victims of sexual violence somehow "asked for it" and focus attention on the behavior of the victim (almost always female) and not that of the perpetrator (male).

Thus, the community, the police, husbands, and even parents blamed victims for attacks undertaken by others, a tactic the Guatemala Human Rights Commission maintains was "used to foster a sense of distrust and skepticism among the general public towards the victims." Even worse, survivors were often forced to live in silence in the same community as their perpetrators.[33]

In its 1999 report *Guatemala: Memory of Silence*, the Guatemalan Commission for Historical Clarification put it thus: "Blaming the women was easier than blaming the military, abandoning the women was a gesture of contempt and sign of superiority of men, to not admit their own shame."[34]

In *Buried Secrets: Truth and Human Rights in Guatemala*, Victoria Sanford writes that the "Guatemalan state, like other military states, had a very gendered response to the political actions of women." She goes on to cite the psychologist Nancy Caro Hollander, who once noted that during the military regimes of Chile, Argentina, and Uruguay, officers, soldiers, and paramilitary forces were given impunity to act according to "the fundamentally misogynist attitudes of the military."[35]

The U.S. government, military, and the CIA also provided indispensable support for the counterinsurgency campaign—training and arming the Guatemalan military and developing much of the strategy behind the destruction of villages and the terrorization and "disposal" of their inhabitants. It therefore comes as no surprise that some of the worst human rights offenders and highly placed Guatemalan government officials are alumni of the School of the Americas, now known under the less inflammatory moniker of the Western Hemisphere Institute for Security Cooperation (WHINSEC). The United States established the institute in 1946, and beginning in 1961 tasked it with the specific goal of teaching "anti-communist counterinsurgency training," a role it would fulfill for the rest of the Cold War.[36]

Although a 1999 FAQ posted on the WHINSEC website insists that, contrary to its detractors, the former School of the Americas has neither supported nor instructed its alumni in methods that ran or run counter to various international human rights agreements, CIA documents tell a different story.[37] Released during a period of relative openness in the 1990s, they reveal that the United States was closely involved in scorched earth policies in Guatemala and elsewhere in Central and South America.[38]

## SCORCHED EARTH

According to Maldonado, the effect on the indigenous community of this new counterinsurgency approach, developed first during the U.S. military campaign in Vietnam, was "devastating."[39] In the Ixil region alone, 70 to 90 percent of villages were razed.[40] Those whose lives were somehow spared fled into neighboring Mexico or into the surrounding mountains.[41] Still others were herded into military-run "model villages" where meetings between more than two people were punishable by death. The Mayan belief system—a mix of pre-Columbian and Roman Catholic beliefs—was prohibited in favor of Ríos Montt's own strange brew of right-wing politics and pentecostalism. Those accused of collaborating with the insurgents paid the highest price—rape and torture or both— often followed by the driving of a stake into his or her heart.

Although human rights groups tend to focus on those who died as a direct result of violence, many more indigenous peoples perished from starvation and disease when the military torched their crops and homes and slaughtered their animals. Tens of thousands were forced to subsist on grass, nuts, and bark while hiding in the mountains. No one actually knows how many Mayans perished in this manner.[42] One Mayan mother, Jacinta Rivera, recounts, "They came for my husband. They tied him up and tortured him. They forced me and my children to watch until they killed him. All my seven children died in the conflict. First I buried my one-year-old son since I didn't have enough milk for him because we had nothing to eat, and he starved in the mountains. The other six died one by one from hunger."[43]

There were other untallied deaths, witnessed primarily by women. Laura (not her real name) recounts this tale:

One story that is always with me is a woman who told me, "It's Rios Montt's fault that I killed my son. I am a murderer!" Because she was pregnant when they had to escape to the mountains. The baby was born in the mountains . . . it's normal for a baby to cry a lot. But the group she was with told her, "Quiet that baby! They are going to hear us! You have got to quiet him!" So she covered his mouth and nose. The baby got sick. He didn't die right away. He died five days later. She remembers this all the time. She says, "I am a murderer. I killed my son. If I hadn't killed him, he would be twenty years old."[44]

In addition to targeting indigenous groups such as the K'iche and the Ixil, the military also reserved special vitriol for what it perceived to be the left-wing intelligentsia, among them professors, teachers, union organizers, human rights activists, journalists, and foreign humanitarian aid workers. Again, women (and female children) were especially singled out.

Julia is a human rights defender whose name has been altered to protect her identity. Now thirty-nine, she recalls the day when a group of soldiers showed up at her parents' house in a middle-class neighborhood in Guatemala City. She and her young brother had returned from school only to find soldiers ransacking the house. Her mother was confined to the bedroom with five other men and did not come out until just before she was spirited away, never to be seen or heard of again.

Before her mother was abducted, however, one of the soldiers took Julia, who was only nine at the time, to her bedroom. "I didn't know what he was trying to do," she says. "It was like he was trying to asphyxiate me with his body. I thought I was dying. I later went to the toilet and saw blood and I thought it was because I had suddenly begun menstruating. It really, really hurt. I didn't know what had happened to me because I was so innocent. Since then, I always thought it was a miracle that I am still alive."[45]

The soldiers then brought her mother out, who, according to Julia, "was no longer recognizable," and tortured her in front of the two children. They pulled out her fingernails one by one with a pair of pliers as Julia and her little brother screamed and sobbed.

Irma Chacon, coordinator of the Guatemala City women's shelter, confirms the widely held popular view that the 1996 peace accords did not go far enough. Indeed, many observers noted at the time that it would be necessary to undertake widespread resocialization and reintegration of the military.

The femicide occurring today in Guatemala is connected to the civil war. Chacon said, "During the war, women were raped and killed in a certain way. Not only were those structures that were responsible never dismantled, but also the people who committed these crimes never received any psychological aid. They continued their work as police officers and were just incorporated without receiving any treatment. Many also became active in government. Today we are seeing the same savagery that we saw during the war."[46]

Mayan men were also complicit. This was because the military and police coerced male youths—often at a very young age, usually at puberty—into committing atrocities against their own people. The Commission for Historical Clarification noted it was

> aware of hundreds of cases in which civilians were forced by the Army, at gunpoint, to rape women, torture, mutilate corpses, and kill. This extreme cruelty was used by the State to cause social disintegration. A large proportion of the male population over the age of fifteen, especially in the Mayan communities, was forced to participate in the [civil patrols]. This deeply affected values and behavioral patterns, as violence became a normal method of confronting conflictive situations and promoted contempt for the lives of others.[47]

The explicit and obscenely brutal targeting of women in the genocide worked. Though the first democratic transfer of power occurred in 1990, and a peace accord ending the civil war was concluded in 1996, it is difficult to conclude that Guatemala is at peace. Because everyone knew but nothing was said and no one held to account for the wholesale assault on Mayan women, the fabric of life in Guatemala has been torn to shreds.

## THE RETURN OF THE GENERALS

On January 14, 2012, Otto Pérez Molina began his four-year term as president of Guatemala after winning the election based on a promise to wield a *mano dura* (hard hand) against crime.[48] It was the first time a military officer had been elected president since the end of the civil war. After many years of escalating crime rates and increasing narcoviolence, many Guatemalans were willing to overlook the former general's less than immaculate past.

During Ríos Montt's reign of terror, Pérez Molina made his military career as the regime's intelligence chief, heading one of the most influential and powerful sections of the army. According to declassified U.S. documents released by the National Security Archive, Pérez studied at the School of the Americas in 1985. He also took classes at and founded the Kaibil training school.

Despite this pedigree, many of those who voted for him hoped that he would bring order to an increasingly disordered country. Even feminists, a group that traditionally eyes all things military with deep suspicion, were willing to give the ex-general a break. "Femicide is being addressed as a matter of state policy, and a message is being sent out to aggressors that their actions will not be tolerated and that they will be punished," declared Mayra Sandoval, a representative of the Observatory against Femicide.[49]

After more than two years into Pérez Molina's term, however, whatever hopes were initially expressed had evaporated. In addition to denying that soldiers had committed acts of genocide against Guatemala's Mayan peoples under Ríos Montt, the president was reallocating funds toward rebuilding the military and away from those ministries associated with prosecuting crimes of violence against women and war crimes.

According to "Esperanza," an indigenous Ixil genocide survivor, "This [the election of Pérez Molina] was the worst news that we received in recent history. He was even elected in those communities that he massacred!"[50]

According to Maldonado, Pérez Molina is also flouting a post-peace accord tradition empowering women's organizations to select candidates for those sensitive governmental posts that directly affect their work.[51] Worse yet, he has also effectively blackmailed foreign governments to withdraw support for various women's organizations that he deems to be subversive to the national interest.

Soon after Pérez Molina was elected, news reports began to appear linking human rights organizations and various foreign embassies to alleged terrorist groups. "So when he first came into power he met with [foreign] diplomats to let them know that his policy would be of reconciliation and that he thanked them for supporting him," said Lucia Moran, whose words were supported by other activists interviewed for this book.

Pérez Molina also cautioned foreign diplomats "to take no part in what was happening and not to support the organizations that fought for human rights," according to a source who prefers to remain anonymous. "It was a disguised threat." The aim, claimed Lucia Moran, was essentially to blackmail foreign governments by threatening their corporate interests. Soon after, the United States, Mexico, Switzerland, Holland, and Norway pulled their funding from these organizations. "They helped us a great deal before but now they shine by their absence," Lucia Moran said, and adds, "Even when we invite them to an event they will not come. We continue to submit proposals, but we no longer receive any financial support."

## THE "HARD HAND"

Human rights activists are also troubled over what they perceive as Pérez Molina's attempt to remilitarize under the auspices of fighting the war on drugs. It is easy to see why. When strolling through the streets of Guatemala's Centro Historico, heavily armed uniformed young men are visible everywhere—lounging in front of banks and ATMs, manning road blocks, and patrolling streets in trucks laden with machine guns and rocket launchers.

Overhead, military helicopters scan city neighborhoods for any sign of unrest, and every day brings reports of military operations somewhere in the country. Despite the display of military muscle, the show of force has apparently done little to stem the tide of violence. According to the U.S. State Department, in 2010 the average number of homicides was 497 per month according to the Guatemalan government's own statistics.[52] As of 2013, the numbers are still climbing, but as we have already noted, the sharpest increase has been in the number of femicides.

Remilitarization is also reviving traumatic memories of the war. During joint U.S. and Guatemalan counternarcotics operations in 2012—which also involved the deployment of 171 U.S. Marines—human rights groups expressed anxiety that the United States was again providing military aid to a state that had, until fairly recently, engaged in widespread massacres and disappearances.

Among those who spoke out at the time was rights advocate Helen Mack, executive director of the Myrna Mack Foundation.[53] "Rural communities in Guatemala are fearful of the military being used to combat drug traffickers because the same techniques are applied that were used in contra [counterinsurgency] warfare," she said. "The historical memory is there and Guatemalans are fearful of that."[54]

A 2012 U.S. State Department report also noted that Guatemala is characterized by widespread institutional corruption, "including unlawful killings, drug trafficking, and extortion; and widespread societal violence, including violence against women and numerous killings, many related to drug trafficking."[55] The end of the civil war did not bring greater peace; it brought greater predation, because it taught those with power just how useful and remunerative predation could be.

The State Department report also confirmed that Guatemala has been deploying the military to support police units in response to a rise in crime and that police involvement in "criminal activities remained a serious problem."[56]

Nevertheless, in an interview with the *Marine Corps Times* during that same year William Ostick, spokesman for the State Department's Western Hemispheric Affairs Office, defended Pérez Molina as "focused on improving citizen security in Latin America." He also insisted that Guatemala's military has "made significant progress on key issues."[57]

"This is what happens," Mack told the *Marine Corps Times*, "when operations about civilian security are used as a means for social control."[58]

"Lots of security, but no security," as one observer dryly noted.


## TRIAL AND TERROR

On May 10, 2013, in a historic first for Central America, a Guatemalan court sentenced the former dictator Efraín Ríos Montt to eighty years in prison for genocide and crimes against humanity—specifically for the slaughter of more than 1,700 indigenous Maya in Guatemala's Ixil region after the 1982 coup.

The ruling also marked the first time a former head of state had been found guilty of genocide within his own country. Significantly—and germane to the current femicide—the tribunal also reaffirmed the findings of the 1999 Truth Commission and directed the government to offer a formal apology to Maya Ixil women who survived sexual violence.[59]

Previous to his arrest and conviction, Ríos Montt had enjoyed immunity from prosecution after he was elected to Congress in 1994, eleven years after he was deposed as president. The moment he resigned in 2012, however, prosecuting authorities swooped down and arrested him. After seventeen tortuous months, the three-judge tribunal ended up convicting the former dictator and sentencing the unrepentant octogenarian to 80 years in prison. It was an important moment in the history of jurisprudence in Central America and indeed the entire world. Nonetheless, the trial itself was "nearly derailed by threats to witnesses, objections by the defense's lawyers, and even criticisms by Mr. Pérez Molina, who denied that there was genocide."[60]

The conviction of Ríos Montt created a real dilemma for Pérez Molina. On the one hand he had to appear as though he played no part in the killings and supported the quest for justice; on the other, he suddenly realized that he would himself be vulnerable to prosecution just as Ríos Montt was the moment he no longer occupied a seat in Congress. As an elected official, President Pérez Molina currently enjoys immunity from prosecution under Guatemalan law. The moment he leaves office, however, prosecutors could arrest and charge the former "El Tito" with crimes against humanity—a scenario that Pérez Molina is doubtless anxious to avoid.

After the verdict, the chief judge instructed prosecutors to launch an immediate investigation of "all others" connected to Ríos Montt's crimes. Her charge to prosecutors could have meant disaster for Pérez Molina, who had already been implicated by witnesses testifying during the trial.

Among them was a former army mechanic, Hugo Leonardo Reyes, who testified that Pérez Molina presided over the burning and looting of Ixil villages in addition to the usual cycle of rape, torture, and the massacre of their inhabitants. In what was to become a familiar litany of horrors, Reyes told the three-judge tribunal that those designated for death were first "beaten, tortured, their tongues cut off and fingernails ripped out."[61]

Three Mayan genocide survivors who agreed to be interviewed for this book confirmed Pérez Molina's involvement in the deaths of their families and friends. All were willing to disclose their identities, but we have changed their names for their protection. When asked "Is your president a war criminal?" all three nodded their heads emphatically and replied yes.

"I am very angry with the people who voted him in because he is directly responsible for the massacres that occurred in our communities," said Luis, forty-seven.[62] Luis was only in his late teens when Kaibiles arrived in his village and killed his wife, his mother, his younger sisters and brothers, and his nine-month-old daughter.[63]

Added Esperanza, fifty-two, "Molina was in charge of the area around my village. They murdered my mother and my father. I still don't know where they are buried. They would come to the villages, abduct the women, force them to cook for them and then rape and kill them. They took young teenagers—children—and would say to their mothers 'give us your daughters, we want to try them out.' They would take them and kill them. He (Pérez Molina) knew it all." Said Elena, "my injuries were so severe I could not bear children. They not only took away everyone I ever loved but my peace of mind. My mind is haunted by what I've seen."

Although Pérez Molina denies all culpability, calls for his resignation immediately followed the sentencing of his former boss—including in an op-ed for the *New York Times*. The writer, Victoria Sanford, recommended that U.S. president Barack Obama "call for Mr. Pérez Molina's resignation and rally support among other members of the Organization of American States to join this call."[64]

In an interview with *Democracy Now*, investigative reporter Allan Nairn, who reported extensively on the massacres in the early 1980s, told the news website that the verdict was "a breakthrough for indigenous people against racism and a breakthrough for human civilization." He also noted, "The judge's order to further investigate everyone involved in Ríos Montt's crimes could encompass U.S. officials [who] were direct accessories and accomplices to the Guatemalan military. They were supplying money, weapons, political support, intelligence. Under international and Guatemalan law, they could be charged."[65]

To date, however, Nairn's prediction has not come true—and likely never will. On May 20, 2013, the Guatemalan Constitutional Court overturned Ríos Montt's conviction and his eighty-year sentence, formally annulling both a few days later.

Some have expressed barely muffled glee at the upending of Ríos Montt's conviction and sentence. Among them was Guatemala's Coordinating Committee of Agricultural, Commercial, Industrial and Financial Associations (CACIF), the largest business association in Guatemala. In an editorial written immediately following the annulment, the CACIF declared: "The business sector defends the importance of knowing how to leave the past behind in order to open a genuine channel to peace and reconciliation."[66] In other words, and as one leftist website observed, "peace can only be guaranteed through impunity for Guatemala's mass murderers."[67]

As we discussed in Chapter 2, this denial of justice in the Ríos Montt case is congruent with the logic of male-bonded groups. Men forgiving other men for what they have done to women or other out-groups is the hallmark of male-bonded nationalist conceptions of peace where both parties have perpetrated widespread atrocities. Indeed, Rigoberta Menchú Tum perhaps puts it best: "An amnesty is invented by two actors in a war. It's hardly the idea of the victims, or of the society. Two armed groups who have been combating each other decide that it is best for each to pardon the other. This is the whole vulgar reality that the struggle for human rights has to go through at this moment. . . . Finding the truth is not enough. What we also have to find is justice."[68]

But justice oft-times also takes a back seat to economic interests, as we shall see.

## MAQUILADORAS AND THE "CORPORATE HACIENDA"

On an average weekday in Guatemala City, the buses and taxis are clogged with commuters on their way to and from work. A good proportion of these are young women who each day head to low-paying jobs in Guatemala's rapidly expanding maquiladoras—transnationally owned factories that began popping up in free trade zones throughout the country during the late 1960s. Many of the buses are festooned with pink ribbons flapping in a burst of exhaust fumes as the vehicles pull away from the curb. The city rolled out "female only" buses in 2011 in an effort to provide safe transport for women and girls after reports of groping, sexual harassment, and rape. The buses are always full.[69]

Although maquiladoras came to Guatemala relatively late in the game, their presence sparked a radical shift in traditional gender relations—which many researchers claim have contributed to today's high femicide rates.

From 1966 to 1982, the Guatemalan Congress passed three laws to attract maquiladora investment to Guatemala, yet substantial growth did not materialize. After Ríos Montt's ouster, the U.S. Agency for International Development (USAID) poured millions of dollars more into the factories, which set Guatemala upon a course that promoters and entrepreneurs then described as "*maquila*-led industrialization."[70]

After Reagan lifted Carter's 1979 bans on foreign assistance to Guatemala, in 1986 USAID revived its maquiladora promotion program as part of its economic aid package. The aim was to cultivate a new class of maquiladora entrepreneurs—a group that would eventually lead and manage the "neo-liberal revolution." The newly established Nontraditional Products Exporters Association (AGEXPRONT) began promoting and assisting companies to export nontraditional products such as raspberries, flowers, and clothing. Funded by millions of U.S. taxpayer dollars, this trade association increased the strength of both domestic entrepreneurs and U.S. corporate interests—further facilitating the expansion of maquiladoras in Guatemala.

In 1984, then U.S. president Ronald Reagan signed the Caribbean Basin Initiative (CBI), which, among other things, offered tariff and trade benefits to a number of Central American and Caribbean countries while punishing those judged to be under the influence of communists or that had expropriated U.S. property.[71]

To secure similar market access and to evade rising labor costs in their own countries, many East Asian investors also set up shop in Central America, sparking a major boom in Korean investment in the late 1980s. Today, Guatemala is home to one of the highest concentrations of Korean-owned apparel plants outside of Korea—at 60 percent of the maquiladora sector. U.S. investors, however, directly own only 7 percent of the maquiladoras in Guatemala.[72] Nevertheless, the trade relationship between all three nations also benefits U.S.-owned companies such as Walmart and other large retailers.

As with many free trade "success stories" greater foreign investment has not necessarily closed the country's substantial inequality gap. For despite the rush of foreign investors that followed in the wake of the CBI, Guatemala still remains one of the most impoverished countries in the Western Hemisphere. More than 50 percent of the population lives below the national poverty line while 13 percent exist in a state of extreme poverty. Indigenous groups are particularly affected. Although they make up only 38 percent of the population, they comprise 73 percent of those living below the poverty line, and 28 percent living in extreme poverty.[73] In 2012, Pérez Molina pledged to keep taxes static—a promise that, perhaps unsurprisingly, delighted the country's establishment.[74]

Although much has already been written about worker conditions and abuses, maquiladoras offered unskilled women and girls an opportunity to enter the labor force en masse. Between 75-80 percent of those employed by the maquiladoras are women—although the ratio of females to males has shifted somewhat owing to the economic downturn.[75]

As with other Central American nations, the entry of large numbers of unskilled females into the labor market was to have a toxic effect on gender relations as women acquired more financial independence and the autonomy that goes with it. Working in the factories was tough and wages low. Despite the fact that many men weren't interested in such menial work, the entry of large groups of women appeared to trigger male rage.

"Generally women are targeted because they are perceived to have transgressed—whether actual or imagined," said Sandra Moran, coordinator of the Women's Sector, an alliance of thirty-four organizations. "If she has a tattoo, or is the sister of a gang member or anything that involves being outside the house after nightfall."[76]

"This also means women who have gone into the so-called 'male domain' of work," she added. "It [violence and murder] is used as a means to punish them but also to use them and discard them. Everything about these crimes is very intimate. Men are shot at long range but women at close range, usually after they have been sexually abused.

They are tortured, mutilated and dismembered. Make no mistake, these are crimes of hate."[77]

Maquiladoras, however, are not the only business sector that has drawn international investors. Guatemala is a country rich in natural resources—crops (particularly coffee), oil, minerals, zinc, hydropower, fish, and timber, most of which are exported to the United States.[78]

On July 27, 2005, the U.S. House of Representatives approved the Central America–Dominican Republic–United States Free Trade Agreement (CAFTA) in a 217–215 vote. This agreement served to expand corporate rights within the poorest countries in Central America, including Guatemala, Nicaragua, El Salvador, Costa Rica, Honduras, and the Dominican Republic. While the trade agreement was ostensibly negotiated to bring prosperity to the Americas and to provide consumers access to less expensive products, detractors accused signatories of using the trade agreement to hawk national assets to their corporate masters at fire sale prices. They also charged that these large transnational corporations were in turn exploiting poor environmental and labor conditions to rake in huge profits.

The various trade agreements also spawned the growth of a "shadow military"—private security companies made up of former military personnel, many of whom committed atrocities during the war. Human rights defenders note that private security personnel are perhaps even more dangerous even than the military because they are not only heavily armed but also wholly unregulated.

Notes Lucia Moran, "There is more private security than public security. No one controls it, no one regulates the way it works." Although the Guatemalan Congress has debated how best to regulate these private security contractors, restrict guns, and how to circumvent bank secrecy laws, in reality few expect that anything will come of it. Anita Isaacs, a political science professor who writes about Guatemala, reported that in April 2014, "security guards for a wealthy landowner shot six unarmed peasants protesting the construction of a hydroelectric dam. In a separate incident just two weeks later, she notes, armed assailants murdered a 16 year old girl, who was the leader of an anti-mining youth movement, and critically wounded her father, who had organized his community to vote against a local mining project."[79]

Moreover, the extraction of valuable natural resources has also meant the expropriation of informal Mayan settlements, whose inhabitants are in turn protesting the wholesale destruction of their ancestral lands. Once again, the government's "hard hand" is falling on unarmed demonstrators as opposed to the "criminal elements" the president pledged to fight.

Thus it is that the seizure of Mayan lands has proven to be a flashpoint between indigenous peoples and the corporations that are profiting at their expense. Most of the disputes involve access to natural resources that just happen to sit on Mayan land. Even where indigenous landowners hold clear title, both the government and transnational corporations have exhibited little regard for the kind of civil engagement necessary to ensure environmental protection and community acceptance. As one indigenous leader observes, "The massacre that there was in the war that lasted more than 36 years, we are living it anew." Attacks against those defending their rights and their land have risen dramatically to levels not seen in more than a decade.[80]

Once again, it is Mayan women leaders who have been targeted by former military personnel now working as private security contractors for mining, petroleum, and hydroelectric giants and their subsidiaries. According to Sandra Moran, "The perpetrators of the murders of the past are now the leaders and chiefs of the businesses that offer private security."[81] As was the case during the war, private security personnel and paramilitary groups are targeting women because they personify the cultural heart of the Maya.

Notes Lucia Moran, "Women are the ones that hold a community together. They hold the family together and it is through their oral history that the Mayan culture is passed from one generation to the next. When you terrorize and rape women, you effectively separate her from her community. When you kill her you kill the Mayan culture."

## NARCOPOLITICS AND
## THE RISE OF NARCOTRAFFICKING

On December 5, 1974, as the Mayan genocide was beginning in earnest, Guatemala's military government established an official Commando School (Escuela de Comandos). Three months later, on March 5, 1975, it renamed it the Kaibil Center for Training and Special Operations (Centro de Adiestramiento y Operaciones Especiales Kaibil). *Kaibil* is derived from Kaibil Balam, a Mam indigenous leader who managed to elude capture by Pedro de Alvarado and his Spanish conquistadores.

Initially, the Kaibil Center was located on two estates, El Infierno (Hell) and La Pólvora (Gunpowder), in the municipality of Melchor de Mencos, Petén. In 1989, it was relocated to the former headquarters of Military Zone 23 in Poptún, Petén.

To become Kaibiles, recruits are pumped through an arduous sixty-day training process. Only 10 percent graduate. The idea is to transform a soldier into a perfect automaton capable of enduring extreme hardship, dispatching orders without equivocation or mercy, and who no longer has any affiliations except with his fellow Kaibiles.

In 1999, the Commission for Historical Clarification slammed the cruelty and degrading nature of Kaibil training and how it was used in counterinsurgency operations that left hundreds of thousands dead. According to numerous reports outlining Kaibil training, methods include bonding with and raising puppies only to kill them later, eat them raw, and drink their blood.

Other methods included extreme sleep deprivation, hardship, and brainwashing. The troops were then deployed to undertake mass rapes, torture, disappearances, and murder—confirming a self-professed tenet of their philosophy: "The *Kaibil* is a killing machine."[82] The kind of training regime favored by the Kaibil school is a variation of that used by religious paramilitary groups—including al-Qaeda and the Islamic State of Iraq and the Levant (ISIL). The objective is to break the recruit and to encourage him to sever all ties with his previous life. It represents the toxic hypermasculinity of male-bonded groups in action and helps explain why militarism and brutal violence against women are twinned.

A good proportion of Kaibil trainees also receive additional training at the School of the Americas and continue to do so today under its new name, the Western Hemisphere Institute for Security Cooperation. So horrific is their record that even the Roman Catholic Church condemned the Kaibil atrocities in the 1998 Interdiocesan Project for the Recovery of Historical Memory. Bishop Juan José Gerardi Conedera, coordinator general of the Office on Human Rights of the archbishop of

Guatemala led the research team that authored *Guatemala: Never Again* (*Guatemala: Nunca Más*). Among its many recommendations was that the government disband the Kaibiles.

> The systems of military instruction for officers, troops, and specialists should be extensively reformed, because they continue to pose a menace to social harmony. In that sense there is a need to reformulate the mindset of military studies, reorient the functions, organization, and armament of the army's bases and special forces, and to close those centers that symbolize aggression against the population, such as the School of Kaibiles.[83]

On April 26, just two days after the report was released, Gerardi was discovered bludgeoned to death in the garage of his San Sebastián parish house.[84]

The bishop's words proved prophetic. Since the close of the twentieth century, if anything, the Kaibiles have only acquired more power: they are now closely linked with the rise of narcotrafficking in Guatemala, Mexico, and indeed around the world.

A plethora of evidence suggests that they were among the founders of the dreaded Zetas, a drug gang made famous for its efficiency, discipline, and brutality. And again, women's rights advocates insist that the same signature of mutilation and sexual torture meted out to Mayan women and human rights workers by Kaibiles during the civil war are once again evident in the work of Guatemala's narcogangs.

"It is very simple," Lucia Moran said. "The narco traffickers have a very macho ethic that women and girls are property. Much of their initiation involves gang raping and murdering girls and women. If a woman or girl wants to join a gang she will then be gang raped and tortured. This does not happen to males."

Moreover, many gangs operate within Guatemala, including the *maras*—easily identified for the distinctive tattoos that cover their bodies. Although they frequently fight over territory and control of the country's lucrative territories, they remain united when it comes to violence and misogyny.

Unlike the Zetas, however, the original *maras* originally hailed from Los Angeles, and were largely made up of the offspring of traumatized refugees and illegal immigrants fleeing El Salvador, Guatemala, and Honduras during the dirty wars of the 1980s. Many were deported back to Central America after doing jail time in the United States. A number also left voluntarily in order to take advantage of the opportunities offered by drugs and human trafficking. The hypermasculinity that these groups promulgate could have been ripped straight from the pages of the Kaibiles training manuals.

Disputes between gangs are often resolved through revenge killings meted out to the female relatives of girlfriends of rival gang members. "Many, many women are dying in this way," Sandra Moran avers.[85] The Guatemalan Human Rights Commission concurs, noting that the patterns of narcogang violence against women closely mimic those of the military and paramilitaries during the civil war. Indeed, in some gangs, members rack up rewards for every woman they murder.[86] Gang initiation often includes killing young women, and many dozens of femicides have been linked to this rite of passage. In some instances, gangs will reward extra points to gang members depending on the brutality of the crime.[87] In other words, terrorize the women and you control the neighborhood.

As is typical in Guatemala, the police provide little assistance. Once police categorize the killing of a woman as a narcocrime, detectives usually are reluctant to investigate—even if the killing meets all the criteria for a femicide. Moreover, investigators tend to classify narco-related crime based on the most trivial of reasons. The case of the still unsolved murder of nineteen-year-old Claudia Velásquez Paiz is a perfect case in point.

On August 13, 2005, Paiz disappeared after calling her mother to tell her she would be home soon. Following many tense hours, her family began a frantic search. They later found her corpse covered in bruises and traces of semen. A single gunshot to the head was officially determined as the cause of death.

In June 2006, the Guatemala Human Rights Ombudsman's Office issued a searing report criticizing the state for "failing in its obligation to respect and guarantee the right to life, security, and due process, including the failure to interview witnesses, conduct a thorough forensic analysis, and preserve the crime scene." The report also revealed that police initially considered Paiz a "nobody" because she was wearing sandals and a belly button ring.[88]

# FEMICIDE LAWS:
## PROGRESS, REDRESS, AND REGRESS

At a distance, the USAID-funded Edificio Control del Ministerio Publico is an imposing structure. Inside, the floors gleam and the walls are spotlessly white. It hums with quiet activity.

Arturo Aguilar is a handsome man but also a busy and impatient one. Despite an almost overwhelming caseload that has him and his staff working far into the night, the then-secretary of the attorney general in charge of strategic affairs agreed to speak about Guatemala's new femicide laws. At the time of his interview with Leidl, he was the right-hand man of then Attorney General Claudia Paz y Paz, so Aguilar knew what he was talking about.

Over two years after Pérez Molina's election, Guatemala still lags when it comes to investigating and prosecuting violent crimes, particularly those perpetrated against women. A faint glimmer of hope, however, once resided with the Office of the Attorney General.

In its *World Report 2013*, the New York-based Human Rights Watch praised then–Attorney General Claudia Paz y Paz and the United Nations International Commission against Impunity in Guatemala (CICIG) for progress made against corruption, femicide, and the prosecution of war criminals. Nevertheless, Human Rights Watch also cautioned: "Yet the progress made by the public prosecutor's office and CICIG in bringing charges against officials has been undercut by the dilatory practices of defendants' lawyers, leading to trial postponements of up to several months or even years. Efforts to reform the criminal code and other laws to limit such practices have not advanced."[89]

Nevertheless, Paz y Paz and her office were lauded for progress in prosecuting war criminals (it was her office that indicted Ríos Montt), extraditing drug lords to the United States, and implementing Guatemala's new femicide law. During her tenure, Guatemala established a DNA lab with state-of-the-art equipment to facilitate rape and murder investigations.[90] Despite making headway against almost insurmountable odds, the maverick prosecutor was forced to step down seven months before her term was to expire because of a technicality stemming from her appointment.[91]

Her departure constitutes a bitter blow for those who are fighting to end femicide. Like other advocates for women's rights, Aguilar blames the current femicidal terror on the legacy of the civil war but avers that the current crisis is in many ways far worse owing to the fact that it has infected almost every city, town, village, and hamlet throughout the country. "No place is safe," he says.[92]

Until very recently, Guatemalan jurisprudence was dramatically skewed in favor of men. Article 200, which was not repealed until June 2006, was a prime example. Among its more salient characteristics, it allowed charges against a convicted rapist to be dropped if he agreed to marry the victim, who could be no younger than twelve, and provided the Public Prosecutor's Office agreed.[93]

The recognition of the gendered nature of the killings and their rapid escalation prompted women's groups to organize and seek allies on the international stage. The aim was to agitate for change by enlisting outside pressure. Among those who joined the fray were Amnesty International and Human Rights Watch. The situation has also drawn the attention of Eve Ensler, author of *The Vagina Monologues*, and celebrity activists such as Jane Fonda.[94]

In response to mounting pressure and a rapidly escalating death toll, in 2004 the Inter-American Commission on Human Rights accused the Guatemalan government of providing only the most limited resources for women seeking help in situations of violence. The left-wing government of President Álvaro Colon responded by creating the Commission to Fight Femicide, which investigates and analyzes femicide cases and makes policy recommendations to eliminate violence against women.[95]

The U.S. Congress, somewhat ironically given previous support for various genocidal regimes, also played a pivotal role in pressuring Guatemalan authorities to bring their criminal code more into line with North American standards.[96] Introduced by U.S. representative Hilda Solis alongside one hundred cosponsors, Resolution 100 was passed by the House of Representatives on May 1, 2007. It condemned the ongoing abductions and murders of women and girls in Guatemala while expressing "condolences and deepest sympathy to the families of victims." It also recognized the "courageous struggle of the victim's families in seeking justice for the victims" and recommended that the U.S. president, secretary of state, and U.S. ambassador to Guatemala "encourage Guatemala to properly investigate, resolve, and prevent these crimes."[97]

Nearly a year later, U.S. senator Jeff Bingaman introduced Resolution 178 with 13 cosponsors, which the Senate passed on March 10, 2008. The U.S. senators denounced the inadequacy of investigations, urging Guatemala to act swiftly to prosecute the perpetrators, hold corrupt officials accountable, and develop a detailed plan directed at attacks against women.

It worked. At least initially.

On April 9, 2008, Guatemala passed its first femicide law. Under Decree 22–2008, the Guatemalan Congress passed the Law Against Femicide and Other Forms of Violence Against Women. It is the first Guatemalan law of its kind and officially recognizes femicide as a punishable crime. It also codifies a more expansive definition of violence against women by identifying four types including femicide and physical/sexual, psychological, and economic violence.[98]

According to Aguilar, the new law led to more arrests, prosecutions, and convictions. Before Paz y Paz was ousted from her position, Aguilar spoke glowingly about his boss, saying, "I don't want to sound as if I'm selling this but our General Prosecutor [Claudia Paz y Paz] is a woman and a feminist, and one of her priorities is to tackle crimes against women." Not only that but she was also "a close personal friend of Hillary Rodham Clinton."

"She [Clinton] has done a great deal to help the women of Guatemala," Aguilar continued. "This building is because she convinced USAID to pay for it and to build our capacity. She hasn't been very vocal publically but she's done a great deal behind the scenes." In a sense, then, Clinton was the first U.S. secretary of state that acted to right some of the wrongs done to Guatemalans—including Guatemalan women—in the name of U.S. foreign policy interests. Her efforts to specifically assist Guatemalan women, detailed in chapter 5, will likely leave a far brighter legacy for that country than that of previous United States administrations.

Because the new law on femicide recognizes gender as the principal motive for the crime, it takes into account the effects of misogyny, machismo, and gender bias, which Aguilar maintains have contributed to the larger issue of gender inequality in Guatemalan society. It allows women, for the first time, to charge their partners with domestic violence, which can also include withholding access to contraceptives.

Guatemala's femicide law also sets out a menu of interventions designed to better protect women and girls from violence—including the establishment of special units tasked specifically with investigating violence against women; the institutional support necessary to operate domestic violence intake centers (Centers for Comprehensive Support for Female Survivors of Violence, or CAIMU) and NGOs; and a national statistics database to collect and collate data concerning violence against women throughout the country.

At the time of his interview with Leidl, Aguilar maintained that 295 men had already been charged under the femicide law since it came into effect. Moreover, if acquitted of femicide, the accused won't necessarily walk away a free man, as regularly occurs in neighboring Mexico. "We can still convict them on the lesser charge of homicide," says Aguilar. "Judges here have less discretion than they do in Mexico."

The question is: Has the femicide law resulted in lower death rates? According to Aguilar, while crimes against women and girls began to fall in 2012, the numbers were growing again in early 2013. "January [2013] was horrible," he said. "Sixty three women and girls were killed. We are trying to investigate why this is so but we don't yet have an answer."

"It is terrible. Because we have historically been so saturated with violence we no longer have the mechanisms to solve our own problems," Aguilar adds thoughtfully. "In a very literal sense violence against women is a very profound way of ensuring social control. It is about resisting change and maintaining a double standard. The killing of women is a form of social domination." The killers who send the decapitated heads of young women to officials trying to enforce the femicide law are, in effect, also relaying a bloody message about who really is in control.[99]

It is no coincidence that both narcotraffickers and the military subscribe to the view that women are no more than objects to be plundered at will. By demonizing the feminine, they also marginalize anyone associated with weak (i.e., effete) members of the social and economic pecking order: human rights activists, intellectuals, artists, indigenous populations, and the very poor. Predation is male and therefore something to be admired. Consensus and respect for human rights, environmental sustainability, and indigenous culture are female and therefore a contagion that must be tightly controlled and neutralized.

As of this writing, and in a move that was widely criticized by the international human rights community, the Guatemala Constitutional Court ruled that Claudia Paz y Paz's term as Attorney General would end in May 2014 instead of December of that same year, and that she is disqualified from holding the post anytime in the near future.[100] Justice has taken a sabbatical in Guatemala.

## THE LILIES OF ANTIGUA

Lovely Antigua was Guatemala's colonial capital under the Spanish, and is now a popular tourist destination. In the courtyard of one of the local hangouts there stood a life size terra cotta statuette that tourists dubbed the "burning boy." He guarded the entrance on scorched legs, childish face curved downwards. Waxy lilies bloomed from his seared head and burnt arm stumps—as if inviting the hope of resurrection and healing. Today that hope continues to elude many who survived the terror only to witness its resurgence in a new and terrible form.

"You can't put an economic price on the ruin that these killers inflict on families," says Iada Batres, a Sobrevivientes social worker. "Even if we managed to convict them all it will not inflict the same pain that the family and children suffer. . . . The mother is not there; the sister is not there; the daughter is not there. A child is left without his mother. They are raped. They are dismembered, asphyxiated. There is a huge amount of brutality in the way they are killed. Who is doing this? We think we know. . . . It is just so horrible. It is unbearable."[101]

But Guatemalan women are still determined to make their own hope, with the rallying cry, "Ni una muerte mas!"—not one more death! Women, and the men who support them, have staged public demonstrations, including carrying coffins symbolizing femicide victims, through the streets of the capital.[102] While the culture of impunity runs deep and those who speak out are threatened or killed, Guatemalan women continue to fight for a national identity that is not based on the valorization of male predation. In this, they follow the wisdom of a Mayan woman elder, who before her death in the genocide, taught her daughter, Rigoberta Menchú Tum, "any evolution, any change, in which women had not participated, would not be a change, and there would be no victory."[103]

Is it even possible that Guatemalan women and the men who support them might forge a new path, one not strewn with the corpses of women and girls? Though at the time of this writing, things appear to be getting worse, not better, perhaps the unceasing efforts of these women and men will one day cause hope to bloom again in Guatemala.

# 4

# A CONSPICUOUS SILENCE

★ ★ ★

*U.S. Foreign Policy, Women, and Saudi Arabia*

So there are these tensions between what the real purpose of foreign aid is: Is it to do development or is it a tool of the geostrategic interests of the United States?

—ANDREW NATSIOS, FORMER USAID ADMINISTRATOR

OR PROPONENTS OF the Hillary Doctrine, no irony was more cruel than seeing Secretary of State Hillary Clinton smiling broadly in her trademark pantsuit as she walked the red carpet from her plane on the tarmac in Riyadh with the Saudi foreign minister, Prince Saud al-Faisal, in February 2010.

It brought to mind an incongruity no less extreme than if Frederick Douglass had been appointed ambassador to the Confederacy and found himself sipping tea and making small talk with Nathan Bedford Forrest. For, to be sure, in Saudi Arabia the subordination of women is as finely calibrated as was slavery in the antebellum South. The question of how Hillary Clinton could so seemingly brush her own doctrine to one side in this case—ostensibly in the name of national interest—is a crucial one.

The either/or vision of foreign aid and diplomacy described by Natsios in the opening quote of this chapter[1] suggests that U.S. foreign policy officials have viewed women's rights as orthogonal to national security. To these officials, "national interests" and "women's interests" occupy different planes entirely, and national interests are viewed as the higher plane. This has played out most vividly with reference to Saudi Arabia and its colonization of Yemen, and in this chapter we will explore whether that stance represents a necessary accommodation to reality.

## A GULAG FOR WOMEN: SAUDI ARABIA AND THE EXPORT OF ISLAMIC EXTREMISM

One day in 2012, Saudi Arabia's Committee for the Promotion of Virtue and the Prevention of Vice made a public announcement. "The men of the committee will interfere to force women to cover their eyes," intoned spokesman Sheikh Motlab al-Nabet. Especially, he added, "the tempting ones." And then, perhaps a little defensively, "[We] have the right to do so."[2]

Especially the tempting ones? Well!

The Committee for the Promotion of Virtue and the Prevention of Vice, otherwise known as the *mutaween* or religious police, has been enforcing moral standards in the kingdom since 1940. Although this Orwellian goon squad, dressed in gold-embroidered muslin and carrying wooden staves, routinely rounds up anyone whose behavior is deemed "morally suspect," it reserves special venom for women and girls, who are routinely beaten, lashed, and thrown in jail for infringements, real or imagined, of the sexual code of conduct.[3]

Saudi Arabia ranks 145th of 158 countries in the U.N. Development Programme's Gender Inequality Index—making it among the worst countries in which to be born female despite its considerable oil wealth.

While Saudi Arabia's maternal mortality rate is similar to that of the United States, child marriage is not uncommon because there is no legal minimum age of marriage. Indeed, the media has highlighted a number of notorious child marriage cases, such as when an eight-year-old girl requested the courts in May 2009 to grant her a divorce from her fifty-year-old husband.[4] Consent in marriage is clearly not required from the bride. And in a slightly surreal twist, in Saudi Arabia, a woman need not even be present for her own marriage, as long as her male guardian and her groom agree.

Complicating matters is that Saudi Arabia has no written criminal code. This vacuum puts human rights activists and women at considerable risk because in the absence of written law, Sharia is applied capriciously depending on the geographic location, gender, wealth, reputation, and kinship ties of both accused and plaintiff.[5]

Nevertheless, in 2011, Saudi women finally gained the right to vote and to run in municipal elections—beginning in 2015. Today, 20 percent of the King's Consultative Council (Majlis as-Shura) is also made up of women.[6] In 2012, women were permitted to work as sales clerks in lingerie and cosmetics shops for the first time. In October 2013, four Saudi women became the first to be licensed as lawyers in the kingdom. The number of women in the workforce has increased ninefold in just five years.[7] At the same time, IKEA in Saudi Arabia removed all images of women depicted in its catalog, literally erasing their very presence, and male professors can teach female university students only by means of video-conferencing, because they are not permitted to be in the same room together.[8]

It is a puzzling set of ill-fitting pieces, to be sure.

Mobility is one of the most vexing problems facing Saudi women. Women are forbidden to drive (apparently it would hurt their ovaries[9]) and may only leave their dwellings while covered top to bottom in the stifling black *abaya* and accompanied by a male guardian (*mahram*), who in some circumstances may be a woman's own son. Women cannot easily move around within their community; they certainly cannot wander about by themselves, ride a bike (unless in a park, in full abaya, and with a male guardian present[10]), or go on a picnic. They cannot travel outside the country nor marry a man of their choosing without the permission of the ubiquitous male guardian.

Gender segregation is extreme. Because of the cultural interdictions against unrelated men and women occupying the same location at the same time, and despite the significant rise in female labor force participation over the past decade, only 17.7 percent of women work outside of the home, compared to 74.1 percent of all males.[11] Eleanor A. Doumato, a professor at Brown University, reports:

> One crime for which women are especially targeted is *khulwa* (the illegal mixing of unrelated men and women), which can occur whether men and women are dining together in a restaurant, riding in a taxi, or meeting for

business. . . . Women are prohibited from most ministry buildings and discouraged from walking along public streets or attending mosques except at pilgrimage. . . . The public spaces in Saudi Arabia that are intended for the enjoyment of the general public, such as parks, zoos, libraries, museums, and the national Jinadriyah Festival of Folklore and Culture, are also segregated by hours of access, with men allocated the greater number and most convenient time slots. . . . Prohibited from driving themselves, unable to afford private taxis or cars, and faced with a lack of accessible public transportation, working women are often forced to walk on the streets, where they may be apprehended by the religious police on accusations of soliciting sex.[12]

The watchful eyes of male relatives and the dreaded *mutaween* circumscribe women's every movement—so much so that in a cable to U.S. diplomats, Wajeha al-Huwaider—a Saudi women's rights activist who recently challenged the ban on female drivers—described the country as "the world's largest prison for women."[13]

Perhaps the most telling example of the extremes to which Arab authorities are determined to enforce their grim code occurred in 2002. It was the middle of the night when a blaze broke out in a girl's school in Mecca. Firefighters arrived on the scene as eight hundred girls fled for their lives. Also in attendance was the *mutaween*. As it turned out, they were not there to help save the girls but to prevent them from leaving because they were not wearing their *abayas*.

The school was locked at the time to ensure the full segregation of the sexes—although male students are not similarly imprisoned. The father of one of the dead girls later told a news outlet that the school watchman even refused to open the gates to let the girls out, while the *Saudi Gazette* quoted witnesses as saying that the *mutaween* had warned, "it is a sinful [*sic*] to approach them."[14]

Fifteen girls died that night because police forced them back into the inferno. Apparently, the police deemed it preferable for schoolgirls to be immolated alive than to risk offending societal norms of modesty by appearing in public improperly attired.[15]

Although the girls' deaths ignited the usual amount of controversy, the religious police remained untouchable. The Saudi royal family publicly supports the *mutaween*. Prince Naif, the heir to the throne who died in 2012, once said: "The committee is supported by all sides. . . . It should be supported because it is a pillar from Islam. If you are a Muslim, you should support the committee."[16] In March 2013, King Abdullah increased the budget for this draconian body by 200 million riyals (about $53 million).[17] Repression is openly encoded in the customary law of the land, as well. In Saudi Arabia, a woman's testimony is worth half of a man's. If she is raped, she needs to produce four male witnesses to corroborate her testimony—effectively giving carte blanche to rapists and pedophiles.

How did this country of 27 million become so repressive of women? And why does the United States apparently refuse to engage in any meaningful dialogue with Saudi Arabia about the clear denial of basic human rights to just under half of its population? As recently as November 2013, Secretary of State John Kerry said at a press conference in Riyadh, "It's no secret that in the United States of America, we embrace equality for everybody regardless of gender, race, or any qualifications. But it's up to Saudi Arabia to make its own decisions about its own social structure and other choices, and timing."[18]

Standing in stark contrast is President Barack Obama's reaction to Russia's recent antigay legislation: "According to news reports, Obama states he has 'no patience for countries that try to treat gays or lesbians or transgender persons in ways that intimidate them or are harmful to them.'" In criticizing a law that prohibits public events promoting gay rights and public displays of affection by same-sex couples, Obama stated without equivocation, "One of the things I think is very important for me to speak out on is making sure that people are treated fairly and justly because that's what we stand for, and I believe that that's a precept that's not unique to America. That's just something that should apply everywhere."[19]

Except where women's rights are concerned?

Saudi Arabia is not only the religious and economic hub of the Islamic world but also the birthplace of Wahhabism, often (incorrectly) used interchangeably with Salafism.[20] Although the two spring from distinct historical movements, both advocate a return to an austere form of Islam whose followers hew more closely to the life of the Prophet Muhammad.

Both schools promote jihad, religious intolerance, a revulsion against idolatry; a return to a medieval Islamism based on the hadiths—and the extreme repression of women and girls.

Muhammad ibn Abd al-Wahhab founded the Wahhabi school of Islamic thought in the eighteenth century in response to what he perceived as the moral decline of Islamic peoples in an attempt to bring about a return to pure Islam as embodied in the Quran and in the life of the Prophet Muhammad.

In a bid to unify the perpetually squabbling tribes of the Arab Peninsula, Muhammad ibn Saud, the ancestral founder of the modern-day al-Saud dynasty, married one of al-Wahhab's daughters in 1744, thereby forging a historic alliance in order to vanquish their political rivals. In return, the al-Saud supported campaigns by Wahhabi zealots to cleanse the land of unbelievers. In 1801, Saudi-Wahhabi jihadists crossed into present-day Iraq and sacked the Shiite holy city of Karbala, killing more than four thousand people. After the Saudis conquered Mecca and Medina in the 1920s, they destroyed shrines that they considered idolatrous, including the Jannat al-Baqi cemetery, where four of the twelve Shiite imams were buried.

After the establishment of the Kingdom of Saudi Arabia in 1932, and in return for endorsing the royal family's authority over politics, security, and the economy, Wahhabi clerics were granted control of the state's religious and educational institutions.

The close political relationship between the House of Saud and the Wahhabis continues to this day. Indeed, in her autobiography, Hillary Clinton has this to say about Wahhabism:

> Like the Judeo-Christian Bible, the *Quran* is open to different interpretations, most of which promote peaceful coexistence with people of other religions; some, like Wahhabism, do not. Wahhabism is an ultraconservative Saudi brand of Islam that is gaining adherents around the world. While I deeply respect the basic tenets of Islam, Wahhabism troubles me because it is a fast-spreading form of Islamic fundamentalism that excludes women from full participation in their societies, promotes religious intolerance, and, in its most extreme version, as we learned with Osama bin Laden, advocates terror and violence.[21]

Salafism shares many of the same goals as Wahhabism but began in the late nineteenth century at al-Azhar University in Egypt. Hassan al-Banna, an Egyptian schoolteacher, founded the Muslim Brotherhood in 1928, and today it remains the oldest organized Salafist-influenced political party in the world. Until his assassination by Egyptian police in 1948, al-Banna continued to call for the Brotherhood to expand beyond Egypt's borders. Until the 1960s, however, these two major bodies of fundamentalist Islam, Wahhabis and Salafis, remained largely isolated from each other until the Saudi monarchy offered refuge to radical members of the Muslim Brotherhood fleeing persecution in Nasser's Egypt, thereby constructing a bridge between the two movements. The Saudis would later regret their decision.

Soon after the Muslim Brotherhood's exile to Saudi Arabia in the 1960s, movement adherents finally obtained what they needed—funding to the tune of billions of dollars, much of it from U.S. purchases of Saudi oil.

Both the Salafi and Wahhabi movements share at their core a philosophy that extols a creed of atavism and purity and thus make common cause of waging jihad against the infidel. According to the scholar and analyst Mohammed Ayoob, "It was the synthesis of the Wahhabi social and cultural conservatism, and Qutbist political radicalism [a strand of Islamic fascism that advocates for global jihad], that produced the militant variety of Wahhabist political Islam that eventually [produced] al-Qaeda."[22] Indeed, perhaps no group exemplifies Qutbist ideology more than the Islamic State in the Levant (ISIL), now carving out a brutal and misogynist caliphate in Syria and Iraq.

During the 1970s, Wahhabi clerics encouraged the spread of this revolutionary and atavistic ideological hybrid into Saudi universities and mosques—ostensibly to counter westernization and the widespread corruption that accompanied the 1970s oil boom. The Saudis eventually discovered, however, that the fundamentalists were becoming increasingly unmanageable.

Their worst fears were confirmed on the morning of November 20, 1979, when extremist clerics, calling themselves the Ikhwan, or the Brotherhood, took control of the Grand Mosque at Mecca. The Saudi military ended up laying siege to one of Islam's holiest sites in order to oust the recalcitrant fanatics, resulting in three hundred deaths and hundreds of injuries during two tense weeks. All captured militants were publicly beheaded.

This is arguably when things changed most dramatically for Saudi women. The crisis convinced the monarchy that it needed the Wahhabi clergy more than ever to control the population and to subvert insurgency by playing to the worst elements in Saudi society. Unfortunately, the price for appeasement was the increased subordination of women. As one Saudi woman expressed it, "After 1979, they decided women have to wear abbayahs always because they allowed the *mutaween* more freedom to impose their ways, and Sharia law was everything. Luckily a lot of us still remember Riyadh before the *mutaween* were so powerful. I used to be free in Riyadh, walking around [with my hair uncovered]. . . . I used to walk alone in Riyadh, no man, no maid, just relaxed like in Paris. Now that is all over, just like that."[23]

After the mosque seizure, the royal family also lit upon the Soviet invasion of Afghanistan as the perfect solution to its surplus jihadists, some of whom were lesser, later sons of elite polygynous families. It was an urgent matter, for "some believed it would only be a matter of time before the Wahhabi clergy of the *mutaween* was sufficiently emboldened to take on the monarchy itself."[24] It was at this time that the Saudis—in coordination with both Pakistan's Inter Service Intelligence agency (ISI) and the CIA—came to the aid of the Afghan mujahideen with both thousands of zealous fighters and billions of dollars in financial backing. Fatefully, the Saudis also began to fund radical madrassas to disseminate neo-Wahhabi ideology and literature in Pakistan's rural areas and sprawling refugee camps, where millions of Afghans had settled to wait out the civil war.

Soon after the withdrawal of Soviet troops from Afghanistan in 1989, the jihadists pursued further victories against unbelievers in Bosnia, Sudan, and elsewhere. Militant Wahhabi preachers invariably accompanied these fighters and preached their own doctrinaire form of Islam in prisons and among whoever else would listen. The Wahhabis brought immense funding to build the infrastructure of mosques and madrassas necessary to ensure that their ideology would persist in these nations long after their fighters had already left for wars elsewhere.

This philosophy of "Quran and sword" would become lethally concentrated in the form of al-Qaeda, the militant terrorist organization founded by Osama bin Laden, a lesser, later son of Yemeni descent. After the Taliban's seizure of Kabul in 1996, Wahhabi missionaries and fighters fled Sudan, which had caved to U.S. pressure and kicked them out, only to retrench to Afghanistan. The goal was to establish a "model Wahhabi state" in a country that had descended into complete lawlessness.[25]

The Taliban's control of Afghanistan offered a safe haven for Wahhabists and an even safer one for Osama bin Laden. From there he launched a series of even more audacious attacks. After the first bombing of the World Trade Center in New York, the Saudi royal family caved in to American pressure and revoked bin Laden's Saudi citizenship in 1994. Despite this, they refused to interfere with related Islamist (i.e., Wahhabi/Salafist) "charities" in the kingdom and abroad.[26] These groups raised money for al-Qaeda, while the Saudi royal family and government continued to pour funds into their various neo-Wahhabist colonial projects.

Even a number of skirmishes between fundamentalists and police, including terrorist attacks within the kingdom, failed to persuade the royal family to turn off the tap. Despite what appeared to be a crackdown on terrorist cells (U.S. pressure again), the kingdom has essentially come to an unspoken agreement between various affiliated jihadi groups. How do we know this? According to the former diplomat Curtin Winsor:

> Hundreds of members of the Saudi royal family jet around the world without fear of assassination. The country's vulnerable petroleum industry has only once been targeted by terrorists, and then in a less than serious manner. In return, and notwithstanding its limited cooperation with Washington in restricting terrorist financing, the Saudi monarchy has maintained its commitment to propagating Wahhabism at home and abroad, providing the terrorist underground with a growing flood of eager recruits.[27]

The kingdom has also been sending men, materiel and money to fund Syria's extremist rebels, especially to those with a fundamentalist ideology—including antiaircraft and antitank missiles from the United States in order to tip the balance toward Sunni hegemony. By backing anti-Assad forces, Saudi Arabia is challenging its main regional foe, Iran, and extending its influence to challenge Shiite dominance in Iran and Iraq. The aim is to ensure Sunni ascendance. By doing so, the kingdom is favoring those rebel groups most in line with Wahhabi beliefs, such as al-Nusra.[28]

The Muslim Brotherhood however, is another story. A number of attacks and skirmishes within the kingdom during the past several decades has soured the originally friendly relationship between the two. The Saudis now perceive their former friend as a foe— and one that has recently promoted the toppling of long-standing autocrats like themselves, such as Mubarak, Ben Ali, and the late Gadhafi. Though the Saudis were not big fans of these three—indeed, the hatred between the Saudi monarchs and Gadhafi was the stuff of legend and assassination plots—the principle of militant grassroots action to overthrow established regimes is anathema to the House of Saud. The Saudis were reportedly furious with the United States for ditching Mubarak, seeing in that act a foreshadowing of what the Americans would do to them if given the chance.

## Colonialism, Saudi Style

The Saudi project of cultural and religious colonialism brings with it a huge price tag. In Yemen, Egypt, and Libya and throughout the Middle East, North and West Africa, and Central and South Asia, increasingly virulent forms of Islam are severely curtailing the rights of women and, by extension, further destabilizing already fragile states.

Regions that previously espoused less draconian views about the role of women are turning toward the Saudi-inspired misogyny. Kyrgyz social philospher Tcholpon Akhmatalieva asserts that the influx of Saudi money has not only produced "a mosque on every block" in Uzbekistan and south Kyrgyzstan, but "now even little schoolgirls are forced to wear the hijab, which had never ever happened in [our] history before. The [Saudi] missionaries tell the patriarchs that all their women must veil now."[29]

And the Saudi-backed messengers also have a message for women in new frontiers such as Indonesia. Wahhabi missionaries are promulgating new restrictions that would prohibit women from dancing in public, from wearing jeans, from appearing without a headscarf, and from riding motorbikes, while other practices such as female genital cutting and virginity testing are now being promoted.[30]

Rania al-Baz, the brave Saudi newscaster who spoke publicly of her own experience with domestic abuse, paints a vivid picture of exactly what is being exported to women in these countries:

> The structure of society—the fact that a woman cannot drive or travel without authorization, for example, gives a special sense of strength to the man. And this strength is directly connected to the violence. It creates a sense of immunity; that he can do whatever he wants, without sanction. The core issue is not the violence itself. It is this immunity for men, the idea that men can do what they like. It is the society of which the violence is an expression.[31]

As we described in previous chapters, it is this impunity for violence against women that breeds unstable, violent societies—the two are joined at the hip. And so, in the end, the Saudis are exporting not just the subordination of women but also violent instability.

Those who argue that our interests in Saudi Arabia are much more important than how women are treated there are suffering from a severe case of short-sightedness. The export of political volatility and violence throughout the international system is not in the interests of the United States of America. As we mentioned in chapter 2, Hillary Clinton herself says it best: "So the next time you hear someone say that the fate of women and girls is not a core national security issue, it's not one of those hard issues that really smart people deal with, remind them: The extremists understand the stakes of this struggle. They know that when women are liberated, so are entire societies. We must understand this too. And not only understand it, but act on it."[32]

Indeed, Fareed Zakaria has gone on record as saying he would award the prize for Most Irresponsible Foreign Policy to our allies, the Saudis. He explained:

> It is the nation most responsible for the rise of Islamic radicalism and militancy around the world. Over the past four decades, the kingdom's immense oil wealth has been used to underwrite the export of an extreme,

intolerant and violent version of Islam preached by its Wahhabi clerics. Go anywhere in the world—from Germany to Indonesia—and you'll find Islamic centers flush with Saudi money, spouting intolerance and hate. In 2007, Stuart Levey, then a top Treasury official, told ABC News, "If I could snap my fingers and cut off the funding from one country, it would be Saudi Arabia."[33]

While many such cases of creeping Wahhabism around the world could be explored, including in Iraq and Syria, it is in Yemen that we turn to see the consequences of Saudi cultural colonialism.

## SOFIYA OF SANA'A

"Welcome, welcome to Yemen!" Ibrahim is a twinklingly friendly resident of Sana'a, the capital of Yemen. The 72-year-old likes to spend his afternoons sitting on a bench in the celebrated Old City—a labyrinth of wattle and daub brick, stained glass and stone fretwork multistory buildings. On any given afternoon Ibrahim enjoys hanging out with his elderly cronies and chewing khat, a mildly stimulating leafy shrub that, in this impoverished country of 2.4 million, is essentially what coffee is for Americans—but much stronger.[34]

Originally a native of Aden, Yemen's most important port city and a former British protectorate, Ibrahim moved his family to Sana'a to find work when the south merged with the north in 1994. Unification, needless to say, was not easy, particularly for the more laid-back southerners who had enjoyed years of secular rule under the Arabian Peninsula's first openly communist government.

Ibrahim's youngest granddaughter, a tiny doll-like toddler dressed in a long pink dress, is sitting on his lap and clutching at the lime green shoots he holds patiently away from her. It is clear that Ibrahim adores the little two-year-old with her solemn stare and dimpled chin, but when he speaks of her future, his mood becomes more somber. "You know," he says in perfect English, "the south used to be very different from the north and from what it is now. My daughters all went to school, they all had jobs, they could move around freely and dressed as they chose."

He shakes his head. "Sofiya here? I don't know." He pauses and then continues quietly, "It is getting worse—much worse. We hoped that the revolution would make things better but it has not. I fear we will become like Saudi but much poorer. We need to leave here, but we cannot."

He has good reason to worry. Chronic instability bedevils Yemen, as does hunger, corruption, and broken educational and health systems. The as-yet-unresolved political stalemate in the wake of the Arab Uprising is further complicating an already complex emergency. With 63 percent of the population under the age of twenty-four,[35] a youth unemployment rate of more than 40 percent,[36] and a water crisis so acute it is among the worst in the world, prospects look dim indeed. Insurgencies in the north and south, a growing al-Qaeda presence, plus a deepening trend toward Saudi-type social conservatism are only contributing to a pervasive sense of gloom.

As Robert F. Worth once put it in the *New York Review of Books*, for most Americans Yemen is "little more than a code word for bizarre terror plots"—the training ground of the "underwear bomber," the attack on the USS *Cole*, and so forth. Many Americans also vaguely remember it as the ancestral home of the bin Laden family and, more recently, the mountainous redoubt of U.S.-born cleric Anwar al-Awlaki, who influenced a generation of al-Qaeda aspirants until a missile from a U.S. drone landed on him in 2011.

Rarely do Westerners hear of the other Yemen—the warmth of its inhabitants, the generosity amid so much want, and the sheer loveliness of the Old City of Sana'a; of phantasmagorical Shabam, with its ancient "high-rises" constructed of mud bricks; of the mysterious isle of Socotra or of the archeological sites that make this country a veritable treasure trove of antiquarian delight.

But Yemen's geostrategic position is what molds its course now. The southwestern corner of Yemen lies on the Bab el Mandeb, a twelve-mile-wide strait connecting the Gulf of Aden and the Red Sea, the latter leading to the southern entrance of the Suez Canal. Each day, three million barrels of oil are shipped through the turbid waters of this international choke point.

To the northwest of the Bab el Mandeb is the Saudi port of Yanbu; around the Horn of Africa and to the southwest are the shipping lanes of the Indian Ocean, a maritime superhighway linking the Middle East to energy-hungry Asian markets; and along the Yemeni coast to the northeast is Aden. (And as far as oil and natural gas production is concerned, Yemen ranks 31st and 30th of 135 countries, respectively.[37]) Although the Port of Aden should—theoretically at least—be an important stopover en route to markets south and east, this is no longer the case because of unrest.

Somali pirates prowl the sea lanes—many of them former fishermen whose traditional livelihoods have been wrecked by foreign overfishing and the unregulated use of drift nets.[38] Continuing and worsening instability in Yemen encourage these disenfranchised but enterprising maritime bandits to disrupt shipping by launching attacks from their own country's long and sparsely populated coastline.[39]

As Robert Sharp and Fahad Malaikah point out in a 2012 article in the *Small Arms Journal*, although the United States has viewed "Yemen almost exclusively through a counterterrorism lens," this has proved "short-sighted and counterproductive." Both authors argue that securing Aden will secure the Suez Canal and by extension help the United States engage with, and perhaps even contain, the growing influence of India and China.[40]

What is missing from most of these geostrategic analyses, however, is the perspective offered by the Hillary Doctrine, which would argue for the necessity of securing the rights and security of Yemen's female population, who are increasingly under siege from the pro-Wahhabi and Salafist political movements largely financed by Saudi Arabia in the north.[41] Ensuring the human and economic rights of women will help stabilize the entire region. But that is not what the Saudis are bringing to Yemen.

## THE WOMEN AT CHANGE SQUARE

In 2011, in a heady response to a Tunisian fruit seller's act of self-immolation, Yemen joined the series of revolutions that toppled despotic governments from Libya to Egypt. Most of those who took to the streets in Yemen, however, were demonstrating against high unemployment, price fixing, and the widespread poverty that was a hallmark of then-President Ahmed Ali Abdullah Saleh's 33-year dictatorship.

For the first time in the history of the Yemeni north, women appeared in public demonstrations. They hefted signs and marched in solidarity with students, human rights activists, and disgruntled citizens of all stripes— and they were among the thousands of demonstrators who camped out at Change Square, as it subsequently became known. One particularly brave woman jumped onto an oncoming tank and pressed her body over the window to prevent army personnel from firing on unarmed protestors. Her identity will never be known because she was wrapped head to toe in a black *abaya* and her face was concealed by her *niqab*. Police quickly hustled her off, and she was never seen or heard of again.

Women took part in the revolution because, quite apart from the lack of opportunities and widespread poverty, Yemeni women are one of the most disenfranchised populations in the entire world.

Yemen scores a miserable last place on the 2012 World Economic Forum's Gender Gap Index (GGI).[42] Sixty percent of Yemeni women are completely illiterate (compared to 20 percent of men).[43] The *Lancet* reports that a quarter of Yemeni women of childbearing age are acutely malnourished, which in turn contributes to the country's fearsome maternal mortality rate.[44] So too does a fertility rate that is among the highest in the world at just over six births per woman—although that figure is an average and doesn't reflect far higher rates in rural areas.[45]

With high birth rates come large cohorts of young people—particularly young men—who could contribute to further violence and instability if they find themselves unemployed, disenfranchised, and unable to wed. As with all of those nations that occupy the bottom rungs of the GGI, Yemen's child mortality and morbidity rates are similarly dismal. According to UNICEF, fully 58 percent of Yemen's children are stunted, and 15 percent are severely malnourished.[46]

Women work from dawn until dusk, rearing children, cooking, cleaning, and tending land and livestock in what economists refer to—apparently without irony—as "unproductive labor." Only 7 percent of Yemeni women earn a wage—despite a lifetime of almost unremitting toil.[47]

Under Yemeni law, women are not fully autonomous human beings, but "sisters of men"; that is, mere appendages or wards of their closest male kin. To date, Yemen has yet to legislate against domestic violence, which puts women and girls at the mercy of male relatives. So-called honor killings are likewise treated leniently—if at all. Article 232 of the penal code of Yemen stipulates that a husband who catches his wife in the act of adultery (otherwise known as *zina*) and then kills her should receive a maximum sentence of no more than a fine or one year in prison.[48] Needless to say, the burden of proof required to support an allegation of adultery is minimal at best. The age of marriage, once set at fifteen, was overturned after reunification and replaced with—nothing. Parliament annulled the marriage-age law in the 1990s, saying parents should decide when a daughter marries.

In 2009, in a response to international pressure, the government attempted to bring in a minimum age of marriage, but the legislation was quickly shelved when fistfights broke out between political progressives and the bearded Islamists who apparently preferred that legalized pedophilia be preserved as the status quo. The upshot is that, particularly in the impoverished countryside, girls are married off well before puberty—even as young as nine, eight, or seven.[49]

In 2010, a group of the country's highest Islamic authorities declared those supporting a ban on child marriages to be apostates—despite a series of sensational cases including that of a thirteen-year-old girl who died of vaginal tearing after being wed days before to a man twice her age.[50] More recently, an eight-year-old died under similar circumstances. But there is still no minimum age of marriage in Yemen.[51]

A man can marry four women and divorce his wives at will while maintaining sole custody of the children. Girls and women have no say over who or when they will marry and face severe social and legal repercussions should they choose to leave. Under Yemeni law, women are entitled to inherit half of what men inherit, but in practice, most women inherit nothing at all.[52] As one female prisoner put it to journalist Janine di Giovanni, a reporter with the *Daily Beast*, "Let's not talk about human rights. Let's talk about animal rights—because that's what we are."[53]

As in the other Arab Uprising countries, Yemen's revolution was initially made up of young, idealistic progressives who were willing to risk their lives for the right to live and work in a Western-style democracy. And die they did—in the hundreds.

In March 2011, President Saleh ordered the military to open fire on protestors, killing fifty. More violence, killings, and disappearances followed, and his international allies—most notably the United States—began to lose patience. Under Hillary Clinton, the State Department initiated what was to become a drawn-out series of Gulf Cooperation Council–brokered negotiations.

Saleh, however, was maddeningly difficult to pin down. The canny despot would initially appear to capitulate only to change his mind at the eleventh hour. In the meantime, he ordered that electricity be cut in Sana'a and in Taiz, a city known for its progressive citizens. Artillery fire shook insurgent strongholds in the former and flattened entire neighborhoods in the latter. The lights would only flicker on for an hour or so every twenty-four hours—usually in the middle of the night. He also ordered ATMs to be closed, severely curtailed gas and oil supplies (insurgents kept cutting the pipelines—or so his government claimed), and generally imposed a blockade of basic goods and services in a bid to contain the country's unruly populace.

Fuel prices shot up by more than 500 percent; fishermen could not afford to power their boats nor could farmers irrigate their crops. Businesses shut down, and inflation and unemployment spiked. Even before the revolution, Yemen had relied on imports for virtually all its staple foods—making its hapless residents even more vulnerable to price fluctuations than in most countries. In the wake of the revolution, food prices soared, and health indicators plummeted accordingly.

Saleh's ploy worked. Thousands of Yemenis could not access clean water. Gastrointestinal illnesses skyrocketed, killing tens of thousands of children. Already in complete disarray, Yemen's health system, such as it is, staggered under the load.[54] The only good that still remained widely available was khat.

As the months dragged on, and as "the president who would not go away" doggedly clung to power, the makeup of the protestors began to change. From mixing freely with the men, women were increasingly corralled into female-only enclosures—a sure sign that the Islamists had co-opted what began as a largely secular uprising.

Women's rights activists told Western media of harassment, smear campaigns, and threats—not only from Saleh's camp, but also from the opposition—including the Al-Islah party, a self-identified Salafist party.[55] The religious force behind Al-Islah is Abdul Majid al-Zindani, who lived in Saudi Arabia from 1967 to 1970, where he was heavily influenced not only by the Salafis but also by the Wahhabis. Indeed, al-Zindani is the founder and president of the Iman University in Sana'a, Yemen, which receives most of its funding from Saudi Arabia and is devoted to the spread of Wahhabi ideology. (A salient fact: Zindani led the opposition to any minimum age of marriage for Yemeni girls.)

While Saleh finally stepped down from power, "The jury is still out on whether we will see significant change in Yemen or a whitewash of just enough reform to keep the public more or less content and a continuation of status quo," said Letta Tayler, a Yemen expert with Human Rights Watch, in a 2013 interview with the *Daily Beast*. "Most of the elites who were in power at the time of the uprising remain in power—just that they played a game of musical chairs."[56]

## A LITTLE FOR WOMEN, BUT IS IT NOW TOO LATE?

When protestors filled the streets of Sana'a and other Yemeni cities early in 2011, women were at the front lines. They volunteered for committees, mixed freely with male protestors, and even challenged long-standing cultural taboos by camping out in Change Square without male guardians.[57] For twelve long months, their sheer numbers became a point of pride for male protestors who, unlike in some other Arab Uprising states, initially welcomed women into their ranks.[58] Before the revolution, women did not even utter their names in public for fear that their families would be shamed by their boldness. During the uprising, women declared their right to speak out on their own behalf, to post blogs under their own name, and to agitate for change.[59] Tawakkul Karman became the first Yemeni of either sex to be awarded a Nobel Peace Prize, which honored her activities promoting freedom.

Kawkab Althabiani was also one of the protestors. At the time, the 24-year-old journalist and women's rights activist said, "We are risking our lives, we are being imprisoned, but we know now that we have power—Yemen will never be the same after this."[60] To date, however, the picture has been a mixed one.

In a widely disseminated Oxfam report based on interviews under-taken with 126 women in July and August 2012, women spoke of being shut out of the political process. Said one, "We don't just want food. We want to know the government is with us and wants to hear our views on how we can be supported to address our problems."[61]

She has cause for concern. Although the power transfer negotiated by Jamal Benomar, U.N. special adviser to the secretary-general on Yemen, made efforts to include women, many activists charge that it fell far short of the 30 percent representation they were looking for. The transi-tion blueprint only called for an "adequate" representation of women from all political parties after the handover. As activists point out, how-ever, "adequate" is very much in the eye of the beholder. "If you are an Islamist, no representation is more than 'adequate,'" says Fatima, a mother of two who took part in the protests but declined to reveal her last name.[62]

The problem, locals contend, is the influence of their powerful neigh-bor to the north—Saudi Arabia. Although Saudi meddling in the affairs of its far weaker neighbor dates back decades, many average Yemenis and human rights activists specifically blame the influx of religious extrem-ism from Saudi Arabia. Unlike the United States, Saudi Arabia spends a fortune on madrassas in Yemen (where girls sit at the back—if they are permitted to attend at all), hospitals, and labor exchange programs that not only provide work for young impoverished male Yemenis but also offer a good dose of Wahhabist indoctrination.

The result, says women's rights activist and scholar Khadjija (not her real name), is a form of cultural imperialism that is further contributing to the erosion of women's rights both economically and within the family. "Traditional tribal culture was no means equal," she says. "But women did enjoy more autonomy. It wasn't okay to beat them . . . in fact it was shameful. They could entertain men alone in the home, they were not forced to wear the *burqa* and their labor was recognized as important to the family."[63]

Moreover, as a result of labor reforms in Saudi Arabia, tens of thou-sands of Yemeni workers have been deported back home, further stirring the situation. These workers, overwhelmingly male, are bringing back attitudes acquired while working in the kingdom. "They leave decent human beings and return as men who have no respect for women," Khadjija said. "Our culture is changing but not in a good way. We can only hope that the uprising will counter these effects."

Indeed, one need only browse old photo galleries from the 1940s, 1950s and 1960s to see that women in rural areas in particular eschewed the smothering cultural exigencies of the *abaya* and the *niqab*. It was the Ottoman Turks incidentally who imported both when they occupied Yemen in the sixteenth and nineteenth centuries—even though both garments are now largely associated with the Sunni Arab Gulf States.

Saudis have long sponsored Yemeni tribal and political figures with money, weapons, and other so-called aid. What is less well known is the Saudi funding of radical madrassas in Yemen, which are almost identical to those found in Pakistan and other near-failed Muslim states. For example, it was allegedly to Yemen that the "underwear bomber," 23-year-old Nigerian national Umar Farouk Abdulmutallab, traveled to receive training and religious instruction from the now-deceased Anwar al-Awlaki.

Many observers note that al-Qaeda took advantage of the destabilization that came with the Arab uprisings to solidify their quasi-colonization of Yemen. According to Yemeni foreign minister Abubakr al-Qirbi, "Saudi Arabia is cognizant that the stability of Saudi Arabia depends on that of Yemen."[64] Many expect that if the Saudi-backed party Al-Islah comes to power, there will be no improvement in conditions for women. "They are all the same," says Khadjija. "The only hope for women lies in a civil democracy."[65] But this is surely the least likely outcome for Yemen.

## DRONES AND DOCTORS:
## THE UNITED STATES IN ACTION

Though Aden was once a busy maritime hub of the Arab world, these days a lack of investment coupled with ongoing unrest has reduced the port to a shabby remnant of its former self. A few rusty freighters float in the waters outside the harbor, but their numbers represent just a fraction of the maritime traffic that once plied the coast. Shortly after the bombing of the USS *Cole* on October 12, 2000, the United States closed its naval base in Aden, and with it went much of the commercial activity that had been keeping the economy afloat. Aden is hanging on—but barely.

Nevertheless, the closure of the naval base has not meant the end of U.S. involvement in the Yemeni south. Since 2011, USAID has been behind various development and stabilization initiatives including the funding of Mobile Medical Teams. The mobile clinics fan out from Aden to service Yemen's growing internally displaced person (IDP) population, who are fleeing the fighting in Abyan and Shabwa. Most of these displaced families wind up hunkering down in abandoned schools, on the dusty outskirts of ramshackle villages, or wherever they happen to find themselves—invariably miserable, minus clean drinking water, and with little hope of finding work.

Part of a $4 billion aid package, the Mobile Medical Teams focus on primary health delivery, reproductive and maternal health, and other low-cost, high-impact health interventions. Chief among these is the provision of contraceptives, maternal health services, and infant and child health care—including immunizations.

Omar Zain, general manager of the government Health Office in Lahj, just north of Aden, said that quite apart from the "excess mortality and morbidity" that has resulted from the political crisis, by far the greatest threat to Yemeni's health and future stability is its high fertility rate. "We have a growth rate of almost three percent," he said. "If we cannot change this we will be facing an economic and social crisis even worse than we are now."[66]

The main stumbling block, he asserted, is inadequate access to reliable family planning methods in hard-to-reach rural areas, combined with insufficient awareness. Inequality and lack of autonomy within the family means that men tend to make the family planning decisions while the average Yemeni woman can look forward to giving birth to six children during her lifetime. What is happening—or not happening—with the women of Yemen will rule that nation's stability for generations to come.

Muwada is among the group of women waiting to see the female doctor who is writing prescriptions and handing out medicine in an RV set up as a mobile medical clinic. At the age of forty-one (approximately; she doesn't know her exact birth date), Muwada has already given birth to twelve children.

Despite years of childbearing, nursing, and rearing, she is an affable woman. The green paste on her face—considered attractive in this part of Yemen—does not detract from her smiling but care-worn beauty. "We need more of these," she says, waving at the Mobile Medical Team RV parked in the thin shade of a desiccated stand of trees. "Maybe if we had them my sisters would still be alive."[67] Muwada belongs to what is a despised minority in Yemen—residents of African descent. Like most of those of her ethnicity, she is hardscrabble poor and, despite her considerable progeny, is now caring for only eight. Two died in infancy, two others were carried away by gastrointestinal infections. All three of her sisters died either during pregnancy or soon after giving birth. "It is lonely without them," she says.

Development experts assert it is these kinds of interventions that really matter to the lives of rural women, and in that respect, these USAID-funded projects are taking a page from the Saudi playbook. "The Saudis are successful in spreading extremism because they give the people what they need," said Khadjija, who also notes that the Saudis rarely focus on reproductive health and thereby miss an opportunity that donors such as the United States could easily exploit. Instead, she said, Saudi aid agencies tend to target prisoners and other marginalized, and thus highly susceptible, populations of young men. They have also opened a number of hospitals where locals can be treated free of charge in a state-of-the-art facility. "The West could be doing the same," she said, "but with messages about human rights, gender empowerment, and how to create a civil society."

USAID has taken note of the situation of Yemeni women. On August 14, 2012, the agency announced that part of its support of the implementation of the new U.S. National Action Plan (NAP) on Women, Peace, and Security would be to create new gender programming in Yemen, Nepal, and the Philippines, saying, "USAID's Implementation Plan and the NAP are part of a suite of policies and strategies that guide the U.S. Government and USAID to pursue more effectively and strategically gender equality, women's empowerment, and the protection of vulnerable populations."[68]

Nevertheless, the amount allocated to do so—$1.5 million—is so negligible that it more or less constitutes window-dressing.[69] Rothna Begum, a Human Rights Watch researcher on women's rights in the Middle East and North Africa, noted that despite U.S. chest thumping, "quite frankly the U.S. is not very responsive when it comes to women's rights in Yemen. We've seen very little from the U.S. in comparison to other [U.N.] member states."[70]

Part of the problem may be that even though USAID unrolled its new "Gender Policy" in 2012, interviews on the ground in Yemen with USAID-funded implementers reveal a sense that the agency has yet to provide the type of in-depth training necessary to explain to contractor staff on the ground why such programming is critical to stability and development.[71] Too often, staff simply do not understand why gender remains such a critical part of their mandate. We will explore this problem further in chapter 5.[72]

Moreover, gains made through USAID's Yemen programming are critically undermined by the U.S. drone program, which continues unabated despite broad international condemnation. Fawzia, an employee who works with a USAID-funded development project in Sana'a, believes that "all the U.S. has to do is be better than everyone else. That's what we once believed but it is getting harder."

## FOR EXPORT ONLY:
## SAUDI MISSIONARIES AND JIHADISTS

A number of commentators have wondered whether Saudi Arabia will eventually find that its chickens have come home to roost with a vengeance. As former U.S. ambassador John Price wrote in a blog:

> Wahhabists helped to build the Saudi kingdom, and exported its fundamentalist teachings. Saudi Arabia's oil brought them wealth, and control of many of the world's economies. Saudi Arabia also brought the world Osama bin Laden. Syria is the next country to go through a regime change, as has taken place in Yemen, Egypt, Libya, and Tunisia. Saudi Arabia may follow, with Osama bin Laden's legacy coming back to its roots.[73]

Not so fast though, say other observers, who claim that Riyadh promotes a policy of containment vis-à-vis its own homegrown Islamists; that is, it will support them as long as they do not challenge the hegemony of the Saudi royal family. Once they cross that line, however, the House of Saud would be only too willing to weigh in with all the considerable resources at its disposal.

That may have already happened. Since the advent of the Arab Uprising, once muted demands for change within the kingdom are now more audible. These include everything from giving women the right to drive to calls for the kingdom to switch to a constitutional monarchy with an elected parliament.[74] In response, Riyadh has been taking a harder line on dissent within its own border—cracking down on progressives and/or threatening and jailing conservatives.[75]

But sticks have been matched by lots of carrots. When the uprisings were at their zenith in 2011, King Abdullah bin Abdulaziz al-Saud, the kingdom's creaky 90-year-old ruler, announced hundreds of billions of dollars in new public spending and wage increases to help quell any discontent. In this way, the Saudi royal family successfully neutralized the potential for Arab Uprising demonstrations on its own soil. It likewise sent billions to the monarchies in Jordan and Morocco, inviting those countries to join the Gulf Cooperation Council in order to strengthen their monarchies. It goes without saying that the Saudi regime openly applauded the July 2013 ouster of the Muslim Brotherhood in Egypt.[76]

Unfortunately, though, the effect on human rights discourse has been obvious. In July 2013, for example, the influential Saudi cleric Salman al-Odah told the *Wall Street Journal* that the government had informed him that his television talk show, *You Have Rights*, would be banned. In March, the popular cleric wrote an open letter to the government that was published online, urging the country's security services to ease their line on dissent. "It is dangerous to restrict people to the point that they feel they have nothing more to lose," he wrote.[77]

On July 10, 2013, King Abdullah delivered a stern speech marking the Islamic holy month of Ramadan in which he warned that Saudi Arabia "will not allow religion to be exploited by extremists." He added, "We will not accept anyone in our country, and in any circumstances, to join political parties which have nothing to do with God, and which only lead to conflict and failure."[78]

Ironically, then, to talk of human rights puts you in the same camp with religious extremists, according to the government—because both threaten the rule of the House of Saud. "They killed the human-rights movement with a stealth campaign," a Western diplomat told the *Wall Street Journal* in June.[79]

## IS SILENCE GOLDEN? THE PARADOXES OF THE HILLARY DOCTRINE

Despite Saudi Arabia's repression not only of women and girls but also of ethnic and religious minorities, the United States has remained singularly mum about its Middle East ally.

Although Hillary Clinton was secretary of state during the Obama administration's first term, this peculiar silence of the United States did not change during those four years. Saudi women activists, for example, had to publicly pressure Clinton to support their campaign to lift the driving ban. Clinton finally went on record as saying, "What these women are doing is brave, and what they are seeking is right. I am moved by it, and I support them."[80] Clinton's spokesperson suggested that, "while Mrs. Clinton's advocacy for women speaks for itself, there were times for 'quiet diplomacy.'"[81] But the activist group Saudi Women for Driving viewed Clinton's silence somewhat differently: "For the United States' top diplomat to make no public statement about such developments sends exactly the wrong message to the Saudi government and, more importantly, to the women of Saudi Arabia."[82]

Clinton then attempted to explain her position in greater detail:

I know there is an active debate in Saudi Arabia on a range of social issues. . . . For our part, we will continue in private and in public to urge all govern-ments to address issues of discrimination and to ensure that women have the equal opportunity to fulfill their own God-given potential. But I want to, again, underscore and emphasize that this is not about the United States. It's not about what any of us on the outside say. It is about the women them-selves and their right to raise their concerns with their own government.[83]

At this point, it is necessary to stop and contemplate this loud silence. If Clinton's proposition, "the subjugation of women is a direct threat to the security of the United States," is true (which we have affirmed by our analyses in chapters 2 and 3) and if her statement that the misogyny of Wahhabism "troubles her" is sincere, then her handling of the Saudi situation is instructive for what it says about Clinton's own understanding of the limits of the Hillary Doctrine—or for that matter, the limits to which she is willing to promote it.

In a WikiLeaks document dated December 30, 2009, a cable from Hillary Clinton states, "It has been an ongoing challenge to persuade Saudi officials to treat terrorist financing emanating from Saudi Arabia as a strategic priority. . . . Donors in Saudi Arabia constitute the most significant source of funding to Sunni terrorist groups worldwide."[84] It is apparent from this cable that Clinton knows all too well that the national interests of the United States and Saudi Arabia do not dovetail. Furthermore, it is also important to remember that despite this fact, it is the United States that is replenishing Saudi Arabia's seemingly endlessly deep pockets. The United States does so by continuing to buy Saudi oil and by selling billions of dollars of arms to a kingdom that not only funds terrorism but also proactively exports a doctrine that disavows individual, and particularly women's, rights and freedoms.

Critics have been scathing in their appraisal of Clinton's silence concerning Saudi Arabia. Mallika Dutt of the human rights group Breakthrough stated, "We've supported Saudi Arabia for decades. . . . Here we are, strong advocates for women's rights, and we're going to rescue women in the global South, while we are creating circumstances that allow these things to occur."[85] Rothna Begum of Human Rights Watch concurs: "Saudi Arabia is incredibly obstructive to women's rights in their own kingdom and that resonates around the world. The U.S. is a key ally of Saudi Arabia and that means the administration has said very little about its human rights record including women's rights. During the 2011 uprising, we saw a real double standard come into play with the U.S. very critical of the human rights records of some countries, but remained singularly silent about Saudi Arabia and its crackdown on human rights and its mistreatment of women."[86] These critics might have said the same thing about U.S.-India, U.S.-China, U.S.-Mexico, or any number of other bilateral relations where the situation of women is deeply problematic and Hillary Clinton said nothing in public.

What does this silence say about the place of the Hillary Doctrine in U.S. foreign policy?

One possible interpretation is that the Hillary Doctrine is in fact merely a rhetorical stance on the part of U.S. foreign policy makers, including, apparently, Hillary Clinton herself—a position that may be jettisoned if its tenets would undermine "real" American national interests in any particular case. Critics point to her similar silence concerning human rights in China. When the press corps posed this question while en route to China for her first trip there as secretary of state, Clinton replied:

> We pretty much know what they're going to say. We know that we're going to press them to reconsider their position about Tibetan religious and cultural freedom and autonomy for the Tibetans and some kind of recognition or acknowledgment of the Dalai Lama. And we know what they're going to say because I've had those conversations for more than a decade with Chinese leaders.[87]

Of course, from the viewpoint of the Hillary Doctrine itself, and as we discussed in chapter 2, there is a much more devastating scourge of oppression in China than that perpetrated among the Tibetans—the scourge of gendercide implemented through sex-selective abortion. As many as a million Chinese girl babies are eliminated from the population either before or after birth every single year in China. Indeed, Clinton spoke of this atrocity in her 1995 speech in Beijing and reiterated her revulsion toward these practices in 2009 in a hearing before the Foreign Affairs Committee of the U.S. House of Representatives.[88] Moreover, in 2005 as U.S. senator from New York, Clinton wrote a letter to President George W. Bush insisting that he raise this very issue with Chinese leaders during his trip to Beijing that year.[89]

It is not known if Bush ever mentioned sex-selective gendercide to the Chinese government. But it also is not known if Clinton ever raised this issue with the Chinese government throughout her entire tenure as secretary of state.

Moreover, Clinton has publicly supported arming the Free Syria Army and other opposition groups even though many are receiving most of their funding from Saudi Arabia and hope to roll back women's rights if victorious. This doesn't quite tally with her rhetorical support for women and women's rights, either.

Given what is now understood about the linkage between misogyny on the one hand and aggression and instability at the nation-state level on the other, diplomatic silence would appear to constitute the tacit endorsement of a shortsighted view of real American national interests. But Clinton is not shortsighted: It is clear that she is well aware of this linkage and acknowledges that violations of women's human rights constitute a threat to American national interests. For example, in a March 2010 interview with Canadian talk show host George Stroumboulopoulos, she noted:

> If you look at some of the large societies, like China and India, where there is a disproportionate number of boys compared to girls—girls don't live to their first birthday in the numbers that they should—and what happens if you have that kind of imbalance where you have too many young men, where you don't have the opportunity for marriage because there's these huge discrepancies, that breeds instability. So there's a lot that goes into my assessment and conclusion that what I believe in passionately—that women's rights are human rights—is also a security issue for my country and yours.[90]

No, then. While perhaps others in the Obama administration might feel that the Hillary Doctrine is some type of rhetorical flourish, it is impossible to believe that is the case for Clinton herself. Some other interpretation for her conspicuous silence is in order. Let's consider the possibilities and what they say about the Hillary Doctrine and Clinton's own perspective on it.

Perhaps Clinton believes that issues of women's status are best left to private conversations at the highest level of diplomacy, conversations to which the U.S. public is not privy. Perhaps she believes the Saudi monarchy is making steady progress for women—progress that would be imperiled by causing them to lose face by publicly chastising them.[91] Caryle Murphy of the Woodrow Wilson Center offers her opinion:

Since coming to the throne in 2005, King Abdullah has made it clear on many occasions that he wants women to have more opportunities and more visibility. He has signaled this in many ways, for example, by including women in the official delegation on his first foreign trip, by appointing the first women to the all-male Council of Ministers, and by founding what will be the world's largest all-female university.[92] The king also made his intentions clear when he posed for a now-famous picture that ran on the front pages of many Saudi newspapers. It showed the king, smiling contentedly, surrounded by a large group of Saudi women, most of them with their faces uncovered. On two occasions, most recently in May 2013, the king publicly fired senior clerics who criticized his moves to advance women.[93]

It must be a terribly delicate balancing act to provide both encouragement for women activists but simultaneously a hand up—as versus a sneer down—for regimes whose pace of progress is much slower than the activists would wish, owing to concerns over internal stability. As Rania Ibrahim, dean of students at the all-female Effat University, put it, "Shocking the whole world by agitating and upsetting the norms the community is used to—it's a recipe for failure."[94] And probably also a recipe for increasing agitation among anti-regime foes—enemies that have shown themselves even less favorably disposed to women than the monarchy.

The Iranian democracy movement's fate is instructive in this regard. Leila Alakarami, aide to Shirin Ebadi, explains:

In 2006, the U.S. Congress declared "it should be the policy of the U.S. to support independent human rights and peaceful pro-democracy forces in Iran." $75 million under the banner of the Iran Freedom Support Act was allocated to support Iranians in their struggles for democracy. The Freedom Support Act not only did not help grassroots movements but also put them under severe pressure from the government. The government used that as a justification to link human rights with West. At that time the One Million Signature Campaign was launched in Iran. Due to the U.S. policy to help human rights in Iran, the Campaign's members were labeled by the government as fifth columns for U.S. interests. Many women's rights activists were prosecuted and arrested and accused of conspiring in a velvet revolution. The grassroots initiatives [must not be] dependent on the assistance of external sources. The only way to support them is to give them voice, to cover their news and bring their efforts to the attention of the world.[95]

Clinton may also calculate that regimes respond best to internal rather than external pressure. Journalist Kim Ghattas, who traveled extensively with Clinton as part of her press corps, explains Clinton's "loud silence" concerning human rights in these terms:

> She didn't want to bang her head against the wall on the issue of human rights with a government [China's] that wasn't listening anyway. She found this approach counterproductive and wanted to advance the human rights agenda in new ways by connecting with grassroots organizations, by using the Internet—anything to bypass the government. It was part of the strategy devised on the seventh floor of the Building by her team to connect American diplomacy with people around the world.[96]

Melanne Verveer concurs:

> You know, I'd love to be able to live in the perfect world, where I can just say and do things on the terms that I find, and then sleep right. But I don't live in that world. And so I have to find ways to compel the countless more who don't share this view. . . . So you do what you can on all these things, which we have done, but does it produce the kind of outcome we want? You know, they are sovereign nations unto their own . . . our voices have been out there bilaterally, multilaterally, privately, and it is what it is. . . . It's not like the United States has been quiet on these issues, nobody can say that. There may have been other times, when you never heard mention of these issues, but we have been consistently there. . . . But are we heeded? That's another part of the equation.[97]

There is also the question of high-profile foreign support for local groups that wind up becoming a lightning rod that attracts the wrong kind of attention. Again, the perfect balance requires taking into account that real individuals may be physically harmed if the United States were openly to voice support for their cause. With respect to Egyptian women activists, Verveer notes:

> There's a whole history of US-supported groups being thrown out, controversies being created, etc. And I said, "We don't want to—in our effort to support you—to cause you greater problems," and that's when we discussed things like using multilateral organizations under the aegis of the UN, for example, to bring support targeted to women so they had what they needed to strategize, to be a more effective force post-revolution in ways that wouldn't come back and provide those who were impeding their progress and give them additional ammunition.[98]

This interpretation of Clinton's resolute muteness when confronted with situations and relationships where a stronger voice might have been expected possibly represents the more prudent course. Being "wise as a serpent and harmless as a dove" must indeed require a lot of painful tongue-biting.

There is one last interpretation, however, that must also be considered: perhaps Clinton wants the Saudi monarchy to fall. After all, from what is understood about the linkage between the treatment of women and the fate of nations, the Saudis will never know peace or stability. Perhaps the Saudis deserve, as do all nations, the right to reap what they have sown regarding women. As Clinton has remarked:

> [Women's issues] have always been security issues, but people haven't quite put them in that context. I actually think the case is easier made today, because if you look at where a lot of this conflict that we are confronting comes from, there's places like Afghanistan or the border area in Pakistan, or Yemen or Somalia—places where women are really treated like second class citizens, where they're not given their voice, where they don't have very many rights. There is a direct correlation between societies like that, that deny women their opportunities, and societies that are breeding grounds for extremism and, unfortunately, terrorism. So I do think it's a security issue. It's a difference between the headlines and the trendlines.[99]

The only incongruity here is that given the widespread nature of the Wahhabi belief system within the country, the fall of the Saudi monarchy would not likely result in an improved situation for women; on the contrary, what little gains have been made for women would almost certainly be lost.

When one assesses the situation, it is salient to note that not a single Arab Uprising country has become a better place for women (though we are crossing our fingers for Tunisia). There may come a time (most notably in Iraq) when the female half of the population in these states may look back upon the days of authoritarianism with yearning.[100] As Rend al-Rahim, the former Iraqi ambassador to the United States, expressed it, "The years from 2005 onward saw a rise in polygamy, unregistered marriages, mut'a (temporary) marriage, child and forced marriages, honor killing, and gender-based violence. Successive Iraq governments after 2005 have done nothing to fulfill their duty to protect women. . . . A culture of impunity regarding abuse of women has been allowed to flourish."[101] Indeed, this attitude has been infectious: the Islamic State 'caliphate' in Syria and Iraq openly sanctions on religious grounds the kidnapping and barter of female sex slaves.

This issue—of whether the autocratic devil you know is better than the democratically chosen devil you do not know—is a critical one for women and their proponents. While long-term autocratic rule may have no impact on the subordinate status of women (think Equatorial Guinea), in other cases such autocrats prove to be the only leaders powerful enough to improve the situation, rights, and status of women, as was observed with Hosni Mubarak in Egypt, who banned female genital cutting, instituted a legislative quota for women, and reformed divorce laws in favor of women. James Smith, a former U.S. ambassador to Saudi Arabia, has commented that, "The country is on a trajectory of modernization, if not too fast . . . [there is] an emerging critical mass of daughters—on campuses and in jobs—who will make a difference." Perhaps the Saudis should be given time, for Smith also suggests that, "The king issues decrees only when he can count on the agreement of two-thirds of the population."[102]

Referring to the Saudis, Ryan Crocker, former U.S. ambassador to numerous Middle Eastern nations, says, "We're not going to change them. . . . Besides, who would be their successors? 'You don't like us? Well, après moi, le deluge.' And we are seeing how right that is [in Syria, Egypt, etc.]."[103] Can it be believed that those who have the will and are gaining the capability to overthrow the House of Saud would appoint women to the highest Shura? Or build the largest, most well funded women's university in the world? Or allow schoolgirls to play sports? These are questions worth pondering.

But also worth contemplating is one other troubling fact. Yes, the Saudi royal family is clearly much more progressive than their subjects on issues of rights for women. But long-term autocracy is fertile ground for the growth of highly toxic, male-bonded nationalist opposition groups that would imperil every advance granted to women by the autocrat— again, as witnessed by the new "caliphate" in Iraq. Indeed, such groups would explicitly target precisely those advances as their first order of business when in power. The Saudis have played midwife to the birth of the male-bonded groups that will one day prove their destruction. These same groups will almost certainly bond over an intensified subjugation of women. Remember, for all its comparative progressiveness, it was the Saudi royal family that embraced the misogynistic Wahhabi viper in the first place.

The case of Saudi Arabia provides an important lesson about the trade-offs involved with public advocacy of women's rights in the international arena. Too much public advocacy breeds defensiveness and even backlash among those one is trying to influence; too little public advocacy— too much silence—suggests to the world these issues are not important after all and leads to despair among those one is trying to empower. To effectively implement the Hillary Doctrine entails squarely facing the paradoxes involved, of which this may be one of the most critical—and in the case of Saudi Arabia, the most cruel.[104]

It is therefore to the implementation of the Hillary Doctrine that we now turn. Given that its most passionate and powerful proponent was the U.S. secretary of state for four full years, enjoying both unprecedented media attention and White House access, how did the Hillary Doctrine fare?

# PART III

★ ★ ★

## POLICY AND IMPLEMENTATION

# 5

# THE GOOD, THE BAD, AND THE UGLY OF IMPLEMENTING THE HILLARY DOCTRINE

★ ★ ★

Hillary Clinton led the transformation of the global security paradigm. The legacy of Secretary Clinton will not be a dictator dead, air assault over Libya, or de-escalation in Gaza. Instead, like Nobel Peace laureate George Marshall, she leaves behind a world more stable because she added women's force as indispensable to "smart power." Like General Marshall, she extended our understanding of security far beyond bombs and bullets. And like Secretary Marshall, she used not only policy acumen but an iconoclastic idea that will outlast generations neither she, nor we, will ever meet.

—SWANEE HUNT[1]

As Clinton's term winds down, women will form the central pillar of her legacy. Alas, Clinton will be remembered not for women's empowerment, but rather for their betrayal. . . . Clinton may cloak herself in the feminist mantle, but her record is something else. Legacies rest more on fact than on handlers and sympathetic journalists. The simple fact is that under Clinton's watch—and largely because of her policies and silence—women in the Islamic world have suffered their worst setbacks in generations.[2]

—MICHAEL RUBIN

The principle of women's equality is a simple, self-evident truth, but the work of turning that principle into practice is rarely simple. It takes years and even generations of patient, persistent work, not only to change a country's laws, but to change its people's minds, to weave throughout culture and tradition in public discourse and private views the unassailable fact of women's worth and women's rights.[3]

—HILLARY CLINTON

THERE IS OVERWHELMING evidence that the premise of the Hillary Doctrine is correct: the security of women and the security of the states in which they live are inextricably intertwined. As we lay out in part 2 of this book, where the security of women is undermined, so too is the security of their neighborhoods, towns, cities and countries.

The question of whether Hillary Clinton was successful in implementing her eponymous doctrine as U.S. secretary of state is a controversial one, as the opening quotes display in vivid fashion. Did the Hillary Doctrine transform the global security paradigm? Or did the rhetoric of the Hillary Doctrine mask a cynical betrayal of women? Or is it too early to say anything much one way or the other? These are the questions that will be addressed in part 3 of this book, beginning with this chapter.

We believe that the Hillary Doctrine can only be evaluated by examining its implementation under its first and most vigorous proponent, Hillary Clinton herself, during her tenure as U.S. secretary of state from 2009 to early 2013.

Even a whole-hearted embrace of the premise of the Hillary Doctrine—that the subjugation of women is a direct threat to the security of the United States—does not lead in straightforward fashion to a programmatic agenda. In a real sense, the Hillary Doctrine *is* what the Hillary Doctrines *does*. And what the Hillary Doctrine would do was a matter of some bewilderment in 2009 when Clinton first became secretary of state.

As Ritu Sharma of Women Thrive relates, for the first couple of years of the Obama administration, she would receive phone calls from State Department personnel, saying, "We know we have to do this gender thing, but we don't know how to do it. What do we do?"[4] As Tobie

Whitman of the Institute for Inclusive Security explained, "[The Hillary Doctrine] also has to be practical—not just why women's empowerment is important but how do you actually do it. The technical training [is needed]—how to write gender-sensitive RFPs [requests for proposals], metrics, collecting gender-disaggregated data."[5]

While Sharma eventually stopped receiving such calls, she nevertheless notes, "Hillary Clinton created a change in the weather from cloudy and rainy to sunny. But the sun being out doesn't mean the plants will grow; you still need to fertilize and weed."[6] So how does her analogy apply to the implementation of the Hillary Doctrine? Did the plants grow?

To answer this question (which is immense in scope and impossible to treat fully in this one book), one must realize that three levels of effort are required in order to implement the Hillary Doctrine. The first is the legal and regulatory framework instituted by officials in Washington, D.C.; the second is program development and contracting, which bridges the U.S. government and recipient countries; and the third is the actual implementation of initiatives in-country.

In this chapter, we will argue that although much has been achieved at the first level serious gaps and inadequacies critically hamper efforts at the second and third levels, despite some real successes. More importantly however, these problems have sometimes radically undermined the Hillary Doctrine in practice.

## JUST GIVE YOUR MONEY TO NORWAY, OKAY?

Before we dive in to that assessment, one must first recognize that a number of observers—both American and foreign—believe the United States is the very *last* country that should be attempting to implement the Hillary Doctrine.

Ann Jones, author of the searing memoir *Kabul in Winter*, put it bluntly:

> Our country shouldn't do anything for women because of our attitude about how good we are despite the incredible damage we have done. . . .
> If the US wanted to help women, it could stop making war—it's the prime

destabilizer, and when it's over, the worst of the "boys" come to power. In Iraq, women have lost one hundred years; in Afghanistan, the gains are already being lost. . . . The Hillary Doctrine is a good one, but we're not the right country to carry it out. Better to give the aid money directly to Norway, and tell them, "Please spend this money on your programs for women, and we won't look over your shoulder."[7]

Nobel Peace Prize laureate Mairead Macguire concurs: "No woman thinks she can destroy a country and then send in the contractors to rebuild it. That's crazy."[8]

Then there's the question of whom the United States has chosen to befriend. Shirin Ebadi, another Nobel Peace Prize laureate, asks, "When the West speaks of human rights and women's rights, I respect that, but I have a question—The most sincere friend of Saudi Arabia is which country?"[9] Lisa VeneKlasen of Just Associates notes, "Obama supported the coup in Honduras. The *first thing* the coup government did was reverse access to emergency contraception for women."[10] Jessica Neuwirth of Equality Now asks, "Why didn't Hillary Clinton ever speak about women's human rights abuses in China?"[11] And Ann Jones, writing in 2011, points to the man the United States supported for well over a decade—Hamid Karzai:

> George W. Bush famously claimed to have "liberated" the women of Afghanistan, but he missed one: Hamid Karzai's wife. Although she is a gynecologist with desperately needed skills, she is kept shut up at home. To this day, the president's wife remains the most prominent woman in Afghanistan still living under house rules established by the Taliban. . . . And what has President Karzai done for the rest of the women of Afghanistan? Not a thing.[12]

If this wasn't enough, there's also the issue of the Convention on the Elimination of All Forms of Discrimination Against Women (CEDAW); namely, the United States is one of the few countries in the world that refuses to ratify it (the others are Iran, Palau, Somalia, Sudan, South Sudan, and Tonga). The United States is also one of only three nations worldwide that has not legislated any paid maternity leave whatsoever, the others being Papua New Guinea and Swaziland.[13] In addition, while reproductive rights in the United States may not be the worst in the world, several U.S. states are currently rolling them back in a dramatic fashion. North Dakota for example, recently passed a law effectively prohibiting abortion after six weeks, with no exceptions for rape or incest.[14]

Not a few observers and activists fervently wish the United States would clean up its own house before it sallies forth to "help" women living outside of its borders.

Underlying this critique is the common view that the U.S. State Department's declared commitment to women's rights is nothing but window-dressing for a foreign policy devoted to more shadowy agendas besides justice and equity. As Ann Jones puts it, "National interests don't always collide with people's interests—look at Scandinavia, Ireland, Germany. It depends entirely on the nation, and the spirit with which they go into another country, such as determining what people really need. The US doesn't go in with that spirit; its aid is wrapped up in foreign policy, which is its military policy. The only interests are those of the military and the free market."[15] Militarism and hypermasculinity go hand in hand, as we observed in Guatemala (see chapter 3). In the opinion of Anne-Marie Goetz of UNWomen, this means militaristic countries such as the United States are simply not capable of empowering women.[16]

Neuwirth observes that even presumably factual reporting is slanted by politics in the United States. The State Department's *Trafficking in Persons Report*, for example, ranks Cuba worse than India—which is quite simply ridiculous. Because of this U.S. tendency to politicize data, increasingly greater numbers of researchers and journalists are choosing instead to rely on other sources, including the U.N.[17]

And despite a foreign aid budget of almost $25 billion per year, Shirin Ebadi is eloquent in her plea to the United States: "We need your love more than your money. We need you to love justice and peace."[18]

These are pretty stout criticisms, and they are delivered at a comparatively high level of abstraction; to wit, the United States shouldn't even think about trying to assist women *through* its foreign policy, for it is incapable of helping them *because* of its foreign policy.

But the question may be a perennial one: If human beings are impelled by both laudatory and self-serving motivations, does the latter render as dross the good that could be accomplished?

Perhaps an alternative view is healthier and more realistic. Could it be that all human endeavors are marred by such inconsistencies and mixed motives, and progress is only measured as these are gradually lessened over time?

After all—speaking of Norway—Louise Olsson, head of the UNSCR 1325 Program at the Folke Bernadotte Academy in Sweden found that of all the Norwegian Provincial Reconstruction Teams operating in Afghanistan, the Norwegian-led one was the least attuned to the needs of Afghan women, despite that fact that Norway was one of the very first countries to adopt a National Action Plan on Women, Peace, and Security:

> The [Norwegian] PRT did not make any distinction between the security situation of men and women. One of the interviewees states that the PRT was probably not very conscious of any such difference in its military analysis and planning, as there had been no discussion of, or reflection on, the fact that women and men may have differing security needs. Accordingly, no gender focus was incorporated into either the planning or implementation of stabilization and security operations. Instead, women were described as being almost invisible. . . . No one [interviewed] reported any discussions about the position and role of women in Afghan society that had resulted in a change in the PRT's work.[19]

Oops.

Some foreign observers are sympathetic to the alternative view expressed earlier. Lena Ag of the Swedish NGO Kvinna till Kvinna suggests, "The statements and rhetoric [of Hillary Clinton] are important. On the other hand, the US is like a huge machine and you couldn't change it in four years. The importance is that she was there; she was talking to women; she was giving the women leverage in their society. It takes a long time span to change, for attitudes have to change. If she hadn't done what she did, what would we have? Nothing."[20]

During an UNWomen brown bag discussion in 2013, one participant opined, "Hillary Clinton walks the talk; she says things no one else will. Yes, it's incoherent, but that's life. . . . You need a critical mass of women in power to change the system, not just a Clinton."[21]

U.S. commentators make the same point. Sarah Taylor of the NGO Working Group on Women, Peace, and Security, states, "Look, it's not add one fantastic and amazing woman and stir. . . . It's up to all the other actors, too."[22] For example, no matter how much Hillary Clinton would have liked for the U.S. Senate to ratify CEDAW, one would have to be stunningly ignorant about U.S. politics to even entertain the possibility—even if innumerable reservations were appended.

Anita McBride, former chief of staff to First Lady Laura Bush, offers another slant: "The alternative would have been *what*? The tough work is to get out there and help."[23] Robin Morgan concurs: "It's worth it because it's better than nothing. The perfect is the enemy of the good, but the bad is the enemy of good, too. There are no magic wands."[24] Melanne Verveer agrees; speaking about the State Department's efforts to raise the issue of women's rights during Egypt's transition, she comments, "You can say until you are hoarse, 'Don't do this,' but it doesn't mean they won't."[25]

Still others suggest that for all its warts, the United States has a special responsibility to speak out for women precisely because it is the current hegemon, with all the militarism that term implies. Shelby Quast of Equality Now put it this way: "We need the US to say these things at the highest levels out loud. The US is the biggest funder of the UN; it's one of the P-5. We do have the responsibility to push the 1325's, the 1888's, etc."[26] While the Russians and the Chinese seem indifferent or actually opposed to elements of the Women, Peace, and Security agenda, Anne-Marie Goetz of UNWomen notes that when Clinton spoke to the U.N. Security Council, other nations were deferential because "they did not want to look churlish. She raised the level of discussion."[27]

Michelle Barsa of the Institute for Inclusive Security adds, "Women come in to [negotiations] with no power network. Men come in with massive networks—arms, narcotics, etc. The US can become part of the women's power network. We can get women on delegations. Behind the scenes, there can be arm-twisting."[28]

Because of its power in the international system, the United States can—when it so chooses—act as an equalizer for women when dealing with powerful men in their own societies. As Melanne Verveer concludes, "Governments are important in moving this agenda forward, because governments are the responsible agents to punish the perpetrators of violence. . . . Don't underestimate the good the US can do."[29]

But is the Hillary Doctrine a Western feminist conceit? Does it impose the values of the West on non-Western women in another manifestation of imperialism? Ironically, it isn't the international feminist community raising this issue—after all, the well-regarded Scandinavians are Westerners themselves. The norms put forward by CEDAW are binding on all of its 186 signatories, which cross all civilizational boundaries. As former coordinator of the Bush administration's Office of International Women's Issues (OIWI), Charlotte Ponticelli, puts it, "What values are you talking about? To get an education? To not die in childbirth? To not be raped? To participate in the political process? What values are you suggesting [these women] don't want?"[30]

Astonishingly, this cultural criticism of the Hillary Doctrine often comes from within the ranks of those charged with implementing U.S. foreign policy—that is, from the U.S. policy-making community itself. It's the U.S. negotiators in Afghanistan who too often say, "Gender will come later; it's too early in the process. You [women] are complicating the process, slowing it down, pissing off the men who can deliver the peace."[31] And this sentiment is not confined to the American segment of the West. It's also when the European Commission investigates the stoning of a woman in Afghanistan, and a female on the delegation pronounces, "This woman was murdered," and the head of the delegation responds, "You know, you really mustn't be so Eurocentric. We're speaking of local customs."[32] Somehow, when it concerns women, it's often the West that believes it's cultural, not criminal, and we mustn't "impose."

As one coalition representative who prefers to remain anonymous put it, "There is no point in pushing gender equality. It will only alienate them [the Afghans]." It is significant that the "them" he was referring to are Afghan men. Rather than dignifying this argument, we'll let Ann Jones have the last word:

What we're up against is not just the intractable misogyny of President Karzai and other powerful mullahs and *mujahideen*, but the misogyny of power brokers in Washington as well.

Take, for example, the second most popular objection I hear from American male experts on Afghanistan when I raise my modest proposal [to include significantly more women at the peace negotiations]. They call this one "pragmatic" or "realistic." Women can't come to the negotiating table, they say, because the Taliban would never sit down with them. In fact, Taliban, "ex-Taliban," and Taliban sympathizers sit down with women every day in the Afghan Parliament, as they have in occasional *loya jirgas* (deliberating assemblies) since 2001.

Clearly, any Taliban who refuse altogether to talk with women disqualify themselves as peace negotiators and should have no place at the table. But what's stunning about the view of the American male experts is that it comes down on the other side, ceding to the most extreme Taliban misogynists the right to exclude from peace deliberations half the population of the country. (Tell that to our women soldiers putting their lives on the line.) . . .

But what becomes of women? Even Matthew Hoh, who resigned his position in 2009 as a political officer in the Foreign Service to protest US policy in Afghanistan, and now heads the Afghanistan Study Group, can't seem to imagine bringing women to the negotiating table. (He says he's "working on it.")

Instead, the Study Group decides for women that, "this strategy will best serve [their] interests." It declares that, "the worst thing for women is for Afghanistan to remain paralyzed in a civil war in which there evolves no organically rooted support for their social advancement." Well, no. Actually, the worst thing for women is to have a bunch of men—and not even Afghan men at that—decide one more time what's best for women.

I wonder if it's significant that the Afghan Study Group, much like the Bonn Conference that established the Karzai government in the first place, is essentially a guy group. I count three women among 49 men and the odd "center" or "council" (also undoubtedly consisting mostly of men). When I asked Matthew Hoh why there are so few women in the Study Group, he couldn't help laughing. He said, "This is Washington. You go to any important meeting in Washington, it's men."[33]

That's the problem the Hillary Doctrine was meant to correct, wasn't it? The dismissive attitude of U.S. foreign policy wonks toward women, their security, and whether they even have the right to be in the room is not, in the end, an argument against the Hillary Doctrine: it's an argument for *why it is absolutely necessary.*

## THE HOUSE THAT HILLARY BUILT

In the good and bad old days, when presidential administrations actually considered a particular foreign policy initiative worthwhile, they would execute it, whether that meant establishing a new office or other institutional entity, developing programming, and/or asking Congress to budget funds.

However straightforward it may initially seem, several problems complicate this approach. Among the most significant are: (a) most of these initiatives are easily dropped by presidential successors, and (b) there is little to no accountability, either in the form of legal obligations to undertake specific actions or a requirement that an external third party monitor and evaluate an initiative to determine whether it produced any of its intended effects.

In a bid to circumvent these problems and establish a legally binding and benchmarked foundation for the Hillary Doctrine, during the Obama administration's first term, the State Department helped develop a framework of laws and commitments relating to women and foreign policy. As Jen Klein, adviser to Hillary Clinton on global women's issues, notes, four principles informed this work:

1. This is a nonpartisan issue.
2. The United States is not imposing its views on other nations.
3. The work must be based in evidence, even though we also feel it's the right thing to do.
4. These efforts must demonstrate that the benefits accrue not only to women but to national interests such as security and prosperity.[34]

Many of the pieces were already in place when Hillary Clinton became U.S. secretary of state—some as a result of her own efforts during her husband's administration, such as the Victims of Trafficking and Violence Protection Act. Nevertheless, in the absence of CEDAW ratification, the United States was not bound by an overarching binding obligation to support the human rights of women on the international stage. U.N. Security Resolution 1325 and its successors 1820, 1888, 1889, 1960, 2106, and 2122 have changed that situation.

In 2004, the Security Council also called on member states to develop National Action Plans (NAPs) to implement UNSCR 1325.[35] In December 2011, the United States unveiled its own National Action Plan on Women, Peace, and Security, for which it is now accountable before the international community.[36] The NAP was the product of more than a year's collaboration between civil society organizations and various executive branch working groups.

As informed by the provisions of UNSCR 1325, the U.S. NAP identifies five primary areas of concern: the national integration and institutionalization of a gender-responsive approach to diplomacy, development, and defense; the strengthening of women's participation in peace processes and decision making; the protection of women from sexual and gender-based violence; the promotion of women's role in conflict prevention; and gender-sensitive access to relief in the case of humanitarian crises.

The U.S. NAP is important because it does not simply talk of objectives; rather it outlines specific outcomes associated with each and then assigns accountability to specific executive branch agencies for the achievement of those outcomes. For example, the Department of Defense is tasked to "incorporate modules on protection, rights, and specific needs of women in conflict into training provided to partner militaries and security personnel." Another, this time the responsibility of USAID, is to "implement the USAID Counter Trafficking Code of Conduct holding personnel, contractors, sub-contractors, and grantees to the highest ethical standards with regard to trafficking, and to develop a new Trafficking in Persons Policy with a focus on increasing anti-trafficking initiatives in conflict-affected areas." The U.S. NAP specifies approximately 80 such outcomes.

Monitoring how the U.S. implements its NAP is thus a considerably more concrete exercise than it otherwise would be. The White House National Security staff (NSS) established the Women, Peace, and

Security Interagency Policy Committee (WPS IPC) to oversee and coordinate NAP efforts. Using indicators chosen by the WPS IPC, agencies report to this body, which in turn notifies to the National Security Council Deputies Committee, which then produces an annual report that it presents to the president. In addition to internal monitoring, this process allows external groups, whether those be civil society organizations or the United Nations, to keep tabs on the process, as well. "Basically what we've given to the outside are the tools now to keep the United States faithful to what obligations we have incurred in the President's launching this National Action Plan and issuing an accompanying executive order," says Melanne Verveer: "this was a major achievement."[37]

The U.S. NAP arguably represents the keystone to the entire framework of U.S. commitment, and like a keystone, it was put into place virtually last. Other component parts of the framework had already been established and, in a sense, were all tied together under the NAP into what is hopefully a coherent whole. The NAP elucidates some of these other pieces:

The Department of State and US Agency for International Development (USAID) are implementing reforms initiated through the 2010 Quadrennial Diplomacy and Development Review (QDDR) related to support for women and girls abroad in the realms of policy development, budget planning, and personnel training. The new positions of the Department of State's Ambassador-at-Large for Global Women's Issues and USAID's Senior Coordinator for Gender Equality and Women's Empowerment ensure that women's rights and concerns remain at the core of US foreign policy. USAID's policy framework highlights a commitment to gender equality and female empowerment as a key operational principle, while USAID's revised Policy on Gender Equality and Female Empowerment will institutionalize our commitment throughout US development and humanitarian assistant activities. In all countries, including those affected by crisis and conflict, USAID mandates that development and humanitarian assistance activities be informed by gender analysis . . . In order to address forced labor and sexual exploitation, USAID is also revising its Counter Trafficking in Persons (C-TIP) Policy, which will include a specific objective aimed at increasing USAID investments in TIP preventions and protection in conflict and crisis-affected areas. Finally, foreign assistance indicators tracking the performance of programs implemented by USAID and the Department of State now include specific indicators on gender equality, women's empowerment, sexual and gender-based violence (SGBV) prevention and response, and women's participation in peacebuilding.

The Department of Defense (DoD) had dedicated staff responsible for addressing gender considerations in keeping with DoD's mission. Within the Office of the Secretary of Defense, the Office of the Undersecretary of Defense for Policy coordinates the development and implementation of DoD's efforts on Women, Peace, and Security. The Office of the Undersecretary of Defense for Personnel and Readiness coordinates the Department's efforts on sexual assault prevention and response, and combating trafficking in persons. For the Military Services, the Defense Advisory Committee on Women in the Services advises on policies related to the recruitment, retention, treatment, and integration of women into US Armed Forces. Around the world, several of DoD's Combatant Commands have made gender issues a focus. US Africa Command has established a Gender Working Group focused on integrating gender considerations across the command's programs and engagements with African militaries. In Afghanistan, US Central Command and NATO's International Security Assistance Force (ISAF) have established gender advisers to assist commanders in identifying the differing effects a potential operation may have on local men and women. In addition, the Marine Corps' Female Engagement Teams and the Army's Cultural Support Teams are providing new avenues for women Marines and soldiers to support ongoing operations and engage women in local populations.[38]

In addition to the above, Clinton also issued a Policy Guidance in March 2012 instructing each bureau, embassy, and office of the State Department to undertake a gender analysis of its respective areas of responsibility, including all current and future USAID-funded projects. The objective was to touch every function of both entities. A regional bureau for example, is now mandated to regularly undertake a gender analysis for each area of responsibility—including all of those initiated by the State Department and USAID. The Foreign Service Institute has also been tasked with developing and rolling out gender integration modules designed to train new Foreign Service officers from the get-go.

More importantly, the Master Indicator List used by the government, including the Office of Management and Budget (OMB), Congress, and the State Department itself, to assess the State Department and USAID includes nine new gender indicators designed to meet guidance requirements. That means, for example, that the monitoring bureau in State Department, "F," will begin formally to evaluate whether its programs are helping to achieve indicators as outlined in the Master Indicator List such as, for example, "the number of local women participating in a substantive role or position in a peacebuilding process supported with US government assistance."[39]

After the U.S. NAP's appearance, other pieces were assembled in 2012 before Clinton's departure as secretary of state. These include a Counter-Trafficking in Persons Strategy, a Policy on Gender Equality and Female Empowerment, an Implementation Plan for the National Action Plan on Women, Peace, and Security, a Strategy to Prevent and Respond to Gender-based Violence Globally, the Equal Futures Partnership in September, and a Vision for Ending Child Marriage and Meeting the Needs of Married Children.[40]

As a final parting gift to his secretary of state the day before Hillary Clinton stepped down in 2013, Barack Obama issued a presidential memorandum institutionalizing a commitment that American foreign policy include a robust attention to gender. He did so in part by establishing the Office of Global Women's Issues (OGWI) as a permanent part of the State Department and reaffirmed its ambassador-level leadership including retaining the direct reporting line to the secretary of state in perpetuity.[41]

All in all, it must be said that Hillary Clinton laid a comprehensive and secure foundation for the continuation of the Hillary Doctrine. The institutions, the obligations, and the accountability mechanisms are all in place. It would be virtually impossible to reverse course regardless of administration: as one staffer at the Institute of Inclusive Security put it, "People don't roll their eyes anymore."[42]

Moreover, the Hillary Doctrine wasn't simply about establishing and implementing policies, but also about putting the right people in place.

As noted by Donald Steinberg, former deputy director of USAID, the first incarnation of the Hillary Doctrine consciously assembled a dream team. With Hillary Clinton at the helm and Melanne Verveer at OGWI, recruiting the top gender analysis talent was easy, and Steinberg—himself a crucial element—was joined by luminaries such as Carla Koppell, Caren Grown, and others.

Notes Steinberg:

> You knew you had a receptive audience for anything you could do [for women]. There was a presupposition that women needed to be at the peace table, that women needed to be consulted. Every Monday there was a staff meeting with the Assistant Secretaries, and we'd go around the table and felt empowered to speak of these things, and if we didn't, we felt we were not discussing the important issues. The atmospherics has changed. [Clinton] approved us doing very expensive programs to address women's empowerment. Her speeches were touted by people in the field and believed so you took action based on those principles. . . . In the [G. W.] Bush administration, gender would be on the agenda, but it would be number five on the agenda. And the last issue on the agenda is the one you never get to because it is not prioritized. The practical impact of Hillary Clinton was that gender issues moved up the agenda and you had to get to them.[43]

The atmospherics were favorable beyond all imagination. The question now is whether sunshine in Washington, D.C., managed to penetrate the gloom of Kabul and Cairo.

## CONTRACTS: THE BRIDGE FROM D.C. TO THE GREAT BEYOND

In terms of the U.S. government, he or she who has money may program. He or she who doesn't, cannot. This truism is critical when attempting to decipher what the government actually did to support the Hillary Doctrine. While the State Department has little pots of money stashed here and there, it doesn't really program: USAID and DoD both do. Indeed, the budgets for these programs often run well into the hundreds of millions of dollars. Since the implementation of the NAP, we now know precisely how much goes to programming to support the WPS agenda. In 2013, the total was $1.9 billion, and the bulk of these funds were earmarked for USAID, not the State Department.

The State Department does nevertheless support some impressive programming of its own, much of which has significant gender implications. For example, following the 2001 invasion, the Office of Afghanistan and Pakistan in the Bureau of International Narcotics and Law Enforcement was placed in charge of justice reform programming. The Rule of Law Team—all female, by the way—oversees fifteen different programs in that country. These programs train and deploy justices, offer education to legal professionals, and promote access to justice. Gender justice has become a program priority over time, and the team has worked with the Afghan Ministry of Women's Affairs to educate law enforcement and religious leaders about women's rights under the law in addition to establishing eight violence against women (VAW) units within the police force, and supporting a number of women's shelters.[44] Nevertheless, even at its budgeting peak, which was $200 million in 2014, its outlays are dwarfed by what USAID, brings to the table.

USAID therefore warrants our close scrutiny as we assess the implementation of the Hillary Doctrine. Ann Jones recalls writing a proposal to expand an ESL (English as a Second Language) program in Kabul: "I made the rounds of funding sources. Later an acquaintance at USAID told me I'd made the mistake of asking for too little money, only about twelve thousand dollars. 'Multiply that by ten or twenty,' she said, 'and somebody might at least take a look at it.'"[45]

Andrew Natsios, former administrator of USAID, was asked about the process;

> State now does the strategic programming and budgeting for USAID, and once that happens, you will sit and you will figure out what you're going to do, how much money is going to whatever country, and then you'll create some kind of contract request for proposals. . . . Then you alert your potential contractors through your field office. So in the countries that AID works in, you have a standing pool of AID contractors who have built a business model around servicing the needs of AID. . . . The contract is

then awarded in the Office of Acquisition and Assistance. [Then] you take the budgeted amount that Congress has appropriated and you obligate it against a contract or grant.

The contract signed, or the grant signed, it goes out to the institution that is our partner. Then we meet with them and tell them, "This is what we really want you to do," in detail. And they assign a person in charge of managing the contract. They're called COTRs (Contracting Officer's Technical Representative). And then they start spending the money. They allocate the money. And there's a heavy reporting requirement, heavy reporting. Every time they spend money they have to go get approval. . . . Furthermore, the program officer will have chosen indicators from a set of 2,400 possible indicators to measure improvement. And the Inspector General of AID has a whole program management review process. And if they decide the program is a failure, then they say you are not supposed to re-fund it, or you're supposed to fire the contractor or reorganize the program. There's a huge amount of money and time spent on collecting and analyzing the data and I argue it may be up to 30 or 40 percent of what AID spends.[46]

USAID has its own Gender Equality and Female Empowerment Policy that sets out three strategic priorities: reduce disparities between men and women; reduce gender-based violence; and increase the capabilities of women and girls.[47] Pursuant to this policy, every USAID solicitation must mainstream gender. Caren Grown, senior gender advisor to USAID at the time of our interview, described two mechanisms by which this is brought to pass. First, USAID is now making efforts to train its contracts and agreements officers about the implementation of the gender equality policy, specifically concerning how to meet the requirements for gender integration when writing requests for proposals. Second, Grown notes that a new chapter in USAID's Automated Directive Services (the "rule book"), ADS 205, explicitly states that "in solicitations, gender equality and female empowerment objectives must be spelled out in the problem statement, reflected in project design, tracked by qualitative or quantitative indicators in performance reporting, and addressed in the evaluation plan and reporting requirements. Moreover, offerers will be evaluated on how well they meet these requirements in each section of their proposal. . . . I have heard informally that contractors have gotten the message."[48]

At the time of our interview in 2013, Carla Koppell, then senior coordinator for gender equality and women's empowerment at USAID noted:

> There's a requirement, for example, for a gender analysis to accompany project design, and [we are working on having] a lot of specificity with regard to when you say "integrate attention to gender," what does that actually mean. . . . So part of it is having gender advisors, and we now have either gender advisors or gender focal points in every mission and operating unit; we have already trained 650. Part of it is enabling our technical specialists in every area to be able to think about those issues on their own. Part of it is ensuring that the gender analysis enables new project design to reflect attention to these issues when they're coming out, and part of it is using monitoring and evaluation systems to enable us to see where there are gaps, and to correct for those gaps.[49]

Koppell is referring to gaps between men and women that are critical to USAID outcomes. These include unequal access to resources, wealth, opportunities, and services in every domain, including the political. USAID is undertaking country surveys to identify shortfalls and then track them over time to determine progress. Furthermore, the nine indicators in the Master Indicator List will be used to determine whether USAID programming is in fact producing the intended effects, with the first such evaluation scheduled to take place in 2017. Nevertheless, even Grown is quick to point out that these nine indicators measure outcomes and outputs as opposed to measuring impact, which is why USAID needs those country surveys.

Carla Koppell maintains it is important to specify what appropriate attention to gender means. Interviews with implementers in the field reveal that gender programming is often little more than an exercise in box ticking. A for-profit implementer could, for example, manage to dodge its gender mainstreaming obligations by simply insisting that a construction project to build a new road will also benefit women because they use roads as well as men!

In a similar vein, Donald Steinberg remembers receiving a proposal to build a dam from a for-profit implementer who insisted it fulfilled the gender requirement: 50 percent of the water, the implementer insisted, would benefit women. Steinberg pushed back, "That's great. Have you looked into what the gender effects will be of displacing people for the dam? You'll be employing mostly men—how will this affect gender dynamics? What will be the effects of electricity on women working on smoky cook stoves?" According to USAID, the gender analyses they are receiving now are far more sophisticated than in those earlier days.[50] Maura O'Neill, a former senior official at USAID, asserts, "Box-checking was a phase, a necessary phase, but we are beyond that now."[51] As we will discuss later on, however, others disagree.

In addition to USAID's intensified scrutiny of its gender programming, the Gender and Development Office of USAID offers its own specialized programming. These include programs to combat child marriage and gender-based violence; the development of mobile phone apps designed to educate girls about violence and to promote life skills; the production of documentaries that profile women and girl community leaders; as well as programs designed to aid disabled women and girls.

One of the most important USAID programs for women is just getting off the ground as we write. PROMOTE is USAID's five-year programmatic response to the impending drawdown of U.S. troops from Afghanistan in 2014 to the new Status of Forces Agreement level of 10,800 troops. PROMOTE is designed to shore up the gains Afghan women have made since the invasion of 2001. Announced in July 2013, the $410 million project is easily USAID's largest-ever gender programming effort, though half of these funds are to be provided by partner nations, which may or may not materialize. Target beneficiaries are primarily Afghan women who possess at least a secondary education.

One of the reasons for developing and implementing such a sweeping program is that the Afghan government has recently agreed to work toward establishing a female quota of at least 30 percent within the civil service. USAID is currently soliciting proposals under PROMOTE to train women to occupy these posts.[52]

Future components of PROMOTE will facilitate the entry of women into the Afghan economy, the establishment and building of women's coalitions, and similar initiatives. To hedge its bets, however, USAID is holding back $175 million in incentive funds that it refuses to disburse unless the Afghan government follows through on promises to protect the rights of women.[53]

At first glance, all seems well and good. The government appears to have transformed the strategic vision of the U.S. NAP into a thoughtful approach to gender equity programming and its evaluation.

And yet, at the ground level, something has gone terribly awry. We argue that the roots of some of the in-country problems discussed below are to be found at this intermediary programming level and are connected to the vast changes in the primary U.S. foreign assistance institution, USAID. Few outsiders understand that USAID is no longer a development agency and has not been for well over a decade. USAID is now essentially a contract management agency, instead. After the end of the Cold War, the U.S. government drastically cut personnel (from twelve thousand in the 1970s to less than three thousand today). At the same time USAID's budget grew immensely, tripling over twenty years. Carol Lancaster, a high-ranking USAID official during the 1990s comments: "USAID has left the retail game and become a wholesaler. . . . In fact, it's become a wholesaler to wholesalers. It takes you far from what's happening on the ground."[54] Ann Jones concurs:

> USAID used to believe in doing work from the ground up by sending highly experienced professionals to the field to work with people there to figure out solutions. Now that it's been brought under State . . . USAID brings in contractors without experience or cultural sensitivity in one-size-fits-all programming. . . . It's overly ambitious but shortsighted; there's pressure to have the proper indicators on your log, and it becomes overwhelming. . . . These people are doing their jobs and have good intentions. But they're there to do things the way Americans know how to do things— top-down, contractors, indicators. . . . Top-down doesn't work! But it's the way USAID programs are implemented.[55]

This wholesaling approach to development has spawned mega-contractors such as Louis Berger, Creative Associates, Development Alternatives Incorporated, and Chemonics—for-profit development companies who often hire retired USAID employees for executive roles. These mega-contractors then partner with subcontractors and sub-subcontractors to win and implement USAID contracts. In her confirmation hearings for secretary of state, Hillary Clinton acknowledged the degree to which USAID had changed: "I think it's fair to say that USAID, our premier aid agency, has been decimated. . . . It's turned into more of a contracting agency than an operational agency with the ability to deliver."[56]

According to Lancaster, it wasn't so long ago that USAID was an operational agency, whose employees went out and "did" development, including building roads and digging wells, a time when, in the words of Natsios, USAID was a "creative, proactive, and technically skilled organization."[57] Now the number of engineers at USAID can be counted on the fingers of one hand, and its employees manage contracts all day. Clinton herself once remarked, "Even when there are not headline-grabbing abuses, there has been a steady transfer of authority and resources from government employees and a chain of accountability to contractors, and we have reaped the very difficult consequences of that."[58]

As a result, the disconnect between USAID and putative beneficiaries has only widened. Helen Mack, founder of Guatemala's Myrna Mack Foundation concurs: "USAID comes in and says, 'Here's our project: Do you want to do it?' They have no interest in asking us what we think needs to be done."[59] Yasmeen Hassan of Equality Now agrees: "So they are doing all this stuff, they are not doing it in consultation, they're doing it in a sort of very hierarchical way, and people in countries that have been very badly influenced by US foreign policy are very, very skeptical. . . . There's immediate conspiracy theories. And so the efforts backfire."[60]

Sometimes the ignorance would be laughable if it didn't involve missing out on real opportunities for change. Patricia Guerrero from the Liga de Mujeres in Colombia approached USAID for funds to support a broader dialogue among women during the peace talks between the Fuerzas Armadas Revolucionarias de Colombia (FARC) and the government. USAID told them, "We only have money for postconflict initiatives." Guerrero replied, "But we are in the middle of the peace process!" No dice, apparently: no money can be spent until there's ink on that peace agreement. She also notes that "The contractors are very conservative, often retired military. They don't establish relationships with the communities in which they work. It's not an equal relationship; they think of themselves as gods: Very hierarchical, very patriarchal, very pyramidal. They came in and wanted to do what they wanted to do."[61]

Indeed, this is one reason why OGWI maintains a Small Grants program; an OGWI staffer relates that the fund has disbursed more than $33 million to NGOs—and not to contractors—in part because of the reasons enunciated by Guerrero and Mack.[62] Unfortunately, $33 million does not go very far, especially when compared with USAID funding.

And the Government Performance and Results Act (GPRA) of 1994 has arguably made the situation worse. GPRA mandates that every government program show measurable results. That sounds eminently reasonable, until one realizes that these quantitative measurements of success will be assessed every twelve months or even sooner. If results are not forthcoming, the program can be shut down. Unfortunately, development often involves timelines of ten to fifteen years, and the impacts may not be quantitative in nature—such as in the case of "building democratic institutions." Natsios comments, "We don't have mathematical formulas for how you build institutions. It's affected by culture and history and region of the world. You can't have some quantitative measurement that works across the whole world."[63]

That's why many development specialists point to the necessity of developing indicators that measure impact and not only output; evaluators should not only be interested in enrollment figures for example, but also whether the students graduated or even learned anything. In 2012, UNICEF reported about Afghanistan that, "Impressive school enrollment figures determine how much money a school gets from the government, but don't reveal the much smaller numbers of enrollees who actually attend. No more than 10% of students, mostly boys, finish high school. In 2012, according to UNICEF, only half of school-age children went to school at all."[64] This is very troubling, yet the Master Indicator List by which USAID measures its success does not include any impact indicators. In the words of Jessica Neuwirth, "They have all these indicators and they have all these reporting requirements so that what actually happens is less important than what it looks like . . . the really good groups don't even apply. The whole thing is so sickening to them that they just don't want to have anything to do with that. So it's a sort of self-feeding cycle of corruption and misinformation and exaggeration, and it's just so unhealthy."[65]

To make matters worse, the compliance paperwork attendant to this annual budgeting and monitoring cycle is enormously time-consuming. In a communication to Andrew Natsios, Ken Schofield, formerly a top official in the Policy and Planning Bureau of USAID, described it thus:

> From the perspective of the officers running programs in the field, two months (October and November) are devoted to reviewing and reporting on past performance; the next four months (December through April) are pretty much devoted to budget and implementation proposals: Preparing the Congressional Budget Justification for the coming year, preparing Mission Strategic Plans for the future year, and preparing Operational Plans for the current year. And of course the final two months of each fiscal year (August and September) are devoted to preparation and signing of contracts and grants to obligate newly appropriated funds that have finally been made available. Almost eight months of every fiscal year are dominated by reporting and budget processes, leaving program and technical experts precious little time to design new programs and monitor the implementation of ongoing programs.[66]

No wonder no one at USAID is digging wells anymore—they are too busy pushing paper. More ominously, employees are under enormous pressure to spend money as fast as possible to avoid future budget downsizing. With its small number of personnel and increasingly higher budgets—$20.4 billion in 2014—our calculation is that each and every USAID employee would have to "burn" almost $6.7 million per year to keep the funds flowing from congressional budgeters. This metric deepens USAID's reliance on mega-contractors, who may be chosen in part because they show great capability when it comes to spending taxpayer dollars hand over fist. While contracts may be put out for bid, there are very, very few organizations that are able to "burn" cash at the rate required. Newer, smaller, or indigenous organizations are therefore perceived as simply unfundable, producing, if you will, a development cartel of mega-contractors that monopolize available funding, thus limiting USAID's choices concerning the implementation of desired programming. Our worst enemy could not have constructed a more perverse set of incentives. Neuwirth comments, "There's billions of dollars and then there's a total dysfunctionality at the bottom."[67]

In theory, perhaps, "top-down, contractors, indicators" should work. In practice, as Ann Jones puts it, "we spend too much, too fast, without a clue," fueling both massive corruption and pervasive cynicism among the very populations USAID purports to aid.[68] Even a policy as enlightened as the Hillary Doctrine can in fact be profoundly undermined by how it is implemented "the American way," as we shall see.

## "WOMEN'S STUFF": THE GOOD, THE BAD, AND THE UGLY

### The Good

Matt Pottinger originally studied Chinese, and wound up working as a reporter with Reuters in Beijing from 1997 to 2005. After all that time writing about catastrophes, corruption and other crises, Pottinger decided to become more actively engaged in solutions. In 2005 he enlisted with the Marines and by early 2007, was deployed to Iraq as part of the surge. Two tours in Afghanistan followed in rapid succession, the first beginning in January 2009.[69]

During his first tour in Afghanistan, Pottinger landed the position of battalion intelligence officer. His job was to track down insurgents responsible for making improvised explosive devices (IEDs). He knew who they were, but not how to find them. Marines typically searched entire villages, but Pottinger realized there would be big problems doing so with Afghan women present.

Pashtunwali, the Pashtun code of conduct, stipulates that women may not interact with men who are not their close kin. Breaking this code incurs a blood debt—which is serious stuff. Pottinger discussed with his captain how best to negotiate what was essentially a gendered minefield. Almost simultaneously they had one of those "aha moments"—the "Lioness Teams"!

The Lioness Teams were made up of female Marines attached to all-male combat units in Iraq. Their primary function was, whenever necessary, to search Muslim women. The teams were somewhat controversial because they had been established before the lifting of the combat ban on women in the U.S. armed forces in January 2013: if shot at, these female soldiers have to engage in direct combat.[70]

Even though he had never heard of the Hillary Doctrine, Pottinger thought the same concept could be very useful in Afghanistan. A number of experts had already told him that Afghan men considered female soldiers to be a "third gender" and therefore inoffensive to male pride. He decided to make it happen.

His first team was made up of seven women—an interpreter, a corpsman, three security personnel, and two women tasked with conversing with the villagers. On the appointed night, the Marines surrounded the village where they thought the IEDs were being assembled. In the morning, Pottinger approached an elder and explained that they would be searching the entire village for the three male suspects.

The elder was informed that, alongside Afghan National Police, U.S. troops would be searching their homes. Because most of the troops were men, villagers were told to move all of the women and children into a large compound where female Marines would guard them, but also feed them and offer medical care.

At first the villagers did not believe that the female Marines were actually women. All had donned headscarves as a sign of respect, but were nonetheless outfitted in full gear, including their weapons. Joanna Schafer, the leader, showed them her long red hair, and one older woman grabbed her breast to make sure she was a woman.

According to Pottinger, after some initial awkwardness, the women began swapping stories while learning more about the village. While the team managed to gather useful intelligence, the primary purpose was to establish good will. The female Marines explained why the United States was there and discovered that none of the female villagers had even heard of the events of September 11, 2001. The village women asked the female Marines whether they were Russians or Christian missionaries, for they had heard both rumors. The female half of the village had never interacted with any International Security Assistance Force (ISAF) soldier—ever.

The male Marines did manage to capture two of the three men they were searching for and discovered an entire IED workshop at the bottom of a dry well. They visited the village again a few days later to assure them the detainees were not being mistreated, and the female Marines treated one of the men's wives for gonorrhea. Surprisingly, a number of Pashtun men saw this "third gender" as kinder and more trustworthy than the male soldiers. Pottinger recalls a conversation with one man, "You guys are all here to fight," he said to Pottinger. "We know the women are here to help." The Afghan men could reveal more to the "third gender" than they could to their own wives or to male ISAF soldiers. Pottinger realized that the presence of the female Marines "softened the interaction with everyone. It was a disarming approach." In a way, added Pottinger:

> The presence of the female Marines brought to the fore issues of human security. Female counterinsurgents are one of the few advantages we have over our adversaries. Women in their culture have second-class status, and thus are not part of the insurgency. Female counterinsurgents thus cannot be matched or responded to; they can't compete with or neutralize that. It's one of the few asymmetric advantages we have.

The other infantry brigades were skeptical at first, but mostly among those whom Pottinger characterizes as, "middle management types who weren't in the field. The top was receptive, and those in the field were receptive, too."

This support was greatly increased when, several months later in July 2009, another unit chased some "bad guys" into a village compound and, after allowing the women of the village to leave, discovered their quarry had donned the women's burqas and slipped away. Brigadier General Larry Nicholson commented, "Why don't we have teams of women?" Someone told him of Pottinger's experiment, and Matt was called in to train the first generation of Female Engagement Teams (FETs).

By the end of 2009, a 45-woman FET contingent was operating in southern Afghanistan. When infantry units began to request FETs, Pottinger and his teams knew that their experiment was a success. The FET idea spread beyond the Marines. Female support teams were organized for the Special Forces, though they were called Cultural Support Teams to get rid of the "F" that might get folks in trouble over the combat exclusion for women still in effect at the time. Nevertheless, the program retained an ad hoc feel. No formal FET position (i.e., Military Occupational Specialty, or MOS) was created, and as a result, Pottinger felt that the FETs "have pretty much died" with the drawdown of troops from Afghanistan.

What Pottinger didn't know is that one young woman on the other side of the planet was paying attention. Alexandra Tenny, the chief of the Eradication, Narcotics Affairs Section of the U.S. Embassy in Bogota, Colombia (whose husband was on contract as the gender specialist for the embassy) believed that the FETs were too good an idea to simply let die: "They have something like 500 female Marines coming back from the 'war theater' with FET experience . . . and they will all scatter to the wind soon, which I keep pointing out is such a waste," she says, adding that FET expertise represents a "broader capability" that the Marines lead and also has "worldwide application."[71] She began to see the possibilities for FETs in Colombia.

"This will be the very first time, to the best of my knowledge, that FETs will be exported to other nations for use in conflict areas," says Tenny, adding that instead of simply providing teams, the U.S. Marine Corps should train host nations in the development and execution of their own teams.[72]

What Tenny was proposing in spring 2012 was for the Marine FET alumni to train Colombian FETs (EFEORs in Spanish[73]) to work with the police in its antinarcotics patrols in Colombia's rural areas—an idea that she pitched successfully to both the Colombian National Police Force and U.S. Southern Command (SouthCom).

It was an easy sell. According to Tenny, the reaction of the deputy director for the Colombian National Police (the number two highest ranking police officer in the country) was "spectacular." He immediately dedicated forty officers to participate in the pilot project. So excited were the army and the navy that, "I had to rein everyone in so as to keep this at a manageable size until we execute it in the field and work the kinks out. . . . And the Marine Chief of Staff at SouthCom said, 'We're doing this. Give them what they want.'"[74] She adds that whenever she heard any nay-saying, she'd think, "If big, bad, super-macho, jarhead Marines see the value of this, how am I going to listen to anybody else?"[75]

It may sound counterintuitive, but as Tenny implies, it may actually prove easier to implement innovative policies such as the Hillary Doctrine through the Department of Defense than through the State Department. Rosa Brooks, former counselor to the undersecretary of defense for policy, comments, "While DoD is certainly male-dominated, it's also a hierarchy, and if someone says 'do it!' they salute and say, 'yes, sir!'" She also notes that those midlevel officers who had seen combat in Iraq and Afghanistan "got it; [gender] was not a hard sell."[76] This was certainly Tenny's experience.

Importantly for the Hillary Doctrine, the Colombian EFEORs will enjoy a number of capabilities that the Marine FETs did not. The Colombian teams, for example, will possess full police authority, which the Marines in Afghanistan did not.

"So one of the challenges I put to my team was for them to conceptualize everything they *wish* they had been able to do in Afghanistan but couldn't because of restraining or lack of authorities, etc., and let's look at how we can do them here," recalls Tenny. One of the EFEOR interventions she is most interested in is investigating and resolving violence and other crimes against women and children.

"We will have to sort this out in more detail as we go along," she says, and further explains, "An EFEOR has to know about NGO services, legal services, everything that's available and make those linkages, that was one thing that we really learned from the Marines is they had to educate themselves on what resources were available so as they heard about needs for the community, they could go and make those connections. So that's going to be a big part of the [EFEOR] training." Noting that U.S. Marine Corps reports show a "direct correlation between the presence of a FET in an area and the reduction of tension and violence against US forces," the hope is that the same white magic would happen for Colombian forces.[77] She elaborates:

Colombia has been in conflict for nearly 50 years. And as in many other countries experiencing internal strife, there is a disproportionately high number of female led households in these areas. Violence against women is also very high, perpetuated by members of both sides so the distrust women in these communities have for men in uniform is deep.

Finally, the FARC—in spite of the recent move for peace talks—actively recruits young women and girls, sometimes forcibly. The FET—a strong woman in uniform with a position of authority and a weapon—provides a symbolic counterbalance to the image of the FARC woman in uniform and can be used as a prevention and counter-recruitment tool. Many demobilized women report in their interviews that they joined the FARC to get out of a bad situation, not realizing that life in the FARC for a woman is not as advertised.[78]

Tenny also believes that the Colombian EFEORs, in addition to engaging in counter-recruitment, will help bring the power of state law to assist rural Colombian women to improve their lives. She says her office will ensure that the new EFEORs will know the law "inside and out" and will also be empowered to arrest perpetrators of gender-based violence. In addition to referring the latter to traveling rural "justice houses," where necessary, the Colombian EFEORs will also inventory the needs of the women through town hall meetings and through door-to-door visits.

The first Colombian EFEORs deployed at the end of 2013. It will be fascinating to observe whether this creative program, inspired by the Hillary Doctrine, will fulfill its promise. In a stroke of golden irony, Tenny's new posting is Kabul, Afghanistan.

Colombian EFEORs are not the only good news for proponents of the Hillary Doctrine. Other examples of creative programming abound. For example, Donald Steinberg, former deputy director of USAID, recounts when Hillary Clinton charged into a meeting room and said, "I'm really concerned about gender in Central America; I'm tired of hearing about femicides; I want to see programs!"[79]

In response, USAID launched a series of initiatives designed to tackle the epidemic of domestic violence in Central America—sorely needed in a clutch of nations characterized by some of the highest female homicide rates in the world. Steinberg recalls how two-and-a-half years later, he and Clinton traveled to Guatemala to observe the results. One of the key projects was a "24-Hour Court" located in downtown Guatemala City that takes domestic violence reports literally twenty-four hours a day—critical in a country where victims have to report a crime within eight hours. If, for example, a woman is beaten at night, she may not be able to report it before the eight-hour window slams shut, nor will she be able to obtain a restraining order.

Steinberg describes the unique nature of this special court:

> When you come in the first door, you go to the first station, and there's a doctor to treat you. Next station is a policeman to take your report. The next station is a judge who will file charges. The next is a psychosocial counselor. The last station is a personal counselor, who will provide money for you to stay in a hotel or safe house, and will go with you back home to get your possessions. The difference in the women at the end of this circuit was nothing short of amazing.

Steinberg sees this initiative as tackling a major problem of national security: "Compare those societies that respect women and those who don't. Who's trafficking in weapons, drugs? Who's harboring terrorists and starting pandemics? Whose problems require US troops on the ground? There's a one-to-one correspondence. Don't tell me there's no relationship between national security and the empowerment of women."

Steinberg knows what he's talking about: As a younger man, he witnessed how the Angolan peace process, which he oversaw, unraveled because the United States failed to empower women, who could in turn pressure government leaders to remain committed to the peace process. "We didn't address girls' education, women's health, justice for violence against women; we didn't include women in reconstruction funding so they could be empowered. . . . We bought into amnesties which destroyed the rule of law, which turned into men with guns forgiving other men with guns for the crimes we committed against women. . . . We didn't have an expansive view of what the peace process meant. It's not the absence of conflict; it's the absence of violence, including domestic violence."

He notes how this lack of support for women is playing out once again in Central America: "There's more domestic violence in Central America than there ever was during the times of civil war due to the way peace was achieved," he says. "Instead of re-empowering the civil society, you re-empower the armed gangs. It's a quick fix that omits what caused the civil war, and it reinforces patterns of male dominance."

All of these experiences were to prove motivational when Hillary Clinton called him back into government: "Some of us promised that if we were ever back in government, we wanted to put into effect the things that we saw were lacking," he says. "The 24-Hour-Court is an excellent example of understanding and addressing the relationship between the security of women and the security of the states in which they live."

Another example of the best of which the United States is capable is exemplified in the person of Princeton Lyman, who recently stepped down as the U.S. special envoy for the postreferendum mediation talks between Sudan and South Sudan. Farah Council of the Institute for Inclusive Security saw Lyman in action in during his tenure from 2011 to 2013 in this position, and relates the details.[80]

As usual, the talks were originally planned without any representation from women and despite the provisions of UNSCR 1325. Women were not even an afterthought: The various stakeholders did not invite a single woman delegate from either country to the 2005 and 2008 donor conferences in Oslo. In order to shoehorn in representation from one half of the population, the Institute for Inclusive Security, UNWomen, and the government of Norway had to join forces and insist that women be present at the talks.

The 2011 donor conference in Washington, D.C., however, was vastly different: Hillary Clinton, Donald Steinberg, and Princeton Lyman all spoke on behalf of Sudanese and South Sudanese women and then tabled their requests. Almost overnight, everything began to change. Whenever Lyman traveled to Sudan or South Sudan, he met with women's groups. Both sides respected him because he shared information—more specifically, he informed women to what degree the peace process was taking into account their concerns; information that they could not get from any other source.

After the referendum, nine agreements were signed, but still, women were unable to offer much input. Lyman then convened a forty-person expert group, which recommended a gender analysis be performed by the United States Institute of Peace (USIP) to evaluate all nine agreements.

Realizing time was of the essence, USIP completed the analysis in three weeks flat, which then enabled Lyman to return to the negotiating table and include the resulting concerns and recommendations in the agenda.

By June 2013, talks were at a stalemate. None of the nine agreements had been implemented. At the annual African Union summit in Addis Ababa, the Institute for Inclusive Security brought women from civil society groups to the meeting and then introduced them to the principals, including current and former African heads of states. Lyman arranged for the women to meet with African Union (AU) High Level Implementation Panel, and Thabo Mbeki, one of the mediators on that panel, told the assembled female delegates, "Your absence is an impediment to this process." The women made six recommendations, all of which Mbeki agreed with and promised to bring to the negotiating table on their behalf.

By acting as a gate opener—and not merely a gatekeeper—Princeton Lyman successfully brought women in even though they had not been invited. By acting as their champion, by sharing information with women's groups when no one else would, by commissioning formal gender analyses to bolster their arguments, by earmarking funds for women's groups to convene, and by leveraging meetings with senior principals, he ensured the voices of women were heard.

Lyman almost single-handedly ensured that women were included in some of the most important decisions affecting the history of their respective countries. The United States balanced the power of the Sudanese and South Sudanese negotiators on behalf of the women in the best tradition of the Hillary Doctrine.

## The Bad

In the first year of the Obama administration, the State Department "voluntold" Peter Van Buren, a Foreign Service officer with twenty-two years of experience, to serve in a rural Provincial Reconstruction Team (PRT) in Iraq. Shortly after Van Buren's arrival, Patricia Haslach also began her tenure as the new assistant chief of mission for assistance transition at the U.S. Embassy in Iraq. Van Buren has a few tales to tell about how their paths intersected.

According to Van Buren, author of the mordantly funny *We Meant Well: How I Helped Lose the Battle for the Hearts and Minds of the Iraqi People*, soon after Haslach showed up, the PRTs were suddenly all told to "do women's programming." In an interview, he described what happened next:

> We were told, "Do women's stuff!" But we were not really given any guidance. In fact, we were told, "You're the local experts." But we weren't. We had to appoint a women's issues coordinator. We had one woman in the PRT—an agriculturalist. She was a 60-year-old retiree from Wisconsin, very conservative and not attuned to women's issues. But at least we had a woman. Other PRTs didn't have any women and were stuck.
>
> My PRT stumbled upon "widows"—we were going to "help widows"—after all, this was in accordance with Islamic values and by golly, widows were women! Okay, what were we going to do for widows? We need something for widows! We already had a beekeeping operation in place, and so we said we'd limit it to widows, which is how our "Bees for Widows" program was born. It was hard to find widows, because we had no access to society because we weren't trusted.
>
> So individuals emerged who could "provide widows." Widow brokers! We filled up our project, and sent photos back to the embassy of hijab'd women doing things. And then we found a woman veterinarian and gave her money instead of the male veterinarians—ta da! Women! Now these things were fed back to D.C. via the embassy in two ways. First, through stats: "we reached 450 women this week." Second, stories on PowerPoints. We got very creative in telling these stories, so for example about the beekeeping, we'd say something like, "This empowered the women and helped change attitudes so that they will participate in the democratic process." The embassy really liked these, and the PRTs would be patted on the head for doing it . . .
>
> I find it difficult to cite any way that we helped women. . . . In Iraq, two large things bumped—Clinton's sincere desires to help women and Iraqi conservative culture. Neither gave ground. And what was between them—the embassy—wanted Clinton to be happy and feel her goals were being accomplished. But there was incredible turnover and so no coherent plan was possible. My boss changed three times in twelve months.

Washington, D.C., has a short attention span. Clinton's in Burma, then she's in China. There's no time to stop and say, is it really happening here? . . . She didn't know, but maybe she didn't care to know. Secretaries of state can't proclaim failure.[81]

If "Bees for Widows" isn't enough to curl your hair, then there's the spotty record the United States has concerning inviting women to the important meetings, where insignificant issues such as their future are decided. We've seen how differently—in a good way—the 2011 donor conference for South Sudan was handled, but the same cannot be said of other conferences during the first term of the Obama administration. As Anne-Marie Goetz of UNWomen put it, "women are always late, uninvited, and outside the door."[82] Goetz recalls how the organizers of the 2010 London donor's conference for Afghanistan failed to invite any women—despite the fact that the United States had used the plight of women as one of its justifications to invade in the first place, and despite the fact that Hillary Clinton was then secretary of state.

Incensed, UNWomen brought them nevertheless: "I was there with a delegation of women from [Afghan] civil society and we had groomed four of them to be super visible on press," recalls Goetz. Goetz provides the backstory to Miriam Mansury's recounting of this incident in chapter 1:

> The [women] had the genius idea themselves of wearing these green heads-carves, so they were immediately identifiable in the press tent, because that's as far as we got them in.
>
> But the night before [the conference] there was a cocktail party at Kensington Palace and I was nearly thrown out physically because I just walked straight up to [Clinton] and guards immediately grabbed me and said, "back off," and "what are you doing, get away," and . . . I just stood there and I didn't move, and I handed her the women's petition, and I said, "they're over there with green headscarves and they would love it if you would meet with them," and I backed off.
>
> And she did, she went over, she said "I'll go at some point," and she did, that night. And then the next day after the conference she had a press conference and she called out and had them stand up, and she had tea with them, separately.

No other foreign minister would ever do something like that. It's striking, and it is a feminist act, and it's an act of solidarity, and it's an act of recognition. And that photograph with Hillary Clinton and the four women in headscarves of course changed their world. Not just them, but it has an enormously huge impact back in Kabul, of course.[83]

This is a terrific story, of course, and with a happy ending, but it's hard not to ask why the United States—why Hillary Clinton—had not insisted on the presence of women to begin with. As Goetz notes, "With foreign affairs, it's negotiations, it's dialogue, it's hunches, it's secrets, it's men."

Goetz also asks some tough questions concerning whether the United States is really sincere about the Hillary Doctrine. "At the State Department, are there hard targets, like a minimum percentage of women at the table? Are there consequences for the desk officer for Afghanistan who clears a report that has nothing in it on gender? Or who agrees to a Taliban reintegration program without a monitoring system to see what's happening to violence against women in communities? Are there consequences? Is there a check system, a review system—is somebody catching that?"[84] The near fiasco at the 2010 donor conference does make one wonder if such a check system for women had been overlooked—even though Hillary Clinton was then secretary of state, and no State Department employee could doubt her sincerity on these issues.

That was 2010; perhaps the check system for women is now in place? Unfortunately, there is reason to believe it's still not there. In April 2012, years after the international community had signed UNSCR 1325, peace talks to help resolve the Malian crisis were held in Ouagadougou, the capital of Burkina Faso. According to Goetz, in what was becoming a depressingly predictable pattern, eighty civil society leaders were invited—but once again, not a single woman. UNWomen had to step in again:

So our head of office said [to Malian women activists], "Okay, I can't guarantee to get you in, but here's a plane ticket; get on a plane." So they landed in Ouagadougou. They had no idea where the peace talks were. They didn't even know where to go. The next morning they figured out which hotel it was, and they walked in, and they were wearing shawls because it was the spring, and they were told to show their badges, and they said, "We're not taking off our shawls to show you what is underneath!," and they walked in, went straight up to President Compaore and said, "you have to give us five minutes," and he did. . . . That's what we do. And I wish we could do more.

But we see these strategic opportunities late, uninvited, almost by accident. . . . We aren't automatically the ones who get called. It would be the same for [OGWI]. You're not the ones that are getting called when they're thinking Syria, you know? You're not the ones getting called when they're thinking Iran. . . . Syria: Whatever happens in Syria, is there going to be a monitoring of levels of violence against women? Or what about Syrian women who give birth in refugee camps and can't pass on their nationality to their children. Anybody going to address that? Is that going to be part of the reconstruction plan? Are women going to have a say?[85]

And as the reader may have guessed, during the first round of the Syrian peace talks, there was barely a woman to be seen. In fact, Sanam Anderlini, cofounder of the International Civil Society Action Network, went so far as to write an open letter in May 2013 to the foreign affairs ministers of Canada, France, the Netherlands, Norway, Russia, Sweden, Turkey, and others urging them to include women, specifically Syrian women, in all deliberations on the civil war in that country.[86] As Syrian activist Hibaaq Osman quipped, "When we talk about women at the table, the men see them as the tablecloth."[87] In the second round, beginning in 2014, it was primarily the United Kingdom that pushed for greater participation by women—even though assessing "the number of local women participating in a substantive role or position in a peacebuilding process supported with US government assistance" is one of those nine new gender indicators put in place for the State Department in July 2013.

A significant degree of slippage is evident between what the U.S. government publicly declares it is doing and the actual reality. In addition to the examples given earlier, one of the best ways to identify the degree of drift is to pose a simple question: Where does the money the United States allocates for gender programming actually go?

Searching for answers, we discovered the larger question of USAID programming to be crucial to our understanding of what might be happening with gender programming. Learning about this arcane subject revolutionized our perspective, so let's wander into the weeds a bit.

When a USAID funds programming in fragile states such as Afghanistan, quite a bit goes for start-up costs; renting and refitting offices to meet ex-patriate expectations concerning housing and security. Typically speaking, foreign contractors enjoy higher standards of living and working than are common in the area. In addition, as we have seen, perhaps 30 to 40 percent of total funds are earmarked for USAID's endless reporting requirements. These indirect costs can be hefty. An example: when all costs were accounted for, the U.S.-based Louis Berger Group built 389 miles of Afghan road for what ended up costing a cool $1 million per mile.[88] Ann Jones estimates that as much as 80 to 90 percent of U.S. government funds goes to U.S. contractors and subcontractors for various services and overhead — and not for program services:

> Contractors understandably tend to charge what the traffic will bear; and the more money they ask for their services, the more valuable their services seem to the donor to be. . . . Successful contractors also know how to value themselves. They believe they're entitled to live well. So when a hot contractor with, say, 98 million taxpayer dollars to spend, brings in one hundred consultants and advisers (all men), it might spend a half million a pop. It might put them up in ten or twelve posh houses, each renting at about ten thousand dollars a month, in the most dollar-drenched part of town . . .
>
> Then it might tack on a little something extra to the six-figure base pay—say something for "danger," something for being "out of location," something per diem, and an expense account. . . . The rationale for squandering tax money in this way is that it's supposed to "buy the best people," but a surprising number of consultants and advisers working for contractors . . . will joke openly about how little they know about the task at hand. Like the high-powered lawyer I met at a party whose contract called for him to advise a government ministry on tax law. "I don't know dick about tax law," he said with a laugh. "Commercial real estate is more my line."[89]

While Jones' observations are accurate, it also depends on the contractor. Many contractors live in conditions of semicaptivity. While working with an agricultural project near the Iranian border, Leidl, for example, lived in a tiny conex (a shipping container converted into simple living quarters) and could only leave the compound accompanied by heavily armed bodyguards and outfitted in a flak jacket. Conditions were adequate, but humble. Moreover, working in a war zone can be dangerous. Andrew Natsios estimates that during his tenure, at least three hundred USAID contract staff were killed while undertaking assignments abroad.[90]

Nevertheless, it is just possible that Leidl was working for the wrong contractor—or, rather, a more responsible one, depending on one's viewpoint. One former Halliburton contractor told her that during the first three years of the so-called reconstruction of Iraq, Halliburton employees hunkered down in five-star hotels in Kuwait and Dubai—at up to $300 per night for two years. The interviewee, who prefers to remain anonymous, told Leidl that at any given time, as many as two hundred were posted in accommodations that can only be described as "beyond luxurious."

So where is the field oversight? Oversight may primarily take the form of USAID employees reading monitoring and evaluation (M&E) reports *prepared by the contractor itself*—a clear conflict of interest but also standard practice. Third-party M&E, as it is known, is rarely, if ever, undertaken, especially in conflict areas. Van Buren notes the State Department required that he bring rural women into the U.S. Embassy to have their photographs taken alongside embassy personnel because mission directors deemed travel to areas outside of Baghdad too dangerous. The same for Afghanistan, where Jones notes, "The well-paid USAID experts . . . live and work in a maze of white shipping containers behind the concrete and razor-wired walls of the Café Compound at Fort Paranoia, the American Embassy."[91]

Jones bitingly observes: "USAID education officials sit in their little white boxes and read the reports (via e-mail) of contractors who enumerate the 'indicators' of their certain success. It's mainly a numbers game: so many million books printed, so many hundred schools built; so many million children in school."[92] Harder-to-count outcomes, such as whether these children actually attended school after being enrolled—or even learned anything—are not part of the scorecard.

And Jones cautions the neophyte to not put much store in the quantitative information that is counted. She cites, for example, USAID reports that showed a marked improvement in the percentage of the Afghan population that now lives within an hour's walk of a health clinic. The reason is not, as USAID reports suggest, the presence of more health care clinics but rather because the percentage of internally displaced persons (IDPs) fleeing the countryside for cities has spiked so dramatically.[93] In other words, the more displaced people who move into neighborhoods with existing clinics, the more people are likely to be within walking distance of one! The fact that they are displaced, homeless, and probably starving is beside the point: They are located closer to a health care clinic than they used to be, and thus, according to USAID indicators, are enjoying improved access to health care.

What we've examined in this section may be the "bad," but there's worse. Besides cases of "looking the other way" and "box-checking," field workers point to the existence of what we will refer to as the "ugly pig problem"; that is, the unfortunate tendency of individual contractors and subcontractors to exploit women—undermining the Hillary Doctrine where it hurts most. Run-of-the-mill greed and indifference pale in contrast.

## The Ugly: Old White Guys

Jimmy loves Afghanistan.[94] At sixty-eight, divorced, and estranged from his two daughters, he has found a sense of belonging in what one U.S. colonel refers to as "the devil's rectum." His employer, a for-profit corporation that implements USAID development projects, pays him generously for doing, well, not so much.

During the short desert evenings and even longer nights, Jimmy likes to stretch out on a plastic chair, cigar clamped between his yellowing canines, and a bottle of smuggled spirits at his elbow. His sexual exploits, he boasts, border on the Herculean. "Seven times in one night," he burbles contentedly. "She was young but she couldn't get enough of me."

Jimmy would be firmly near the bottom of the dating sweepstakes in North America. But he doesn't care. "Girlfriends" come for five bucks a pop in this part of the world, and they'll do "anything." There are plenty of brothels in Kabul—otherwise known under the euphemism of "Chinese restaurants"—where women are trafficked in to service U.S. contractors and other foreign workers. When Jimmy is in the mood to splurge, he might splash out on higher-priced hookers in Dubai or Thailand, but generally speaking, he prefers to stick to Cambodia or Laos where the action is cheaper.

Jimmy likes them young and is none too troubled about whether his "girlfriends" are trafficked or not. "It's their culture," he replies airily, "they do it to support their family. Besides, I've never met a girl who says to me 'Look, I'm being held against my will.'"

The Jimmys of the world—noxious though their views may be—are not necessarily as harmless as they may seem. Because Afghanistan is a hardship post, recruiters find it difficult to locate seasoned and experienced staff. Although the recession has made it a little easier to hire and retain people, USAID requirements still stipulate minimum years of service in "fragile environments" plus education and technical expertise that is often so specific that it doesn't allow for much flexibility.

For more senior posts, in particular, this means that many promising female candidates won't qualify because women haven't been working in sufficient numbers or for long enough in hardship posts. For-profit contractors also earn a percentage for every position they manage to fill with any warm body that qualifies—with Americans at the top of the heap. It doesn't matter how committed these recruits are or are not so long as they possess the requisite experience in the right kind of post. Although not particularly captivating in person, Jimmy is a golden goose.

"I'd happily toss him off the roof or throw him down a well," says one of his former colleagues, a chief of party (COP; project heads hired by for-profit contractors to oversee the implementation of a USAID program) who is now working in Africa.[95] "Guys like him make all of us look bad." While, as we have seen, both contractors and subcontractors are strictly prohibited by U.S. law from purchasing commercial sex—even when off-duty—enforcement is lax to nonexistent.

Donald Steinberg, former deputy director at USAID, acknowledged that contractors are a problem, but anticipates the Obama administration in its second term would announce dramatic measures against those who procure sex. Indeed, the very last thing Steinberg did before leaving USAID in July 2013 was to e-mail every single mission director a copy of the antitrafficking code of conduct.[96] Nevertheless, serious problems remain, even though the inspector general's office at USAID maintains it is willing to take any and all complaints.[97] Equality Now has even threatened to sue the U.S. government over the behavior of its contractors. Indeed, this type of strategic litigation may be the only way of forcing the government to act. But again, how the government will actually enforce any new regulations is another matter.

"The biggest obstacle to implementing programs that will benefit women is USAID itself," declares Molly, a fifteen-year veteran of USAID-funded projects who requested anonymity because she fears for her job. "It's stacked with old white guys."[98]

Molly has been working as a gender advisor on a USAID-funded project in Kabul for years now. Formerly stationed in Pakistan and other hardship posts, she is fully cognizant of the good, the bad, and the ugly of USAID programming. She also knows that the stakes in Afghanistan are unusually high. But although Molly says the State Department made welcome progress under Hillary Clinton and Mary Fontaine, USAID's senior gender advisor for Afghanistan, too few in-country USAID employees fully understand why gender programming is so critical. The primary reason behind this lack of knowledge lies, she says, in the "gender composition of the mission and projects themselves."

"It seems like a lot of COPs are selected because they have gray hair and a penis," observes Molly. "It doesn't seem like they are vetted for quality, development skills or a sound development philosophy. I don't think they even think about women enough to have some kind of hard line position against women. They are dealing with their political world," she adds thoughtfully. "Because there are no women, women are kind of a non-entity. It just doesn't even enter their universe."

In 2011, under the leadership of Fontaine, USAID required that all projects new and ongoing undergo a gender analysis to determine to what extent implementers were mainstreaming gender into existing projects and into the proposals of those up for tender. The response? There has, Molly says, "been enormous resistance within the Mission" not only to gender analyses but to gender programming in and of itself. "When we have the interim or exit briefings it is not only USAID, but also Afghans and Americans who insist that 'Oh no, we cannot do that. It's not within the scope of the project!'"

"It [the gender analysis] was supposed to be a baseline study, with concrete recommendations about how implementers should proceed," says Molly. "But what we found was that USAID didn't share the analyses with project heads. Even though the gender analysis had been finished nine months before the project was awarded, the [implementers] couldn't integrate it because they never received it until it was too late!"

Moreover, according to Molly, even the few women working for USAID tend to back down in the face of pushback owing to a combination of ignorance and fear that they will risk "career suicide" for "sympathizing with those gender people."

"I expect it isn't the way to get ahead," she muses. "They look at [gender programming] as a social program rather than a development objective."

But Sarah, another gender expert, asserts that attention to gender is the only way to undertake successful development programming.[99] "Development is really a long-term transformational process," she says. "But in the USAID way of doing things it is much like the American car company take to car manufacturing where success is determined by car sales. Development doesn't work like that. It isn't just about how many people received how many days of training or cookstoves: it's about people doing things in a different way and it takes time."

Delia is a 53-year-old grants professional who initially cut her teeth in NGOs such as CARE and Save the Children. During the past fifteen years, she has worked almost exclusively with USAID in Africa, Pakistan, and Central Asia.[100] Although the "gender situation" is now "better," she confirms that a lack of awareness both within the USAID mission and at the project level is why "gender programming just isn't getting off the ground."

Not only does Delia continue to see multimillion-dollar project proposals that don't so much as mention women—a shocker in a country where half the population is severely disadvantaged—but when they do, it usually involves teaching women kitchen gardening, sewing, or hairdressing. "Not exactly a decent livelihood," she notes dryly.

The end results often tell the tale. In one project for example, implementing agricultural experts came up with the idea of training farmers in high-value greenhouse horticultural techniques. Upon the completion of training, each male farmer received a brand new, full-size greenhouse, along with seed and other farming "inputs."

The women? "Our (green) houses were very small and some of us have to share," says Malala, head of the local women farmer's cooperative gesturing at a greenhouse the size of a tall pup tent. "We make up at least one third of all the farmers here," she adds bitterly. "We have mouths to feed and no man to provide for us. The US ignores us and gives money to village men who are already very rich." As Ann Jones comments, "what passes for development is delivered from men to men, affirming in the strongest possible terms the misogynist conviction that women do not matter."[101]

Another case in point is the Land Reform in Afghanistan (LARA) project. When it was first tendered in 2010, the $140 million contract placed unusually progressive stipulations on contractors: that women title holders increase by 50 percent, and that the importance of women's land rights be regularly covered in the media and in the curricula of secondary schools and universities. This requirement was critically important not only for Afghanistan but is arguably of global importance. Women grow an estimated half of all food worldwide (in sub-Saharan Africa that number jumps to 80 to 90 percent) yet own less than 2 percent of the world's agricultural land.[102]

Before the contract was awarded, however, USAID reversed itself and stripped the bid of all gender-related stipulations—even though the implementer had done its due diligence, budgeted and planned accordingly, and already enjoyed a decent reputation for successfully implementing gender programming. For reasons that still remain obscure, USAID then altered the tender to require that the implementing agency only "study the issue" of female inheritance, even though the original contract itself fatalistically stated, "meaningful reform may not be possible."[103] Soon after, the *Washington Post* infamously quoted an anonymous U.S. senior official who said, "Gender issues are going to have to take a back seat to other priorities. There's no way we can be successful if we maintain every special interest and pet project. All those pet rocks in our rucksack were taking us down."[104]

"Basically, if some aspect of the program is going to be jettisoned it will be gender," says Delia. "Some of the (implementing) companies actually take it more seriously than USAID, but unless you have a mission director who is actually invested and understands, it just won't happen." Currently, about 46 percent of mission directors listed on the USAID website are women, so there's potential for turning this situation around.

Perhaps more important for our analysis, more and more COTRs are actually hired locally and are overwhelmingly male—which means they may be as blind to the gender injustices of their own region as those they are mandated to enlighten. Needless to say, these types of attitudes fly in the face of the evidence about what works in development programming. Numerous studies show that when more women are involved in the planning, implementation, evaluation, and monitoring of development programs, not only are the needs of female beneficiaries more likely to be taken into account and met, but the project as a whole benefits from a more equitable and less corrupt management style.[105]

"The fact of the matter is that if you are really looking for stability, then you have to empower women," says Molly.

## Addendum: Boneyards and Burn Rates

Things are winding down in Afghanistan. As the date of the coalition drawdown nears, even though 10,800 U.S. troops will remain for the foreseeable future, the watering holes where diplomats, aid workers, journalists, and contractors all used to rub shoulders are looking a bit worn. No longer are the bars stocked with the most expensive liquors, while the pool of restaurants that serve booze continues to shrink as demand withers. Many are closing their doors altogether as their owners try to figure out where to go next. Syria perhaps, or Iraq, Burma would be nice. . .

Local staff are bored and barely able to contain their resentment of "the occupiers" who will soon return to their homes in the United States, Canada, or Europe far away from the violence that grows ever worse by the day. The more friendly (or terrified) among them are more likely to pepper irritated customers with anxious queries about immigration and visas than to serve drinks or food.

The age of patrons has likewise undergone a dramatic change from those early years—these days they are either very young and just out of college or older, white, and invariably male. "We are scraping the bottom of the barrel," said one U.S. diplomat on the condition of anonymity. "Most of USAID staff are not here willingly. They are either obligated to be here before they can get a promotion or are about to retire."

"A preponderance of the COPs and DCOPs [deputy chiefs of party] are here because of the money," avers Molly. "They pretty willingly share that information with anyone who will listen. They talk about how they hate the place; how they hate the people. . . . Even if they aren't motivated by idealism or the desire to help, at least they could make sure that those objectives are followed—but they don't even do that."

While USAID implementers such as Jimmy and his ilk might be considered antediluvians pretty much anywhere else in the world, they still wield tremendous power in hellholes where no one else wants to go.

"You have to understand that these COPs are like gods," says Delia. "Most contractors are hired and can be fired at will, for no reason and for no cause," she says. "These contractors can be incredibly abusive, and many female staff just learn not to push the gender thing too hard because they can get canned."

Ibrahim S. is a chief of human resources who works with a large for-profit implementer that, for legal and security reasons, cannot be named.[106] In his early thirties, he is tall, well built, and articulate. "USAID projects are losing good people because they [staff] can't stand what they are seeing," he says, adding that contracts are written in such a way as to "effectively silence women." Furthermore, if the DCOP or a COP is an Afghan, "then they will bring all of their relatives into the fold." "Everyone," he says, hires according to "kinship ties and tribal affiliations." If the COP or DCOP is an expatriate, then he usually will stack the project with his cronies or "the women he wants to sleep with."

"Too many COPs and DCOPs prefer to wield power at the expense of programming," Ibrahim S. notes. "It is like a powerful clique or mafia. All it is doing is making people [Afghans] angry. How can we have faith in 'democracy' when this is what it looks like?"

"If I were an American taxpayer I would be very concerned," he adds.

For locals, who are daily bombarded with messages about democracy, human rights, rule of law, and equal pay for work of equal value, the way USAID projects are run is nothing short of bewildering and not a little horrifying. "We were always led to believe that you [Americans] were better than us," Ibrahim S. says. "But we are experiencing the same problems at your hands that we did from Afghans. What then do we have to aspire to? Nothing."

Marina, a former COP with fifteen years of experience, blames old-fashioned chauvinism and misogyny for the problem.[107] "If a man behaves a certain way—takes hookers back to his room, screams at local staff, harasses female staff—it's fine, but if a woman wants to bring more of a gender focus into a project? Forget it: she's a 'bitch' or a 'feminist.'"

"One guy was evacuated from multiple countries with multiple Viagra overdoses but they kept on hiring him back," adds Delia, who maintained she has witnessed working staff fired for no cause aside from "the usual abuses that go with total power."

Sexual harassment is another issue that tends to get "disappeared." One young contractor, twenty-eight, who still lives in Afghanistan and prefers to remain anonymous out of fear that no one will ever hire her again, was working for one of the largest for-profit USAID implementers in the world when her COP took an "unpleasant" interest in her. "He made passes at me, he was always calling me up to his room for a drink and just wouldn't leave me alone." One evening, after he returned to Dubai, he presented her with a gift of lingerie. "I was so shocked," she says. "I didn't know what to do." Concerned that the situation was getting out of hand and her job was in peril, Maya (a pseudonym) contacted the company's human resources department for instructions about how to proceed. "They did absolutely nothing," she said.[108]

Well, not quite. The human resources department notified the COP, who became so incensed he arbitrarily moved the young woman's sleeping quarters right next to the "poker" room (or as they called it, the "poke her" room) where she could hear every word of the sexually explicit discussions between male personnel about female staff—including herself.

"I finally had enough," she says. "I was a wreck and he [the COP] was intentionally trying to get to me." She left but has not yet been hired for another USAID-funded post. "I can't say for certain, but I think the COP blackballed me. It [development] is such a small world and everyone knows everyone else." Yet another female staff member with yet another USAID-funded project recalls one COP who used to quietly "creep up" on female staff—including Afghans—and "sniff us."

"It was the oddest thing," she says.

Adds Laura, who used to work in logistics, "One of our local staff, a really great enlightened guy, once came up to me and said, 'You seem like a really nice woman. How can you work with such pigs?'"[109]

"Apparently the COP and the DCOP used to discuss how they would pay young girls to have group sex with them in Dubai and Thailand right in front of the Afghan male staff."

" 'Good question,' I said to him. 'How do I work with such pigs? I ask myself that every single day but bottom line: if I wasn't here then we'd have no female staff at all.' "

Although Marina credits the State Department under Hillary Clinton for the fact that it "has gotten better," she adds that, "just because it's better than before, it's not as good as it could be. We can't let that be enough. It still doesn't make it right."

Why are USAID and its contractors scraping the bottom of the barrel when recruiting personnel in fragile states such as Afghanistan and Iraq? As we have mentioned earlier, part of the reason is simple: These are war zones, and even during a recession it's still difficult to recruit people to work there. But we opened this chapter with a survey of other, larger forces at work that are also shaping how U.S. foreign aid is actually administered on the ground. It's time to talk more in depth about *burn rate* and how this plays into the ugliness we've described in the programming world.

To understand burn rate, recall our earlier discussion about the GPRA system, signed into law under President Clinton, which puts all agencies, including USAID, under a framework where for every dollar given, the agency has to come up with quantitative measures to show the effect that dollar bought. Remember, too, that during the G. W. Bush administration, USAID's budget effectively tripled, and the budget has gotten even larger under the Obama administration. And lastly, remember the law of government budgeting: if an agency does not spend its allocation for the fiscal year, not only will the government take back what remains at the end of that year, but it will cut off the offending agency's budget for the upcoming fiscal year. Keep these three facts in mind, and the problem will begin to come into focus.

On the surface, this all sounds good. If an agency can't show that it utilized government and taxpayer funds effectively it raises the specter of embezzlement, which in turn jeopardizes government credibility and leads to accusations of corruption. Moreover, a bigger foreign aid budget represents good PR—especially for the United States, whose percentage of GNP dedicated to foreign aid is nothing to brag about. And lastly, why should Congress give an agency any more of the taxpayer's hard-earned money if it hadn't spent it the previous year? It all sounds pretty reasonable and would improve the U.S. foreign aid system.

Alas, put it all together, and the result is a system of perverse incentives. An agency like USAID is only rewarded—or even just not punished—by the system if it spends a lot of money, fast, and counts only those outputs that are easy to count and look the most impressive. And because there are fewer USAID personnel, they can't possibly monitor all projects. As we have seen, this means the contractors are responsible for most of the legwork—including monitoring and evaluating their own efforts, which represents a clear conflict of interest.

"There's just so many things you can go to jail for now," said Natsios, explaining why USAID turns to contractors for the very information it needs to monitor the contractors. The contractors are then responsible, not USAID, if outcomes are questioned by government inspectors.

This, explains Natsios, is why our foreign aid system is fundamentally incapable of living up to our own principles. "It may be irretrievably broken at this point," he says.[110] "That is why we build up a lot of schools and print up a lot of textbooks, but we actually aren't looking to see if anyone goes to school or reads the books or even becomes educated. Just count the number of schools built and books printed, and burn through that budget as fast as you can so you can justify asking for more money next year to do it all over again." Natsios comments,

"The oversight process was not designed for foreign development programming, where there's simply not the technical expertise for the type of compliance the IG and GAO are looking for, and where you need to take a longer-term perspective than that of year to year."[111]

He continues:

While I [was at USAID] we moved to shorter time horizons of five years because we were trying to do more crisis management and conflict resolution programming which by nature has shorter time horizons. Since I left office and the new budgeting system was put in place controlled by the State Department, USAID program officers tell me programs are reviewed annually and so every program is at risk each year if it doesn't produce results. It is a crazy system; given one year, it's impossible to produce a serious development program. The State Department has a time horizon of two years at most because of the nature of diplomacy, which is reactive. So the more intimately State controls AID, the shorter the time horizons have grown.[112]

"The sole objective is to meet the numbers and that is what a project is judged on," says Molly, who describes working on one project where the implementing firm was struggling to meet its burn-rate requirements. The contracting firm would hire a second organization every time it would do a training—effectively hiring two organizations to teach the same subject to the same people.

"They figured they could bring up their numbers that way and it worked because all they needed to record was numbers—and not whether the people they trained knew more about the subject after than they did before. . . . It is transactional development versus transformational," she adds, noting that the former simply counts the numbers of beneficiaries while the latter measures the impact on the community; on the economy; and in terms of the lives of the individuals it seeks to assist.

The system contains other, equally perverse incentives. In Yemen and Afghanistan, for example, USAID tends to focus programming efforts on only the most unstable provinces. Again, this makes a certain amount of sense; after all, development leads to stability, and stability is needed most where it's unstable, right? But as Leidl found out, Yemenis and Afghans tend to see it slightly differently. "It seems that the only way to attract American aid is to shoot them," says Ibrahim S. "It's become a joke here. You want US dollars, then go plant an IED."

Within this larger context of contractor self-M&E, the burn-rate sword of Damocles hanging over every project, and all the various built-in perversities, the check box for gender looks very trivial indeed. "It all depends on leadership," says Marina "If a COP says we're going to do this seriously, then it will get done. But again, in the leadership you have a lot of older guys who essentially say we've ticked this box, plopped this paragraph into the RFP, and we're done."

"They don't understand that this isn't just about women," says Marina. "It's not part of the 'feminist agenda'—which we hear *all* of the time—but it is about empowering men and women and the community, it's about making a society better."

Molly is even more blunt: "These old angry guys are ripping off an entire country of opportunities. Me, I can take care of myself, but what they are really doing is robbing Liberia, Pakistan, Afghanistan of its opportunity and US taxpayers of their money: and that is what really pisses me off."

This survey of the good, the bad, and the ugly of the Hillary Doctrine's implementation is instructive. It teaches us that even a smart, well-intentioned policy can founder when it butts up against indifference, antipathy, a perverse incentive structure, and home-grown misogyny.

What can be done? Is the system irretrievably broken? Before presenting recommendations for the future, in the next chapter we will address the issue of political will. We write this volume at a pivotal time. In a sense, the litmus test of the Hillary Doctrine will come in the short term, and it will take place in Afghanistan, after the drawdown of U.S. troops.

# 6

# AFGHANISTAN

★ ★ ★

*The Litmus Test for the Hillary Doctrine*

We will not abandon you, we will stand with you always . . . it is essential that women's rights and women's opportunities are not sacrificed or trampled on in the reconciliation process.

—HILLARY CLINTON[1]

The return of the Taliban will not undermine progress. . . . I have no doubt that there will be more Afghan young girls and women studying and getting higher education and better job opportunities. Even if the Taliban come, that will not end, that will not slow down.

—HAMID KARZAI[2]

Under the Taliban, a woman unaccompanied by a man would have her breast cut off. Now at the peace negotiations, the Taliban will get four ministries. What was the use of the fighting?

—SHIRIN EBADI[3]

I T IS HARSH land, occupied by a people as tough as the few sinewy trees that manage to struggle up through the parched desert. But it is Pashtun women—downtrodden, beaten, hidden behind burqas, and denied the most rudimentary education—who are the toughest of all.

One day in November 2009, in Helmand Province's capital city of Lashkar Gah, a group of widows and divorcees met with Patricia Leidl, who had been commissioned to write a series of success stories about USAID programming for Afghan women. All of the women were in their twenties, thirties, and forties but looked to be in their sixties.

Until very recently, none of them could work outside the home because they possessed no marketable skills, could neither read nor write, and were unable to leave their homes for fear of being killed. Not one of them had less than five children, and three of the seven women had more than nine. Some of the women mentioned that prior to taking part in the USAID program—which focused on tailoring and basic literacy—their children used to weep at night from hunger.

As Leidl prepared to leave, the women fluttered around her like dry moths, touching her sleeves and speaking all at once. "What are they saying?" she asked the young Pashto-speaking interpreter. "They are telling you to go back to your country and to ask your people not to abandon them. The women of Afghanistan don't want you to leave. They will quite literally die if the Taliban return," she said.[4]

During a question-and-answer session at a U.S. university in 2010, a student bluntly asked then-CENTCOM commander General David Petraeus whether anyone thought to ask the women of Afghanistan how they felt about U.S. hopes to incorporate reformed Taliban into governance structures as the United States draws down its forces in the country.[5] In an answer that carefully sidestepped the most important noun—*women*—the general assured the questioning student that only moderate Taliban would be eligible for such rehabilitation. Left unaddressed was the definition of *moderate*, which clearly depends, at least in part, on your sex.

As for *rehabilitation*, what exactly does that mean? That the Taliban will no longer terrorize women and deny girls the right to be educated— is Hamid Karzai's assertion to be believed on this point?[6] Before talks were even slated to begin, Karzai told Zainab Salbi, founder of Women for Women International, that Afghan women would have to "compromise on mobility and dress" for there to be peace.[7] But given no women were even involved in any negotiations with the Taliban, who exactly was offering such compromises on behalf of Afghan women? Derrick Crowe speculates:

> There is a very powerful set of anti-women's-equality caucuses already nested within the Afghan government that the U.S. supports. These individuals and groups are working to reassert the official misogyny of the Taliban days *already*, independent of the reconciliation and reintegration process. Given the opportunity, these individuals and groups in the U.S.-backed government will manipulate the reconciliation and reintegration process and leverage armed-opposition-group participation in the process to push through policies they'd prefer already as *compromises* with their "opponents."[8]

For the women Leidl met that day, the return of the Taliban combined with the drawdown of U.S. forces—whose presence had signaled that the U.S. was involved enough in Afghanistan to pay attention to any backsliding on women's rights—will likely foreshadow an end to their nascent independence and possibly the end of their very lives. Every female foreign aid worker in Afghanistan we have met shares this view, even now that the Karzai regime has stepped aside in favor of the Ghani/Abdullah power-sharing government.[9] The 2014 Status of Forces agreement, providing for 10,800 U.S. military advisers to remain, most to be stationed in Kabul, does not really change that calculus, despite Ashraf Ghani's more forward-thinking views on women.

Said the young interpreter as Leidl climbed back into the armored SUV, "They [Afghan women] will be killed or starved to death. Their [daughters] will be treated like dogs. They want you to return to your country and tell your leaders that the coalition is their only hope."

Donald Steinberg, former deputy administrator of USAID, admits, "If I were an Afghan woman, I'd be petrified, too."[10] Ryan Crocker, who served as U.S. ambassador to both Afghanistan and Iraq, puts it even more bluntly: "One graduate who goes to the American University [in Kabul] said to me, 'I'd die before I'd wear a burqa.' And what occurred to me is, 'Maybe you will. And we will be responsible because you know it was at our urging and with our support that women stepped forward.'"[11]

## THE LITMUS TEST

There is no U.S. foreign policy issue more closely tied to the Hillary Doctrine than that of the plight of Afghan women, which the Bush administration made part of the justification for the original invasion by U.S. troops. Since then, U.S. government has invested the better part of a billion dollars to ensure a brighter future for women and girls of Afghanistan,[12] and the American media and public have also consistently demonstrated a high level of continuing interest. While it was the Bush administration which first organized gender programming in Afghanistan, former Secretary of State Hillary Clinton and Ambassador Melanne Verveer were even more adamant in their stance that the future of Afghanistan is tied to the future of its women.

In other words, unlike other policy issues that fade after several news cycles, high-level officials were focusing more attention on this country's women moving from the Bush administration into the first term of the Obama administration—not less. As noted at the beginning of the chapter, Clinton even promised Afghan women that the United States would never abandon them and would stand with them "always." If there is any place on Earth where it should be possible to evaluate the promise of the Hillary Doctrine, it would be here.

## THE PEACE OF THE BURQA

While virtually no Americans now remember, many Afghans recall that in the late 1980s before the civil war and the subsequent Taliban takeover, "70 percent of teachers, about half of all civil servants, and 40 percent of doctors in Afghanistan were women."[13] Until the mujahideen and then the Taliban imposed severe restrictions on their ability to work, Afghan women actively headed humanitarian relief organizations and worked as journalists and university professors.[14] Although many today cite "cultural reasons" as to why the United States and its partners should not intervene to protect the rights and physical security of Afghan women and girls, the truth is that before the advent of the mujahideen, Afghanistan was one of the most socially progressive societies in the entire region.

During the 1920s, women won the right to vote and the first school for girls was opened in Kabul, and as early as the 1960s, the Afghan constitution guaranteed gender equality. In 1977, women constituted 15 percent of Afghanistan's highest legislative bodies—something many Western democracies had not yet achieved by that date.[15]

The Soviet invasion of Afghanistan in 1979 ushered in a decade of proxy war. Although popular wisdom tends to mark the start of CIA support for the mujahideen as beginning after the former USSR invaded Afghanistan in 1979, in fact the intelligence agency was funneling resources into the Saudi-backed fighting force for at least seven months beforehand.[16]

In his 1996 memoir *From the Shadows*, Robert Gates, a former director of central intelligence, contends that the United States designated $500 million in nonlethal aid to counter the billions that Soviets were pouring into the puppet regime they had installed in Kabul.[17] The idea, he wrote, was to lure the Soviets into a Vietnam-like quagmire that would divert men, materiel, and resources while destabilizing the Afghan government.[18]

As is often the case, however, the United States did not then fully recognize that it was effectively making a "deal with the devil." As the cold war deepened in Afghanistan, it attracted fanatical Saudi jihadists—including Osama bin Laden—who brought with them their doctrinaire brand of Wahhabi Islam, which would eventually form the basis for the Taliban movement.[19]

In a 1997 interview with CNN, Jimmy Carter's former national security adviser, Zbigniew Brzezinski, admitted that during the 1970s, the United States organized and supported the mujahideen to fight the Soviets even before the 1979 invasion. Operation Cyclone involved not only American assistance, but also assistance from "the Saudis, the Egyptians, the British, and the Chinese."[20] Indeed, during the Carter years, Brzezinski had praised the mujahideen, saying, "We know of their deep belief in God—that they're confident that their struggle will succeed—that land over there is yours—and you'll go back to it some day, because your fight will prevail, and you'll have your homes, your mosques, back again, because your cause is right, and God is on your side."[21]

The United States did not stop with military aid but also undertook a fantastical indoctrination program in a bid to create subsequent generations of anti-Soviet jihadists. According to a 2002 *Washington Post* article, the U.S. State Department and the CIA spent millions of dollars during this time period to supply Afghan schoolchildren with smuggled textbooks stuffed with violent imagery and militant Islamic teachings. "The primers, which were filled with talk of jihad and featured drawings of guns, bullets, soldiers and mines, have served since then as the Afghan school system's core curriculum."[22] Even the Taliban used these U.S.-produced books when they came to power to indoctrinate young would-be fighters.

With the United States, Saudi Arabia, and Pakistan providing considerable financial and military support, the mujahideen inflicted a heavy toll on the Soviet Union, including the loss of an estimated fifteen thousand soldiers. In 1989, Soviet troops withdrew from Afghanistan, and the puppet government led by President Sayid Mohammed Najibullah was subsequently overthrown. The mujahideen alliance formed a new Afghan government and appointed Burhanuddin Rabbani as interim president. Within months, the alliance collapsed.

More fighting erupted, and within a year Ahmed Shah Massoud, a military leader and ethnic Tajik from the Panjshir Valley in Northern Afghanistan, surrounded the Afghan capital. Although Massoud had already proved his mettle as a military leader (and a war criminal), the United States continued to support Gulbuddin Hekmatyar, a religious fanatic favored by Pakistan. During this period of intensive civil war, Kabul changed hands several times, suffering wave after wave of artillery bombardment.[23] Ryan Crocker notes Kabul began to resemble 1944 Berlin, and that the death rate among women was probably higher than among men because the women were forbidden from leaving their homes to save themselves from even the worst of the shelling.[24]

After this bloody free-for-all, which involved countless war crimes and atrocities—including widespread rape[25]—Massoud and his men finally formed a coalition government with other warlords. Eventually, Massoud served as President Burhanuddin Rabbani's defense minister but retreated north when, with the help of the usual suspects such as

Pakistan and Saudi Arabia, the Taliban toppled the government and assumed power in 1996.[26]

The Taliban had by 1994 already emerged from among the rival mujahideen factions as a formidable fighting force, with their moniker roughly translating as "students of religious studies." The Taliban were originally poorly educated rural Pashtun youths primarily recruited from refugee camps and madrassas in neighboring Pakistan. Led by a mysterious character known as Mullah Mohammed Omar, the "Talibs" claimed that they would restore peace and security through the imposition of a strict Islamic code.

By the time the Taliban came to power in 1996, the population was weary of the three years of endless fighting, stealing, rape, massacre, and the endemic corruption of the mujahideen. With no functioning judicial system, many municipal and provincial authorities wearily turned to the Taliban's interpretation of Sharia (Islamic law) and traditional tribal codes of justice. It was harsh but it filled a vacuum. Few realized that the Taliban would become one of the most brutal and repressive regimes ever to wield power on Afghan soil, especially in relation to women.

But the Taliban were not the only ones who oppressed women in Afghanistan: their foes were vicious as well. This is important to remember: Nearly all of the anti-Taliban warlords wound up in positions of authority in the current government, and not one has been prosecuted for crimes committed during the 1990s civil war. Indeed, in January 2010, Karzai quietly arranged an official amnesty for all, Talib and anti-Talib, who had been involved in armed conflict before the formation of Afghanistan's Interim Administration in December 2001.[27]

Despite the cruelty of all players, it was the Taliban who systematized the oppression of women into a form of social, emotional, and economic control that represented something akin to misogynist genius. They moved against women to shore up their legitimacy within the country, paralleling the syndrome we explained in chapter 2, putting an end to education for girls while banning women from employment with only few exceptions, such as midwives. The Taliban enforced a dress code that included the muffling burqa, and women had to be accompanied by a male relative when in public. Violations of these rules would lead to public beatings—or worse. Maternal mortality soared to astronomical levels. The gender apartheid imposed by the Taliban meant, for example, that male doctors could not attend to women or girls. If there were no female health workers available, women were simply out of luck.

Jamila, a 48-year-old gender specialist who prefers to keep her identity secret, remembers when the Soviets controlled Afghanistan. "We could do almost anything we wanted," she says. "We were poor but we had freedom. When the Taliban came were still poor but had no freedom at all."[28]

After the Taliban fighters rolled into Kabul, Jamila, who worked as a teacher and helped support two daughters, was suddenly out of work overnight. She could no longer go out unaccompanied by a male relative nor send her daughters to school. All females, even girls as young as nine, were forced to don the tent-like burqa on pain of being beaten or killed. Massacres and other human rights violations continued—but in a far more systematic fashion than the atrocities undertaken by the mujahideen. Unlike the latter, however, the Taliban did not condone rape and severely punished anyone accused of it.[29]

The Taliban did not permit women to wear noisy shoes, and the windows of their houses had to be blacked out. If a woman accidently exposed an ankle or a forearm, Taliban enforcers would cut her arms or legs off.[30] The smallest infraction of the Taliban's dour code could lead to severe beating, immediate death, or public execution. Male doctors were forbidden to attend to women and girls, and hospitals closed all over the country as the health status of women and girls deteriorated and maternal and infant death rates shot up. "We lived in fear," says Jamila simply.

Without the extra income Jamila brought in, her formerly affable husband became withdrawn and angry. Before long, he began to internalize the prevailing Taliban culture and took to beating his wife. It didn't last long, though.

One day he fell ill with a gastrointestinal infection, and within months Jamila was a widow—with no income, nothing to eat, and responsible for two small girls. Because of Taliban interdictions against unaccompanied women collecting food from international donors, she was unable to even obtain food aid to feed her children.[31] Jamila fled across the border into Pakistan where she and her daughters eventually wound up in a United Nations High Commission for Refugees (UNHCR)-operated refugee camp. "I learned English," she now says of her time there. "So did my daughters. That's the main thing."

Some argued that the Islamists, though repressive, had at least brought order and security to the anarchy that characterized the post-Soviet collapse. But there was pushback: In the late 1990s, the U.S. group Feminist Majority under Eleanor Smeal waged a well-publicized campaign called "Stop Gender Apartheid in Afghanistan," attracting the support of numerous Hollywood celebrities. And of the few human rights groups that continued to operate in the country, Physicians for Human Rights (PHR) condemned the willful indifference that allowed the international community to ignore the plight of Afghan women. In a 1998 report, PHR stated:

> For nearly twenty years, the Afghan people have suffered the health con-
> sequences of armed conflict and human rights violations. That Taliban offi-
> cials now claim to be "restoring peace" to Afghanistan is perhaps one of
> the cruelest ironies of our time, as they have virtually imprisoned Afghan
> women in their homes and threaten their very survival. The "peace"
> imposed on that portion of the country under Taliban rule is the peace
> of the burqa, the quiet of women and girls cowering in their homes, and
> the silence of a citizenry terrorized by the Taliban's violent and arbitrary
> application of their version of Shari'a law.[32]

Shortly after the attack on the World Trade Center on September 11, 2001, the United States and its allies invaded Afghanistan and, with the help of the Northern Alliance, quickly drove the Taliban out of power. At the time, the Bush administration made it clear that although the primary aim of the United States was to rout Osama bin Laden, the liberation of Afghan women from the shackles of tyranny was another important objective. On March 12, 2004, President George W. Bush lauded the progress made in protecting and advancing the rights of women and girls: "Today, the Taliban regime is gone, thank goodness. Girls are back in class. The amazing accomplishment, though, is that Afghanistan has a new consti-tution that guarantees full participation by women. The constitution is a milestone in Afghanistan's history. It's really a milestone in world history, when you think about it. All Afghan citizens, regardless of gender, now have equal rights before the law."[33]

But in the time-honored U.S. tradition of "the enemy of my enemy is my friend," the United States made what human rights organizations roundly condemned as a serious mistake. In a bid to bring aboard the various warlords from among the anti-Taliban mujahideen, the State Department renewed its pact with the devil and invited them to join the fledgling government of President Hamid Karzai. Mariam Mansury of the Institute for Inclusive Security still feels a sense of incredulity even thinking about that critical decision:

> I wouldn't have brought the warlords to the table to decide Afghanistan's future. We brought every single one of these people to Bonn [in 2001]. I'm a realist and know this was important, but why *only* them? Why not ask anyone else? It baffles me. I want to ask Ryan Crocker [former U.S. ambassador to Afghanistan] why. It borders on stupid. The bad guys would be at the table, yes I understand, but they sure as hell wouldn't have been the only ones. I would have out-numbered them [with others].[34]

One of the problems with the U.S. strategy was that many of these warlords had also committed atrocities against women and men. Most, if not all, were clearly war criminals. As the *Guardian* noted in a 2010 editorial:

> Repressive patriarchy is not exclusive to the Taliban, nor is it simply foisted on Afghan society by a minority religious junta. Many features of Taliban rule that are most distasteful to western political sensibilities are common also in areas controlled by tribal leaders and warlords loyal to President Hamid Karzai.
>
> There is not a clear line where political rights end and fundamentalist dogmas take over. There is not a clear distinction between those Taliban who are driven by ideological Islamism in the al-Qaida mould and those who have been recruited out of ethnic Pashtun loyalty, as mercenaries or to serve some labyrinthine local vendetta.[35]

According to an 800-page report compiled by the Afghan Independent Human Rights Commission (AIHRC), the new government included a rogue's gallery of former warlords who had raped, pillaged, massacred, and bombed their way into power during the post-Soviet civil war. In 2005, Karzai had reluctantly commissioned the study as part of a reconciliation and justice effort. Top forensics experts from around the world trained and advised the forty researchers who worked on the report from 2005 to 2011. They unearthed massacre sites, identified remains, and interviewed witnesses and family members. Unsurprisingly, the report never saw the light of day.[36] Karzai stripped its author, Ahmed Nader Nadery, of his position on the commission.[37] One of Afghanistan's vice presidents—named in the report—argued that Nadery should have been shot in the face instead.[38]

Although the report was suppressed, the *New York Times* managed to obtain a leaked copy. Among the high government officials named were First Vice President Fahim, a Tajik from the Jamiat Islami Party, and Second Vice President Karim Khalili, a Hazara leader from the Wahdat Party; General Atta Mohammed Noor, a Tajik from the Jamiat Islami Party and now the governor of Balkh; and General Abdul Rashid Dostum, a colorful Uzbek warlord from the Jumbush Party who holds the honorary title of chief of staff to the supreme commander of the Afghan Armed Forces.[39] Dostum enjoyed considerable notoriety for ordering his men to tie a soldier suspected of stealing "to the tracks of a tank that then drove around until he was reduced to mincemeat."[40] Indeed, their impunity is so complete that a number of these men ran for president in the April 2014 Afghan elections.[41]

In terms of the Hillary Doctrine's application to Afghanistan, it is fateful that for the warlords and mujahideen that make up the upper echelons of the Afghan government, the issue of gender equality was always a completely unwelcome appendage to U.S. involvement. As Christine Fair of Georgetown University quipped, "The way the US tells whether they are good or bad is whether they take our money."[42] Whether they are war criminals or misogynists was not part of the calculus. These suboptimal decisions in the early days of the invasion would jeopardize some of the loftier U.S. goals, including those concerning Afghan women, as we will describe.

But first, the positive side of the ledger.

## GAINS

The U.S. invasion of Afghanistan in the wake of September 11 would focus the world's attention to the plight of Afghan women. Laura Bush's historic radio address in November 2001 highlighted the Taliban's repression of women as a significant element that underpinned the moral case for invasion. While we have noted in Chapter One that the Bush administration's efforts on behalf of Afghan women were sometimes fitful, important gains were made during its tenure, and further gains were made during the Obama administration.

Eager to demonstrate its commitment to democracy, in December 2003 the United States established a constitutional *loya jirga*, the most inclusive in the entire region and quite possibly the world, which included 100 women delegates out of a total of 502. The constitution approved in January 2004 guaranteed equal rights to men and women, not just to "citizens." The International Crisis Group interviewed Massooda Karokhil, an MP from Herat, who noted, "We thought it better to specify men and women and not just all citizens. We felt that if we didn't, men would say this is a male-dominated society, so the term all 'citizens' does not apply to women."[43]

From there, the newly created Afghan political system, with the prodding of the Bush administration, established a quota system ensuring that 25 percent of parliamentary seats be set aside for women.[44] Afghanistan also signed on to the Convention on the Rights of the Child (CRC), the Convention on the Elimination of All Forms of Discrimination Against Women (CEDAW), and the International Criminal Court (ICC)—which is noteworthy given that the U.S. government has refused to adopt any of these three international treaties. In the case of CEDAW, the Afghan government astonishingly signed the treaty without any formal reservations, which have been used by other Islamic countries to assert that anything in CEDAW that appears to contravene their interpretation of Sharia law will not be accepted. The Afghan government was, at least on paper, committing fully to implement women's rights in a way many other countries had not.

The constitution also called for the establishment of an independent human rights commission to monitor the implementation of these and other laws. The AIHRC is headed by Dr. Sima Samar, whom Ryan Crocker describes as "one of the most formidable women" he has ever met. "She and Karzai have a significant relationship. She always has access to him, and will tell him just what she thinks."[45]

In addition, the new Afghan government also established a Ministry of Women's Affairs (MOWA). Women also initially headed several other ministries, including public health, labor, social affairs, and the ministry for the disabled, though most of these positions were later transferred to male cabinet members.[46] Women have also made inroads in local politics: the first female governor of an Afghan province is Habiba Sarobi in Bamyan Province, appointed in 2005, who ran for vice president in 2014. In early 2013, the Karzai government also appointed the first-ever female district governor. Crocker describes other women in positions of influence and authority as well:

> A woman was chair of the Afghan Parliamentary Defense Committee. And boy, was she hands-on—touring installations, watching training, challenging the Afghan military leadership, challenging the American military leadership about the quality of training. . . . And the best provincial prosecutor in the country is Maria Bashir in Herat, backed by Karzai, protected by us. She is absolutely incorruptible, which is something that can't be said about very many in the judicial system in Afghanistan. And she is absolutely fearless in going after significant figures. But under constant threat of assassination. We fund a detail for her, including an armored car.[47]

Furthermore, Afghanistan now has a National Action Plan for the Women of Afghanistan (NAPWA), approved by its cabinet in 2008, which sets goals for the advancement of women in the country. One benchmark, for example, is that women to make up 30 percent of the civil service by 2018. Women are increasingly participating in the police force (1,974 women police officers in 2013, compared to less than 500 in 2007) and in the legal field (150 female judges in 2012; 300 female defense lawyers and 250 female prosecutors in 2013).[48]

In 2009, an important piece of legislation was passed by presidential decree (not by the legislature) called the Elimination of Violence Against Women law otherwise known as EVAW. This law criminalizes various practices that harm women, including underage marriage, rape, and the denial of inheritance. (It should be noted that this was the first time rape had been formally criminalized in Afghan history.) Afghanistan is now home to a small network of shelters, some run by MOWA and others operated by a variety of Afghan NGOs— though services are clearly insufficient to meet the need.

In addition to the expansion of women's rights, education and health indicators for women have greatly improved. Haidari notes, "Of nearly 5 million children in grades one through six, 36.6 percent are girls. The number of girls in high school almost doubled from 2007 to 2008, from 67,900 to 136,621 students. Some 8,944 university students graduated in Afghanistan in 2008. Of them, 1,734 were female students. These numbers continued to rise in 2009, 2010, 2011, and 2012."[49] Haidari adds that infant mortality has decreased by 23 percent since 2001. Maternal mortality has dropped as well: the World Bank estimates 327 deaths per 100,000 live births in 2013, down from 1,600 deaths per 100,000 live births in 2001. Though still ranking next to last in global maternal mortality, this is a stunning improvement.[50] As Melanne Verveer puts it, "Afghan women have said to me, 'We've gained more in the last ten years than we have in the last fifty years.' "[51]

The years since September 11 have without a doubt seen immense positive change for women in Afghanistan, particularly in urban areas such as Kabul. But what will the U.S. drawdown bring, even with the small number of military advisers to remain under the 2014 SOFA? Worrying signs abound.

## WORRYING SIGNS

Ethnic Tajiks live in the Deh Salah region of Baghlan Province in Afghanistan. This is anti-Taliban territory, where the Northern Alliance once held sway. But the local religious council issued a fatwa in summer 2013 that shut down all cosmetics shops and barred women from leaving their homes except when accompanied by a male relative. The response of the Afghan government? None whatsoever.[52]

This is but one of the many signals that concern Afghan women and their supporters. More ominously, in July 2013, the election law was amended to lower the quota for women in the provincial councils from 25 percent down to 20 percent. Says Oliver Lough of the Afghan Research and Evaluation Unit,

> Parliament has grimly carried on snipping away at guarantees of women's rights at every available opportunity. It's a similarly depressing demonstration of just how desperate the international community is to make the next elections presentable that no mention of the quota's reduction has made its way into the relieved briefings accompanying the Law's passage. And it's a worrying sign of where things are going that the erosion of the quota—which only a couple of years ago seemed relatively secure—suddenly feels like par for the course.[53]

Given talk in Afghanistan about how quotas for women are un-Islamic and even un-democratic, this does not bode well for the future: Indeed, unless Ashraf Ghani rallies stronger support, national quotas may also eventually wind up on the chopping block. As Melanne Verveer commented to Hudson, "As I sit here looking at you, I have no idea, nobody does, what's going to happen there with the withdrawal."[54] Heather Barr of Human Rights Watch is not so equivocal; in her view, these pre-drawdown setbacks for women are "making me think that the predictions of doom we have . . . are not dire enough."[55]

More alarming, the Afghan parliament has also set its sights on the Elimination of Violence Against Women (EVAW) law, possibly the most monumental gain for women's rights in Afghan history. In May 2013, when attempting to have parliament fully instate the EVAW presidential decree so that a new president in 2014 could not reverse it, female MP Fawzia Koofi brought the legislation before parliament. Two hours of contentious debate ensued, during which male MPs attempted to strip the law of provisions that curbed polygamy, early marriage, forced marriage, domestic violence, rape, and so on. They did so on the grounds that these provisions are, in their opinion, un-Islamic.[56]

The Karzai administration shelved the bill, sending it back into committee before parliament could vote on it, predicting—correctly—that it would be eviscerated otherwise. Female MPs worry what Karzai's successors will be tempted to do as they jockey for ascendance in the new power-sharing government; as we discussed in chapter 3, a common technique for new leaders to consolidate power in an unstable environment is to attempt to bond with other powerful men by subordinating women. With respect to the current political situation, Jenny Nordberg observes, "Taking a conservative stand on women's rights has become the necessary norm for every politician or influential power broker who wants to demonstrate his or her nationalist and Islamic credentials."[57] Reversing the presidential decree that led to EVAW might be seen as a master stroke by some hoping to out-maneuver Ashraf Ghani, who has been viewed in many quarters as "too Western." Indeed, in 2013 the International Crisis Group (ICG) interviewed a Wolesi Jirga member who noted how tricky this issue had been under the previous government,

> We asked the president [Karzai] to intervene [on behalf of EVAW], but he said the people from Helmand had told him they respected him because he didn't let his wife out in public, and visitors from Baghlan province had told him they disapproved of him signing the EVAW law. This means Bonn was only a slogan, the president is backing away from the pledges he made twelve years ago, and the conservatives are getting stronger.[58]

There is precedent for such a betrayal. The Shia Personal Status Law, signed in 2009 but revised in 2010, is an example of how an Afghan leader used the status of women as a political football, this time on the eve of the 2010 presidential election. While Shia are less than 20 percent of the population in Afghanistan, their political support is useful. The original law, which met with outrage from women's advocates both within and without Afghanistan, enshrined the right of men not only to control women and children, such as by mandating a wife ask permission of her husband to leave the house for any reason, but also to rape their wives. The resulting outcry led Karzai to place the law under advisement, but this tactic proved insincere; in March 2010, a revised version of the law was approved by parliament and signed by the president. Now a wife can deny her husband sex, but then he has the right to deny her financial support and even food.[59]

This is not the only case where Karzai waffled, and where other would-be Afghan leaders might see fit to follow suit. The Ulema Council, the highest religious body in Afghanistan, has recently opined that women should be forced to wear veils and that a male relative must accompany them outside of the home. The Congressional Research Service notes that Karzai endorsed their statement on March 6, 2012.[60] Another contentious issue is the new criminal procedures law, whose Article 26 makes it impossible for relatives—including the victim herself—to testify against an accused abuser. Karzai signed the law but then issued a presidential decree asserting that all witnesses in such cases can provide "voluntary" testimony, opening the door for the coercion of possible witnesses by perpetrators or angry relatives.[61]

If these shenanigans are not worrying enough, violence against prominent women is also rising. As described by the ICG,

> In 2012, there was a 10 percent decrease in civilian casualties, the first reduction since the UN started recording such casualties in 2007. Yet female civilian casualties increased by 20 percent, with 200 women and girls killed and 560 injured. In the first six months of 2013, the decrease in overall civilian casualties was reversed, and female civilian casualties increased further by 61 percent compared to the same reporting period in 2012.[62]

There is a real fear that women will be the battleground for extremist forces as the United States turns its attention elsewhere. Among those targeted are women who appear to have somehow transgressed into traditional male-dominated roles. Islam Bibi, the senior female officer in Helmand, was assassinated in July 2013; her successor, Nigara, was murdered under similar circumstances two months later.[63]

Bibi was only thirty-seven when she was attacked while riding a motorbike with her son in Lashkar Gah and was just one of a clutch of 32 female officers out of a 7,000-strong police force battling crime in one of the most conservative provinces in the Pashtun Belt. Like many of her female colleagues, Bibi faced unending opposition—not only from colleagues, extremists, and opium smugglers but from her own family as well.

In an interview with the U.K.-based *Telegraph* earlier in 2013, she told a reporter, "My brother, father and sisters were all against me. In fact my brother tried to kill me three times. He came to see me brandishing his pistol trying to order me not to do it, though he didn't actually open fire. The government eventually had to take his pistol away."[64]

Asked why she continued even when her life was in danger, she replied, "Firstly, I needed the money, but secondly I love my country. . . . I feel proud wearing the uniform and I want to try to make Afghanistan a better and stronger country."[65]

Bibi's death and the death of her successor are clear signals that women who have stepped beyond cultural boundaries could well be targeted despite the election of President Ashraf Ghani, who although a progressive, is in a weak and contested position despite purported primacy in the power-sharing government. Zohra Rasekh, former general director of the Foreign Ministry's Office of Human Rights and Women's International Rights, is pessimistic:

> With the US withdrawal and in the absence of a legitimate moderate government in place, there is no doubt that most of the Afghan women's gains, specifically, some of the protective laws, Action Plans and policies as wells as programs and services for women and girls, will either be abolished or ignored. Talibanism, other hardliner/fundamentalist regimes, corruption and continuing conflict poses great risks that would strip Afghan women from rights to public life, access to justice, healthcare, education and economic empowerment now and post US withdrawal.[66]

In addition to the steady erosion of hard-won gains, endemic violence and intimidation all but silence those women who dare to participate in public life. Male lawmakers often ignore or even threaten female lawmakers. Security threats keep women from voting or running for office. While women may sit on local councils, it is the men who are in charge of any development funds offered by the central government. MOWA is underfunded and lacking in influence. In 2012, UNICEF reported that "Only 20 percent of women aged 15–24 are literate more than a decade after the Taliban were ousted from power, and that number is three times lower in rural areas."[67] Only a tiny fraction of crimes against women are reported. Prosecutions and convictions are even more rare. For example, according to the AIHRC, only 400 of the 2,135 registered cases of violence against women in the second half of 2012 were prosecuted.[68]

To make matters worse, women who run away from their abusers may be accused of "attempted non-marital sex" (*zina*) and either returned to their abusive families or prosecuted for that crime. Police themselves are accused of perpetrating rape and honor killings.[69]

There are still not enough female police officers, too often because their male colleagues threaten violence, and not enough women's shelters, which have been attacked by the government and religious factions as being covers for brothels. Rural areas remain largely untouched by the progress women have made in urban areas. Women own only 5 percent of all businesses and remain significantly underrepresented in the formal labor force.[70] Female teachers and students are constantly threatened with violence, with incidents of acid attacks and even suspected poisonings recorded. A majority of brides in Afghanistan are still under the age of sixteen, which is the legal age of marriage, and estimates are that 70 percent of all Afghan marriages are forced.[71]

Indeed, Mariam Mansury suggests that part of the reason many in the West do not endorse an emphasis on Afghan women as leaders of social, cultural, and political change is because they see clearly the immense obstacles they face: "Women are at the forefront of changing Afghanistan, but the context is increasingly difficult for them to do so, especially in rural areas where there's been no change in women's status in forty years. Some men look at this reality and don't see how the women matter. There's a truth there. Look at what these women are facing. It's more than a rejection of the notion that women's empowerment could help change things."[72]

## LOOK AT WHAT THESE WOMEN ARE FACING

In far-off Kabul, Herat, and other larger urban centers throughout Afghanistan, the arrival of coalition forces signaled the end of the Taliban night and the dawn of an era with new opportunities and new hope. This was especially true for women and girls who, after years of virtual imprisonment and the denial of even the most basic rights and freedoms, were suddenly sprung from the shadows. For women and girls living here in the remote villages surrounding Farah, however, the transition from Taliban to post-Taliban barely even registered.

Fatima is among those who noticed little difference. "For us nothing changed," she says quietly. "Women have always suffered and we always will. The only thing we can hope is that our lives will be short and that we do not give birth to daughters. I would rather kill my daughter at birth than have her live a life like mine."[73]

The town of Farah in the southwest of Afghanistan is a bare place. Surrounded by bony hills and vast stretches of desert, it is a world and mentality away from the far-off capital to the north. Long ago, far back into antiquity, Alexander the Great trod this land along with a huge army that eventually conquered the entire area, known in those days as the breadbasket of Central Asia. The wetlands, flowing rivers, rich green foliage, jaguars, and herds of antelope are all gone now. Gigantic crumbling forts that appear from a distance like massive rectilinear mountains melt into an expanse that seems to march off into an infinity of stony beige.

Despite its unsparing ruggedness, however, Farah is home to an estimated 500,000 people, mostly Pashto speaking, who scrabble out a lean existence growing nuts, grapes, mangos, and other agricultural products, which, to an untrained eye, seems nothing short of magic given the unremitting bleakness of the environment.

Fatima was born in a tiny hamlet just west of here. The youngest of nine children, she grew up more or less confined to the family compound. As a small child, she was sometimes permitted to wander to and from the community well, occasionally searching for errant goats or hunting for chicken eggs. Only rarely did she partake of either: Protein was jealously hoarded for the men and boys of the family. Her belly constantly rumbled with hunger, and she would often spit up blood owing to the corrosive effect of stomach acids on her empty stomach. Her brothers all went to school, but she was prevented from doing so because she was "just a girl." Sometimes, at night, when no one was watching, one of her brothers, who is close to her own age, would read to her by the light of a single guttering lamp. She longed to go to school, to become a doctor . . . to be a boy.

On Fatima's ninth birthday, her father dressed her up, took her to a local imam, and, in a cursory ceremony, married her to a man forty years her senior. The man took Fatima away from her home, away from her parents, her brothers and her sisters—to a village sixty kilometers from the little dab of a community where she had spent her entire short life.

It was the first time she had seen the world outside of her own village. Her mother-in-law was an angry woman who beat her almost as soon as she entered the household. What followed, however, was even worse.

Her "wedding night" left her ill for weeks. Subsequent assaults left her almost unable to walk or to undertake the endless chores her new in-laws and husband demanded of her. She toiled from dawn to dusk, often doubled over in pain.

A few years passed, and despite numerous venereal infections and chronic cystitis, she somehow became pregnant at the age of twelve. "I stopped growing," she says, offering a wide white smile that contradicts the sadness of her story. At less than five feet tall, Fatima's pregnancy was almost too much for her tiny frame. Nonetheless, despite all she managed to give birth to a healthy boy—a miracle given she delivered unattended squatting over a hole in the ground specially prepared for her in a ramshackle outbuilding among the goats.

While pregnant, Fatima had hoped that the birth of a prized boy would change how her in-laws and her husband treated her. But the daily abuse, overwork, lack of food, and constant violent rapes did not cease. At fourteen, she was kicked out of the house when her husband sold her to another man. Her "second husband" soon abandoned her also.

At the age of seventeen, Fatima is now alone. She cannot read, she cannot write, and she has no skills. Her husband's third wife, who is little more than a child herself, cares for Fatima's son, named Mohammed, after the prophet himself, whom Fatima in a rare display of rebelliousness calls "the Prophet for men."

Fatima's first and legal husband is also a heroin addict and will not divorce her unless she pays him. The authorities also require a $500 bribe to hear her case. In Afghanistan, a man need merely declare "I divorce thee" three times in order to sever all ties with a wife and gain sole custody of any offspring. Not so for Afghan women. Without a divorce, Fatima cannot marry; without marriage she will not survive.

"Inshallah," she says, before her smile collapses into bitterness and she bursts into sudden tears.

Fatima's story is the kind of personal history that is so typical of Afghan women that it barely even warrants retelling in a country that still ranks among the lowest with respect to gender equality in the entire world.

In May 2013, Human Rights Watch reported that more than six hundred women had been imprisoned for the "moral crime" of running away from home or having sex outside marriage, a 50 percent increase from the previous eighteen months. According to the press release that accompanied the report, *"I Had to Run Away,"* these usually involved fleeing forced marriages or domestic violence.[74]

The New York–based activist organization described abuses including beatings, stabbings, burnings, rapes, forced prostitution, kidnapping, and threats of honor killing. Police rarely, if ever, investigated the abuse that forced victims to decamp in the first place, instead subjecting them to humiliating virginity tests or charging them with *zina* (non-marital sex) under the assumption that a woman or girl who is unaccompanied by a male guardian (or *mahram*) is looking to have sex outside of marriage. In Afghanistan, the latter is still a crime punishable by up to fifteen years in prison. "Virtually none of the cases had led even to an investigation of the abuse, let alone prosecution or punishment."[75]

Fully half of the women imprisoned in Afghanistan are in jail because they have been charged with moral crimes—including rape victims who are typically accused of *zina*. A case in point is the celebrated case of nineteen-year-old Gulnaz, a young woman sentenced to twelve years in prison after she reported that a cousin by marriage had raped her. The case came to light after the birth of her child, the offspring of repeated attacks. After the decision of the European Union to withdraw a documentary that it had funded exploring the plight of Gulnaz and women like her, the subsequent outrage over its suppression ironically wound up forcing Karzai's hand.

Authorities would release her, he said, provided that she and her attacker undergo mediation—the implication being that she would be freed if she agreed to become wife number two. Says Clementine Malpas, the documentary's British director, "She has told me that the rapist had destroyed her life because no one else would marry her after what happened to her. She feels like she has no other option than to marry him and it's the only way to bring peace between her and his family."[76]

In yet another case that made international headlines, in 2013 an Afghan court overturned the conviction of three family members accused of torturing, burning, and starving a young teenager in the factory town of Puli Khumr.

Like all too many Afghan girls, Sahar Gul was married off at the age of twelve to a total stranger in exchange for the equivalent of $4,000. Her stepbrother sold her, hoping that the dowry would settle the family's financial difficulties. Once ensconced in the home of her in-laws and far away from her family, Gul's life took a predictable turn.

Her new husband, a thirty-year-old soldier by the name of Gulam Sakhi, tried to force her into prostitution, but when she refused, he chained her to a basement toilet. For two years she endured almost constant torture at the hands of his mother and sister. When her uncle came to visit unexpectedly, he found little else but skin and bones. Photographs show a tiny girl, so savagely abused that she resembled not a teenager, but an enfeebled crone in the terminal stages of some horrible disease.

The fourteen-year-old could no longer speak or walk. Both her hands were broken, and her in-laws had yanked out her fingernails with pliers. They had also ripped out most of her hair. Gul was covered with deep bruises, and her left eyelid had been burnt with a hot metal rod. "In short, marks of torture and beating were visible all over her body."[77]

Despite the fact that her case sparked an uproar, women's right advocates point out that what happened to Gul is hardly atypical in a country where child brides are treated worse than livestock. Most are bought or are exchanged to resolve feuds or repay debts.

Among the more disturbing details was how local authorities responded to Gul's plight *before* her uncle discovered her in the basement toilet. According to Jon Boone of the U.K.-based *Guardian*, Gul had managed to escape before, but when she told local authorities of the abuse, they simply visited her in-laws and extracted a promise to "stop hurting her." According to a local community leader, the family felt they owned Gul and therefore she was obligated to "do as she was told."

According to the community leader, the family also paid hush money to local police and politicians to make the problem go away. Among these were Rahima Zarifi, chief of women's affairs in Baghlan Province, who told the *Guardian* that she could not remember the details of the case or why Gul was sent back home.[78]

Fawzia Koofi, an MP and women's rights activist, noted that even then, local authorities attempted to resolve the abuse through "traditional means. Basically they wanted the relative to sit down with his sister's abusers and work out an agreement," she said. Koofi also claimed there was strong community pressure not to publicize the case: "Many people don't take these sorts of crimes seriously and don't think they should be reported."[79]

Nevertheless, international outrage again spurred Karzai publicly to denounce all of those involved with Gul's prolonged torture. Once more, he vowed that the perpetrators would be punished accordingly. As usual, however, his words appeared to be more calibrated to international media and donors than based on legitimate concern.

One year after Karzai's declaration, the much-vaunted prosecution withered before the predictable blast of political, social, and judicial misogyny. On July 11, 2013, an appellate court let Gul's tormentors go free on grounds that there was insufficient evidence to support their sentences—even though Gul was not told of the new hearing or given a chance to submit her case. As it turned out, aside from the judge, the defense, and the accused, the court was almost entirely empty.[80] Though the original indictment was initially considered a landmark case upholding the prosecution of violence against women, the appellate court decision has only confirmed just how naive expectations of justice are in Afghanistan.

Gul's case has also attracted some international heavy hitters. After the release of the in-laws, U.S. lawyer Kimberley Motley joined the girl's legal team. Motley is determined to put the three back behind bars either through appeals or by pressing charges not included in the original indictment—including false imprisonment and underage marriage. She notes, however, that Gul's case is only one of a rising number of assaults and murders involving women that have never been properly prosecuted because of the "inertia or indifference" of those authorities tasked with protecting them. "I'm seeing more and more cases of women victims of . . . severe violence," she told the *Guardian*. "Things are going downhill really fast for the protection of Afghan women."[81]

Women who stand up for women are especially at risk. In a somber 2013 report, the United Nations noted:

Especially egregious was the killing of two directors of the Department of Women's Affairs in Laghman province in July and December by Anti-Government Elements. Both killings followed threats by Anti-Government Elements against the women in relation to their work with the Government on women's issues. On 13 July, Anti-Government Elements detonated a magnetic IED against the vehicle of the director of the Department of Women's Affairs, killing her and wounding her husband and daughter. Similarly on 10 December, two armed Taliban members shot and killed the acting Director of the Department of Women's Affairs in Laghman province.[82]

Needless to say, the two examples above are only a few of a growing number of attacks on women human rights workers—most of whom are not nearly as high profile. These activists, many of whom are very young, toil in the country's rural areas, working with the most impoverished women while having to deal with suffocating fear and the ever-present threat of assassination.

Hosiy Sahibzada, an eighteen-year-old living in Kandahar, was one these.[83] Kandahar is among one of the most dangerous urban centers in all of Afghanistan. A sprawling town of 500,000, it lies, or rather glowers, at the base of the southernmost knees of the Hindu Kush—"Killer of Hindus" in Urdu. At once impoverished and very wealthy, this extremist stronghold sports potholed dirt streets alongside concrete drug lord mansions that bristle with concertina wire and bad vibes.

For years now, Kandahar's warlords have become wealthy by operating illegal tolls and roadblocks and by smuggling drugs, weapons, and foreign jihadists in and out of Pakistan. Their houses, which resemble malevolent wedding cakes, are monuments to narco kitsch (and not at all dissimilar to those found in other narco strongholds in Mexico and elsewhere) and testify to the skill with which extremist criminals have manipulated foreign aid to suit their own economic and political agendas.

In 2009, Sahibzada described working for a USAID-funded project in the south of the country. Tiny and delicate, she nevertheless was preternaturally wise for her years. Every week she would cover herself in a worn burqa and make the long trek by bus and taxi from Kandahar to

Spin Boldak, a Taliban stronghold bordering Pakistan's Federally Administered Tribal Areas.

Although terrified, Sahibzada said she felt that she had no choice. She was teaching two hundred local women basic literacy and numeracy under the guise of training them in basic hygiene and pickling. All of her students, most of whom were adults, concealed this fact from their male kin. The reason? They would be killed—murdered—for simply wanting to learn how to read or write.

Despite her youth, Sahibzada instinctively grasped what few policy makers, development experts, and conflict researchers are either unwilling or incapable of doing. "I do this," she told Leidl, "for no other reason than because I believe that the only hope for my country lies in its women."

"I am very afraid but my anger is greater than my fear," she said. "No one should have to live as we live. This country will never have peace and it will never have security if we die for no other reason than wanting to be treated equally. It isn't right and it isn't fair."

A year later, Sahibzada was dead. Although initial reports pinned the blame on the Taliban, further investigation revealed it was her younger brother who threw her onto her bed, pressed a pillow to her face, and shot her in the chest. Apparently, his schoolmates had taunted him. His sister, they said, was "no better than a whore."

## THE KNIFE'S EDGE

The warlords are re-arming, and the Taliban grow increasingly bold in their attacks. At the time of this writing, a status-of-forces agreement that would keep about 10,800 U.S. military advisers in Afghanistan until 2023 has just been successfully concluded. Hanging over these deliberations was the historical precedent of the United States pulling up stakes and leaving Iraq without any status-of-forces agreement at all, a turn of events that Ryan Crocker calls "the height of diplomatic incompetence."

Is the situation of Afghan women hopeless if the Americans turn their attention elsewhere? Some think so. The ICG interviewed a female MP who states, "The mujahideen and the Taliban share the same stance on women. It's only because of the pressure of the B-52s that [they] accept women's rights, because they need US air support to maintain their military superiority over the Taliban."[84] What will that mean when the B-52s are gone? As Crocker puts it, "It is a fundamentally chauvinistic, traditionalist society. And that applies to those who hate the Taliban as well as those who are them."[85]

Christine Fair of Georgetown is likewise pessimistic: "The gains outside of Kabul are totally reversible," she says.[86] The mood of the average American is pretty grim as well. Steve Steiner of the United States Institute of Peace (USIP) describes it well: "After the Taliban period, we could talk to Americans, and maybe they didn't like our military involvement there, but we'd say, what about the women; you have to support the women, and they would agree. . . . But now it tends to be, yes, I'd like to support the women, but it's hopeless."[87] One unnamed official concurs, "Nobody wants to abandon the women of Afghanistan, but most Americans don't want to keep fighting there for years and years. . . . The grim reality is that, despite all of the talk about promoting women's rights, things are going to have to give."[88]

The Afghan peace process does not inspire confidence at this point. Even though the preconditions for Taliban leaders to enter negotiations are a renunciation of violence, a complete, formal break with al-Qaeda, and respect for the Afghan constitution, including its provisions for the protection of the rights of women and minorities, Ann Jones observes:

> In Afghanistan, Karzai names a High Peace Council [HPC] to negotiate with the Taliban. Sixty men. The usual suspects: warlords, Wahhabis, mujahideen, long-bearded and long in the tooth, but fighting for power to the bitter end. Thomas Ruttig of the Afghan Analysts Network reports that among them are 53 men linked to armed factions in the civil wars of the 1980s and 1990s including 13 linked to Gulbuddin Hekmatyar's Hezb-e Islami, currently allied with the Taliban. An additional 12 members of the High Peace Council held positions in the Taliban's Emirate government between 1996 and 2001.
>
> Under some international pressure, Karzai belatedly added eight women, the only members of the High Peace Council with no ties to armed militias past or present; they represent the interests of civil society, which is

to say the people who might actually like to live in peace for a change and do their utmost to sustain it. The U.S. signed off on this lopsided Council. So did Hillary Clinton, a woman who, as Secretary of State, has solemnly promised again and again never to abandon the women of Afghanistan, though she never remembers to invite them to a conference where international and Afghan men decide the future of their country.[89]

This is very worrisome. As Ryan Crocker pointedly notes, "You're not going to get peace, or certainly not a sustainable peace, if you don't have the whole population engaged. I mean if you exclude women, leave aside the fundamental injustice of it, you're going to get more of what you had. And what you had was pretty incredibly nasty. So, you know, we've seen what Afghanistan can look like when it's just the boys."[90]

Unfortunately, it looks like it's still just the boys. The women on the HPC have been relegated to public outreach and have not participated in any direct talks, with one male provincial council member interviewed by the ICG opining, "What can we do if the Taliban don't want to talk to women? We can't force them."[91] (Of course, women actually do negotiate with the Taliban—when a relative must be ransomed from them.)

There is good reason for women to fear that their exclusion will result in women's status becoming a bargaining chip within the negotiations. Rumors abound, for example, that the Taliban will allow the education of girls as long as their education is primarily religious in nature, girls and boys are strictly segregated, and the girls are prohibited from learning any English.

Mariam Mansury knows why educational restrictions are so important to the Taliban:

> The Taliban know what their threats are—it's not our bombs and drones. The biggest concern is their women with books. That's why they carry out attacks on women in schools and attacks on women in official positions. It's not just a belief that women are inferior. It's a fear that people will discover that [the Taliban's] beliefs are not based in the Koran. If women read the Koran and say [their beliefs are] bullshit, that will be the death of their movement in a very real way. The killing of these women show there's a recognition that there's a tipping point at hand. It's a tactic based in real fear.[92]

Malala Yousafzai, the young student shot by the Pakistani Taliban, concurs: "The extremists . . . are afraid of women. The power of the voice of women frightens them. . . . They are afraid of the change and equality that we will bring to our society."[93] Her conclusion? "A deal that goes against the rights of women is unacceptable."

But if the peace process isn't looking favorable for women, there's also a real concern that the absence of a peace process will be even worse. Why should the Taliban negotiate at all or agree to any U.S. "red lines," including respecting the rights of women? Perhaps they can have what they want without negotiating for it. Perhaps, as Esther Hyneman of Women for Afghan Women puts it, "They don't want a role in the Afghan government—they want the Afghan government."[94] According to Ryan Crocker,

> The High Peace Council—well, the good news there is it's going nowhere fast. . . . There was a deep suspicion on the part of women and minorities as what's going on. Is this going to be a sellout to the Taliban? Well, it's not. In fact, it's so much not a sell out that it's been very difficult to get Taliban officials to come out and play. . . . But Taliban-types [may be thinking], Why reconcile in a way that gives legitimacy to the new Afghanistan when all we have to do is outlast the Americans and we can get it all back? . . . [Some I have spoken to] said it was definitely the preponderant view in the Taliban leadership.[95]

It was all supposed to be so different. When the United States and its allies announced the end of the Taliban regime in November 2001, then-President George W. Bush declared, "The mothers and daughters of Afghanistan were captives in their own homes, forbidden from working or going to school—now they are free."[96]

Today, however, the same president who signed the multibillion-dollar Afghan Women and Children Relief Act on December 12, 2001, is far less sanguine about the future of the country's women and girls.[97] In a 2011 interview with Fox News, Bush told talk show host Greta Van Susteren: "My concern—is that the United States gets weary of being in Afghanistan, it is not worth it, let's leave. . . . And Laura and I believe that if that were to happen, women would suffer again. We don't believe that's in the interests of the United States or the world to create a safe haven for terrorists and stand by and watch women's rights be abused."

He added, "The idea of liberating women, empowering women, encouraging women, educating women in Afghanistan is all part of laying a foundation for lasting peace."[98] Peace may not last, then, in Afghanistan, for women's rights and women's safety are already being eroded well before the U.S. drawdown. The pace of that erosion will, we predict, only accelerate over time. The light is dimming for Afghan women once more, and the path ahead is unclear.

## THE WOMEN THEMSELVES

But even if fighting breaks out again, there are some who believe the women of Afghanistan will not be defeated easily. Ryan Crocker is one of those: "[Afghan women] certainly don't think it's hopeless and that it's all going down the drain and they're going to lose everything and it's time to emigrate. They're—you know, they're digging in for the fight."[99] Fariba Ahmad Kakar, a female MP held hostage by militants and then freed in a prisoner exchange, is proof of this: "I am even braver than before. . . . I will defend Afghanistan, especially the women, until the last drop of my blood."[100]

The factor that weighs most heavily in favor of a cautious optimism for Afghan women is the sheer length of time the Americans have been in their country—a dozen years and counting. Many see great promise in the generation that grew up without the Taliban ruling their lives; those who were able to attend school and experience the sense that there was a wider world beyond the borders of their own repressive country. Mariam Mansury comments:

> Last year, when I saw the policy direction moving somewhere else, I was terrified. Our mistakes like this always bite us in the ass. This is a repeat of the early 1990s. You'll have different competing warlords and mujahideen leaders vying for power. And somehow Americans are going to suffer for it due to a power vacuum. Now I'm just skeptical and disappointed. The 5- to 10-year approach to change was stupid. So many lives have been lost

and money spent—that sacrifice warrants us being smarter about moving forward. The concerns about abandonment are real.

But Kabul is not the same as in 1991. There's a new generation of inter-connected, tech-savvy young Afghans who won't go back, even if there is a return to violence. I'm hopeful. It will be 10 steps back, but not 30. Exam-ple, there was a recent student-led campaign against sexual harassment at Kabul University. It was an incredibly sophisticated multimedia campaign, LinkedIn, Twitter, sit-ins, etc. Very strategic. The women are not backing down and the young men are supporting them. This is the change we were hoping to see. The young don't want to go back. And they won't, even if there is a return to violence.[101]

A State Department official concurs: "It won't be like 1989. The forces of globalization are stronger now—Afghanistan can't go back to being an abandoned and isolated country. The cell phone coverage is amazing and they all have one. Everyone watches Bollywood and their kids are on Facebook. Once you have a cell phone, you won't give it up."[102]

Crocker, too, feels that the wind has changed in Afghanistan:

You know, Afghanistan's future, more than any other country, does lie in its twenty-somethings and early thirty-somethings—those who came of age and had their education post-Taliban. They are completely different from those guys and from their own parents, simply because they've had an exposure to an open media, open access to the Internet, a free exchange of ideas that has never existed in Afghanistan before.

[And] it's not [just Kabul]. The proliferation of cell phones and smart phones is ubiquitous in the country. And you know, one of the smart things we did—I won't say there were many—but one of them was to put up a robust telecommunications infrastructure country-wide. You know, there was one of the major private TV stations has a call-in show which is fun, I mean, because . . . the substance of it is, "What's wrong with this coun-try?" And there was a guy who called, who from, you know, Khas Kunar, you know, out there in the east just to say, "The country's gone to hell, the government is corrupt, you know, life has never been worse, yadda yadda yadda," and you know, the moderator said, "Where are you calling from?" and the guy says East Jesus Nowhere Kunar. He said, "Oh that's interesting, so how are you making the call?" The guy says, "Well, on my cell phone," and the response from the moderator was, "Just think about it a minute."[103]

Just think about it a minute—and see how far Afghanistan has come: that change in perspective may be important as we look toward the future. As Mansury sees it, "It's not a success or a failure. It's a blending of both, but more a success than a failure. This is a 50- to 75-year process and to think otherwise does a disservice to the reality on the ground. But it's a success given where we've been and where we are now. We must recognize where we are on the spectrum and what the trajectory is. Yes, [an indicator like] maternal mortality is still almost at the bottom, but the change is still real and still important."[104]

A recent survey underscores that change may be occurring right before everyone's eyes, even though few may recognize it. A survey done by the Asia Foundation in 2012 shows that 87 percent of respondents—male and female—agreed that women should enjoy the same rights to education as men.[105] And this is not simply conceptual: more than half of the graduates of the American University in Afghanistan in 2013 were female.[106]

And Afghan women are a force to be reckoned with, educated or not. One State Department official suggests, "We can't be paternalistic—or maternalistic—about Afghan women. We can't infantilize our partners. They may not have had our educational opportunities or exposure to media, but they are smart, canny women."

Says a female police chief, "I know what the danger is. I choose to fight for my country."[107] Sanam Anderlini insists that people should listen to what this chief is saying: "This 'my pet Afghan woman' attitude is very damaging. I despise the fact that people here think they are going to bequeath the gift of empowerment on these who have such courage. We undermine them in this way."[108]

Sima Samar, the redoubtable chair of the AIHRC, has this to say: "[Whether we hold] the gains in the last 12 years depends on the overall security and political situation in Afghanistan. It looks fragile for the moment. And I think it strongly depends on the women in Afghanistan and how strongly they stand to keep the gains and improve more on the gains that we have."[109]

But will they stand alone?

## THE HILLARY DOCTRINE
## AND AMERICAN WILL

There is no doubt that the U.S. invasion of Afghanistan altered the course of Afghan women's lives, opening up new opportunities that could never have existed under the Taliban. "There are a lot of reactionary forces out there that our presence, our influence, our engagement and our resources have done an enormous amount to keep at bay and to allow women the space to develop," says Ryan Crocker, and that space is worth defending.[110] Mariam Mansury agrees, "We did mess up. We are messing up. But we created a space for the women themselves. They own it and they're not going to give it up."[111]

But looking back a few decades in time will serve as a reminder that gains for Afghan women can disappear relatively quickly. Afghanistan before the Soviet withdrawal was a time of great advances for women in terms of rights and education and personal freedoms, but these were all swept away as the country plunged into civil war and then Talibanism. Will the same be said of the U.S. drawdown or is there a chance things could be different this time around? One of the eight female members of the High Peace Council, Hawa Alam Nuristani, puts it this way, "It's a men's country. Our only support is from the international community. What is the guarantee that we won't be faced with a similar regime as the Taliban when the Americans withdraw?"[112]

What is the guarantee, indeed? But remember, this time around the United States has espoused the Hillary Doctrine, with a detailed and legally binding framework obligating the United States to stand with Afghan women. The United States has also specifically earmarked hundreds of millions of dollars to help Afghan women during the transition, such as for the PROMOTE initiative.[113] Donor commitments base aid levels on the degree of protection afforded women's rights by the Afghan government, and there exist high-profile bipartisan declarations that "we must not abandon the women of Afghanistan."[114]

By all accounts, things should be different this time.

What seems to be lacking, however, is probably the most important element of an effective implementation of the Hillary Doctrine—U.S.

resolve, manifested from the Oval Office itself. U.S. foreign policy is a presidential affair in the end, and no secretary of state can effectively implement a set of priorities without steadfast support from the president of the United States. Did the Hillary Doctrine receive that kind of support from Barack Obama? The answer is no.

Unless asked a direct question from a reporter about Afghan women, Barack Obama ceased talking about them sometime in 2010, as if ditching a blind date gone bad on his way out of town. Charlotte Ponticelli, former senior coordinator of the Office of International Women's Issues (OIWI) in the Bush administration, quips, "Forget the walk; we don't even have the talk anymore."[115] Ryan Crocker is scathing in his critique:

> This is a disengaged president. You know the Obama that ran that 2008 campaign, which was I think probably the finest presidential campaign we've seen in 100 years, and the Obama who then occupied the Oval Office are two different people. And he's become more withdrawn, more disengaged with passage of time. . . . If I hear any more about ending wars—well, you don't end wars by disengaging. You end wars by prevailing! And that means you may shift from a military instrument to economic and political instruments but you're not going to end them if you just abdicate the field.
>
> And that's what we seem to be doing in Iraq and in Afghanistan and I've worked pretty damn hard in both countries to set in place the architecture for sustained, long-term US engagement but those agreements only have meaning if they are given content and we are not giving them content. . . . You know, any time you hear the president talk about Afghanistan it is about ending the war in Afghanistan—by leaving. You know, that isn't going to end the war; that is simply going to let our adversaries have a field day. But he reads the American mood and either doesn't know or doesn't care what the consequences could be.
>
> Because we didn't fumble the ball in Afghanistan in terms of [gains for] women. We're about to fumble by not stepping onto the field. You know, it's not that we're trying hard and might screw up. I don't see us as trying. . . . And a lot can be done just with the bully pulpit. Again, we are not without influence even without troops. But you've got to use the influence.

So, you know, please, administration, recognize what we've done and recognize that it has to be protected, and nowhere is that more important than for the women of Afghanistan. You know, the forces of darkness are just waiting and as we agree, they are not just the Taliban, it's the thrust of Afghan society. And the only entity can stand against that is the one who has stood against it so far, and that's us.[116]

Gayle Tzemach Lemmon suggests a possible explanation for this unaccountable stance: Perhaps the mindset of the president has become synched with the mindsets of the men with whom he has surrounded himself. She quotes an unnamed senior official as saying, "These guys don't get it. Ten years on we still have to make the case that women are additive."[117] That infamous photograph of Obama in the Oval Office surrounded entirely by male cabinet members—and the one leg of Valerie Jarrett visible—may not be the context in which the Hillary Doctrine will flourish.[118]

Sanam Anderlini concurs: "Her president isn't behind her. You're raising expectations of the women, you're making it part of the American agenda, and then your own guys don't follow through. They're the first ones to sell you down the river. One US official told me, 'The issue of Afghan women is not our issue.' They didn't take it seriously, they were late to it. . . . Don't just talk about it and then behind the scenes let it all go."[119]

As Ryan Crocker phrases it, "No one is going to be dumb enough to say, 'Oh, forget the women. That's not important.' But the extent to which you have the commitment, you know, to actually get things done, is a little harder to gauge."[120] To expect these men, who have spent all of their professional lives almost exclusively in the company of other men, to champion women's rights is perhaps asking too much. Ironically, that's what is said about Afghan men, too, isn't it?

Esther Hyneman of Women for Afghan Women is unhappy with this state of affairs, noting, "I am at my wit's end at the lack of discussion by the media, by our government, by our president on the issue of women's rights in Afghanistan. . . . I am appalled that [Obama] has not mentioned Afghan women's rights since his speech on withdrawing US troops. . . . We are in favor of peace, but this is not the road to peace, it is the road to bloodshed and subjugation and civil war, a repeat of the years past. Everyone will be sitting in front of their TV sets wringing their hands as we see women brutalized."[121]

In a very real way, Obama's abandonment constitutes a betrayal of the women of Afghanistan—as well as of all those women and men who dared hope that Afghanistan would be the Hillary Doctrine's proving ground. The rights of women and girls continue to be cynically disregarded even as the coalition mumbles about the necessity of gender equality in almost the same breath as it speaks of engaging "moderate Taliban." Ann Jones poses the question: "We can bomb the hell out of their country and set up a puppet government, but we can't interfere in how they treat their women?"[122]

Plainly, something is amiss. A shameful U.S. tradition is developing, one of leaving women no better off (Afghanistan)—or even much worse off (Iraq)—than before U.S. troops intervened. When Crocker is asked point-blank whether the United States did any good for women in Iraq, he lets out a bitter chuckle, "No!"[123] On the basis of the U.S. track record, it is hardly surprising that women worldwide no longer have any faith that U.S. intervention will improve their security. The Obama White House has indeed fumbled the ball for women: it was dropped as if it were a "pet rock" instead.

In a sense, then, Afghanistan is not the litmus test for the Hillary Doctrine and cannot be; for that, the United States would need a president as committed to the Hillary Doctrine as Hillary Clinton herself. Perhaps there will be such a president in the future. But for Afghan women it could be a few years too late.

## IF THE UNITED STATES WERE SERIOUS

If there were a proponent of the Hillary Doctrine in the Oval Office, how would she or he support Afghan women?

First, the deafening silence on the subject would end. The president would be talking—incessantly and publicly—about how America's eye is fixed on the future of Afghan women. Ryan Crocker puts it this way:

What I'm not hearing are senior administration voices saying, we understand reality, but here's reality that we also have to understand: if we do not continue to support Afghan women, they're going to get it in the neck, literally. . . . These women stepped forward because we encouraged them to do so. And in so doing, implicitly we said, We got your back. And if we decide that we don't have their backs, then we're responsible for what happens. Do we want to live with that as an administration? As a people? I don't think we do. It isn't a hard case to make. But I don't see the White House or the State Department or the administrator of USAID standing up and saying it.[124]

The U.S. secretary of state, John Kerry, would also be speaking out about these issues. Although Kerry met with Afghan women entrepreneurs while attending to other state business less than two months after his confirmation, eight full months of silence followed. Indeed, the hush had become so loud, rumors abound that it was Hillary Clinton and Laura Bush who arranged for Kerry to join them on November 15, 2013, at Georgetown University to speak about the future of Afghanistan's women. That very morning, Laura Bush had published an op-ed in the *Washington Post*, entitled "Afghan Women's Gains Are at Risk," in which she penned, "I worry that the message we are sending to Afghan men, women and children is that their lives are not worth our time or attention. That message must change. We cannot abandon them."[125] And Hillary Clinton introduced Kerry warmly by hopefully asserting, "We have an advocate for the women and girls of Afghanistan in Secretary John Kerry."[126] Kerry then spoke:

Creating opportunities for women is not just the right thing to do, it's also a strategic necessity . . . there is no question in my mind that investing in Afghan women is the surest way to guarantee that Afghanistan will sustain the gains of the last decade and never again become a safe haven for international terrorism. . . . I say to you today . . . we have to be determined that they will not stand alone. America will stand up with them. . . . Our responsibility is clear. We need to make sure that they succeed. Because this is one of those benchmark moments, not just for them but for all of us, and what we care about, what we fight for and who we are.[127]

While the content of Secretary Kerry's speech would seamlessly integrate with that of any speech delivered by Clinton during her time at the State Department, his long months of prior silence on the subject of Afghan women does not reflect the emphasis given them by Secretary Clinton.

Any proponent of the Hillary Doctrine in the Oval Office would also jettison fuzzy indicators in favor of concrete benchmarks with respect to women's rights. And failure to hit those targets would result in tangible loss to the government in Kabul. Crocker notes:

> Protect the gains they've got. Figure out where they're most vulnerable and then put the resources and the diplomatic energy into shoring up their defenses. You know, we have got an enormous amount of leverage. Even without forces, you know, we were the ones who organized the Chicago summit in May of 2012 that produced international commitments over the long term for the support of Afghanistan's security forces. Those commitments will be made good as a direct result of how enthusiastically we go after the donors. Same thing with the Tokyo Economic Ministerial in July of 2012. I was present for both. $16 billion on pledges of economic assistance. That will be delivered on to the extent that we make this a cause. And you know, if Hillary Clinton were sitting in the White House— because she represented us in Tokyo and of course was the number two in Chicago—she would be saying we will put our backs into this to the extent that you give us solid assurances that we can trust, that the position of Afghan women is secure and that you will neither take any step nor permit any step to be taken that would affect the gains they have made. Are we clear, Mr. President? As only Hillary Clinton could say.[128]

Rhetoric and benchmarks are intertwined; the former demonstrates the will to enforce the latter. As Crocker puts it, "The architecture is there. What is critical is American will—because again, let me tell you something learned through hard experience: If we don't lead, others are going to wander away, too, and those pledges will vanish like smoke. Absolutely guarantee it."[129]

In an interview with Razeshta Sethna of the *Guardian*, Afghanistan Human Rights Watch researcher Heather Barr reaffirmed the importance of benchmarking: "If at the 2012 NATO summit the international community came together to make a 10-year plan for supporting the Afghan security forces, then why hasn't it also come up with a similar roadmap supporting women's rights in Afghanistan?" She added, "Making sure that Afghanistan continues to have an army seems important to other countries because of their own national security concerns—and women's rights just don't matter to them as much."[130]

In this regard, it is noteworthy that a technical group focused on the elimination of violence against women and human rights was established in July 2013 as part of the Afghan donor framework. If handled adroitly, this mechanism could be a very useful means of tracking the establishment, implementation and monitoring of benchmarks.[131] It is also imperative that Afghan women's organizations be included as indicators are developed and evaluated.

Crocker also suggests that we use our resources to buy some hope for the Afghans: "Support for Afghan women, for civil society, for social and economic development is also pretty cheap insurance to prevent a spirit of hopelessness from taking hold among the general population that makes it easy for the Taliban."[132] The drawdown of the troops will result in profound reductions in expenditures; nevertheless, some of this insurance should be obtainable even within the context of budgetary constraints. While the United States has been spending $110 billion per year on security in Afghanistan to date, that amount is projected to fall to about $2.5 billion per year after the drawdown. During this key transition period, a shifting of resources to programs with the potential to curb an expected upsurge in violence against women—such as rule of law programs—is eminently justifiable.[133] Indeed, when Oxfam surveyed Afghans about their highest priorities, respondents listed the establishment of the rule of law at all levels, a crackdown on corruption, and an end to the culture of impunity.[134]

Also on the to-do list would be a U.S. insistence that Afghan women belong at the peace table in respectable numbers, as part of Afghanistan's legal commitments under U.N. Security Council Resolution 1325—not to mention those of the United States. The donor checklist for any conference or jirga would include the significant presence of women; apparently, it does not. Manizha Naderi, director of Women for Afghan Women, points out, "Women comprise 50 percent of [the] population, and they have not been consulted in any of this, not the transition, not reconstruction, not the negotiations. They haven't been consulted at all."[135]

Just as Asha Hagi Elmi pioneered the concept of the Sixth Clan in Somalia, in societies where clans are run exclusively by men—as is the case in Afghanistan—it is time to think of women as an Afghan clan of their own, but one that represents fully half the population. They have a right to representation in all the councils of the nation not only based on their sheer numbers but also owing to the relationship between the status of women and the security of the state.

As the future of Afghanistan is being decided, the mothers and daughters of the nation deserve and indeed have a right to have a voice. Therefore, the international community must insist they have a place at the table under the mandate of U.N. Security Council Resolution 1325. A gender support team that can offer a gender analysis of any peace agreement would be a useful adjunct to these negotiations as well, with the United States or the international community providing the services of such a team. As Zohra Rasekh states,

> The United States has a moral responsibility towards Afghan people, and in particular Afghan women and children, during and after its war against terrorism inside the Afghan soil. The US government needs to stand firm about Afghan women human rights during its negotiations with the Taliban. Compromising women and human rights for the sake of peace and security will only bring the peace and security of a concentration camp, which was [our] experience before during [the time of] Taliban power in Afghanistan.[136]

Indeed, Hillary Clinton promised as much, asserting, "Women have to be involved in every step of the way in this [Afghan peace] process"[137] and "We certainly . . . cannot be part of blessing any deal that turns the clock back on women in Afghanistan."[138] Only if women are at the table will they be in a position to prevent men from bargaining their hard-won gains away.

Critically important, also, is the gender composition of the large multilateral donor conferences, which are held annually. The track record has not been exceptional to date and could be much better. When NATO leaders, the government of Afghanistan, donors, and the United States convened in Chicago on May 12, 2012, to plan the coalition withdrawal from the country, not a single woman was invited. Only after Afghan women protested did Hamid Karzai quickly shoe-horn in two at the last minute.[139]

The July 8, 2012, Tokyo Donor's Conference turned out to be even worse. Despite ongoing corruption, insecurity, cronyism, and human rights abuses, the international community pledged $16 billion beginning in 2014 to assist the hapless nation to get a grip on its many problems. Conspicuous for their absence, however, were any hard requirements and benchmarks regarding protecting and advancing the human rights of women.

In her opening speech to delegates, then-Secretary of State Hillary Clinton said:

> Obviously, the future of Afghanistan belongs to its government and its peo-ple. And I welcome the clear vision presented by President Karzai and the Afghan Government today for unlocking Afghanistan's economic potential by achieving a stable democratic future. That must include fighting cor-ruption, improving governance, strengthening the rule of law, increasing access to economic opportunity for all Afghans, especially for women.
>
> On this point, let me emphasize that the United States believes strongly that no nation can achieve sustainable peace, reconciliation, stability, and economic growth if half the population is not empowered. All citizens need to have the chance to benefit from and contribute to Afghanistan's prog-ress, and the United States will continue to stand strongly by the women of Afghanistan.[140]

Given Afghanistan's inability to meet even the most basic require-ments, critics charged that the pledges made in exchange for aid verged on fantasy. Without concrete benchmarks and goals, vague promises will likely prove hollow. As Anthony H. Cordesman wrote in a Center for Strategic and International Studies opinion piece, "This is the most criti-cal failure of both the Tokyo Conference and the transition effort to date. There is no real plan, and there is no one in charge."[141]

But there are specific benchmarks that could be used to bring the pledges back from fantasyland and into reality—and the first benchmark would involve hard targets for female representation during peace talks and related donor conferences. Other measures could follow on from an analysis of the shortcomings of United States support thus far. The United States must, for example, engage the Afghan government over EVAW.[142] It must not be eviscerated by the Afghan Parliament. This is non-negotiable: benchmark number 2.

It is also time for a renewed commitment to the independence of the AIHRC. In June 2013, that independence was compromised by the addition of five new presidential appointees to the commission, one of whom is a former Taliban commander. Only time will tell whether these appointments have undermined the commission's effectiveness, and donors must monitor that situation closely. If Sima Samar indicates the commission can no longer function, donor action must be taken: benchmark number 3.

Another situation needing attention is the procedure by which "rehabilitated" Taliban are to be given positions within the Afghan Local Police (ALP) force. This gives the Taliban a golden opportunity to undertake tremendous mischief. Already a majority of Afghans believe the ALP to be thugs kept on the government payroll so that they will commit their depredations only at the local level and not the national level, according to the International Crisis Group (ICG).[143] Because international donors are the primary funders, this effectively means that former Taliban insurgents will never account for their crimes, and, to add insult to injury, will draw a salary from the countries whose soldier sons and daughters they killed. We agree with the ICG that at a minimum, Afghan women should reserve the right to vet any candidates for the ALP. There must be some accountability before women for the crimes committed against them by men who will be ostensibly tasked with protecting them. The worst should not be permitted to sign up. An official regulation mandating women's presence on the ALP vetting committees should be benchmark number 4.

And accountability to women concerns not only crimes of the past but crimes of the present as well: "There should be concrete terms for them to demonstrate the changes," activist Palwasha Hassan told the *Guardian* in June 2013: "Girls' schools have been under attack, teachers have been killed, women leaders have been assassinated. The real change will show in stopping these actions . . . we will remain concerned until the end."[144]

Enforcing laws to protect women will be key to halting such crimes. In addition to the training of female Afghan lawyers and judges, it is imperative that women see a career path for themselves in the Afghan National Police (ANP). This will necessitate action by the government to combat sexual harassment and threats made against those women who join the ANP. Michelle Barsa of the Institute for Inclusive Security suggests an emphasis on increasing the number of women in law enforcement may help this situation: "The US has appropriated $52.8 billion to support the Afghan National Security Forces (ANSF), but has not specifically targeted the recruitment and retention of women in Afghan forces. . . . It is time for a change."[145] The fiscal year 2014 Defense Appropriations Bill earmarks $47.3 million toward the recruitment and retention of women, which is an important step forward, but it deserves expansion and careful follow-through.

Furthermore, law enforcement efforts on behalf of women are unlikely to succeed without a robust monitoring capability to collect statistics on cases reported, estimate reporting rates, and tally prosecutions, convictions, and sentences. Not only should gender-based violence be monitored but also cases involving the violation of women's property and marriage rights . Monitoring levels of violence against women is therefore number 5. Donors will need to closely cooperate with Afghan civil society groups in this task.

While withholding aid is one way of dealing with failure to reach benchmarks, there is yet another remedy should the situation become intolerable. Through its membership on the U.N. Security Council, the United States could support the pursuit of International Criminal Court indictments against top Taliban and even mujahideen leaders even though it is not party to the Rome Statute. Crimes against the female half of humanity still count as crimes against humanity, and the resumption of widespread atrocities against Afghan women should put into play all former atrocities as well, despite the 2010 amnesty accorded by the Afghan government.

In addition to benchmarks for accountability, we also need to be thinking in concrete terms about how to provide some measure of physical safety for high-profile Afghan women. To a certain extent the Diplomatic Security branch of the State Department is already doing so.

Diplomatic Security provides bodyguard training to the male relatives of such women, arming and paying them as well. In certain cases, hardened vehicles are also provided. We suggest a significant expansion of this program for high-profile women as the transition nears.

There are other measures that would help shore up women's security as well. For example, the United States might consider an explicit asylum policy for Afghan women facing the threat of femicide. To save the gains made by Afghan women of this generation, it may be necessary to save the women themselves, hopefully to return once their deaths would no longer serve a political purpose for the warlords and the Taliban. Another possible initiative is a scholarship program to take the best and brightest female Afghan students into U.S. universities; currently, the U.S. government provides scholarships for girls to attend college in Afghanistan only. But as Christine Fair advocates, "Get those girls out. Give them scholarships to India, the US, Tajikistan, etc. Sure, the program would no doubt be self-selecting—only those parents who are willing to send their daughters away from the family would be the ones interested in this program. But such a program could build a progressive diaspora, which becomes a tool for engagement. Then the international community could also invest in Afghan women outside of Afghanistan."[146]

It's also time to push for a course reversal on the diminished quotas for provincial councils in order to prevent additional erosion of women's participation in the political system. Donors must push back, understanding that any changes to the quota system that go unchallenged will encourage a broader campaign against the political participation of women after 2014. Donors should also engage with the National Action Plan for the Women of Afghanistan (NAPWA) goal of 30 percent female civil servants. Nevertheless, numbers alone are not enough; donors need to pay attention to which ministries and at what level the female civil servants operate.

But Mariam Mansury cautions us about reifying these numbers:

We need a different idea of nation-building. We did it for about six years and gave up. It got difficult because we thought of it too grandly. The objectives and indicators shouldn't have been to get 75 percent of children in school in two years. We should have had 20 year performance indicators, but we tried to do it in 2 to 3 years. Since we can't measure incremental change, so it creates an air of failure. If you shoot for 15 percent women police and you only get 2 percent, that's seen as failure. But it's not—women are coming forward, there's public awareness of them, retention of women means there's change. We're not capturing these kinds of things. We really missed an opportunity not measuring against what we should. Sure, need results-based development—if you are timing it correctly. Two to five years is not the correct time horizon. You're forcing results on measures that didn't add up.[147]

She has a point, and the topic of development planning horizons will be taken up in chapter 7. Nevertheless, even incrementally higher levels of participation for women in key institutions such as the civil service and the ANP will be critical in safeguarding progress made for Afghan women. The flagship AID program for Afghan women in the drawdown period is called PROMOTE, and it will focus on training women for the civil service positions that will be opened to them through the NAPWA quota and on continued entrepreneurial training for Afghan businesswomen.

But there is more to be done. Michelle Barsa notes that without security, women will be pushed out of the public square; for example, they will almost surely be unable to cast votes at polling stations or to attend public meetings. As the International Security Assistance Force (ISAF) pulls back causing NGOs to leave transitioned areas, women are pulling back as well: More than two hundred women journalists quit their jobs during the past year, and monitors observe that women can no longer travel by taxi and cannot access clinics and vocational centers. There are stories of midwives being killed in rural areas along with an increased number of early forced marriages. Reports of threatening letters and telephone calls have spiked dramatically.[148]

Female MP Fawzia Koofi notes, "You hardly see women on the streets nowadays. As a woman, you feel everyone is looking at you. Even going to restaurants has become tense. . . . We're more at risk, and I think as we get closer to [the U.S. drawdown] the risk of being targeted and attacked will increase."[149]

Creative means to circumvent these mobility problems will be key. Ensuring cell phone coverage and radio coverage could be useful because both are essential to the informational infrastructure that benefits the women of Afghanistan. Kaiya Waddell of Facebook estimates that 45 percent of the world's population will have access to a smart phone by 2016. While that seems high for Afghanistan, research has shown that 83 percent of Afghans already own a radio, 37 percent own televisions, and 6 percent have access to the Internet.[150] Radio has proved indispensable, for example, in reaching rural Afghan women for teacher training, which was problematic owing to lack of mobility. As educator Suzanne Griffin notes:

> In the BESST teacher training project, a radio station in Kabul made CDs of the training models and sent them by taxi to 11 provinces every week where they were broadcast in all the districts. We reached 77,000 teachers in that five-year project with a combination of face-to-face training (using a cascade model) and radio broadcasts to reinforce the training. The female teachers often told us that they listened to the broadcasts while cooking meals for their families.[151]

Especially if Afghanistan descends once again into a bloody internal war, funding for something akin to a Radio Free Women of Afghanistan station would be crucial to help maintain gains for women, especially in rural areas where progress is much more easily reversed. Such communications strategies should also target men, encouraging them to support the dignity and human rights of the women in their lives.

Last but not least, we cannot overlook demographic pressures, pressures that Afghan women know all too well due to lack of reproductive planning. Afghanistan is grappling with the same demographic time bomb that bedevils close neighbors India and Pakistan. With a median age of 17.8 years, a sex ratio of 104 males to every female, and 42 percent of the population under the age of 14, Afghanistan faces a huge youth bulge coupled with high unemployment, a masculinized sex ratio, and a lack of skilled workers.[152] It is a recipe for further conflict that will only be mitigated with the integration of women into all spheres of social and economic life and, of course, discussions that will affect their security.

Fortunately, this is something the United States knows how to do. As Andrew Natsios notes, "Seventy percent of all the family planning money spent in the world is AID [USAID] money. It's the biggest in the world, much bigger than the UN program and, by the way, much better run."[153] While USAID's premiere post-drawdown program for women is PROMOTE, which as we have discussed is focused on leadership training, more mundane needs such as family planning should not be given short shrift: such programs will be imperative for future stability.

In conclusion, while it is true that, ultimately, only Afghan women can protect their rights, they, like human rights defenders everywhere, require partners, public support, and material assistance—the more so because they remain so profoundly disenfranchised. These women are not pet rocks, weighing us down.[154] Their situation is one of the most critical measures by which U.S. foreign policy toward Afghanistan should be judged. There is no denying that the United States bears a special responsibility toward the women of Afghanistan, one that cannot be shirked. As U.S. representatives Martha Roby and Niki Tsongas have written, "Having elevated women's place in Afghan society . . . the U.S. must depart the country in a responsible way that secures these gains. When history grades America's involvement in Afghanistan, the status of Afghan women in the coming years will weigh heavily on that judgment."[155]

Amen. It is unfortunate that the White House undermined the full implementation of the Hillary Doctrine in Afghanistan. But that can be changed, if the United States is prepared to muster the will. Plenty remains to be done to ensure a softer landing for Afghan women after the 2014 drawdown. The United States is not helpless and the situation is not hopeless—unless Americans choose to believe so.

While no one can foretell the fate of Afghanistan's women, Ryan Crocker sees it thus: "If we can buy them another decade, this [progress for women] probably is sustainable on its own momentum. . . . It's up to us. It could go either way, and it's really up to us."[156]

# 7

# THE FUTURE OF THE HILLARY DOCTRINE

★ ★ ★

*Realpolitik and Fempolitik*

So the United States has made empowering women and girls a cornerstone of our foreign policy, because women's equality is not just a moral issue, it's not just a humanitarian issue, it is not just a fairness issue; it is a security issue. It is a prosperity issue and it is a peace issue. And therefore, when I talk about why we need to integrate women's issues into discussions at the highest levels everywhere in the world, I'm not doing it just because I have a personal commitment . . . I 'm doing it because it's in the vital interest of the United States of America.

—HILLARY CLINTON[1]

We had our moment in the State Department's sun with Hillary Clinton, and for now it's over.

—ROBIN MORGAN[2]

WE HAVE EXAMINED the history of the Hillary Doctrine and its premise that the security of women and the security of states are linked. We have also analyzed the implementation of the Hillary Doctrine during the four years in which Clinton was U.S. secretary of state and probed its potential and its limits. It is now time to ask: What is the future of the Hillary Doctrine in U.S. foreign policy?

As historian Karen Garner reminds us, "The question first posed by American feminists in the 1970s remains: Do 'women' matter in US foreign policy making or not?"[3] This is not a question of whether women *should* matter—we hope that point has been settled in the affirmative. Instead, we are asking whether the Hillary Doctrine will persist beyond its creator's tenure, and what should be on the to-do list of subsequent U.S. secretaries of state who take its premise seriously.

## WILL WOMEN CONTINUE TO MATTER IN U.S. FOREIGN POLICY?

There are several ways to approach this question, and some lend themselves to more hopeful answers than others. For example, if we were to ask whether it would be possible for successors to Secretary of State Hillary Clinton or to President Barack Obama to undo the web of institutions and legal obligations established during Clinton's tenure, we would have to answer, "no."

As one National Security Council (NSC) staffer put it, "The shifts that have been made are irreversible."[4] What this means is, first, the legal obligations will likely persist for the long term, and second, it would be politically foolish to attempt to unravel many elements of the web; for example, is it likely that even the most recalcitrant president would attempt to formally downgrade the ambassadorial rank of the head of the Office of Global Women's Issues (OGWI)? The political fallout would simply be devastating.

Shelby Quast of Equality Now concurs: "[The] foundation already exists, and it makes it so much easier to implement if it's already there. So in that sense, I think it's being done very strategically and very cleverly; we have people who are looking out toward the future."[5] The visibility and transparency of these commitments empower civil society actors as well as multilateral and foreign actors to hold the U.S. government accountable for what it has promised.

A less hopeful answer is that no successor to Secretary of State Clinton need do anything that foolish, when all that is necessary is to acknowledge the web of institutions and obligations but remain indifferent to them.

Yes, the ambassador-at-large heading OGWI reports directly to the secretary of state, but what if the secretary is not interested in what the ambassador has to say? What if that annual National Action Plan (NAP) report to the president languishes unread because of an unwillingness to engage with these issues?[6] What if even a sympathetic president is convinced that Realpolitik, with its emphasis on power, trumps the Hillary Doctrine's Fempolitik, with its insistence that women are a core national security interest? What if he or she simply decides not to insist that women be invited to the negotiating table, even though the United States is bound by U.N. Security Council Resolution 1325?

Indeed, one could make the argument that such indifference already exists on the part of the Obama White House, that it was present before Hillary Clinton even stepped down, and that it has only worsened since then.

Rosa Brooks, former deputy assistant secretary of defense during the Obama administration's first term, opines, "I'm very disappointed in this administration. There is no high level interest in any of this; there are occasional spurts of rhetoric, but it hasn't translated into longer-term commitments. It certainly hasn't translated into executive branch decision-making. Hillary Clinton was definitely interested, but it is not clear now that anyone else has picked up the ball. . . . There are more people in DoD who care about the fate of Afghan women than there are in the White House."[7] It is even possible, now that Hillary Clinton has stepped down from the State Department, that there might be more people at the Bush Institute at Southern Methodist University who care about Afghan women than there are in the Obama White House.[8]

If the White House did take the Hillary Doctrine seriously, why was it Foreign Secretary William Hague of the United Kingdom who led the push for women to be included at the 2014 Syrian peace talks?[9] Why has the United States allowed Afghan women to be marginalized during the peace talks with the Taliban? Why hasn't the United States insisted that women be at the table for the Sudan–South Sudan negotiations? And we are not just talking about Syrian, Afghan, and Sudanese and South Sudanese women: where are the American women at these tables?

It is almost as if the Obama administration is constructing the issue as an either/or proposition—that Fempolitik is the antithesis of a Realpolitik approach.

But that stance betrays a serious lack of imagination and also serious ignorance of the extant research. For example, if the U.S. government truly believed that a lasting peace accord in Afghanistan is in the national interest, then the United States would insist that women be represented at the peace talks, in numbers sufficient not only to preserve the gains made, but also to ground diplomatic rhetoric in the truth that this conflict has produced incalculable suffering, oppression, and corruption. Research shows that peace agreements forged from negotiations that included both sexes are more durable than those that did not.[10]

In other words, Fempolitik is no "pet rock": it is a pillar of Realpolitik.[11]

Some might suggest that the track record of the post-Hillary administration proves that any U.S. secretary of state who is not a woman cannot effectively advance the Hillary Doctrine. We are not convinced that this is true. Dara Kay Cohen of Harvard University agrees: "I wonder if in the end when people say, it takes a Nixon to go to China, I wonder if it really takes a male leader to really make progress on these kinds of gender issues for the same reason, that it's sort of hard for a women to make this her central focus because she is just simply perceived as less credible because she is a woman."[12]

Cohen is suggesting that when men join the chorus of voices advocating the importance of "women's issues," other men are more likely to pay attention and take these issues seriously as well. There is no doubt that the Donald Steinbergs and Princeton Lymans we have spoken of in the preceding chapters played this kind of critical role. Rosa Brooks concurs: "It's a rare man that is truly committed to these issues. Don Steinberg is one of those rare exceptions. He brought to the table a tremendous amount of personal energy on gender."[13] That male energy matters.

And men will continue to matter for some time to come because Washington is still a "city of men." In 2011, Micah Zenko enumerated this reality:

To get a sense of the scope of this problem, I looked at the gender breakdown at 10 prominent think tanks with a substantial foreign-policy focus. After crunching the numbers, which were culled from their publicly available rosters, I found that women constituted only 21 percent of the policy-related positions (154 of 723) and only 29 percent of the total leadership staff (250 of 874) . . .

Given this disparity, it should come as no surprise that women are also underrepresented in the halls of power. The Pentagon's "Senior Defense Officials" website lists 129 positions, of which 21 (16 percent) are filled by women. John M. Robinson, the State Department's chief diversity officer, recently wrote that "Twenty-two percent of senior leaders at the Department of State are women." Of the 171 chiefs of mission at U.S. embassies, 50 are women (29 percent).[14]

As long as men wield the preponderance of economic, political, and military power, men's voices and men's priorities will inevitably be privileged.[15] The men who choose to use their advantage on behalf of women are crucial to the future success of the Hillary Doctrine. Yet this takes a level of commitment that many men—even men sympathetic to the Hillary Doctrine in theory—may not be willing or able to muster.

Perhaps this is best exemplified by current Secretary of State John Kerry, who started out of the gate strong in his first month as secretary by writing an op-ed on International Women's Day in March 2013 and by flying back from an overseas trip in order to present the State Department's International Women of Courage Awards. All well and good, but his Policy Planning Staff reportedly no longer has a gender expert among its members, as it had under Clinton.[16] Moreover, ever since meeting with Afghan businesswomen and the women's soccer team in Kabul two months after he became secretary of state, John Kerry became notably and ominously silent about Afghan women and their fate for almost eight months—until, that is, Hillary Clinton and Laura Bush hosted a symposium on the topic where he was pointedly invited to present the keynote address, as discussed in chapter 6. And rather tellingly, on the anniversary of the announcement of the Equal Futures Partnership, when the new $10 million Safe from the Start program to help fund UNHCR (the UN High Commissioner for Refugees) to hire gender experts to help women in conflict zones was unveiled, Kerry couldn't stay. "I want to emphasize that high-level meetings like this are critical to our ability to be able to identify where and how we can generate systemic change. It helps all of us to organize and coordinate our energies to that end. And so I regret that, because of the schedule, I'll be leaving here to go—I'm meeting shortly with President Obama."[17]

Playing off on what has been famously said about Hillary Clinton, one civil society group leader put it this way: "John Kerry doesn't wake up in the morning wondering how to empower women worldwide."[18]

But maybe we should not only focus on the here and now in order to perceive the future of the Hillary Doctrine; perhaps we should cast our gaze toward the longer term, where generational change may catalyze the transformation of existing mindsets. As Caren Grown of USAID observes, "The educated younger generation that is entering government service 'gets' gender equality, in large part because their own mothers were educated, strong women who did not hesitate to raise their voices in the public square."[19] Experimental evidence supports her assertion: The role model effect is a powerful means through which to ameliorate gender stereotypes and inequities.[20]

Rosa Brooks has also witnessed this generational change in the Department of Defense, but attributes it to a different cause. According to Brooks, midlevel officers who served in Afghanistan and Iraq understood how engaging women is critical to stability, even though senior officers and those who were never in the field might not have learned this lesson. "They had seen how women were deprived of opportunities, and what the costs were from shutting women out of the political and economic life of their communities."

Mariam Mansury of the Institute for Inclusive Security notices this effect as well:

The guys on the ground [in Afghanistan] see that women have a more straightforward agenda. These guys get disillusioned with the tribal elders because they have multiple allegiances—they're connected with warlords, the Taliban, etc. The guys get that they can trust the women more because their agenda is, how do my kids get to school, where can lights be placed for greater safety, where not to place the well because the land is contested and that can imperil those who fetch water, and so forth.[21]

Brooks observes that even before the lifting of the combat exclusion for women, men serving side-by-side with women in battle was changing minds and hearts. She'd hear men say things like, "I was in a firefight with my female first sergeant, and I'd trust her any day over fifty men."[22]

She is hopeful that the kind of bonding that has historically resulted from serving together in combat situations will be a game-changer. She also notes that many senior officers now have daughters serving in the military, and that a new generation of female leaders—even generals—will now emerge with the lifting of the combat exclusion. Indeed, to what extent would gender relations improve if the type of bonding men enjoy in combat were extended to include women? Might this even dampen the epidemic of rape and assault in the military?

Combat experience and strong mothers are not the only reasons why the younger generation better understands the need for gender equality. Hillary Clinton also established an extensive program of gender training for State Department and USAID employees, as mentioned in chapter 5. Jen Klein, formerly with OGWI under Clinton, explains:

> We actually changed the Foreign Service Institute training. If you think of this as a multi-year endeavor, what you want to do is train the next generation of Foreign Service Officers to actually do this work. And so what we did was the first-ever session on gender integration. It was a three day course at the Foreign Service Institute, which was a partnership between the Foreign Service Institute and our office. . . . The next stage of this is to break up that course into modules that could then be inserted into the political and economic statecraft courses, which are not self-selecting, which are *required* of every Foreign Service Officer.[23]

In other words, from virtually day one on the job, the State Department now educates Foreign Service Officers about why integrating a gender perspective is so critical to their work.

And it's not just a topic raised with entry-level personnel. An example: USAID's Office of Conflict Management and Mitigation has developed special training for USAID personnel involved in designing development programs in conflict-affected areas (the Office of Transition Initiatives has its own gender training called "Gender in Political Transitions"). Cybele Cochran, who developed the modules, describes how it works:

> We discuss how we as US government representatives can either squash progress [for women] or assist it, depending on how we behave in contexts

where we are foreigners and don't really understand what is happening on the ground. So we dive into how to uncover some of the assumptions we might not even realize we have, such as when you say "victim," do you think of a man or a woman? How about "combatant," do you think of a man or a woman? How about "judge?" Community leaders? Religious leaders? How might that affect your programs? If you think combatants are only men and that victims are only women, then how might you be disregarding the needs of the men victims and the female combatants? . . .

We have an activity called "what would you do?" where each person is given a quote they would have to read to another person, such as "Gender doesn't matter here" or "We'll have a gender specialist look at it later," and they have to be able to respond to one another about how they would handle a situation like that.[24]

This type of training, coupled with the legal obligations incurred under the National Action Plan (NAP), has turned gender from an add-on into something much more central. As Cochran describes it, "The NAP implementation plan goes office-by-office and process-by-process. The word that I personally like to use is 'infect.' So that we infect the inside processes and procedures so that gender isn't a stand-alone thing, and it's not something that can go away when the political winds blow another direction."[25]

But has it worked? Cochran thinks it has:

I've got to tell you, it is a sea change in attitude that I have observed over at least the almost four years that I've been at USAID. I mean, honestly, in the beginning, it was me and a couple of colleagues . . . trying to rally, trying to convince, trying to beg, trying to advocate. Because some of these requirements were already on the books, but they were kind of obscure, and again, people didn't know how to apply them. There was this fierce resistance—"Gender isn't relevant here"—mostly USAID people, and again, I do not think there's any ill will here. I think it's just a lack of understanding of the issues. . . . You really have to study and think about these issues, and if you have not been trained to know what you don't know, in a sense, to ask questions about gender, you don't realize how important it is to you.

So we had this speakers' series, we brought in folks who were working on the vanguard of these issues to help the agency see, "this is what goes wrong when you don't look at gender and here are ways to do it right." So there really is this sea change in attitude where people realize, "Okay, okay, I get it, gender is important, it matters. But I don't know how to do it." So USAID has responded by pairing gender advisors at almost every office and mission or having a gender point of contact [which can range from fairly inexperienced people] to an expert we brought in with a Ph.D. who's been doing this for twenty years . . .

For example, I was at a meeting recently at the State Department, I was brought in to be like sort of a, I hate the word expert, but to present on gender and help them understand better some of these concepts. And so someone, a young woman, raised her hand and said, "I have a question. I think this is really important, this is great, but the thing is, when we go into the country, get on the ground, we have to talk to a lot of local leaders. And local leaders are all men, you know, so what are we supposed to do?" I said, "You need to examine what the word 'leader' means and how you're defining that. Because I will guarantee you that every single country that you're going into, there are women civil society activists who have made tremendous progress before you got there. If you do not recognize their efforts, if you do not recognize them as leaders, you will turn back the clock on the progress they have made, you will squash future progress, and you will solidify patriarchal regimes."[26]

Tobie Whitman of the Institute for Inclusive Security concurs on both accounts, to wit, that such training is essential to the continuation of the Hillary Doctrine, and that it must emphasize not only that women are important but also how to implement gender programming:

Changing hearts and minds of those who've been at it for decades is very difficult. True changes to how business is done will really only come with the next generation. . . . So I think the training and education that new professionals receive is game changing. But it also has to be practical—not just why women's empowerment is important but how do you actually do it. The technical training—how to write gender-sensitive RFPs [requests for proposals], metrics, collecting gender-disaggregated data.[27]

A tipping point, Cochran says, has definitely been reached. One of the authors (Hudson) participated in her speakers' series, and Cochran relayed the following: "Do you remember speaking at the workshop? One of our more senior folks in our policy bureau emailed several other people. I got the email train a couple of emails later, where he said, 'You know, I've heard Hudson speak, I really was impressed with what she had to say, can someone tell me why this is considered controversial? It seems really obvious to me.' "[28]

This is what a tipping point looks like—a discussion of the relevance of gender to U.S. foreign and development policy seems unremarkable and obvious to a senior male USAID official. From where Cochran sits, this immense change in consciousness took only four years. It is difficult not to be optimistic that at the very least, a foundation has been set that could lead to the persistence of the Hillary Doctrine over time—despite indifference at the highest levels.

## THE TO-DO LIST

So what should U.S. foreign policy makers convinced of the wisdom of the Hillary Doctrine have on their 'to do' list? Our research, our travels, and our interviews have helped us develop a personal vision of what works and what should be included in the toolkit, as well as where the United States falls short. The latter will require significant policy attention.

### The Powers That Be

To start with, there are some powers that only states can utilize, and the United States should consider wielding them on behalf of women. The first is the bully pulpit afforded by the (current) hegemonic status of the United States and its membership in the P-5.

Hillary Clinton set an admirable example when she spoke up on the behalf of women before the U.N. Security Council and in virtually every public speech she made as secretary of state. She explains her rationale in this way: "It is why I mention the issue in every setting I am in, and why I mention it with every foreign leader I meet. It is like any challenge. You just keep at it, take it piece by piece, seize the ground you can, hang onto it, and then move forward a little bit more. And we are heading for higher ground."[29]

This rhetoric both discourages and sometimes even silences those who disagree, while at the same time greatly heartening those world-wide who agree with her view. It lends legitimacy and even protection to those who are working toward a better world for women (and by extension men and boys), and holds other national leaders to a higher standard.[30]

We hope that all subsequent U.S. secretaries of state will take up the challenge and speak out on behalf of women and girls at every possible opportunity. And this is especially true if the secretary is male. For those who believe gender does not matter, sometimes only the authoritative voice of a highly ranked man can persuade them otherwise. As Anne-Marie Goetz of UNWomen puts it, "I know that there's many countries that would dismiss [Clinton's statements on women] because she's a woman and so on and they just sort of say, of course she would say that because she's a woman. Therefore it's crucial that John Kerry carries on with the rhetoric."[31] (As we have suggested, it is far from clear that Kerry has done so.)

Related to the power of the bully pulpit is the power of the demarche—the power to "tell it like it is" in private, state-to-state communication. As former FSO Deborah Cavin, now with the Institute for Inclusive Security, relates, "As somebody who delivered lots of demarches over the years to foreign governments telling them how they should vote at the UN, develop their Ministry of Health or not, accept GMOs [genetically modified organisms], allow American licenses to proceed unfettered for some commercial transaction, whatever the issue . . . the people who run the State Department, no matter the administration, historically, have no problem telling the world how they ought to act."[32]

If the U.S. can demarche over GMOs, surely it can do the same over women's rights, which are certainly not only more central to U.S. core values but also vital to the nation's security interests.

Another critical power of the state is the authority to insist that women and their concerns be included in events in which the United States—or its NATO and major non-NATO allies—plans to participate, mediate, or facilitate.[33] The United States can mandate that its own officials and representatives meet with women's groups when they are overseas. Swanee Hunt suggests that "Kerry could insist that whenever there's a dinner given for him by a country, which will happen like three times a week probably, that he will be sure that between 20 and 40 percent of the professional people at the table or at the reception are female. He wouldn't need to say anything—his staff would convey that. So he doesn't have to spend any capital on that. It'd be staff-to-staff. . . . It's more than optics. Because the women that are invited there, their status will skyrocket."[34]

Dinners aside, women's presence at the negotiating table should be non-negotiable, though it currently is not. That's because major players—including the United States—have never insisted on it. Though in principle bound by U.N. Security Council Resolution 1325, the United States—even during Hillary Clinton's tenure as secretary of state—has a very spotty record. The ambassador who originally presented Resolution 1325 to the U.N. Security Council in 2000, Anwarul Chowdhury of Bangladesh, laments "the disappointing record of its implementation," and speaking in 2012 he stated, "Twelve years after 1325, progress on the implementation of the resolution seems minimal."[35] The inclusion of women—both from other countries and from the United States—should be a higher priority for U.S. foreign policy makers. The U.S. should set hard targets for the participation of women, within the range of 20 to 30 percent to start with. This will require attentive monitoring and record keeping.[36]

Why is there still so little progress on the inclusion of women? One ISAF PRT commander probably summed it up when asked if he engaged women in his province (Bamyan, Afghanistan): "Yes, women are half of the population. Do we need to influence them? Probably not. . . . Women will not kill us."[37] According to this mindset, the only players needed at the table are the players prepared to kill people to get their way. Tobie Whitman could not disagree more: "Norwegian researchers looked at 80 peace negotiations, and those that had included civil society representatives had the most durable peace agreements. The 'worst' should not be allowed to establish the framework for the future."[38]

Nation-states are not powerless to insist on the inclusion of women at important gatherings of decision makers. Pressure can range from the overt, such as threatening to pull out of events, to a more gentle prod, such as allocating additional seats to delegations if women occupy them. And in terms of including women's issues at the highest levels of diplomacy, we have seen how Hillary Clinton effected this by bringing along the ambassador-at-large for global women's issues on visits to foreign countries, such as for bilateral strategic dialogues, which forces the other country to come up with a counterpart with whom the ambassador can meet to discuss issues at the highest levels.[39]

This inclusion mandate carries with it some ancillary responsibilities. If the event is to produce an agreement, such as a peace accord, the United States should take it upon itself to have its own gender experts available to perform a gender analysis examining the implications of the document before signing off. Indeed, we could go even further and urge the U.S. government to emulate the World Bank, whose environmental analysts have veto power over any proposed loan made to a foreign country (though, ironically, not their gender analysts!). Imagine a world where the ambassador-at-large for women's issues has the power to exercise a similar veto on U.S. foreign policy initiatives and agreements and where the secretary of state's policy planning staff would not be complete without an OGWI gender expert.

Furthermore, gender benchmarks must be integrated into annual performance reviews. If women aren't at the table, someone must be held accountable for that fact. We hope the nine new gender indicators adopted for the State Department and USAID in 2013 will produce a new culture of attention to these important matters—but hard targets are yet to be attached to any of them. And, as we have already noted, these are output, and not impact measures. For example, the very first is, "Number of laws, policies, or procedures drafted, proposed, or adopted to promote gender equality at the regional, national, or local level." Surely more important than the number of laws is whether such laws are enforced, but no such measure is incorporated into any of the nine indicators.[40]

Another important state power that should be wielded more frequently and to greater effect is bringing women into "the loop"; that is, transmitting important information to and from women on a regular basis. For example, one NSC staffer spoke about how the United States facilitated the creation of a "Women's Situation Room" in Sierra Leone and Senegal during the recent elections. This was essentially a communications hub where local women could report election violence and from there transmit information to official electoral commissions and observers.

But the situation room also operated in reverse: information also flowed down to local women from the national level.[41] This two-way exchange of information is well worth replicating. Even a one-way exchange of information can, in some regions, constitute a major breakthrough while enhancing the goal of including women in the political process. Moreover, as we have seen, women are often capable of gathering information that men can't. Mobilizing female U.N. peacekeepers, for example, has opened up entirely new networks that previously went untapped. Kristen Cordell, who served in U.N. missions in the Democratic Republic of the Congo and Liberia, describes what it was like to work with all-women peacekeeping forces in that country:

> People were actually safer in Congotown with the women [peacekeepers] there, compared to other towns with male peacekeepers. There was a dramatic difference. Women peacekeepers described their work differently— for example, they set up after-school programs for girls so that they could marry later. The principal of the school said, "Their presence is our safety." That's not just a sweet sentiment; that's human security.
>
> The male peacekeepers had a more limited vision; their attitude was, "We do night patrols; if we see something, we investigate; if we don't, we don't pry." They did not interpret their task broadly. If they were asked, "Tell me about your community—what are the needs of the women and girls?" they didn't know. But the female peacekeepers could see the issues of early marriage and other problems; there was better communication. For example, there was a battalion of female Ghanaian peacekeepers in an area of Liberia called Buchanan. A woman there told them about a weapons stockpile. The male peacekeepers—who had been in the country for a year—didn't even know this community was Muslim.[42]

Talking to women on the ground is also essential. Alexandra Tenny tells how she learned this lesson through her experiences in Turkey and Colombia:

You hear people coming out of Iraq and Afghanistan and [they say], "Oh, well, we met with this village tribal leader and we couldn't convince them of this, that, and the other," and I literally looked at one guy one time and I said, "Did you ever talk to the women?" "Well, you know, we talked to tribal leaders!" And I said, "That was your problem." Because I remember very distinctly [in Turkey], sitting down with all these women, and it was like, "The men, all they do, they're lazy, they just work in their fields, and then they come in and they drink tea and whatever and we have to do all the work," so when you've got to decide where you're going to build a school or a hospital or a well, the men are all about the politics and who's going to get the credit for it and the women are like, "No, no, no, we have to walk there! We're the ones that have to take the kids to the hospital, so put it here."

Colombia has the second largest problem with IEDs and landmines in the world after Afghanistan. The FARC uses them to protect the coca fields, for cocaine production. And again, it was a similar conversation, where I was speaking with some folks from the Ministry of the Interior, and I said, "Well, do you ever engage the community in finding out where these [mines] are?" "Oh, well, they're too afraid or whatever." . . . I finally said, "Does anybody talk to the moms and say, 'Where do you not let your kids play?' And I guarantee you that they don't let their kids play where they know there might be mines." And so that was all kind of the genesis of [the idea] that we've got to engage the women and the mothers in these communities through the security forces much more than we have been. Not the usual communities, not the civilian entities, but the security forces, for a lot of reasons.[43]

Engaging women is also imperative in terms of documenting more than the location of land mines. Women also know where the bodies are buried, and we mean this literally. Rigoberta Menchú Tum, a Nobel Peace Prize laureate from Guatemala, tells of how Mayan women preserved evidence that was used during the ill-fated trial of former dictator José Efrain Ríos Montt. She notes that it was the women who kept the most important evidence. They remembered where the mass graves were and how many were buried there and how to identify the bodies based on what remained—fragments of clothing, identifying jewelry, and so forth. And when the graves were exhumed, the women made sure the evidence was not removed.[44] It is critical that the U.S. government facilitate the preservation of evidence in postconflict situations by ensuring that there is official outreach to women who may not only have witnessed atrocities and experienced them firsthand but also carefully husbanded memories in the hope that justice would eventually be served.

Another way to marry inclusion and information flow is through the power to convene. This is not a power exclusive to states. While researching this book, we have come across excellent examples of how NGOs, such as the Institute for Inclusive Security, have brought the right people together in the same room or how the Bush Institute's African First Ladies Initiative has mobilized the wives of African presidents to work together to improve women's lives.

But the state and multilateral state institutions such as the United Nations have a special role to play in terms of convening, and arguably, Hillary Clinton herself was a master of the art: she understood the concept of "vital voices." As Tobie Whitman explains:

> I think connecting policymakers directly with women from different parts of the world is important as well. We can all say how important including women is at the macro-level but I think making individual connections is what really helps make these issues a priority. It's why as an organization we bring delegations of women to Washington and try to foster human connections. As advocates we can be persuasive, but more compelling is when actual women leading change in their own environments speak about their circumstances and their priorities. Learning from them of the different experience they have of a development project is what will make a policymaker think twice the next time that they embark on a project without consulting with women. I think the practice that HRC started of actually meeting with local women's groups has been very significant and should be supported moving ahead.[45]

The United States Institute of Peace (USIP), a government-funded institute located right next to the main State Department building, is technically part of the executive branch of government but neverthe-less occupies an interesting and useful niche in terms of state convening power. It has been effective in providing a bridge between policy makers and civil society; for example, USIP was instrumental in forging the U.S. Civil Society Working Group on Women, Peace, and Security, which cre-ated an opportunity for Obama administration policy makers to convene with civil society groups and listen to their requests for a NAP and ideas about what such a document should include. This role has grown over time. Kathleen Kuehnast at USIP explains:

> On the average of twice a month I'm contacted [by the State Department] to ask if I would convene the civil society working group to meet with a delegation from this country or that. . . . So they lead, we house. It's a perfect symbiotic relationship. . . . Three weeks ago, an EU representa-tive was here, their gender advisor. A week ago we met on Afghanistan with the Open Society Foundation, because they want to do funding of women in Afghanistan post-2014, so they're trying to get a beat on what they should be working on. . . . It's just such a win-win. Everyone benefits.[46]

Kuehnast calls USIP a "think and do tank" because they are able to request funding for small programs. One of these programs offered a fascinating exercise in the art of convening:

> We wanted to bring Afghan women leaders and Iraqi women leaders together . . . and when the Afghans and Iraqis first heard that they were going to come together, they were, like, "Why do we have to meet with those Afghans?" and "Why do we have to meet with those Iraqis?" But within a half day, they were, like, "Why didn't this happen before?" Because even though they're in such different countries, when it came to the impact of these wars on women's livelihoods, their identities, their families, their work, everything, they had so much in common, and to step out of the microcosm of their world and talk across a table as regional players is an empowering process . . .

So the next part of the puzzle, they wanted also to bring women from the Arab Spring in because they said, "We don't want them to have to go through what we've gone through." Isn't that amazing? Look at the hell that they've lived, and who are they looking out for? They want to talk to the Tunisians, they want to talk to the Libyans, they want to talk to the Yemenis, they want to talk to Egyptian women. Because they really want their lives to be different. To me, that's profound, given all the burdens of their everyday life, if they could prevent others from going through what they have, they want to make a difference.[47]

Notably, Kuehnast maintains that the topic of most interest to participants concerned the differing translations of the Quran and the interpretation of particular verses—especially those pertaining to women.

This brings up a important point: As former president Jimmy Carter has argued, to empower women worldwide, it will be essential for the state to engage religious figures on the subject of women's status and rights.[48] Way back in 1984, activist Robin Morgan created the Sisterhood Is Global Institute, which attempted bridge that gap by, among other activities, distributing information on women's rights under Sharia law that was translated into thirteen languages. Newer organizations, such as Women Living Under Muslim Law and Sisters in Islam, have picked up that baton. Nevertheless, even though USIP includes a Religion and Peacemaking program, it doesn't include a gender component. While the U.S. government is a secular entity, there is no question that some of the most powerful figures determining how women are treated are male religious figures. Notes Shirin Ebadi, a Nobel Peace Prize laureate from Iran, "In the Koran, the punishment for rape is death. Sexual harassment is *haram*. Even looking at women with sexual desire is *haram*. We must ask religious leaders to perform this part of Islam. They only enforce the parts to their benefit, and not those parts to their detriment."[49]

Leymah Gbowee, another Nobel Peace Prize laureate, speaks of how when she was a little girl, the Lutheran Church she attended was engaged in an anti-apartheid campaign. Every Sunday, the pastor would deliver sermons that she credits with sparking her own sense of social justice. "We must engage religious institutions; they wield so much power," she says. "We must engage their space. Our pastors must preach against rape and sexual violence. Give them reasons they should care."[50]

Might innovative programming offer religious leaders "reasons they should care" about the lives of women? In 2009, the *New York Times* profiled an effort by the NGO Marie Stopes International to speak to Afghan mullahs about lactational amenorrhea and birth spacing. The mullahs were paid to show up, and a mullah taught the class: "This was a useful and friendly discussion," said Mullah Amruddin, a tall man in a dramatic turban. "If you have too many children and you can't control them, that's bad for Islam." Maybe they were so receptive because a mullah led the class, using their own language—scripture from the Quran. Mr. Massoom, the mullah trainer, put it most directly. "This is an Islamic country," he said. "If the clerics support this, no one will oppose it."[51]

While there may be backlash if the U.S. government funds these programs directly, perhaps the United States should take a page from Ann Jones—perhaps it should, in fact, give some of its money to the Norwegians and ask that country to undertake what the U.S. government cannot—or let the Norwegians route funding to recipients that would be endangered by accepting support from the U.S. government. Take, for example, Women Under Siege, a project that chronicles in real time the violence against women in conflict zones such as Syria. Lauren Wolfe, creator of this important endeavor, recalls that although the U.S. State Department has offered to fund her efforts, she simply cannot take the money because others would believe that her program has links to the CIA. She can, however, take money from Scandinavians. Perhaps it is time for the United States to allocate funds to augment the budgets of the Nordic countries in order to support international efforts to empower and protect women.

## Harnessing the Power of Information

We have already spoken about the need to use state power to keep women "in the loop." Advanced communication and data analysis capabilities encourage us to raise our sights. Both governmental and nongovernmental actors can advance this objective. For example, the Women Under Siege project just mentioned is also a good example of how the creative use of technology can be harnessed to gather information about violence against women in real time. This type of data collection uses social media, such as Twitter feeds and cell phone footage, to document events as they evolve, such as the use of rape in the Syrian civil war.[52] HarassMap, created in December 2010, is another innovative project that uses technology to document and then to organize reaction to sexual harassment and assaults in Egypt. Rebecca Chiao, one of the founders of HarassMap, writes, "None of us wanted to start a new initiative, but at the same time, we could not continue to stand by and quietly tolerate the damaging effect sexual harassment was having on our daily lives, our choices, and our feelings of safety and pride in this country."[53]

Chiao notes that in the past, Egyptian communities curbed this type of behavior by mobilizing bystanders to stop street harassment. The traditional punishment meted out to a perpetrator involved bystanders who would chase him down then forcibly shave his head as a mark of shame. She notes that while today bystander reaction can still be mobilized to combat thievery, no longer do crowds mobilize to stop sexual harassment on the street. It is now considered normal behavior.

HarassMap members realized that in such a context, legal remedies would be ineffective, as there would be no enforcement. So Chiao and her colleagues hit upon a four-pronged approach. First, they would create on online reporting system, soliciting crowdsourced data about when and where the harassment and assaults were taking place, mapping the data and making it instantly available online. They also helped mobilize volunteers through Operation Anti-Sexual Harassment to perform rescues of women being assaulted by crowds on the basis of the HarassMap data.[54] Teams of fifteen male rescuers would wear special identifying vests and carry flares and extra clothing to help victims, who would be spirited to safe houses. Rescuers then attempt to form a human chain around the woman in order to get her to safety. Some may carry sticks to deter offenders.

HarassMap goes further, attempting to change perceptions that street attacks on women are normal. They "go door-to-door in harassment hotspots identified by the map and ask bystanders to take a stand against sexual harassment and create visible, zero-tolerance 'safe areas' in their communities." HarassMap volunteers also hand out hotline numbers on the street, so that women know how and where to access frees services offered by NGOs, such as legal aid, psychological counseling, and even a how-to guide for registering a police report. This marriage of real-time data with mobilization and the attempt to change social norms is inspiring.

Another creative use of technology is the Eyes on Darfur project, created by Amnesty International. This project uses high-resolution commercial satellite imaging to allow people from around the world to keep tabs on developments in and around twelve villages in Darfur.[55] And on the ground, organizations like mwomen.org develop cell phone interfaces and applications for women in rural Africa who are functionally illiterate. For example, mwomen has developed a Mobile Vital Records System that allows female agents to register the births of children within just a few minutes, allowing families to access state benefits for the child.[56]

Along this same line, Google Ideas is using its data streaming and visualization capabilities to help create a real-time picture of human trafficking in the United States, as is the Defense Advanced Research Projects Agency (DARPA).[57] Is it possible for the State Department, with its extensive network of employees and access to intelligence streams and the U.S. government's fleet of satellites around the world, to extend its current monitoring of the situation of women to involve real-time updating? This would enable a more rapid and creative reaction to the changing circumstances of women.

Even without advanced technology, creative responses can be crafted when the situation of women matters to those involved. Consider this rapid reaction by U.N. peacekeepers in Eastern Congo who demonstrated what Anne-Marie Goetz calls "a tactical determination to stop rape":

> [The peacekeepers] were driving trucks full of soldiers into the forest at night, when the Mai Mai rebels were around. And they would blare their lights and play music all night, and villagers would come, sometimes 3000 villagers would come and sleep around the trucks because it was safer to be out in the open around a truck than in the village where the Mai Mai were targeting women and girls. Also in early mornings [the rebels] would target women and girls going to collect water.

And these peacekeepers, somebody had commanded them to engage in this tactic, and suddenly we understood, *sexual violence can be prevented.* It absolutely can. It can be anticipated and prevented through deliberate use of intel, using women informants, using local translators, using early warning signs, like another peacekeeper was issuing women with whistles, because they didn't have phones or anything, but with whistles they could whistle from village to village to get to some kind of peacekeeper. And that it was about changing the time and space of peacekeeping. . . . So if you want to protect women, you do not patrol the main road at 2 PM in the afternoon, [because] you're going to catch the coal traffickers but you're not going to stop the rapists. [To stop the rapists] you have to go at a different time and a different space—between the village and the water at 4 AM and 5 AM. So that was a huge revelation.[58]

In addition to developing new technologies to quickly discern and react to the situation on the ground, the U.S. government already possesses incredible capabilities that it could deploy to further the Hillary Doctrine, but which have yet to be explored. Jane Mosbacher Morris, for example, focuses on human trafficking in her work for the McCain Institute for International Leadership.[59] She notes that most efforts to combat trafficking focus on the rescue and rehabilitation of victims, which is absolutely necessary. What was not being examined, however, was strategic prevention.

Morris realized that the same actors involved in human trafficking were also involved in other illicit trafficking, such as drugs and arms. But while drug trafficking and arms trafficking were considered national security concerns, human trafficking was not. It was treated as a human rights concern, and was not given the same priority on the intelligence collection list. In other words, policy makers were unable to draw the connection between human trafficking and national security. In order to see the link, one has to look for the link—and the United States wasn't looking.

As a result, the tools of strategic disruption honed by the U.S. government during the many years of the war on drugs were not being used to combat human trafficking. For example, notes Morris, the president has the authority to freeze the assets of entities posing a national security risk to the United States. The U.S. government has long used these types of strategies to disrupt terrorist and narcotrafficking networks. Among other things, these measures prohibit U.S. banks from executing transactions with entities so designated, and most foreign banks respect those measures and will freeze their activities with them. If the United States deployed these capabilities against human trafficking, it could be more effective in their disruption.

In this case, the United States already possesses the intelligence capabilities to collect and disseminate trafficking information within the U.S. government for response. What has been lacking is the vision provided by the Hillary Doctrine—that human trafficking is a national security threat.

Lastly, there is work to be done in a more traditional data collection mode: Implementing the Hillary Doctrine requires a strong evidentiary base. As we have noted, the Master List of Indicators now contains nine new gender indicators that should, within a few years, help the State Department and USAID evaluate their efforts in the area of gender. These are an excellent first start, but as noted, the indicators are not impact oriented and are steadfastly quantitative in nature. Charlotte Ponticelli comments on the need for a more nuanced approach to the collection of data that focuses on women: "I suppose it's hard to measure how much progress you're making on women because it's not just how many women in Parliament, it's, are they getting the legislation passed, and are they getting it implemented? So numbers, it's not always quantitative in terms of women, it's qualitative. And it's reconciling that gap between the de jure and the de facto implementation of women's rights and freedoms."[60]

This is an important point to which we will return later in the chapter. It is also fair to note however, that numbers are better than nothing. For example, under the legal framework developed while Clinton was secretary of state, particularly the U.S. NAP, it is now possible to determine how much the U.S. government is spending on targeted gender programming. The State Department began this practice in 2010, but the NAP has extended it to the rest of the U.S. government. This information will be very helpful when tracking funding levels from administration to administration.[61]

In addition to these welcome changes, Hillary Clinton also announced the Data 2X Initiative in July 2012:

> We keep statistics on everything we care about, from RBIs to ROI, the daily ups and downs of the Dow and our bank accounts. So if we're serious about narrowing the gender gap and helping more girls and women, then we must get serious about gathering and analyzing the data that tell the tale.
>
> Now, the data already provides strong evidence that demonstrates the links between gender equality and increased prosperity and security. This has been a real focus for us at the State Department. We have been clear from day one that when we're making the case for elevating the roles of women, we can't just rely on moral arguments as important and compelling as they might be. We have to make a rigorous case, backed up with solid evidence and data.
>
> For too many countries we lack reliable and regular data on even the basic facts about the lives of women and girls—facts like when they have their first child, how many hours of paid and unpaid work they do, whether they own the land they farm. And since women make up half the population, that's like having a black hole at the center of our data-driven universe.
>
> It keeps us from fully realizing how advancing the status of women affects women, their families, their communities, their countries, and the rest of us. And it keeps those of us looking to close the gender gap from getting the most out of our investments from either the public or the private or the not-for-profit sector. Because ultimately data are a means to an end to a more peaceful, prosperous world where women are full participants who, like men, can reach their God-given potential.
>
> Data not only measures progress, it inspires it. As we have learned in this country, what gets measured gets done. Once you start measuring problems, people are more inclined to take action to fix them because nobody wants to end up at the bottom of a list of rankings. So data are critical on both sides of the question—knowing what to do, and how to do it. . . . Getting the gender-sensitive data we need is a critical starting point.[62]

There is so much we still do not know about women's lives. For example, the staff at Equality Now was interested in whether the HIV/AIDS rate had decreased in nations such as Sweden since the imposition of an abolitionist policy against prostitution, but they were unable to locate any such research. One of us (Hudson) was interested in the prevalence of patrilocal marriage in traditional societies, which is an important indicator of a woman's status in marriage. No dataset existed. The information we eventually compiled for the database of the WomanStats Project was far from complete and took over a year to collect.[63] Dara Kay Cohen is currently developing a pioneering database identifying which combatant groups deploy sexual violence in conflict and when, a very difficult and complex task. As with so much pertaining to sexual violence, no such data existed prior to her efforts.

In other words, we have done an appalling job of collecting some of the most basic information about the lives of women around the world. This is one area in which a major initiative, such as Data 2X, is most welcome, for programming without foundational information is an exercise in futility. Policy making on behalf of women will only improve as we understand more about their lives, and this should remain a priority for Clinton's successors at the State Department.

## Reconceptualizing State Responsibilities Under Just War Theory

After conducting the research for this book, we have come to the conclusion that the Hillary Doctrine must inform our traditional concepts of just conduct by the state in war, including armed interventions. If we accepted the premises of the Hillary Doctrine, what would change?

Take *jus ad bellum*, that is, how a state is to justify the resort to war. The Hillary Doctrine would suggest that any decision to use military force that emanates from councils with little or no representation by women cannot be considered just decisions. Women may not be inherently pacifist, but they have different perspectives and priorities simply from having lived their lives as women. State decisions to resort to force are some of the most momentous a nation will ever take and cannot be considered legitimate if women—one half of the population—are excluded. Furthermore, recent research finds decision-making quality correlates with gender composition of the group, and decisions that exclude women are very likely to be suboptimal.[64] As Leymah Gbowee has said, "It's time for women to stop being politely angry. No more kneeling down in front of men asking for peace—or anything else." There is a great truth here, one forged in her experience of refusing to wait patiently for Liberian warlords to make peace. Gbowee would not have been forced to fight for peace if she had had the power to combat the decisions to go to war in the first place. For all of these reasons, we must revisit our concept of *jus ad bellum*.

*Jus in bello*, or concepts of justifiable state conduct during war, would also get a thorough makeover. In an age where the principle of discrimination (which stipulates that noncombatants cannot be targeted) is falling by the wayside owing to advances in technology and changes in war-fighting style, the perspective offered by the Hillary Doctrine would compel us to look for ways to resurrect it creatively.

For example, Anne-Marie Slaughter, formerly director of policy planning at the State Department, has championed revisiting the concept of "no-kill zones." Established along the borders of countries embroiled in a civil war, such as Syria, the principle undergirding these zones would be one of "defensive defense," where the purpose of arms is not to kill, but to defend against all killing by either side. No offensive use of arms would be permitted in these zones. As Slaughter puts it, "The international community can draw on the power of nonviolence and create zones of peace in what are now zones of death."[65] The location of these zones by the borders would prevent them from being surrounded and besieged by hostile forces (as happened in Bosnia, China, and elsewhere), while allowing for the creation of shorter humanitarian corridors, permitting food and medicine to be brought in and the heavily wounded to be evacuated. As possible using only defensive defense, these zones would be slowly expanded.

It's an interesting idea worth examining, and we do not think it is a coincidence that the idea has been revisited and revised by a female scholar. This issue of safe spaces and havens for women is a subject with great but underdeveloped potential. We also know that with proper planning, it is possible to minimize the risk of rape in displacement camps by the strategic placement of lights, barriers, and even the very layout of the camp buildings. Indeed, in recent years feminist geographers, planners, and architects have been promulgating this vision of planning for women's safety.

Beyond ideas on safe space, women's insights on what constitutes security could lead to an important reconceptualization of *jus in bello*. Anne-Marie Goetz, for example, asks some *jus in bello* questions not typically considered by the international community: "Whatever happens in Syria, is there going to be a monitoring of levels of violence against women or Syrian women who give birth in refugee camps and can't pass on their nationality to their children? Anybody going to address that? Is that going to be part of the reconstruction plan?"[66] Male-dominated governments and militaries typically don't ask these questions, which is precisely why it is so important to discover how women define security as opposed to a male-only definition. Defining security from a male perspective will inevitably leave women insecure, and leaving women insecure leaves countries insecure.[67]

Finally, given the U.S. military drawdown in Afghanistan, it is imperative that the United States develop a justifiable *jus ex bello* strategy that specifically includes planning for the physical safety of women after what may eventually become a new descent into regional strife among warlords, and perhaps even the outbreak of open conflict. Darrel Moellendorf expresses this well:

> There is a peculiar, and possibly more important, moral issue that arises when a war that satisfies just cause should be ended on grounds of the unlikelihood of success or disproportionality. For to end such a war is to admit failure for the cause of justice. Justice either cannot be achieved or only at excessively high moral costs. But the considerations that make the cause just also serve to make it appropriate to mitigate the resulting injustices of failure, to whatever extent this can be done within the constraints of the likelihood of success and proportionality.
>
> On the assumption, then, that national protection against terrorist attacks and rescuing the Afghan people from Taliban domination are just causes for continued prosecution of the war, an argument on behalf of ending the war should pay attention to the manner in which the resultant injustices—such as greater room for terrorist organizations to operate freely and poorer prospects for women, girls, minorities, and dissidents—might be mitigated.[68]

If Moellendorf is right, and we think he is, someone in the U.S. government must be tasked with thinking about the physical safety of Afghan women after the U.S. drawdown. As noted, we have seen no sign that this discussion is taking place in the Department of Defense. If not the Department of Defense, then surely the State Department and USAID have taken seriously the peril in which the United States is leaving Afghan women? USAID's PROMOTE program, which is the flagship program for Afghan women after the drawdown, includes no programming to protect the physical security of its beneficiaries.[69]

Economic development is critical, but even more so is life itself. Even if USAID is not in the business of physical safety, the success of its projects depends on it. The Afghan Women's Network already notes: "The number of female students at vocational training centers have decreased [since July 2012] because the husbands tell the women they [the husbands] will be killed by the Taliban at night if their wives go to courses. . . . It is said that the ALP [Afghan Local Police] is banning girls from accessing schools and vocational training centers by using insecurity as an excuse, instructing communities that girls must remain at home because it is not safe for them to be outside."[70] The forces of darkness that Ryan Crocker alluded to in chapter 6 want women to adopt a form of voluntary house arrest, and they may well succeed. For that reason, donors and all other concerned parties must be engaged in creative efforts to safeguard the physical security of women without constructing a new prison for them.

In chapter 6, we discussed how the Bureau of Diplomatic Security in the U.S. State Department is one of the only (if not the only) government entities active on this issue. It has been tasked with training and equipping bodyguards for high-profile Afghan women in advance of the drawdown. Generally, these bodyguards are male kin of the women. In some cases, even hardened vehicles have been provided.[71] But it is clear that barring buying an army to protect women, the U.S. government needs to be thinking in concrete terms about the physical safety of the women it encouraged to stand up and stand out while greater numbers of troops were there. The 2014 Status of Forces Agreement will leave 10,800 U.S. troops in Afghanistan. We challenge the Department of Defense to think creatively about how their assets can be used to provide some measure of safety for Afghan women.

In chapter 6, we also spoke of a robust asylum policy for Afghan women facing the threat of assassination, and this also touches on U.S. obligations under *jus ex bello*. Furthermore, if Afghanistan devolves into civil war, we believe Christine Fair is right in arguing it will be important to develop a scholarship program to take the best and brightest female Afghan students into universities outside of Afghanistan to return only when the situation becomes less volatile (and they are less likely to be targeted for assassination). While PROMOTE insists that its female beneficiaries receive their education and training in Afghanistan, it may well be that the United States should open a way through which to ensure the physical survival of those who represent the promise of Afghanistan's future by allowing some young Afghan women to leave their country for a time. While there may be but few families willing to allow their daughters travel to other countries for education, there have been enough successful training programs for Afghan women based on this very model to conclude some do exist. The United States should open that door for those prepared to use it.

Physical safety may be effected by these physical means, but there may also be diplomatic means that will reduce the probability that women will come to harm. In chapter 6 we enumerated five benchmarks by which donor nations can assess whether further aid to the Afghan government is warranted, offering some leverage to those concerned with the safety of women. These include hard targets for Afghan women's participation in peace talks and donor conferences, tracking the fate of Afghanistan's Elimination of Violence Against Women (EVAW) law and its Independent Human Rights Commission, mandating female participation in the vetting of former Taliban for employment by the Afghan Local Police, and overall monitoring of the level of violence against women after the transition.

In addition to these benchmarks, there are other important components of any *jus ex bello* strategy for Afghanistan. For example, it may well be time to up the ante in terms of standing with Afghan women against the return of darkness; it may be time to let it be known the United States will pursue International Criminal Court (ICC) indictments against top Taliban leaders who order the targeted killing of women and girls after any peace accord is negotiated. (While not a signatory to the

Rome Statute of the International Criminal Court, the United States, as a member of the P-5, has the right to refer incidents to the ICC for possible prosecution.) As a first step, the collection of witness and evidence from Afghan women concerning these crimes would mean far more than its instrumental value to the ICC. It would signal to Afghan women that the United States is not willing to overlook these crimes for the sake of political expediency.

Rule of law for women is also a cause in which the United States should heavily invest in terms of ensuring greater levels of physical safety for Afghan women under *jus ex bello*. The United States will be ramping up its funding for rule of law projects in Afghanistan from roughly $25 million a year over the past several years to approximately $200 million for the 2014 fiscal year.[72] Although this money will not be spent solely on programs to benefit women, it will still have a tangible and positive impact. Over and over, researchers have found that women simply do not know their rights, nor do they know how to exercise them. Men don't know much about the rights of women either, and even if they do, they don't necessarily care. This is precisely the environment in which male impunity with respect to crimes committed against women can flourish. Despite the fact that Afghanistan has ratified the Convention on the Elimination of All Forms of Discrimination Against Women (CEDAW) with no reservations whatsoever, judges may be sincerely or willfully ignorant of their country's resulting international legal obligations. The United States can help by making sure the means are in place by which women can learn what rights they have under Afghan law—and by which men can learn those rights as well. The Afghan Women's Network explains why a focus on men is so important:

> Few men are aware of the laws that protect women in Afghanistan and that men do not receive severe punishments for crimes against women even when they are caught. . . . Nothing has been done to educate men about women's rights. This is a mistake. Men should have been educated as well. When women ask for their rights their husbands beat them because nothing has been done to raise the awareness of men together with women.[73]

In a country with significant female illiteracy, radio is critical to the dissemination of such information. While most Afghan women enjoy access to radios, they are substantially less likely to use cell phones than men—especially in rural areas. Even when they do have access, illiteracy limits the extent to which they can make use of the phone's features. But while UNESCO, the United States, and other states such as Canada have provided substantial funding for independent community radio stations, some with programming focused specifically on women, these will likely be targeted by the Taliban and other extremist Islamic forces if Afghanistan unravels.[74] For the purposes of contingency planning under the principles of *jus ex bello*, establishing something akin to a Radio Free Women of Afghanistan station is something to be considered—even if it means broadcasting from outside the Afghan border.

The establishment of the rule of law for women will also necessitate greater participation by women in the legal and law enforcement fields, especially in Family Response Units that respond to domestic violence. While PROMOTE may help with the first, it is also important for the United States to fund projects that will encourage the Afghan National Security Forces (ANSF) and the Afghan National Police (ANP) to recruit, train and retain women.

In sum, a core part of the Hillary Doctrine must be hard-nosed thinking about the principles and logistics of *jus ex bello* for women.

## Fostering Accountability and Change by States and by Men

Throughout this book, we have noted that male impunity is critical to the ongoing subjugation and oppression of women. Holding men and male-dominated institutions accountable for the harm they cause women is integral to advancing the vision of the Hillary Doctrine. Indeed, such accountability may be too important an issue to leave to governments alone. The efforts of the U.S. government to improve the rule of law for women is usefully complemented by the work of strategic litigation carried out by NGOs—against the U.S. government itself. It was Equality Now, for example, that successfully sued the U.S. government in 1996 for imprisoning a young woman who had fled to the United States for asylum owing to her justifiable fears of undergoing genital mutilation/ cutting in her homeland of Togo. Legal pressure is often effective in goading national bureaucracies into greater accountability for what happens to women within their borders.

Equality Now is preparing to sue the U.S. government for ignoring the fact that so many contractors purchase commercial sex while working on USAID-funded projects. As Shelby Quast of Equality Now's Washington, D.C., office puts it, "A big key . . . is contractor compliance. There are laws that exist, and they are required to abide by these things 24-hours-a-day, but there's zero implementation. . . . We need to hold them accountable in a way that impacts their ability to do business. We can say, 'You have to do this because it's the right thing to do,' and that's nice, but we have to hold contractors to more."[75] Equality Now and the Service Women's Action Network (SWAN) are also working on the issue of sexual assault within the U.S. military. If the U.S. military cannot or will not enforce its own regulations designed to ensure perpetrator accountability, then a lawsuit might help the process along.[76]

It is not only U.S. soldiers, contractors, and NGO personnel that should be held to account, which brings us to the issue of malfeasance by U.N. peacekeepers. We have all heard the stories of "blue helmets" sexually abusing women and children. Most often, this is survival sex, where victims trade their bodies for food to survive one more day. Currently, the response is to pack offenders back home to their own countries where they will face little to no censure. Equality Now is also preparing to sue the United Nations on behalf of women who were raped by U.N. peacekeepers, because the onus should be on that organization to change its procedures to more effectively deter and punish those who perpetrate or enable sexual violence. Equality Now will also seek reparations, which funds will be used to improve the economic standing of survivors.

It is clear that the United Nations needs the legal authority to vet peacekeeping candidates and punish the offenders among the ranks; after all, it has already given itself plenty of authority to hold conflict participants accountable for sexual violence through several U.N. Security Council resolutions. As Anne-Marie Goetz remarks, "If you can punish deserters, you can punish sexual violence."[77] Moreover, the United Nations doesn't seem to have any difficulty disciplining whistleblowers such as the three former staff who coauthored *Emergency Sex and Other Desperate Measures: A True Story from Hell on Earth*, a stinging indictment of, among other things, the abuses perpetrated by peacekeepers in Liberia and the Democratic Republic of the Congo.[78]

Adele Kibasumba of the Democratic Republic of the Congo puts it bluntly, "We'd rather not have the UN peacekeepers in Congo. They date the girls. They rape the girls. They stand by while others kill and rape them."[79] Given the unevenness with which the United Nations holds perpetrators accountable, it is probably time it established a victims' compensation fund; indeed, it is probably time for the United States to follow suit with regard to contractors and military personnel. A reparations system has been creatively used in countries such as Uganda and the Democratic Republic of the Congo to provide victims the physical and psychological rehabilitation they need.[80] Reparations and compensation can be a powerful means of focusing attention on a previously neglected issue and can simultaneously serve the cause of economic empowerment.

More important, however, it is also time to realize that the Hillary Doctrine cannot be pursued by only paying attention to women. The oppression of women and girls originates in a toxic and dysfunctional conception of manhood. It is those narratives of masculinity that must also be addressed in any attempt to improve the situation of women— and of men—worldwide. After all, many would argue that given the high rates of violent deaths among men, hypermasculinity harms all of us, not just women.

Tawakkul Karman, a Nobel Peace Prize laureate, referred to this when she noted that in her country, Yemen, men are prized for having "red eyes"; that is, an aggressive, even hostile, character. She offered the opinion that there is no way to achieve peace without changing customs and traditions that valorize and reward male aggression. In other words, peace building means reducing conflict before it erupts into armed insurgency, wars, or widespread criminality.[81] Kathleen Kuehnast of USIP concurs: "I think we really need to engage men in this conversation about where they fit in the *Men*, Peace, and Security agenda, and offer new notions about manhood, because a lot of our problems are based in rites of passage: how do you define yourself as an adult male? And especially if all you've known for 30 years of your life is conflict and violence and that part of making your manhood is having a gun and using it. How do you separate out these identities?"[82]

The NGO Promundo is actively engaged on these very issues, implementing programs to help men redefine their manhood in a more socially constructive manner. Indeed, Steven Steiner of USIP believes this is an area in which a male U.S. secretary of state could make great strides.[83] As Joseph Vess of Promundo's Washington, D.C., office puts it, "We teach men to respect women's boundaries. On a macro level, we must as a state respect boundaries, as well."[84] Promundo sees the two goals as going hand in hand. Vess points out, "There's just no psychosocial support for men" who want to change what it means to be a man in their culture.[85]

Moreover, women and girls aren't the only victims of sexual violence. A growing body of research, including studies undertaken in the Democratic Republic of the Congo, show that men steeped in a toxic form of hypermasculinity also target other men and boys. As bad as the stigma is surrounding female survivors of male sexual violence, just as destructive is that surrounding male survivors of male sexual violence, whose very "manliness" is called into question and who often contend with a humiliation and physical trauma equal to that of their sisters.[86] Male-on-male rape is also a feminist issue because the objective of perpetrators is to emasculate the victim; in other words, to reduce him to the lowly status of female.[87] Thus, the very same mindset that sanctions sexual violence against women and girls also victimizes out-group males.

Intervention programs to help men reconceptualize masculinity have been attempted, and with good results. For example, one program in Peru involved men meeting together and questioning their own use of violence against women. In a sense, the program used the concept of male bonding to encourage men in a close-knit group to find common cause over the renunciation of domestic violence. Through this strategy, participants eliminated behavior that involved physically and sexually abusing their partner.[88] Women for Women International has also invested in a Men's Leadership Program designed to train men to educate other men to advocate for women's rights. More than two thousand participants have already graduated.[89]

Indeed, inattention to the male half of the equation will likely render Hillary Doctrine–based programming less effective. Palwasha Kakar of the Asia Foundation believes "the biggest problem that was not adequately tackled by US funding/support was to help build grassroot support for legislations and policies on gender equality and justice therefore engendering a gap between legislation and practice and between the government and the common people. The common people knew the US policy to support women's rights but weren't/aren't convinced; in fact as the US presence and support wanes, they now see it as interference and have strong reactions against laws and policies . . . wanting to purge them."[90] This happened with the Afghan EVAW law, as described in chapter 6.

Policies are likely to be more successful if men are involved from the start. Deborah Derrick, formerly with the Gates Foundation, recounts how in one region in India, rates of stunting among newborns, as well as levels of malnutrition among women of childbearing age, dropped significantly when the husband of each pregnant woman was sent a letter that read, "Dear Dad: I'm your baby. If Mom doesn't get enough food to eat, I won't be as healthy."[91] And Sanam Anderlini posits that one of the most effective ways of engaging men is to ask them a simple but thought-provoking question: In ten years' time, what do you want for your son and your daughter?[92]

This type of educational effort is not only for men in "less-developed countries." Louise Olsson describes an innovative program in Sweden called Gender Coach. Under the program, "key Defense forces personnel (at the level just under the Supreme Commander) and civilian leadership working with peace and security get a personal gender coach (mentor) for a year to improve their knowledge and skills. The rationale is that it is the leadership that sets the example in addition to setting priorities and distributing resources."[93] We would heartily endorse the import of such a program to the United States. Furthermore, it is not only the top leaders who could profit; after all, as Michele Flournoy, former undersecretary of defense for policy, explains: "The military is a supporting actor, but often it is the first actor on the ground. Education and sensitivity on these issues is important for operations. . . . People understand that this is an issue of effectiveness; they saw different results when they went down that path [of incorporating gender]."[94]

Kathleen Kuehnast of USIP notes that sometimes men tempted by the siren song of hypermasculinity to become terrorists and agents of violence need the psychosocial support of women who have been empowered to think of themselves as capable of reclaiming a radicalized loved one. This USIP program educates daughters, wives, and sisters of such men about how to recognize the signs of radicalization and provides instruction in ways to effectively intervene.

Encouraging men to change their definition of masculinity and to become more accountable is vital to the success of the Hillary Doctrine approach.

## Looking Inward

There are other initiatives, both large and small, that should be on the U.S. to-do list; several of these involve domestic affairs. The appointment of women to top posts in foreign policy and national security is necessary in order to change the atmospherics. After all, as some have noted, the glass ceiling in these fields could be more accurately described as a "thick wall of men."[95]

Nevertheless, and although Washington is, as we have already noted, still a city of men,, the U.S. government is doing better than it has in the past. A woman serves as the acting chief of the National Clandestine Service, and two other women head academic affairs at the National Defense University and the U.S. Air Force Academy.[96]

These high-level appointments and others like them should be applauded and follow-on efforts devised. One major game-changer has already taken place. In January 2013, the combat exclusion regulation was lifted for women, making it likely that there will be a higher percentage of women field officers. The integration of a female perspective at the highest levels of military service will offer a more comprehensive view of security than the United States has heretofore experienced.

Yet another item on the domestic to-do list would be the passage of the International Violence Against Women Act (IVAWA), which has not yet been brought to the floor of Congress for a vote, despite the bill's bipartisan introduction in the 110th, 111th, and 112th congresses. Because of this lack of congressional action, in 2012 USAID articulated a *United States Strategy to Prevent and Respond to Violence Against Women Globally*, and in 2013, Secretary Kerry announced the Safe from the Start initiative as a programmatic initiative of this strategy.[97] Nevertheless, the passage of IVAWA would symbolize that the Hillary Doctrine is more than simply an emphasis of the executive branch. Under IVAWA, Congress would authorize appropriations for training, monitoring, preventing, and responding to violence against women and girls, targeting five specific nations over a several-year period. Furthermore, in addition to these five countries, capacity building to address gender-based violence (GBV) would be included in all U.S. efforts in the areas of humanitarian relief, conflict, postconflict, and disaster relief programs. At one point, then-Senator John Kerry was a cosponsor of IVAWA, which makes it all the more puzzling that he has not championed the passage of this bill since becoming secretary of state.

While it may be controversial in some quarters, it seems clear that the Hillary Doctrine must also proceed hand-in-hand with greater attention to domestic issues if the United States is to be credible as a spokesnation for women worldwide. Several U.S. states now offer paid maternity leave; is it possible an administration could prioritize this issue? Isn't it also time for the Treasury and Commerce departments to count women's unpaid caretaking labor (the so-called unproductive labor mentioned earlier) as part of the GDP? Wouldn't it be possible for the Labor Department to offer greater protections for part-time workers, most of whom are women with small children? The Obama administration convened a White House Summit on Working Families in spring 2014 to tackle some of these long-standing problems, and they are well worth the attention.

These efforts to reconcile the talk with the walk could have a salutary effect in both the domestic and foreign policy realms. The perceived irony of the United States promulgating the Hillary Doctrine globally centers around such inconsistencies with our own country's practices—the United States is a glass house at which it is all too easy to lob stones. It never fails to amaze observers, for example, that the Iraq and Afghanistan constitutions that the United States helped draft stipulate quotas for women that have resulted in significantly higher representation in both countries than can be found in the U.S. Congress, and that families in both nations enjoy paid maternity leave, while the United States offers none. It's time to build that house of sterner stuff.

## Reforming the U.S. Foreign Aid System

It's also time to examine more closely how bureaucratic procedures have combined to produce less than satisfactory U.S. foreign policy outcomes, which undercut the impact of the Hillary Doctrine. For example, the short tours of State Department personnel abroad, as so devastatingly chronicled by Peter Van Buren in chapter 5, undermine the ability of the U.S. to put forward coherent and consistent programming on the ground.

The most crucial transformation in our opinion, however, is a complete overhaul of the way the United States conducts its foreign assistance programs. Three major issues loom large: (1) the unintended perverse incentives created by the Government Performance and Results Act (GPRA), (2) the transformation of USAID into a contracting agency through extreme cuts to staffing levels, and (3) the uneasy fit between the State Department and USAID. We will describe each in turn.

We have already discussed how GPRA—ironically enacted during the Clinton administration—has led to a U.S. style of "big RFP, big contractors, quantitative indicators, high burn rate, short-term outcomes." This approach needs to be rethought—that is, if peace and stability really are the objective. What seems like a rational programming system under GPRA has, in far too many cases, produced irrational outcomes. In the words of Andrew Natsios, former administrator of USAID, "measurability should not be confused with development significance."[98]

The next administration should question the GPRA approach, especially as it relates to long-term development initiatives. And, using the terminology employed by Natsios, it is imperative to examine how, in particular, the compliance "counter-bureaucracy" is undermining the credibility of U.S. foreign aid efforts.[99] What Natsios is referring to is how the United States currently ensures compliance—that is, through a simplistic monitoring and evaluation mechanism—is harmful to its objectives. The United States may legitimately prefer long-term objectives, but because of GPRA, the government has been legally forced to become shortsighted, with time horizons of twelve months in most cases.

In addition to the now-legislated inability to ever look beyond the short-term time horizon, the concept of rewarding burn rate (see chapter 5) must be one of the most pernicious output indicators ever devised. It incentivizes waste, corruption, and sheer lunacy: It also generates a demand for large, for-profit institutional development contractors that spend money as if it was water, with next to no accountability whatsoever. Natsios observes:

> Senior AID officers would protest at these meetings about how foolish and counterproductive this metric was for judging program performance, as it created a powerful incentive for USAID officers to use mechanisms to spend money quickly as opposed to mechanisms that were the most programmatically successful over the long term. Fast disbursement would avoid any Afghan or Iraqi input, management, or leadership in program decision making (essential to getting local ownership), because such activities inevitably meant long debates, negotiations, and delays, slowing the burn rates to a crawl. This perverse incentive encouraged money to be spent through large NGOs and contractors that could spend the money faster than virtually any other international aid agency and certainly much faster than developing country governments.
>
> This practice has restricted newer, smaller, and local organizations from competing for grants and contracts, because these organizations lack the business systems to follow U.S. federal law and regulation, to account properly for all funds, to disburse money quickly, and to produce measurable and auditable results. The notion that a developing world company can easily comply with the requirements of the Federal Acquisition Regulations and the Foreign Assistance Act . . . is preposterous. . . . This has meant more funding for Bechtel Corporation in Iraq (at least as a prime contractor) than a local Iraqi company, or to large established NGOs such as CARE, Save the Children, Catholic Relief Services, and World Vision, rather than to Mother Teresa's charity or a local social entrepreneur. . . . Equally important, the transactional costs of funding a $1 million grant to a small NGO is the same as a $20 million contract to a large established partner organization because of the nature of federal regulatory requirements, and so it makes little management sense with a limited staff to fund smaller grants and organizations.[100]

The GPRA approach guarantees that the United States will be for-ever counting textbooks printed rather than knowledge gained. Service delivery will always be prized over institution building, because it can be measured quantitatively and institution building cannot. It also means that USAID winds up not in the business of empowering the Education Ministry of, say, Yemen, but of empowering a large for-profit contractor instead. Something is amiss.

Which brings us to the next issue. USAID wasn't formerly a contract management agency; as we have discussed, it used to be an operational agency. But since the 1970s, USAID has suffered a 75 percent reduction in staff.[101] Currently, a small number of employees are scrambling to meet high demands to push paper in order to comply with federal regulations. A perfect storm consisting of GPRA plus plummeting personnel levels, combined with vastly enlarged budgets stemming from the engagements in Afghanistan and Iraq, means that USAID cannot be or do what was intended. Shannon Beebe notes that his colleagues at USAID remind him "that there are fewer full-time staff employed by USAID than there are members of US Army marching bands."[102] Natsios asserts that at least a third of the small number of USAID employees are hired to work on compliance with GPRA alone. Because of this lamentable situation, as Christine Fair of Georgetown University expresses it, "Institutional con-tractors hand it off to institutional subcontractors. As long as the money is allocated, USAID is done. It's the allocation rate that matters."[103] This must change.

And finally, it may be time to rethink the uneasy relationship between the State Department and USAID. During the Clinton administration, USAID, which was originally a stand-alone agency, was folded into the State Department. All USAID appointments are now decided by the State Department, and the State Department is now responsible for USAID's budgeting and its strategic planning. But this may not be the optimal arrangement. Natsios observes:

> Both defense and diplomacy share a common short-term time horizon inconsistent with that of development, which requires a longer time-frame for planning and success. The demands made by the U.S. defense and diplomatic establishments of development agencies (usually the U.S.

Agency for International Development [USAID] in the case of the U.S. Government) during and following conflicts contradict good development practice and the dynamics of collapsed states. Defense and diplomacy demand more immediate results than what are achievable given the nature of social change and institution-building in the postconflict setting. When the results produced by aid programs are not what the other agencies of the U.S. Government expect, aid or development is said to have "failed" when in fact the demands were inconsistent with historical and developmental reality.

The bureaucratic weakness of the development function in the U.S. Government has meant operationally that it will lose bureaucratic and policy battles, not because its perspective is less legitimate than those of diplomats and military officers, but because it is not at the table or its positions contradict those of its State Department superiors. Unless policymakers seek out development expertise, the short planning requirements of American diplomacy and military operations will overwhelm the long-term development requirements to create a sustainable peace.[104]

The situation is not hopeless, but it certainly is dire. Natsios' analysis of the situation lends itself to some obvious workarounds, such as gaining congressional exemption from the quantitative measuring of certain categories of long-term projects, such as institution-building projects and governance programming. These types of programs should be evaluated through field impact evaluations, which are more appropriate for such purposes. This is not unprecedented—Congress exempted all CERP funds (Commander's Emergency Response Program funds, disbursed by the Department of Defense Provincial Reconstruction Teams). Hillary Clinton herself once explained why: "In Afghanistan, the Pentagon has a fund that allows a young American officer to take $100,000 in discretionary funds and rebuild a school on his own authority. By contrast, a diplomat or development expert trying to rebuild a school would spent months filling out forms, and probably still wouldn't get the money out of Congress."[105]

These workarounds, however, are only Band-Aids; there are still larger reforms that need to be tackled. In addition to exemptions, the two most important reforms are, at least to these outsiders, (1) to return to a more decentralized USAID programming and procurement model , which will (2) necessitate a substantial increase in USAID field personnel. Field missions should once again be the most important decision-making node for USAID; right now, it is the State Department that calls the shots even though the requisite expertise still lies with the agency.

How the Hillary Doctrine plays out on the ground, then, may be vastly different from how Washington officials envision it in part because of the profound dysfunctionality inherent in the current U.S. foreign aid system. It is therefore necessary to move beyond the concept of the burn rate and easily assessed, but superficial, indicators of success. The State Department and USAID need to steer the ship of state back on course, and that means a high-level rethinking of the context in which foreign aid is administered.

## *Mustering Presidential Will*

The most important ingredient of all may be the most elusive, at least for now. And that is the will to implement the Hillary Doctrine, which can only come from the White House itself.

Yes, the State Department has to be committed, at levels both high and low. Says Yasmeen Hassan of Equality Now, "You either feel it or you don't. You need to put people in place who care. But their promotion is not based on caring about these issues."[106]

But it could be. A good first start would be to base performance criteria on the achievement of hard gender targets, such as matching the United Nations' goal of spending 15 percent of any postconflict budgeting on the empowerment of women.[107] Otherwise, as Michelle Barsa of the Institute for Inclusive Security put it, "with Kerry, we may lose the white male middle management who were only doing this to please their boss, who was Hillary Clinton."[108] But this is also an opportunity for Clinton's successor. According to Kathleen Kuehnast of USIP: "Kerry can carry this agenda even further because he's a guy. He has all the credibility of Washington. . . . He can take it to the next level—making gender part and parcel of all we are doing, and not silo it."[109] If anyone could integrate gender as vital enough to warrant inclusion in an annual performance evaluation, it would be someone like John Kerry.

The Obama White House itself, however, would first need to prioritize gender itself in order for Kerry to follow suit. We have already seen how Clinton was denigrated for having focused on "small-bore" interests such as women. Some smirked at her championing of cookstoves as a "little" issue even though pollution from cooking fires disproportionately hurts women on an immense scale worldwide.[110]

If Kerry is aiming to be another Acheson or Kissinger because his boss is intent on solidifying his legacy as a "foreign policy president," the United States will be stuck with the same old metrics that resulted in our current dysfunctional foreign policy. Although the jury is still out, thus far Kerry's rhetoric in support of women's rights comes across as increasingly hollow: it hasn't been accompanied by obvious benchmarks, such as including women in peace negotiations, whether in Syria, in Afghanistan, or in numerous other countries. The Office of Global Women's Issues under Ambassador Catherine Russell operates with a budget of $3.4 million and a staff of twenty-four. It is grossly underfunded considering that it is supposed to represent the interests of one half of the world's population.[111]

But this remains a larger issue that goes way beyond the narrow confines of State Department politics—as important as that is. This snippet of conversation between Valerie M. Hudson and Ryan Crocker is illuminating:

HUDSON: You feel that American foreign policy should be concerned about what happens to women.

CROCKER: Absolutely.

HUDSON: And you also feel that it's feasible, although at times, like with Saudi Arabia, not expedient.

CROCKER: Or doable.

HUDSON: But that where it's doable we have the leverage to not only create these gains, but sustain them if we want to.

CROCKER: Yeah.

HUDSON: What stands in our way?

CROCKER: Lack of focus. Ignorance. And simply being overburdened. Somebody of influence has to explain to the president and his key advisers what's at stake here.[112]

We'd like to suggest, with all due respect, that Crocker may be wrong on this one. It may be that the only way truly to implement the Hillary Doctrine is if the president of the United States is that "somebody" who explains to the key advisers what's at stake. The United States needs a president capable of asserting, without any prodding or coaching, "I believe that the rights of women and girls is the unfinished business of the twenty-first century," and "Give women equal rights, and entire nations are more stable and secure. Deny women equal rights, and the instability of nations is almost certain. The subjugation of women is, therefore, a threat to the common security of our world and to the national security of our country."[113] But the United States is not there—yet.

In the meantime, there is much that can be learned from the attempts of the United States to implement the Hillary Doctrine. We have learned a great deal about what works and also about what doesn't. As Michele Flournoy, the former Undersecretary of Defense for Policy puts it, "I'd look to see where we've succeeded and where we've failed. I'd like to see the US government press on this as a major area of focus with foreign and security policy."[114] There's a substantial to-do list for current and future secretaries of state (and defense) unwilling to see the Hillary Doctrine lost to the slipstream of time.

## A FARTHER SHORE? THE RESPONSIBILITY TO PROTECT WOMEN

Even with this list in hand, there may be larger issues to contemplate. For example, David Rothkopf, editor of *Foreign Policy*, offers a different set of metrics. His elegant but direct prose lifts our sights to a higher horizon: one where Realpolitik and Fempolitik are not from Mars and Venus:

> The underrepresentation of women in positions of power is proof not so much that men still dominate the top of the pyramid as it is of a system of the most egregious, widespread, pernicious, destructive pattern of human rights abuses in the history of civilization. There is no genocide against any people that has produced more victims than the number of females who have lost their lives to discrimination against the birth of girl babies

(in Pakistan alone, for instance, there is a culturally encouraged "shortage" of an estimated 6 million females), or who have died from the unwillingness of societies to provide the health care women need, or who die as a result of social customs that allow fathers to kill daughters for "shaming" families, husbands to kill wives for adultery, and men to perpetrate other horrific violence against women. That countless millions of women are also regularly raped, beaten, and abused by men only compounds these atrocities.

The systematic, persistent acceptance of women's second-class status is history's greatest shame. And for all our self-congratulations about how far we have come, we live in a world where even in the most advanced countries, deep injustices against women remain. These injustices, of course, have other costs beyond the purely human ones. Nothing would help societies grow more than educating and empowering women economically. Democracy is a sham until the planet's majority population actually achieves equitable representation in deliberative bodies and executive positions of government. And the absence of women in positions of power is also, of course, a guarantee that women's interests will continue to be minimized, ignored, or repressed.

We're talking about nothing less than an epoch-long war on a people here, an effort to hold back the economic—and social—progress of the majority of humanity. So how come the tough guys of the foreign-policy community continue to denigrate this as a "soft" issue, one of secondary importance at best?[115]

Rothkopf is suggesting that what some have seen as "small" or "soft" issues are not small at all and neither are they soft—adjectives that are ironically used to describe the female body itself. No, these are the largest, hardest issues of all. Yet Americans avert their gaze and tell themselves that gendercide is either normal or at least unremarkable. Americans tell themselves that "real men" are concerned with any issue but this one. Cindy McCain reflects, "When I talk about rape in Congo, people turn their backs and run, especially the men."[116] Americans tell themselves that U.S. national security interests may well depend on ignoring the enormity of this horror. After all, bringing up these inconvenient truths simply "pisses off the men you need to make peace." Americans have told themselves there is nothing that can be done about it anyway. As Dee Dee Myers describes this mindset, "We'll fix the 'real' problems and then we'll worry about women."[117]

Is the United States really that helpless in the face of genocide, just because it is perpetrated not against an ethnic minority, but against *women*?

In the field of security studies, Realpolitik dominates. In addition to its emphasis on power as the ultimate national interest, those who adhere to this worldview are committed to accepting empirical evidence when it is placed before their eyes—that is to accept the world as it really is and not what it ideally should be. As Walter Lippmann wrote, "We must not substitute for the world as it is an imaginary world."[118]

It's ironic, then that Realpolitik is set up as the foil to the Hillary Doctrine,[119] for there is copious empirical evidence that the security of women and the security of the states in which they lived is closely linked. As elucidated in chapter 2, research reveals that the very best predictor of a state's peacefulness is not its level of wealth, its level of democracy, or its ethno-religious identity; the best predictor of a state's peacefulness is the security of its women. What's more, democracies with higher levels of violence against women are as insecure and unstable as non-democracies.

Our findings echo those of other scholars, who have found that the larger the gender gap between men and women, the more likely a country is to be involved in intrastate and interstate armed conflict, to be the first to resort to force, and to resort to higher levels of violence in conflict. Concerning issues of national health, economic growth, corruption, and social welfare, the best predictors are also those that reflect the situation of women. The status of women affects the security, stability, prosperity, bellicosity, corruption, health, regime type, and (yes) the power of the state. The days when one could claim that the situation of women had nothing to do with matters of national or international security are, frankly, over. The empirical results to the contrary are just too numerous and too robust to ignore. Americans owe it to themselves to be realistic about the world in which they live.

It's ironic that authors such as Steven Pinker, who claim that the world is becoming much more peaceful, have not recognized that everyday violence against women is, if anything, becoming more prevalent, and not less so, and that it dwarfs that which results from war and armed conflict.[120] To say a country is at peace when its women are subject to widespread domestic violence, rape, and femicide—or to ignore violence against women while claiming, as Pinker does, that the world is now more secure—is simply to abandon realism.

The evidence is clear: The primary human rights challenge of the twenty-first century is to eliminate violence against women and remove barriers to developing their strength, creativity, and voice. A bird with one broken wing or a species with one wounded sex will never soar—nor solve the many crises that now afflict the world's societies and the planet. It is incumbent upon Americans—it is incumbent upon all—to try a different path, one we have every empirical reason to believe will lead to greater well-being, prosperity, and security for international and national systems alike. Realpolitik and Fempolitik are not foes—the Hillary Doctrine is a fundament of Realpolitik.[121]

Perhaps now is the time to rework foundational concepts as democracy and national interest, and even more recent concepts such as R2P—the Responsibility to Protect.

Consider democracy, for example. As secretary of state in 2011, Hillary Clinton asserted that, "Any democracy that does not include half its population—its women—is a contradiction in terms."[122] Perhaps it is time to treat those nations that exhibit such contradictory tendencies with the same diplomatic opprobrium reserved for those who constrain the civil liberties of their male citizens. And perhaps it is time to reconsider whether continued close relations with nations that make no pretense concerning their subordination of women contribute to U.S. national interests or not. Remember what Donald Steinberg said, "Compare those societies that respect women and those who don't. Who's trafficking in weapons, drugs? Who's harboring terrorists and starting pandemics? Whose problems require US troops on the ground? There's a one-to-one correspondence. Don't tell me there's no relationship between national security and the empowerment of women."[123]

Steinberg is challenging the U.S. definition of *national interest*. Surely, if the security of women is integrally linked to the security of the states in which they live, then nations are insecure and unstable to the degree to which women's security is compromised. And the degree to which the international system or its regional subsystems are dominated by states in which women are insecure, so too do those systems become insecure and unstable. Is it really possible, for example, for China to "rise peacefully" while culling almost 15 percent of its daughters from the birth population and continuing the practice of government-mandated forced abortions and sterilizations of women? Using the lens of the Hillary Doctrine, we think not.

This brings us to back to the central question we have posed in this final chapter: Is the United States really that helpless in the face of genocide, just because it is perpetrated not against an ethnic minority, but against women?

Even feminists who would not consider themselves hawks sometimes find themselves admitting, as Lauren Wolfe did during an interview with Hudson, "I get so angry. Our red line is chemical weapons in Syria, and not the mass assault of women. I don't want intervention, but how can we not advocate for something to be done? And in the meantime, NGO workers trade food coupons for sex in the Syrian refugee camp—of course."[124]

If Fempolitik is in fact integral to Realpolitik, could the treatment of women ever reach the status of a vital national interest, for which we would be prepared to do something more than talk?[125]

As noted earlier in this book, even Hillary Clinton and Laura Bush articulated a stance that could reasonably be placed in this camp with regard to the Taliban's treatment of women. If the extreme oppression of women is antithetical to U.S. national interests and the stability of the international system, how can states remain quiescent over this threat?

And yet the United States continues to remain silent in the face of the mass violation of the rights of one half of humanity in various parts of the world. In 2011, even mentioning that the new regimes that came to power in the wake of the Arab Uprising threatened women's rights provoked retorts (by Westerners!) that mentioning this constituted a cynical ploy to keep corrupt allies in power. When the Muslim Brotherhood was overthrown by Egypt's military, Western commentators called it a coup—the very same pundits who remained silent as the Brotherhood summarily fired women from government posts and sought to reinstate child marriage during its brief reign.

This is the same inscrutable reaction that met *Time* magazine's 2012 cover story of the young Afghan woman, Bibi Aisha, whose father-in-law, husband, and others sliced off her ears and nose.[126] Anyone who expressed second thoughts about what the U.S. drawdown would mean for the women of Afghanistan was accused of being a puppet of hegemonic militarism; indeed, some critics labeled the article itself as "war porn." A male Afghan national working for USAID responded incredulously: "I don't think westerners understand what it was like under the Taliban. I saw one old woman pulled off the bus because when she reached up to steady herself part of her forearm showed. They took her right then and there and chopped off her arm."

To worry about the fate of Afghan women when U.S. troops draw down is a reflection of the best instincts of Americans, not their worst instincts. As journalist Soraya Chemaly puts it, "There has to be a place for American women to say, 'We stand in solidarity with women in the Middle East' without being labeled racist, imperialist, etc. Liberal Westerners need to get over their fears of Western imperialism and stand up for women's rights."[127] Americans—especially American women—are right to ask why they sent their sons and daughters to fight and die so that Afghan women can continue to be treated like an inferior subspecies of humanity.

At the same time, there are those who will justifiably say, if it's hypermasculinity that causes militarism, how can one possibly rationalize being hawkish on behalf of women? Isn't the cure going to cause more harm? After all, when asked whether the U.S. invasion of Iraq had helped that country's women, former ambassador to Iraq Ryan Crocker leaned back in his chair and chuckled bitterly before answering with a simple "No!" Iraqi women concur: activist Yanar Mohammad asserts, "Although people in this part of the world think that Iraqi women are liberated, actually, we have lost all of the achievements and all the status that we used to have."[128]

But the opposite course—inaction—seems to bring its own moral complexities. If babies were being aborted simply because they were French, there would be an international outcry followed by action. If Swedes were targeted for assassination because they dared to leave their homes and venture outside, the U.N. Security Council would act. Are Americans simply unwilling to see gendercide as the genocide it really is because victims just happen to be women? Is the violation of their rights so accepted that inaction seems justified?

Such inaction seems to be at odds with the concept of an international "responsibility to protect."[129] In 2005, the U.N. General Assembly adopted the principle of R2P, or Responsibility to Protect. It establishes three pillars of international conduct: first, that states protect their citizens; second, that the international community assist states in protecting their citizens when conflict threatens to break out within the nation; and third, that the international community step in to protect citizens whose states are waging war against them. This last was based on data showing that most victims of conflict die in civil wars or are killed by their own governments.

Arguably, it was NATO that undertook the first military intervention launched under R2P. This followed a U.N. Security Council resolution authorizing the enforcement of a no-fly zone to prevent the Libyan military from killing its own people. Notably, based on information gleaned from insiders, it was not Secretary of Defense Robert Gates who pushed for the intervention (initially, he appeared to oppose it), but rather Secretary of State Hillary Clinton.[130] This position mirrored an earlier historical situation, in which another female secretary of state, Madeleine Albright, likewise pushed a reluctant military to protect Bosnian civilians from Serb atrocities.

We find it interesting that in these cases it has been female leaders in the United States who have advocated proactive intervention to blunt egregious human rights violations. It is as if they offer a different answer to the question, "What's a military for?" Their answer is that it exists to protect those who cannot protect themselves—in the name of justice and in order to bring about peace. Indeed, security scholars are beginning to discuss a new paradigm for intervention, one that emphasizes human security over state security and defense over victory. This approach might include innovative programs such as the arms-for-development program in Sierra Leone, where villages were offered their choice of development projects in exchange for allowing community-based volunteers to collect weapons. As Beebe and Kaldor explain, "Human security operations, even in the midst of war, are in support of law and order where law and order is based on human rights. This has profound implications for the rules of engagement, [which] are shaped by domestic law rather than by the laws of armed conflict."[131]

Even so, the consequences for women of the overthrow of Libya's Muammar Gadhafi, Iraq's Saddam Hussein and other autocratic but secular tyrants caution against destroying state power—even authoritarian state power—without seriously considering the long-term ramifications. This is because it is usually women who come out the worst. As noted earlier, Gadhafi's ouster resulted in that nation's women losing what few rights they possessed—something that could be said of the Arab Uprising in general. Even more disappointing, as Sanam Anderlini notes, "The US did nothing to push the Libyan leaders on gender. You had the NAP in place, you have a real-live case in front of you—why didn't we say, 'Where are the women?'"[132]

Military action in and of itself against regimes violating human rights will not protect women. If anything, it unleashes new and usually even more vicious male-bonded groups intent on stripping them of even the most basic human rights. The realization that such interventions to promote human rights and/or democracy have results that differ so drastically by sex—that they actively hurt women by empowering the very men who seek to profit politically from their subordination—is stunning.

In light of this, we propose the "Steinem test," named after Gloria Steinem's revelation about the Afghan mujahideen presented in chapter 1: In a conflict where one side aspires to create (or has created) a worse situation for women than the other side, *the United States should not back that side*. We can think of a number of instances where that simple rule would have saved our nation tremendous regret. The first question to ask any opposition group seeking U.S. support is very simple: What is your stance on women?

That Secretary Clinton is both an advocate of R2P and the author of the Hillary Doctrine prompts a natural question: Is there an international Responsibility to Protect Women (R2PW)? If not, should there be? If the security of states is rooted in the security of women, as we have argued and hopefully also demonstrated, is not the international community of states obligated to stand with women when their own governments and countrymen subjugate, oppress, cull, and kill them? The concept of an R2PW would be, in essence, the Hillary Doctrine rewritten for the world stage.

We argue that it is time acknowledge the status of women as one of the foremost issues facing the international community today. It is time for the U.N. Security Council and General Assembly to hold nations accountable for how women are treated within their borders. Fully 50 percent of humanity is affected both directly and personally—something that cannot be said about any other international security problem. Not only is it time to make plain the link between the security of women and that of states and the international system, but also to clarify the responsibility of the international community to undertake stronger actions to pressure countries into more proactively safeguarding women's rights.

If an R2PW mindset had already been established, the international community would not have waited until after the events of 9/11 to move against the Taliban: It would have done so as soon as women were stripped of their livelihoods, their education, their autonomy and even the most basic of rights. This type of action need not be military in nature, but might resemble the international community's vigorous campaign against the South African apartheid regime during the 1980s and early 1990s. Regimes with atrocious records in defending the security and the rights of women must be held to account, publicly named, and materially punished.

The groundwork for such an R2PW is already being built. U.N. Security Council Resolutions 1325, 1820, 1888, 1889, 1960, 2106, and 2122 are important milestones in the development of a nascent R2PW consciousness. But it must also be acknowledged that the United Nations is as flawed a champion of an R2PW as the United States is of the Hillary Doctrine.

As we have seen, even the binding nature of U.N. Security Council resolutions pertaining to women, such as UNSCR 1325, have been systematically sidestepped by even those Security Council members who initially voted for them. Indeed, as Anne-Marie Goetz of UNWomen notes, "Russia and China dispute everything [about the Women, Peace, and Security agenda]; they really want it all to stop."[133] Moreover, Member States refuse to regularly monitor and report their obligations under UNSCR 1325: antipathy and indifference appear to rule the day.[134] Similarly, even though the United Nations has set a target of 50/50 representation of women within its own ranks, it is nowhere near achieving this goal. The percentage of women occupying senior positions is especially low, hovering stubbornly around 25 percent.[135] Indeed, very few U.N. organizations have even established a timeline by which to reach this goal.

To make matters worse, United Nations peacekeeping troops continue to be implicated in the sexual and physical abuse of women, girls, and boys in areas where they have deployed. While many laud the excellent work of female peacekeepers, especially in regions characterized by high levels of gender-based violence, only 2.7 percent of U.N. peacekeepers and 9.8 percent of U.N. police are female.[136] Plainly, the United Nations has work to do.

Regional international governments such as the European Union will play an important role as well. The European Union (EU) adopted a resolution in March 2012, calling for gender equality in economic affairs, governance and decision making in addition to an end to gender-based violence.[137] Although the EU is tackling domestic violence and harmful traditional practices such as female genital cutting (FGC), and attempting to ensure that all member states harmonize their laws with respect to women's rights, Europe still struggles with human trafficking, the forced sterilization of minority women (such as the Roma), and enclaves where forced marriages and honor killings continue.

Similarly, although twenty-eight of fifty-three states in sub-Saharan Africa ratified The Maputo Protocol on the Rights of Women in Africa, that leaves twenty-seven states that have failed to do so.[138] In 1994, the Organization of American States adopted the Inter-American Convention on the Prevention, Punishment, and Eradication of Violence Against Women, yet femicide rates in Latin America continue to soar. Even global summits ignore women; the World Economic Forum in Davos is a case in point. That august convocation takes place every year in Switzerland, where it gathers together global leaders, business leaders, and celebrities to discuss the "big" problems facing humanity. Nevertheless, women remain conspicuously underrepresented (less than 5 percent in 2009 and in 2013, only 17 percent were participants), while the agenda remains largely bereft of any content addressing the perspectives or concerns of women.[139] Although this gaping void sparked the establishment of a parallel shadow meeting for women in Deauviille, France, the fact that it was even necessary for one half of humanity to meet at a separate summit is staggering.[140] How long will women and those issues that concern them—and by extension concern all of humanity—continue to be infantilized and relegated to the little table, while the "adults" at the big table carry on completely unaware?

If indignation doesn't work, then maybe evidence will. One of the very first steps necessary in order to establish R2PW on the international and national stage is to gather the data necessary to justify its implementation and to rank nations according to what degree each takes its responsibilities seriously.

Moreover, such ranking efforts must be multivariate—meaning involving more than one variable. This will ensure that researchers and policy makers have access to as accurate an accounting as possible. After all, South Africa's national legislature is made up of nearly the highest percentage of female parliamentarians in the world, but does that compensate for the fact that the country has among the highest rates of rape in the entire world?

These types of rankings would not only serve as a mechanism to rationalize action against states that flout their obligations, but could also focus state efforts in areas of particular concern. For example, while most view Sweden as a haven for women, reports indicate that levels of domestic violence in that country have spiraled upward in recent years.[141] A detailed and comprehensive analysis of R2PW-relevant measures could help spot such problems early on, hopefully prompting state intervention or, in its absence, regional or international community censure.

In addition, such an analysis would promote the development of "impact-on-women" studies that should take place before the enactment of any new national or international economic or security policies. If this indicator system were longitudinal, it could also monitor and even forecast the probable consequences to women of new policy initiatives. This would promote a more holistic approach to policy evaluation than that which currently exists. Measures of GDP for example, often exclude the reproductive unpaid labor of women, masking policy effects on the rationality of caregiving in society. A new set of measures would cease "invisibilizing" women's labor, the value of which is imputed at almost half of global calculated GDP, and in this way promote more effective policy making.

It is imperative also to track the discrepancy between a state's international obligations to women, national laws, and the real situation of women on the ground.

For example, do those who recommend and implement military interventions monitor whether doing so improves or detracts from the security of women? Is anyone asking whether an influx of International Monetary Fund or bilateral loans changes the situation of women for the better? No one really knows—but this information would provide crucial input for quality policy making.

Similarly, there are several important historical questions that have been neither raised nor answered. When nations make the transition to greater levels of gender equality, which changes do they implement first? What changes then follow? Do these depend on region or religious affiliation? Can researchers trace the path dependence of nations that have more fully made that transition to greater gender equality? Can nations learn from one another? For example, what measures did nations such as Morocco and Tunisia take to curtail polygamy, and could those be deployed in other Islamic countries? These types of historical inquiries should not shy away from pointing out how those nations that currently enjoy relative gender equality can improve their own situation. In terms of gender equality, there is not a single nation on the planet today that can claim that women and men enjoy equal economic, social and political rights within their borders.

Armed with pertinent knowledge and a tracking and monitoring indicator system that actually works, concerned citizens, states and multilateral organizations would be poised to do more than simply ruminate on the most pervasive abuse of human rights in the world. They would be in a position to effectively pressure—perhaps by the application of sanctions—those states that failed in their application of R2PW.[142]

It is high time for nations that signed onto the Women, Peace, and Security agenda to call out other nations for their indifference or even hostility to women. Violence against women cannot remain the price to be paid for international comity. And through the regional and international organizations of which they are members, states should begin to treat these violations as the grave threat to national and international security that they truly are. The abuse, marginalization, impoverishment, and discrimination of women should be condemned as harshly as any other breach of an important treaty—such as the Non-Proliferation Treaty (NPT). A wide array of diplomatic and economic instruments can and should be deployed to support R2PW— just as they would be if the treaty in question were the NPT. This, to our mind, would constitute the "doing something" that Lauren Wolfe envisioned but could not articulate.

R2PW, then, may well be the true destiny of the Hillary Doctrine.

## FINAL THOUGHTS

The Hillary Doctrine helps create a new standard for analyzing the national interest, one that we would argue is more realistic than previous metrics. What some see as soft and small issues are, in fact, some of the most vital interests facing the United States and the international community of nations today. As Donald Steinberg noted, there is a one-to-one correspondence between countries of greatest concern to the United States and countries in which women are treated poorly: the Fempolitik encoded in the Hillary Doctrine is a central pillar of clear-eyed Realpolitik.

Nevertheless, the scorecard for the Hillary Doctrine is mixed, and the United States can learn from that record. While there have been victories, such as the creation of the U.S. National Action Plan, there have also been troubling inconsistencies and lapses. As we have seen, the issue of proper implementation dogged the Hillary Doctrine from the very beginning. The analysis of what worked and what didn't—and why—will be an essential task for any future U.S. president who cares deeply about these issues.

But the mixed scorecard may simply be the result of growing pains. It may be too soon to tell. The more worrying issue may be whether there is still time to tell if it is too soon to tell. Michelle Barsa puts it this way: "Was the acceptance of women as a focus driven by operational realities or by rhetoric? If the former, it will survive."[143] And what Barsa implies is also true: If most in the American foreign policy establishment felt it was only rhetoric and did not understand the operational realities, the Hillary Doctrine will be as ephemeral as Clinton's four-year tenure as secretary of state.

We believe there is reason for optimism, at least in the long term. As Donald Steinberg believes, "time is on our side."[144] What he means by this is that there is a younger generation that has been trained to internalize gender in a way that preceding generations were not. And as we argued earlier in this chapter, the structure of institutions and legal obligations built during Clinton's tenure will be almost impossible to reverse, even if it is still possible for the White House to use indifference to undermine it.

In the final analysis, though, the Hillary Doctrine's legacy will be judged by whether the phrase "the Hillary Doctrine" disappears from the vernacular. Tobie Whitman explains: "The goal is that it no longer is the Hillary Doctrine, or attached to any specific individual, but it's just the standard operating practice."[145]

The hope is that what is now known as the Hillary Doctrine will one day become an accepted, indeed standard, frame of reference founded on a firm evidentiary base. What is currently thought of as the 'revolutionary' Hillary Doctrine should become just another day at the office for those who succeed her in the halls of power. And when that day comes, seeing women as integral to national and international security will have become as natural and unremarkable as not seeing them once was.

Here's to that day.

# NOTES

★ ★ ★

## PREFACE

1. Hillary Clinton, "Remarks at the TEDWomen Conference" (speech at Ronald Reagan Building, Washington, D.C., December 8, 2010), accessed September 15, 2013, http://www.state.gov/secretary/rm/2010/12/152670.htm.
2. Ibid.

## 1. HOW SEX CAME TO MATTER IN U.S. FOREIGN POLICY

1. Hillary Clinton, 2010, "Remarks at the TEDWomen Conference." Ronald Reagan Building, Washington, D.C., December 8, 2010, http://www.state.gov/secretary/20092013clinton/rm/2010/12/152671.htm.
2. "Clinton Addresses State Department First Day on Job."
3. "Subjugation of Women Is Threat to US Security."
4. U.S. Department of State and U.S. Agency for International Development, *Leading Through Civilian Power*.
5. Tétreault, "Justice for All."
6. See, for example, Beevor, "'They Raped Every German Female from Eight to 80.'" See also Morrow, review of *Taken by Force*.
7. Tétreault, "Justice for All."
8. Sanger, "Wako Journal." The issue continues to reverberate: In May 2013, the mayor of Osaka declared that wartime sex slavery was "necessary" and that "anyone would understand" that soldiers need "a rest." Armstrong, "Japanese Politician Calls Wartime Sex Slaves 'Necessary.'"
9. Poston, Conde, and DeSalvo, "China's Unbalanced Sex Ratio."

10. "Hillary Clinton U.N. Women's Conference Beijing."

11. Grant, "20 Minutes That Changed the World."

12. It should be noted that the Chinese government was not thrilled with her speech. Clinton notes, "I learned later that the government had blacked out my speech from closed-circuit TV in the conference hall, which had been broadcasting highlights of the conference." Mention of her speech was pointedly absent from all Chinese newspapers and media, as well. See Clinton, *Living History*, 306.

13. Clinton noted in her biography, *Living History*, "What I didn't understand at the time was that my twenty-one minute speech would become a manifesto for women all over the world. To this day, whenever I travel overseas, women come up to me quoting words from the Beijing speech or clutching copies they want me to autograph" (306). It should be noted that the phrase about women's rights being human rights was originally coined by the Filipina women's movement in the 1980s. Robin Morgan, telephone interview by Valerie M. Hudson, January 30, 2014.

14. Garner, *Gender & Foreign Policy in the Clinton Administration*, 160.

15. Gloria Steinem, e-mail to Valerie M. Hudson, February 5, 2013.

16. L. Jordan, "Real Hillary Clinton."

17. Flaherty and Flaherty, *First Lady*, 38.

18. Sheehy, *Hillary's Choice*, quoted in Lowen, "Hillary Rodham Clinton's Legacy."

19. Swanee Hunt, telephone interview by Valerie M. Hudson, March 19, 2013.

20. Lemmon, "Hillary Doctrine."

21. Robin Morgan, interview by Valerie M. Hudson, May 14, 2013, New York City.

22. In an e-mail dated January 30, 2014 to Valerie Hudson, feminist activist Robin Morgan remembers, "Just remembered a meeting of Gloria Steinem and me with Andy Young, then US Ambassador to the UN (1/77 to 9/79), lobbying for women to be included by Security Council mandate in peace-making and peace-keeping. It was engineered by Gloria's and my friend, Koryne Horbal, then the "woman's affairs" person at the US Mission and the real author of CEDAW: Koryne actually did the formulation of and drafting of the Convention—and never got credit for that. At the time, she was Ambassador for Women in the US Mission, under Andy Young/Carter administration). I remember that we also talked about FGM [female genital mutilation]— a barely heard of subject in those days—and Andy Young kept nervously crossing and uncrossing his legs."

23. Catherine Bertini, presentation at the George Bush School of Government, October 10, 2013, at Texas A&M University, College Station.

24. Charlotte Ponticelli, interview by Valerie M. Hudson, June 28, 2013, Washington, D.C.

25. See, for example, Riding, "Rights Forum Ends in Call for a Greater Role by U.N."; Ferraro, "Human Rights for Women."
26. Garner, *Gender & Foreign Policy in the Clinton Administration*, 111.
27. Ibid., 114.
28. Clinton, "Remarks of First Lady Hillary Rodham Clinton at a Special Event at the UN Social Summit."
29. Crossette, "U.S. to Help Girls in Poor Lands Stay in School."
30. Clinton, *Living History*, 169.
31. Purdum, "Hillary Clinton Discovers A New Role." The trip was from March 26 to early April.
32. Clinton, *Living History*, 278.
33. Melanne Verveer, e-mail correspondence with Valerie M. Hudson.
34. Clinton, *Living History*, 170.
35. Purdum, "March 26–April 1; On the Road in Hillaryland."
36. Purdum, "Hard Choice for White House on Hillary Clinton and China"; Ferraro, "Women's Rights, Human Rights"; Pelosi, letter to the editor.
37. Lemmon, "Hillary Doctrine."
38. Garner, *Gender & Foreign Policy in the Clinton Administration*, 144–45.
39. Lemmon, "Hillary Doctrine."
40. Melanne Verveer, interview by Valerie M. Hudson, May 21, 2013, Washington, D.C.
41. U.N. Security Council, "Resolution 1325 (2000)."
42. There were other steps taken after Beijing by the U.S. government that are worthy of mention, including new commitments by USAID in 1996 to make women central to their work of fostering development by conducting gender analyses of all existing and proposed programming, new guidelines for asylum that included domestic violence, rape, and genital mutilation as possible justifications, and so forth. The President's Interagency Council on Women (PICW), under Theresa Loar, became "a formal mechanism especially for implementation and follow-up." Garner, *Gender & Foreign Policy in the Clinton Administration*, 167. In September 1996, the PICW sponsored a national teleconference that allowed women across the nation to receive an update on how their government was doing in implementing the U.S. commitments to women made at Beijing (for the summary report, see "The President's Interagency Council on Women," September 1997, U.S. Department of State Archive, http://secretary.state.gov/www/picw/archives/sept96.html). Garner estimates that seventy thousand participated across the country (169). Also in September 1996, Congress declared female genital cutting to be a federal crime. Loar transitioned to become head of the OIWI in October 1996.
43. Verveer, interview.
44. Clinton, "Remarks by the First Lady International Women's Day."

45. See, for example, "Bosnia-Herzegovina: Mass Rape, Forced Pregnancy, Genocide."
46. Leatherman, *Sexual Violence and Armed Conflict.*
47. O'Kane, "The Mistake of Being Muslim."
48. Simons, "U.N. Court, for First Time, Defines Rape as War Crime."
49. "UN Commissioner for Human Rights Delivers 2013 Bram Fischer Lecture."
50. Hunt, interview.
51. Ibid.
52. Ibid.
53. Nelson, *Vital Voices,* 46.
54. Albright and Clinton, "Special Program in Honor of International Women's Day with Secretary of State Madeleine Albright and First Lady Hillary Rodham Clinton."
55. Garner, *Gender & Foreign Policy in the Clinton Administration,* 193.
56. Nelson, *Vital Voices,* 44.
57. Albright and Clinton, "Secretary of State Madeleine K. Albright and First Lady Hillary Rodham Clinton."
58. Ibid.
59. Andrew Natsios, interview by Valerie M. Hudson, March 27, 2013, College Station, Texas.
60. Beebe and Kaldor, *The Ultimate Weapon Is No Weapon,* 133.
61. Verveer, interview.
62. Sanam Anderlini, telephone interview by Valerie M. Hudson, November 21, 2013.
63. Hudson, *Gender, Human Security, and the United Nations,* 12.
64. U.N. Security Council, "Peace Inextricably Linked with Equality Between Women and Men Says Security Council, in International Women's Day Statement," press release SC/6818, March 8, 2000, www.un.org/News/Press/docs/2000/20000308.sc6816.doc.html.
65. Hudson, *Gender, Human Security, and the United Nations,* 13.
66. Ibid., 15.
67. The Norwegian minister of international development made up the funds withdrawn by the Bush administration. Gro Lindstand, executive director, FOKUS (Forum for Women and Development), May 28, 2013, in discussion with Valerie M. Hudson at the Nobel Women's Initiative Conference, Belfast, Northern Ireland.
68. Paula Dobriansky, interview by Valerie M. Hudson, June 28, 2013, Washington, D.C.
69. Ponticelli, interview, June 28, 2013.
70. Ryan Crocker, interview by Valerie M. Hudson, September 23, 2013, College Station, Texas.

71. Paula Dobriansky, interview by Valerie M. Hudson, June 28, 2013. When Condoleezza Rice became secretary of state, she renamed OIWI the Office of Women's Empowerment.

72. Ponticelli, telephone interview by Valerie M. Hudson, June 2, 2013.

73. Ponticelli, interview, June 2, 2013.

74. Hunt and Posa, "Iraq's Excluded Women."

75. Jessica Neuwirth, interview by Valerie M. Hudson, May 14, 2013, New York City.

76. Young, "The Logic of Masculinist Protection."

77. See Finlay, *George W. Bush and the War on Women*, and Riley, Mohanty, and Pratt, *Feminism and War*.

78. Young, "Logic of Masculinist Protection," 19–20.

79. Ritu Sharma, telephone interview by Valerie M. Hudson, June 5, 2013.

80. Anita McBride, telephone interview by Valerie M. Hudson, June 14, 2013.

81. Dobriansky, interview, June 28, 2013.

82. McBride, interview; L. Bush, *Spoken from the Heart*, 238.

83. G. W. Bush, "Radio Address by Mrs. Bush."

84. McBride, interview. In her autobiography, Laura Bush notes about this similarity, "Not everyone was quite so willing to let my voice be my own. Writing in *Newsweek* after the White House event, reporter Martha Brant said, 'If I had closed my eyes, I could have sworn it was Hillary Clinton talking'" (L. Bush, *Spoken from the Heart*, 252).

85. Dobriansky, interview, June 28, 2013.

86. Dobriansky, interview with Valerie Hudson, Washington, D.C., May 23, 2013.

87. Ibid.

88. Sharma, interview.

89. McBride, interview.

90. Charity Wallace, telephone interview by Valerie M. Hudson, June 19, 2013. Melanne Verveer was appointed vice chair of the council during the Obama administration. The Bush Institute hosted two meetings in 2010 and 2011 and at the time of this writing was planning to host another in 2014.

91. Garner, Karen, "The Clinton Administration's Global Gender Policy: Promise and Change." Unpublished 2012 draft of Garner, *Gender & Foreign Policy in the Clinton Administration*, 384.

92. Lemmon, "Hillary Doctrine."

93. Ponticelli, interview, June 28, 2013.

94. The Bush Administration instituted the three-tier system of assessing nations according to their efforts to reduce trafficking.

95. Sharma, interview.

96. Natsios, interview.

97. Neuwirth, interview.

98. Natsios, interview.
99. U.S. Department of State, Bureau of International Organization Affairs and Bureau of International Information Programs, *Working for Women, Worldwide*.
100. Finlay, *George W. Bush and the War on Women*.
101. G. W. Bush, "Commencement Address at the University of South Carolina in Columbia, South Carolina."
102. Wallace, interview.
103. Ibid.
104. G. W. Bush, "Commencement Address at the United States Military Academy at West Point."
105. Clinton, "New Hope for Afghanistan."
106. Jodie Evans, interview by Valerie M. Hudson, May 29, 2013, Belfast, Northern Ireland.
107. Zunes, "Hillary Clinton on International Law." The International Criminal Court allows for the prosecution of individuals for war crimes, crimes against humanity, etc.
108. Lawrence and Rose, *Hillary Clinton's Race for the White House*, 32.
109. Bernstein, *A Woman in Charge*, 553.
110. The *New York Times* suggests, "Clinton vacillated for days, at one point deciding to decline. (Her aides say Obama would not take no for an answer; he avoided at least one phone call from her, the story goes, by having an aide explain he was in the bathroom.)" See Myers, "Hillary Clinton's Last Tour as a Rock-Star Diplomat."
111. Garner, "Clinton Administration's Global Gender Policy," 418.
112. "Hillary Sees Subjugation of Women as Threat to Security."
113. Lemmon, "Hillary Doctrine."
114. U.S. Department of State and U.S. Agency for International Development, *Leading Through Civilian Power*, x.
115. Ibid., 23.
116. The aforementioned Security Council resolutions were followed by UNSCR 2106 and 2122 in the year 2013, after she had stepped down from being secretary of state. UNSCR 2106 urges all actors in armed conflicts, including international organizations, to do more to end sexual violence during war. UNSCR 2122 underscores the need to include women in conflict resolution and related peace processes.
117. In addition, she added the United States as one of the countries covered in the U.S. State Department *Trafficking in Persons Report*.
118. See Steinberg, "USAID's Steinberg on Empowering Women Globally."
119. Combe, "At the Pinnacle of Hillary Clinton's Career."

120. See, for example, Gettleman, "Rape Epidemic Raises Trauma of Congo War."
121. U.S. Department of State, Office of Global Women's Issues, "Fact Sheet: Promoting Gender Equality to Achieve Our National Security and Foreign Policy Objectives."
122. Klein, interview.
123. J., interview conducted in confidentiality by Valerie M. Hudson, summer 2013.
124. Ibid.
125. Jamille Bigio, interview by Valerie M. Hudson, May 21, 2013, Washington, D.C.
126. Rosa Brooks, telephone interview by Valerie M. Hudson, October 8, 2013. However, it is also important to remember that the issue of sexual violence in the military was brought to public attention during these years as well, most effectively by a documentary called *The Invisible War*. It should also be noted that the Defense Department lifted the combat exclusion for women in January 2013, only a few days before Hillary Clinton stepped down from state.
127. M. Jordan, "'Hillary Effect' Cited for Increase in Female Ambassadors to U.S."
128. Ibid.
129. Lena Ag, interview by Valerie M. Hudson, May 30, 2013, Belfast, Northern Ireland.
130. Referenced in Deborah Cavin, e-mail correspondence to Valerie M. Hudson, March 27, 2013.
131. K. P. Vijayalakhshmi, interview by Valerie M. Hudson, May 6, 2013, College Station, Texas.
132. Coleman, "A Powerful Voice for Women Around the World."
133. Clinton, "Remarks at the Women in the World Summit."
134. Lemmon, "Hillary Doctrine."
135. Gbowee, speech at the Nobel Women's Initiative Conference, May 27, 2013, Belfast, Northern Ireland.
136. Evans, interview.
137. Cooper and Myers, "Obama Takes Hard Line with Libya After Shift by Clinton."
138. Dreyfuss, "Obama's Women Advisers Pushed War Against Libya."
139. McKelvey, "Hillary Clinton, State Feminist?"
140. L. Bush, "Don't Abandon Afghan Women."
141. "UN Women Brown Bag," discussion, May 14, 2013, New York City.
142. Natsios, interview.
143. Neuwirth, interview.

## 2. SHOULD SEX MATTER IN U.S. FOREIGN POLICY?

1. Andrew Natsios, interview with Valerie M. Hudson, College Station, Texas, March 27, 2013.
2. See Davis, trailer for *It's A Girl*.
3. Hudson, Ballif-Spanvill, Caprioli, and Emmett, *Sex and World Peace*.
4. World Bank, *World Development Report 2012: Gender Equality and Development*.
5. U.N. Food and Agriculture Organization, *State of Food and Agriculture 2010–2011*.
6. Caren Grown, interview by Valerie M. Hudson, May 20, 2013, Washington, D.C.
7. Ibid.
8. The database of the WomanStats Project is available at http://womanstats.org /index.htm.
9. Enloe, *Bananas, Beaches, and Bases*; Elshtain, *Women and War*; Cohn, "Sex and Death in the Rational World of Defense Intellectuals"; Peterson, *Gendered States*; Peterson, "Gendered National"; Sylvester, *Feminist Theory and International Relations in a Postmodern Era*; Sylvester, *Feminist International Relations*; Sylvester, " 'Progress' as a Feminist International Relations"; Tickner, *Gender in International Relations*; Tickner, *Gendering World Politics*; Tickner, "Hans Morgenthau's Principles of Political Realism"; Grant and Newland, *Gender and International Relations*; Pettman, *Worlding Women*; Zalewski and Papart, *The "Man" Question in International Relations*; see also Fukuyama, "Women and the Evolution of World Politics."
10. See, for example, Hansen, *Security as Practice*; Whitworth, *Men, Militarism, and UN Peacekeeping*; Zarkov, *The Body of War*; Mazurana, Raven-Roberts, and Parpart, *Gender, Conflict, and Peacekeeping*.
11. Fish, "Islam and Authoritarianism."
12. Caprioli, "Gendered Conflict."
13. Caprioli and Boyer, "Gender, Violence and International Crisis."
14. Caprioli, "Gender Equality and State Aggression." These results were replicated by Melander, "Gender Equality and Interstate Armed Conflict"; see also Marshall and Ramsey, "Gender Empowerment and the Willingness of States to Use Force."
15. Caprioli, "Primed for Violence."
16. Caprioli and Trumbore, "Human Rights Rogues in Interstate Disputes, 1980–2001"; Caprioli and Trumbore, "Hierarchies of Dominance"; Caprioli and Trumbore, "Ethnic Discrimination and Interstate Violence."
17. Sobek, Abouharb, and Ingram, "The Human Rights Peace."
18. McDermott and Cowden, "The Effects of Uncertainty and Sex in a Crisis Simulation Game."

19. D. Johnson et al., "Overconfidence in Wargames."
20. Florea et al., "Negotiating from Mars to Venus."
21. Inglehart and Norris, "The True Clash of Civilizations"; Inglehart and Norris, *Rising Tide*.
22. Hudson et al., "Heart of the Matter." Huntington operationalizes civilizational identity according to a scheme that includes categories such as Western, Latin American, Eastern Orthodox, sub-Saharan African, Islamic, Buddhist, Confucian, etc.
23. Charles Bowden, interview by Patricia Leidl, January 17, 2013, El Paso, Texas.
24. The analysis provided here follows Hudson and Den Boer, *Bare Branches*.
25. These are 2010 figures. For more information, see U.N. Population Division, Department of Economics and Social Affairs, *World Population Prospects: The 2012 Revision*, http://esa.un.org/unpd/wpp/unpp/panel_indicators.htm.
26. Hudson and Den Boer, *Bare Branches*, 60, table 2.3.
27. Ibid., 176–77.
28. Murray and Lopez, *Global Burden of Disease*, 448; Rosenthal, "Women's Suicides Reveal Rural China's Bitter Roots."
29. See Breslaw, "Where Are India's 60 Million Missing Girls? The Tragic, Obvious Answer."
30. The material in this section was originally published in a piece by Patricia Leidl entitled "Silent Spring: The Tragedy of India's Never-Born Girls," which first appeared in 2005, written under the auspices of the U.N. Population Fund (http://www.unfpa.org/swp/2005/presskit/docs/india.doc). Leidl conducted all the interviews for this essay. All subsequent references to India's sex selection in this section can be attributed to Leidl, "Silent Spring."
31. "Shenzhen's Newborn Sex Ratio More Balanced," *People's Daily Online*, last updated April 15, 2005, http://english.people.com.cn/200504/15/eng20050415_181218.html.
32. See McCurry and Allison, "40m Bachelors and No Women . . . The Birth of a New Problem for China"; Poston Jr. Conde, and DeSalvo, "China's Unbalanced Sex Ratio at Birth, Millions of Excess Bachelors and Societal Implications."
33. Poston, Conde, and DeSalvo, "China's Unbalanced Sex Ratio."
34. In certain Middle Eastern societies and other adjacent countries such as South Sudan, it is not a dearth of females, but rather the upward spiral of marriage costs that are creating serious dislocations in the marriage markets that mimic those we see in China and India, where sex ratios are the major issue. See, for example, Richmond and Krause-Jackson, "Cows-for-Bride Inflation Spurs Cattle Theft Among Mundari in South Sudan." Prevalent polygyny, of course, exacerbates marriage market tensions as well, acting as an imitation of abnormal sex ratios favoring males.
35. For a wide-ranging literature review on the phenomena explored here, see Hudson and Den Boer, *Bare Branches*, 192–200.

36. Edlund et al., "Sex Ratios and Crime."
37. See Lu, "Excess of Marriageable Males and Violent Crime in China and South Korea, 1970–2008"; Dreze and Khera, "Crime, Gender, and Society in India."
38. Taylor, "Rising Protests in China."
39. Hudson and Den Boer, *Bare Branches*, Chapter 5.
40. This account stems from Elizabeth Perry's work on revolutionaries in North China. For more information, see Perry, *Rebels and Revolutionaries in North China, 1845–1945*.
41. Hudson and Den Boer, *Bare Branches*, Chapter 5.
42. Ibid.
43. Ibid.
44. "China's 1-Child Policy to be Loosened: Labour Camps Closed."
45. See Mokuwa et al., "Peasant Grievance and Insurgency in Sierra Leone"; Hudson, Bowen, and Nielson, "Clan Governance and State Stability."
46. "Hillary Clinton: Helping Women Isn't Just A 'Nice' Thing to Do."
47. Camia, "Clinton Warns of 'Extremists' Out to Control Women."
48. Jones, *War Is Not Over When It's Over*, 160.
49. Jones, *War Is Not Over When It's Over*, 161–163.
50. Leatherman, *Sexual Violence and Armed Conflict*.
51. Jones, *War Is Not Over When It's Over*, 27, 37–38, 76–77.
52. Lindholm, *Generosity and Jealousy*, 148–49.
53. Morgan, *Demon Lover*, 121.
54. See Locke, "Valentine de Saint-Point and the Fascist Construction of Woman."
55. Okin, "Inequalities Between the Sexes in Different Cultural Contexts," 282.
56. Morgan, *Demon Lover*, 81–86.
57. Olsson and Tejpar, *Operational Effectiveness and UN Resolution 1325*.
58. See Mill, *Subjection of Women*; Hudson et al., *Sex and World Peace*.
59. Robin Morgan, *The Demon Lover: The Roots of Terrorism* (New York: Washington Square, 2001).
60. Center on Law & Globalization, "Voices from Rwanda."
61. Wrangham and Peterson, *Demonic Males*, 2–5.
62. Ibid., 125.
63. Ibid., 159.
64. Neil Boyd, interview by Patricia Leidl, July 7, 2013, Vancouver, Canada.
65. Wrangham and Peterson, *Demonic Males*, 146.
66. Jones, *War Is Not Over When It's Over*, 37–38.
67. Miller, *Sex and Gender Hierarchies*, 22.
68. Smuts, "The Evolutionary Origins of Patriarchy."
69. Thayer, *Darwin and International Relations*.
70. Wrangham and Peterson, *Demonic Males*, 249.
71. Ibid., 233.
72. Ibid., 125.

73. See Alexander, "Evolution, Culture, and Human Behavior," 509–520; Hartman, *Household and the Making of History*; and Greene and Pole, *Colonial British America*.

74. Raymond, "International Norms: Normative Orders and Peace," 290.

75. Erchak, "Family Violence"; Erchak and Rosenfeld, "Societal Isolation, Violent Norms, and Gender Relations"; Levinson, *Family Violence in Cross-Cultural Perspective*; Cockburn, "The Gendered Dynamics of Armed Conflict and Political Violence."

76. Elshtain, *Women and War*; Ruddick, *Maternal Thinking*; Reardon, *Sexism and the War System*; Brownmiller, *Against Our Will*.

77. Caprioli, "Primed for Violence."

78. Stojsavljevic, "Women, Conflict, and Culture in Former Yugoslavia."

79. See, for example, Joshua Ramos, "Demographics as Destiny."

80. Peterson, "Gendered National."

81. Tickner, *Gender in International Relations*; Tickner, *Gendering World Politics*; Papanek, "To Each Less Than She Needs, From Each More Than She Can Do"; Tessler and Warriner, "Gender, Feminism, and Attitudes Toward International Conflict"; Caprioli, "Primed for Violence."

82. Clinton, "Remarks at the UN Commission on the Status of Women."

83. See Hunt and Posa, "Women Waging Peace"; Tickner, *Gender in International Relations*.

84. A. Johnson, "Freedom in Egypt?"

85. Human Rights Watch, "Egypt: Epidemic of Sexual Violence."

86. See Brightman, "The Sexual Division of Foraging Labor."

87. Hannagan and Arrow, "Reengineering Gender Relations in Modern Militaries."

88. Human Rights Watch, "Egypt: Epidemic of Sexual Violence."

89. Saudi men are also arranging temporary marriages for themselves with young girls from the Syrian refugee camps. These Saudi men, in their forties, fifties, sixties, and even seventies, prefer twelve-year-olds, whom they "marry" for a few months, often for as little as $100, before returning them to their parents in the camps. See Virk, "Why Old Saudi Men Are Marrying Syrian Teenage Refugee Girls"; Chumley, "Islamic Cleric Decrees It OK for Syrian Rebels to Rape Women."

90. In Syria, of course, there is a horrific level of gender-based violence taking place, but that nation is also in the midst of an active civil war, with women from "other" ethnic groups being primarily targeted. In Egypt, the "other" group being targeted is defined exclusively by sex.

91. See, for example, "Libyan Men Now Allowed to Remarry without Consent of First Wife: Court Rule"; Eltahawy, "Why Do They Hate Us?"

92. Shirin Ebadi, speech at Nobel Women's Initiative Conference, May 27, 2013, Belfast, Northern Ireland.

93. de Silva de Alwis, "Some Lessons from Other Post-Conflict Communities."

94. Bower, "New Protest Statement Builds in Iran—Men in Head Scarves."
95. Mayton, "Egypt: Muslim Brotherhood and Women."
96. Khattab, "For Women, the Arab Spring Has Yet to Arrive."
97. Ibid.
98. Equality Now, "TAKE ACTION: Ensure Egyptian women's fair representation on the new constitutional committee," e-mail sent to Valerie M. Hudson and others, September 18, 2013.
99. Benmehdi, "Maghreb Women Fear Regression of Rights."
100. Ibid.
101. See, for example, North, Wallis, and Weingast, *Violence and Social Orders*.
102. Hudson, Bowen, and Nielsen, "Clan Governance and State Stability."
103. Leatherman, *Sexual Violence and Armed Conflict*, 141.
104. Ibid., 156.
105. Jones, *War Is Not Over When It's Over*.

### 3. GUATEMALA: A CASE STUDY

1. Estimates of the death toll in El Salvador vary greatly across academia. For more information on the various estimates, see McElhinny, "Low Intensity Warfare, High Intensity Death." For information about deaths in Honduras, see Thompson and Cohn, "Canada Moves to Expel Honduran Torture Figure."
2. McDonald, "Quiet Guatemalan Prosecutor Takes on Dictator, Drug Gangs."
3. Reynolds, "Femicide Courts in Guatemala."
4. Thomson, "Guatemala: Region's Highest Rate of Femicide."
5. CIA, *World Factbook: Guatemala*.
6. de Pablo and Zurita, *Invisible Genocide of Women*.
7. Irma Chacon, interview by Patricia Leidl, February 9, 2013, Guatemala City, Guatemala.
8. CIA, *World Factbook: Guatemala*.
9. Ibid.
10. Alba Estela Maldonado, interview by Patricia Leidl, February 19, 2013, Antigua, Guatemala.
11. These figures from Maldonado are verified in Pablo and Zurita, *Invisible Genocide of Women*.
12. Maldonado, interview.
13. It is ironic that, despite having married two Spanish wives in succession, Alvarado's only offspring were the children of an indigenous woman who had been "gifted" to him by her father, a Mayan chieftain.
14. Las Casas, *A Brief Account of the Destruction of the Indies*.
15. Lucia Moran, interview by Patricia Leidl, February 20, 2013, Guatemala City, Guatemala.
16. Menchu, *Crossing Borders*, 181.

17. Cullather, *Secret History*.
18. Commission for Historical Clarification (CEH), "Caso Ilustrativo No. 31."
19. Ibid.
20. The U.N.-sponsored Commission for Historical Clarification asserted that the army committed genocide against four specific language groups: the Ixil Maya, the Q'anjob'al and Chuj Maya, the K'iche Maya, and the Achi Maya. These were the Maya that lived in the areas of active guerrilla insurgency. See note 19.
21. Martin, "The Right Way to Fight Anti-Guerilla Warfare"; see also Castillo, "Guatemala's Rios Montt Guilty of Genocide."
22. According to Agence France Presse, "Montt also used his office to preach every Sunday night. Dressed in a combat uniform, the dictator would take to the airwaves and talk about God, morality and politics. In one particularly creepy presentation he claimed that a 'good Christian' was that person who carried out their life 'with a bible and a machine gun.'" See "Rios Montt, Guatemalan Dictator from Humble Start."
23. "Rios Montt, Guatemalan Dictator from Humble Start."
24. Chelala, "Rios Montt's Conviction Will Change Guatemala."
25. Castillo, "Guatemala's Rios Montt Guilty of Genocide."
26. McDonald, "Former Guatemalan Dictator Rios Montt Convicted of Genocide."
27. Robin, "Ronald Reagan"
28. Commission for Historical Clarification, "Caso Ilustrativo No. 31."
29. Maldonado, interview.
30. See Mendez, "'I Don't Want to Die Without Seeing Justice.'"
31. Maldonado, interview.
32. Maldonado, interview.
33. Proyecto Interdiocesano de Recuperación de la Memoria Histórica (REMHI), "Botín de Guerra."
34. Commission for Historical Clarification, *Guatemala: Memory of Silence*.
35. Sanford, *Buried Secrets*, 53.
36. "U.S. Army School of the Americas Frequently Asked Questions."
37. Ibid. In response to the question "Why the controversy over the School?" the 1999 FAQ responds: "According to leaders of the opposition movement, the controversy is not limited to the School nor its graduates; but rather with U.S. foreign policy in Latin America. In their view, that policy is responsible for all the violence and repression that characterized many countries during the Cold War. The School is the easiest target for those people who believe solutions lie in eliminating military or police forces in the region. Many of the critics supported Marxism—Liberation Theology—in Latin America—which was defeated with the assistance of the U.S. Army. In other words, their objective of achieving socialist revolutionary governments failed, and they now are going after one of the mechanisms which assisted in promoting and maintaining democratic ideals."

38. Doyle and Osorio, "U.S. Policy in Guatemala, 1966–1996."
39. Maldonado, interview.
40. Commission for Historical Clarification, *Guatemala: Memory of Silence*, 40.
41. It must be noted that the CEH determined that at least 3 percent of the atrocities were committed by the insurgents. For example, survivors assert that the massacre at Chacalte in the 1980s, in which more than one hundred men, women, and children were slaughtered in their beds before dawn, was in fact committed by the guerrillas provoked by the participation of the young men of that town in the army's militias. See Guzaro and McComb, *Escaping the Fir*, 130.
42. Maldonado, interview.
43. Pablo and Zurita, *The Invisible Genocide of Women*.
44. "Laura," *What War?*
45. Interview by author, 2013; other details will not be printed to ensure anonymity.
46. Chacon, interview.
47. Commission for Historical Clarification, *Guatemala: Memory of Silence*, 27.
48. Maldonado, interview.
49. Valladares, "Guatemala Heeds the Cries of Femicide Victims."
50. Leidl interviewed Lucia Moran and "Esperanza" during separate interviews on February 20, 2013, in Guatemala City, Guatemala. All quotations from Esperanza throughout the remainder of the chapter derive from an interview with three Ixil genocide survivors. Similarly, all quotations from Lucia Moran throughout the remainder of the chapter derive from this interview.
51. Maldonado, interview.
52. U.S. Department of State, Bureau of Diplomatic Security, *Guatemala 2012 Crime and Safety Report*.
53. Myrna Mack Chang was a Guatemalan anthropologist who met her end when a military death squad knifed her twenty-seven times for criticizing the Guatemala government's human rights abuses, massacres, and the disappearances of indigenous Maya. The Inter-American Court of Human Rights identified her killers and the reasons behind her murder on November 25, 2003, in Washington, D.C. In April 2004, the Guatemalan government publicly acknowledged that its agents had murdered Myrna Mack and ultimately paid her family financial compensation. One man, a lower-level sergeant, was eventually convicted and three upper-level superiors tried in precedent-setting cases before the Inter-American Court of Human Rights in Costa Rica. One of them, Colonel Juan Valencia Osiro, was convicted and sentenced to 30 years in prison.
54. Ruiz-Goiriena, "Rights Groups Fear Marines in Guatemala."
55. U.S. Department of State, Bureau of Democracy, Human Rights, and Labor, "2011 Human Rights Reports: Guatemala."

56. Ibid.
57. Ruiz-Goiriena, "Rights Groups Fear Marines in Guatemala."
58. Ruiz-Goiriena, "Rights Groups Fear Marines in Guatemala."
59. Sanford, "Victory in Guatemala? Not Yet."
60. Ibid.
61. van Auken, "Guatemalan High Court Upholds Overturning of Rios Montt Conviction."
62. Although all three were willing to disclose their identities, we have altered their names for their own safety.
63. Interview with author, 2013; other details will not be printed to ensure anonymity.
64. Sanford, "Victory in Guatemala? Not Yet."
65. Nairn, "Ríos Montt Guilty of Genocide."
66. Committee of Agricultural, Commercial, Industrial and Financial Associations (CACIF), "Saber Dejar Atrás el Pasado."
67. van Auken, "Guatemalan High Court Upholds Overturning of Rios Montt Conviction."
68. Robert F. Kennedy Center for Justice and Human Rights, "Guatemala: Rigoberta Menchú Tum."
69. Valladares, "Guatemala: Women-Only Buses Against Sexual Harassment."
70. Mattson, Ayer, and Gerson, "The Maquilla in Guatemala," 481–487.
71. Ibid.
72. Ibid.
73. CIA, *World Factbook: Guatemala.*
74. Perez, "Otto Perez Molina, Former General, Wins Guatemala Presidential Elections."
75. Gonzalez, "Central America: Crisis Chews Women Up, Spits them Out."
76. Sandra Moran, interview by Patricia Leidl, February 2, 2013, Guatemala City, Guatemala.
77. Ibid.
78. CIA, *World Factbook: Guatemala.*
79. Isaacs, "New Bad Old Times for Guatemala?"
80. Davis, "In Guatemala, A Mass Grave for the Truth."
81. S. Moran, interview.
82. Commission for Historical Clarification, "Caso Ilustrativo No. 31."
83. Proyecto Interdiocesano de Recuperación de la Memoria Histórica (REMHI), "Botín de Guerra."
84. Bathanti, "Bishop Gerardi: A Life Devoted to Social Justice."
85. S. Moran, interview.
86. Guatemala Human Rights Commission/USA, "Guatemala's Femicide Law."
87. Ibid.
88. Ibid. See also Guatemala Human Rights Commission/USA, "Fact Sheet."

89. Human Rights Watch, *World Report 2013: Guatemala*.

90. Tran, "Guatemala: One Woman's Campaign Against Violent Crime and Corruption."

91. McDonald, "Quiet Guatemalan Prosecutor Takes on Dictator, Drug Gangs." See also "Claudia Paz y Paz Ousting Puts Spotlight on Guatemalan Justice System."

92. Aguilar, interview by Patricia Leidl, February 11, 2013, Guatemala City, Guatemala. All quotations from Aguilar throughout the remainder of the chapter are from that interview.

93. Guatemala Human Rights Commission/USA, "Guatemala's Femicide Law."

94. "Jane Fonda Visits Guatemala to Put Spotlight on Murders of Women in Guatemala."

95. Guatemala Human Rights Commission/USA, "Guatemala's Femicide Law."

96. Ibid.

97. Ibid.

98. Ibid.

99. Yerman, "Women in the World Summit 2012."

100. Avakian, "Guatemala's Praised Attorney General to Step Down Under Controversy."

101. Iada Batres, interview by Patricia Leidl, February 9, 2013, Guatemala City, Guatemala.

102. Batres, interview.

103. Menchu, *I Rigoberta Menchu: An Indian Woman in Guatemala*, 230.

## 4. A CONSPICUOUS SILENCE: U.S. FOREIGN POLICY, WOMEN, AND SAUDI ARABIA

1. Andrew Natsios, former administrator of USAID, interview by Valerie M. Hudson, March 27, 2013, College Station, Texas.

2. Keyes, "Saudi Arabia's Religious Police Outlaw 'Tempting Eyes.'"

3. WomanStats Project, "High Rape-Scale in Saudi Arabia."

4. In May 2009, an eight-year-old girl made headlines by securing a divorce from her fifty-year-old husband, a marriage brokered by her father to settle old debts. See Doumato, "Saudi Arabia."

5. Rothna Begum, interview by Valerie M. Hudson, September 21, 2013, New York City.

6. See, for example, Buchanan, "Women in Saudi Arabia to Vote and Run in Elections"; "Saudi Arabia (Majlis Ash-Shura)."

7. Easton, "Saudi Women Find a Way."

8. Quinn, "Ikea Apologises over Removal of Women From Saudi Arabia Catalogue"; Mills, "Reforms to Women's Education Make Slow Progress in Saudi

Arabia." For more information on Saudi Arabia's Princess Nora Bint Abdul Rahman University in Al-Riyadh, visit www.pnuproject.com.

9. See Jamjoom, "Saudi Cleric Warns Driving Could Damage Women's Ovaries."
10. See "Saudi Arabia Eases Ban on Women Riding Bikes."
11. U.N. Development Programme, "Saudi Arabia."
12. Doumato, "Saudi Arabia," 5, 8.
13. "Saudi Arabia Is 'World's Largest Women's Prison.'"
14. "Saudi Police 'Stopped' Fire Rescue."
15. Ibid.
16. Keyes, "Saudi Arabia's Religious Police Outlaw 'Tempting Eyes.'"
17. Ibid.
18. "Saudi Arabia Must Decide on Women Drivers: Kerry."
19. Ehrenfreund, "Obama Cancels Meeting with Vladimir Putin."
20. Contemporary Saudi Wahhabism combines the teachings of its founder Abd al-Wahhab (1703–1791) and other religious and cultural traditions. Salafism, or Salafiyya as it is more generally known among Arabs, is a puritanical Islamic movement that evolved in Egypt but is now so similar that, in the West at least, it is synonymous with Wahhabism.
21. Clinton, *Living History*, 273.
22. See Ayoob, "Political Islam: Image and Reality."
23. Ahmed, *In the Land of Invisible Women*, 59.
24. Ibid., 248.
25. Winsor, "Saudi Arabia, Wahhabism and the Spread of Sunni Theofascism."
26. "Osama Bin Laden: A Chronology of His Political Life."
27. Winsor, "Saudi Arabia, Wahhabism and the Spread of Sunni Theofascism."
28. Clark and Nassar, "Analysis: Who's Backing Who as Syria's Civil War Threatens to Spread."
29. Tcholpon Akhmatalieva, interview by Valerie M. Hudson, July 12, 2013, Orem, Utah.
30. See, for example, Marwan, "Virginity Tests for Indonesian School Girls?"; Schonhardt, "Indonesian Women Told How to Ride Motorbikes."
31. Ahmed, *In the Land of Invisible Women*, 390.
32. "Hillary Clinton: Helping Women Isn't Just a 'Nice' Thing to Do."
33. Zakaria, "Zakaria: The Saudis Are Mad? Tough!"
34. Ibrahim (would not give last name), interview by Patricia Leidl, August 19, 2011, Sana'a, Yemen. All subsequent quotations are from this interview.
35. CIA, *World Factbook: Yemen*.
36. World Bank, "World Bank Grant Supports Employment Creation for Yemen's Neediest Youth and Women," press release, April 2, 2013, www.worldbank.org /en/news/press-release/2013/04/02/world-bank-grant-supports-employment -creation-yemens-neediest-youth-women.
37. CIA, *World Factbook: Yemen*.

38. Chivers, "Seized Pirates in High-Seas Legal Limbo, With No Formula for Trials."

39. Lister, "Why We Should Care About Yemen."

40. Sharp and Malaikah, "Yemen: A U.S. Strategic Partner?"

41. Abdullah, "Iran and Saudi Arabia Allegedly Funding Proxy War in Yemen."

42. Hausmann, Tyson, and Zahidi, *Global Gender Gap Report 2012*.

43. "Oxfam in Yemen."

44. Burki, "Yemen's Hunger Crisis."

45. "Fertility Rate, Total (Births per Woman)."

46. UNICEF, "Yemen Statistics."

47. Semlali, "Yemen's Women Make Their Voices Heard from Revolution to Constitution."

48. Amnesty International, *Yemen's Dark Side*.

49. Sheffer, "Yemen's Youngest Divorcee Says Father Has Squandered Cash from Her Book."

50. Mail Foreign Service, "Child Bride, 13, Dies of Internal Injuries Four Days After Arranged Marriage in Yemen."

51. Habboush, "Child Bride in Yemen Dies of Internal Bleeding on Wedding Night."

52. Amnesty International, *Yemen's Dark Side*.

53. di Giovanni, "After the Arab Spring, Yemen's Women Are Left Behind."

54. Coauthor Patricia Leidl was working in Yemen at the time. Information is based on her eyewitness accounts.

55. Stanford, "Women's Rights Campaigner Warns of Islamists Behind Yemen Uprising."

56. Salama, "Abdullah Saleh."

57. Alwazir, "A Long Road Ahead for Yemeni Women."

58. Ibid.

59. Ibid.

60. Kawkab Althabiani, interview by Patricia Leidl, September 15, 2011, Sana'a, Yemen.

61. S. Begum, "Still Waiting for Change in Yemen."

62. Fatima (would not give last name), interview by Patricia Leidl, August 21, 2011, Sana'a, Yemen.

63. Khadjija (not her real name), interview by Patricia Leidl, December 19, 2011, Sana'a, Yemen. All information provided by Khadjija is from this interview.

64. Mukhashaf and McDowall, "Yemeni Troops Advance; Donors Pledge $4 Bln Aid."

65. Many Yemeni progressives prefer the term *civil democracy* or *secular democracy*, which they believe suggests Western imperialism and an anti-religious stance despite the fact that for all practical purposes they are one and the same.

66. Omar Zain, interview by Patricia Leidl, December 26, 2012, Sana'a, Yemen.
67. Muwada (would not give last name), interview by Patricia Leidl, September 10, 2011, Sana'a, Yemen.
68. USAID, "USAID Implementation of the United States National Action Plan on Women, Peace, and Security," press release, August 14, 2012, www.usaid .gov/news-information/press-releases/usaid-implementation-united-states -national-action-plan-women-peace.
69. Ibid.
70. R. Begum, interview.
71. Interviews with USAID-funded gender specialists in Yemen were conducted by Patricia Leidl on November 15, 2011, in Sana'a, Yemen. Additional interviews with gender specialists in Afghanistan, Sri Lanka, and Washington, D.C., were conducted via Skype by Patricia Leidl on June 16, 2013.
72. "'Pipelines' and 'Burn Rates.'"
73. Price, "The Kingdom of Saudi Arabia—Wahhabism and Oil Exports."
74. Ibid.
75. Knickmeyer, "Activists Are Feeling Squeezed in Gulf Kingdoms."
76. Al-Rasheed, "Saudi Arabia Pleased with Morsi's Fall."
77. Knickmeyer, "Activists Are Feeling Squeezed in Gulf Kingdoms."
78. Ibid.
79. Ibid.
80. Myers, "Clinton Adds Her Voice in Support of Saudi Women."
81. Ibid.
82. Ibid.
83. Ibid.
84. Spillius, "WikiLeaks: Saudis 'Chief Funders of al-Qaeda.'"
85. McKelvey, "Hillary Clinton, State Feminist?"
86. R. Begum, interview.
87. Ghattas, *The Secretary*, 43.
88. See "Sec. Clinton Repeats Her Strong Opposition to Forced Abortion and Sterilization in China."
89. Clinton, "Letter from Hillary Clinton to President George Bush on China's Human Rights Violations."
90. "U.S. Secretary of State Hillary Clinton on Women's Issues."
91. Clinton might well feel as John F. Kennedy did, who, only two months before his death, visited the Tabernacle at Temple Square in Salt Lake City, Utah, and gave a speech in which he stated: "We must recognize that foreign policy in the modern world does not lend itself to easy, simple black and white solution. If we were to have diplomatic relations only with those countries whose principles we approved of, we would have relations with very few countries in a very short time. If we were to withdraw our assistance from all governments who are run differently from our own, we would relinquish half the world

immediately to our adversaries. If we were to treat foreign policy as merely a medium for delivering self-righteous sermons to supposedly inferior people, we would give up all thought of world influence or world leadership. For the purpose of foreign policy is not to provide an outlet for our own sentiments of hope or indignation; it is to shape real events in a real world." John F. Kennedy, "Address in Salt Lake City at the Mormon Tabernacle," speech, September 26, 1963, Salt Lake City, Utah.

92. That university is the $11.5 billion Princess Nora Bint Abdul Rahman University, which opened its doors in 2011. It aims to enroll 60,000 students and is supervised by women rectors. Notably, women can drive on its campus. Mills, "Reforms to Women's Education Make Slow Progress in Saudi Arabia." For more information on Princess Nora Bint Abdul Rahman University, visit www.pnuproject.com.

93. Caryle Murphy, "Arab Awakening Brings Hope, Change to Saudi Women," in *Is the Arab Awakening Marginalizing Women?*, Middle East Program Occasional Paper Series, Woodrow Wilson International Center for Scholars, 2012, accessed November 15, 2013, available at http://www.wilsoncenter .org/sites/default/files/Arab%20Awakening%20Marginalizing%20Women_0 .pdf, 20.

94. Ibrahim, interview.

95. Leila Alakarami, e-mail correspondence with Valerie M. Hudson, July 27, 2013.

96. Ghattas, *The Secretary*, 43.

97. Melanne Verveer, interview by Valerie M. Hudson, May 21, 2013, Washington, D.C.

98. Ibid.

99. "U.S. Secretary of State Hillary Clinton on Women's Issues."

100. Brown, "Nostalgia for Saddam Hussein's Rule."

101. Rend al-Rahim, "Iraq: Frustrated Expectations," in *Is the Arab Awakening Marginalizing Women?*, Middle East Program Occasional Paper Series, Woodrow Wilson International Center for Scholars, 2012, accessed November 15, 2013, available at http://www.wilsoncenter.org/sites/default/files/Arab%20 Awakening%20Marginalizing%20Women_0.pdf, 18.

102. Easton, "Saudi Women."

103. Ryan Crocker, interview by Valerie M. Hudson, September 23, 2013, College Station, Texas.

104. Indeed, in March 2014, President Obama "chose not to raise the issue of human rights during a two-hour discussion with King Abdullah of Saudi Arabia" while in Riyadh. On the very same trip, however, he presented an International Women of Courage award to a Saudi woman who works to promote women's rights. Shear, "Obama Ends Overseas Trip with Award for Saudi."

## 5. THE GOOD, THE BAD, AND THE UGLY OF IMPLEMENTING THE HILLARY DOCTRINE

1. Swanee Hunt, "Marshall and Clinton: A Shared Legacy," *Huffington Post*, January 30, 2013.
2. Michael Rubin, "Hillary Clinton's Legacy," *Commentary Magazine*, July 17, 2012.
3. Hillary Clinton, "Remarks at the UN Commission on the Status of Women," UN Headquarters, New York City, March 12, 2012
4. Ritu Sharma, telephone interview by Valerie M. Hudson, July 13, 2013.
5. Tobie Whitman, e-mail correspondence with Valerie M. Hudson, July 25, 2013.
6. Ritu Sharma, telephone interview by Valerie M. Hudson, July 5, 2013.
7. Ann Jones, telephone interview by Valerie M. Hudson, July 8, 2013.
8. Mairead Macguire, speech at Nobel Women's Initiative Conference, May 27, 2013, Belfast, Northern Ireland.
9. Shirin Ebadi, speech at Nobel Women's Initiative Conference, May 27, 2013, Belfast, Northern Ireland.
10. Lisa VeneKlasen, speech at Nobel Women's Initiative Conference, May 28, 2013, Belfast, Northern Ireland.
11. Jessica Neuwirth, interview by Valerie M. Hudson, May 14, 2013, New York City.
12. Jones, "Can Women Make Peace?"
13. We have received conflicting reports on Lesotho, Liberia, Suriname, and several Pacific islands.
14. Mears and Killough, "Judge Blocks North Dakota's Restrictive Abortion Law."
15. Jones, interview.
16. Anne-Marie Goetz, interview by Valerie M. Hudson, May 14, 2013, New York City.
17. Neuwirth, interview.
18. Shirin Ebadi, speech.
19. Olsson et al., *Operational Effectiveness and UN Resolution 1325—Practices and Lessons from Afghanistan.*
20. Lena Ag, interview by Valerie M. Hudson, May 30, 2013, Belfast, Northern Ireland.
21. UNWomen Brown Bag, discussion, May 14, 2013, New York City.
22. Sarah Taylor, interview by Valerie M. Hudson, May 15, 2013, New York City.
23. Anita McBride, telephone interview by Valerie M. Hudson, June 14, 2013.
24. Robin Morgan, interview by Valerie M. Hudson, May 14, 2013, New York City.
25. Melanne Verveer, interview by Valerie M. Hudson, May 21, 2013, Washington, D.C.

26. Shelby Quast, interview by Valerie M. Hudson, May 21, 2013, Washington, D.C.

27. Goetz, interview.

28. Michelle Barsa, interview by Valerie M. Hudson, May 21, 2013, Washington, D.C.

29. Verveer, interview.

30. Charlotte Ponticelli, telephone interview by Valerie M. Hudson, June 2, 2013.

31. W., interview conducted in confidentiality by Valerie M. Hudson, May 2013.

32. Jones, *Kabul in Winter*, 202.

33. Jones, "Can Women Make Peace?"

34. Jen Klein, interview by Valerie M. Hudson, May 20, 2013, Washington, D.C.

35. See, for example, U.N. Security Council, Presidential Statement 2004/40, "Statement by President of the Security Council"; and U.N. Security Council, Presidential Statement 2005/52, "Statement by President of the Security Council."

36. Office of the White House Press Secretary, "United States National Action Plan on Women, Peace, and Security," press release, December 19, 2011, www.whitehouse.gov/the-press-office/2011/12/19/united-states-national -action-plan-women-peace-and-security.

37. Verveer, interview.

38. Office of the White House Press Secretary, "United States National Action Plan."

39. The nine indicators are (1) Number of laws, policies, or procedures drafted, proposed or adopted to promote gender equality at the regional, national, or local level; (2) Proportion of female participants in U.S. government (USG)-assisted programs designed to increase access to productive economic resources (assets, credit, income, or employment); (3) Proportion of females who report increased self-efficacy at the conclusion of USG-supported training/programming; (4) Proportion of target population reporting increased agreement with the concept that males and females should have equal access to social, economic, and political opportunities; (5) Number of laws, policies, or procedures drafted, proposed, or adopted with USG assistance designed to improve prevention of or response to sexual and gender-based violence at the regional, national, or local level; (6) Number of people reached by a USG-funded intervention providing gender-based violence (GBV) services (e.g., health, legal, psychosocial counseling, shelters, hotlines, other); (7) Percentage of target population that views GBV as less acceptable after participating in or being exposed to USG programming; (8) Number of local women participating in a substantive role or position in a peace-building process supported with USG assistance; (9) Number of training and capacity-building activities conducted with USG assistance that are designed to promote the participation of women or the integration of gender perspectives in security sector institutions

or activities. See USAID, *Integrating Gender Equality and Female Empowerment in USAID's Program Cycle*.

40. See Steinberg, "USAID's Steinberg on Empowering Women Globally."
41. Office of the White House Press Secretary, "Presidential Memorandum—Coordination of Policies and Programs to Promote Gender Equality and Empower Women and Girls Globally," press release, January 30, 2013, www.whitehouse.gov/the-press-office/2013/01/30/presidential-memorandum-coordination-policies-and-programs-promote-gende.
42. Sarah Chatellier, interview by Valerie M. Hudson, May 21, 2013, Washington, D.C.
43. Donald Steinberg, telephone interview by Valerie M. Hudson, July 12, 2013.
44. See U.S. Department of State, Bureau of International Narcotics and Law Enforcement, "Afghanistan Program Overview"; see also International Development Law Organization (IDLO), "Justice Training Transition."
45. Jones, *Kabul in Winter*, 236.
46. Andrew Natsios, interview by Valerie M. Hudson, March 27, 2013, College Station, Texas.
47. USAID, *Gender Equality and Female Empowerment Policy*.
48. Caren Grown, e-mail correspondence with Valerie M. Hudson, October 8, 2013.
49. Carla Koppell, interview by Valerie M. Hudson, May 23, 2013, Washington, D.C.
50. Steinberg, interview.
51. Maura O'Neill, speech at Futures Without Violence Conference, October 3, 2013, Washington, D.C.
52. For more information on PROMOTE, see USAID, "Promoting Gender Equality in National Priority Programs (PROMOTE)."
53. However, in recent weeks, Hudson has been hearing rumors that PROMOTE will be scaled back to $315 million or less. We are not able to corroborate those rumors at the time of this writing. For more information on Afghanistan Promote and USAID's commitment to women, see USAID, "Afghanistan Promote"; and USAID, "USAID Announces Long-Term Commitment to Afghan Women," press release, July 18, 2013, www.usaid.gov/news-information/press-releases/usaid-announces-long-term-commitment-afghan-women.
54. Dilanian, "Short-Staffed USAID Tries to Keep Pace."
55. Jones, interview.
56. Dilanian, "Short-Staffed USAID Tries to Keep Pace."
57. Natsios, "Time Lag and Sequencing Dilemmas of Postconflict Reconstruction."
58. Dilanian, "Short-Staffed USAID Tries to Keep Pace."
59. Helen Mack, interview by Valerie M. Hudson, May 28, 2013, Belfast, Northern Ireland.
60. Yasmeen Hassan, interview by Valerie M. Hudson, May 15, 2013, New York City.
61. Patricia Guerrero, interview by Valerie M. Hudson, May 28, 2013, Belfast, Northern Ireland.
62. T.T., interview conducted in confidence by Valerie M. Hudson, May 2013.

63. Natsios, interview, March 27, 2013.
64. Jones, "The Forgotten War."
65. Neuwirth, interview.
66. Natsios, "The Clash of the Counter-Bureaucracy and Development."
67. Neuwirth, interview.
68. Jones, "Remember the Women?"
69. Matt Pottinger revealed his experiences with FETs during a phone interview with Hudson on July 14, 2013. All content and quotations used throughout the remainder of the chapter regarding Pottinger's experiences are from that interview.
70. In fact, female army personnel did engage in combat even before the lifting of the ban. The military, however, could not acknowledge this publicly, thus putting female personnel in the unpleasant position of risking their lives but nevertheless denied promotions owing to a lack of combat experience, based purely on a ban that was in name only. See Lee, "Battleground: Female Soldiers in the Line of Fire."
71. Alexandra Tenny, e-mail correspondence with Valerie M. Hudson, October 5, 2012.
72. Ibid. Indeed, for those of you with LDS background, Tenny views the Colombian FET program as "visiting teaching on steroids."
73. EFEOR, Escuadrón Femenino de Enlace Operacional Rural.
74. Alexandra Tenny, interview by Valerie M. Hudson, April 26, 2013, Washington, D.C.
75. Ibid.
76. Rosa Brooks, telephone interview by Valerie M. Hudson, October 8, 2013.
77. Tenny, interview.
78. Ibid.
79. Steinberg, interview. All subsequent quotes from Steinberg are from the July 12, 2013, phone interview by Hudson.
80. Farah Council, interview with Valerie M. Hudson, May 28, 2013, Belfast, Northern Ireland.
81. Peter Van Buren, telephone interview by Valerie M. Hudson, July 16, 2013.
82. Goetz, interview.
83. Ibid.
84. Ibid.
85. Ibid.
86. The letter is available at http://kvinnatillkvinnafrontend.qbank.se/deployed Files/e45823afe1e5120cec11fc4c379a0c67.pdf.
87. Benjamin, "Should Syria's Future Be Decided by Men with Guns?"
88. Jones, *Kabul in Winter*, 243.
89. Ibid., 249, 254–255.
90. Andrew Natsios, written remarks, Lone Star National Security Symposium, March 22, 2014, College Station, Texas.

91. Jones, *Kabul in Winter*, 260.
92. Ibid., 261.
93. Jones, interview.
94. The interview with Jimmy (a pseudonym) by Patricia Leidl was conducted in confidentiality. The individual's name and the location, and date of the interview are being withheld by mutual agreement.
95. The interview with Jimmy's supervisor by Patricia Leidl was conducted in confidentiality. The individual's name and the location, and date of the interview are being withheld by mutual agreement.
96. Steinberg, interview.
97. Cybele Cochran, interview by Valerie M. Hudson, May 22, 2013, Washington, D.C.
98. Molly (a pseudonym), Skype interview by Patricia Leidl, October 21, 2012, Kabul, Afghanistan. All subsequent references to Molly and her experiences with USAID can be attributed to the Skype interview in Kabul.
99. Interview with Sarah (a pseudonym) by Patricia Leidl, July 25, 2012, in Kabul, Afghanistan.
100. Delia (a pseudonym), Skype interview by Patricia Leidl, March 27, 2013, Washington, D.C. Delia's insights throughout the chapter came from this interview.
101. Jones, "Remember the Women?"
102. Weisfeld-Adams, "Factsheet: Women Farmers and Food Security."
103. Chandrasekaran, "In Afghanistan, U.S. Shifts Strategy on Women's Rights as It Eyes Wider Priorities."
104. Ibid.
105. Eagly, Johannesen-Schmidt, and van Engen, "Transformational, Transactional, and Laissez-Faire Leadership Styles."
106. Ibrahim S., Skype interview by Patricia Leidl, August 1, 2013, Kabul, Afghanistan. The following story is an account of their discussion, and all quotations are from that interview.
107. Interview with Marina (a pseudonym) by Patricia Leidl, October 15, 2013 and November 10, 2013, via Skype.
108. Interview with Maya (a pseudonym) by Patricia Leidl, November 18, 2012, Sana'a, emen (recollecting her experiences in Afghanistan).
109. Interview with Laura (a pseudonym) by Patricia Leidl, August 10, 11, and 15, 2012, Kabul, Afghanistan.
110. In a subsequent conversation, Natsios has expressed that he is not sure he actually believes that, but rather may have spoken out of frustration. Andrew Natsios, personal conversation with Valerie M. Hudson, Lone Star National Security Symposium, March 22, 2014, College Station, Texas.
111. Ibid.
112. Andrew Natsios, e-mail to Valerie M. Hudson, October 21, 2013.

## 6. AFGHANISTAN: THE LITMUS TEST FOR THE HILLARY DOCTRINE

1. Hillary Clinton, "Clinton Pledges to Not Abandon Afghan Women," *MS Magazine*, May 14, 2010.
2. Hamid Karzai, "Karzai Lashes Out at the U.S. for Its Role and Focus in Afghanistan," *New York Times*, October 8, 2013.
3. Shirin Ebadi, speech at Nobel Women's Initiative Conference, Belfast, Northern Ireland, May 27, 2013.
4. This encounter took place on November 1, 2010, in Lashkar Gah, Afghanistan.
5. The question-and-answer session took place at the Wheatley Institution, Brigham Young University, Provo, Utah, on March 26, 2010. At the time, General David Petraeus was on a tour of sixty American universities, discussing the situation in Afghanistan and Iraq.
6. Indeed, a Taliban spokesman has already stated, "it is too early to discuss" whether the group would support the education of girls. See Macinnis and Ferris-Rotman, "Insight: Afghan Women Fade From White House Focus as Exit Nears."
7. See Yerman, "Women in the World Summit 2012." Oxfam published a report in late 2014, *Behind Closed Doors*, which Rod Nordland of the *New York Times* summarizes thusly: "Oxfam's report details 11 instances of direct or indirect peace talks between the international community and the Taliban or other insurgents since 2005, none of which had any confirmed participation by women. It also lists 16 such efforts carried out by the Afghan government, only three of which involved any female delegates, and those were fewer than 10 percent of the government representatives involved." See Nordland, "Peace Effort with Taliban Is Excluding Women." At the time of this writing, Ashraf Ghani has not resumed any peace talks, so it is too early to tell whether he will change this situation or not.
8. Crowe, "TIME's Epic Distortion of the Plight of Women in Afghanistan."
9. As does Bibi Aisha, the young woman whose mutilated face was shown on the cover of *Time* magazine in 2010. According to Aryn Baker writing in *Time*, "Talk that the Afghan government is considering some kind of political accommodation with the Taliban is the only thing that elicits an emotional response [from her]. 'They are the people that did this to me,' she says, touching the jagged bridge of scarred flesh and bone that frames the gaping hole in an otherwise beautiful face. 'How can we reconcile with them?'" Baker, "Afghan Women and the Return of the Taliban."
10. Donald Steinberg, telephone interview by Valerie M. Hudson, July 12, 2013.
11. Ryan Crocker, interview by Valerie M. Hudson, September 23, 2013, College Station, Texas.
12. Back-of-the-envelope calculation based on assorted figures, such as $96.57 billion spent on Afghan Reconstruction from fiscal year 2002 to June 2013;

$60.7 billion spent by the Department of Defense; $16.5 billion spent by USAID; $4.2 billion, State Appropriated, Obligated, Disbursed. See Special Inspector General for Afghanistan Reconstruction, *Quarterly Report to the United States Congress*. Combat costs now run about $100 billion per year. P.L. 111–8, an Omnibus Appropriation, required a State Department report on the use of funds to address the needs of Afghan women and girls (submitted by September 30, 2009). See Special Inspector General for Afghanistan Reconstruction, *Quarterly Report to the United States Congress*; Katzman, *Afghanistan: Politics, Elections, and Government Performance*.

13. International Crisis Group, *Women and Conflict in Afghanistan*, 2.

14. U.S. Department of State, Bureau of Democracy, Human Rights and Labor, *The Taliban's War Against Women*.

15. See Rhem, "Women's Rights a Priority; Humanitarian Aid Improves."

16. See Alterman, "'Blowback,' the Prequel."

17. Gates, *From the Shadows*.

18. Ibid.

19. "Analysis Wahhabism."

20. CNN, interview with Zbigniew Brzezinski, June 13, 1997, http://www2.gwu .edu/~nsarchiv/coldwar/interviews/episode-17/brzezinski1.html

21. "Sleeping with the Devil."

22. Stephens and Ottaway, "From USA, the ABC's of Jihad."

23. It is hard not to be stung to the heart when a former mujahideen commander, Abdul Hafiz Mansoor, asserts, "If this war and all these killings were so bad, then why aren't we putting their international backers on trial? If we talk about violation of human rights, we should accuse the U.N. special representative for Afghanistan, who supported the mujahideen at the time and now calls them warlords. Or President Ronald Reagan, who provided these warlords and human rights violators with Stinger missiles." Nordland, "Top Afghans Tied to '90s Carnage, Researchers Say."

24. Ryan Crocker, interview by Valerie M. Hudson, October 20, 2013, College Station, Texas.

25. There were abuses on all sides, and the jury is out as to whether Massoud personally ordered or personally took part in atrocities against civilians—including women and girls.

26. Human Rights Watch, "Crisis of Impunity."

27. Crowe, "TIME's Epic Distortion."

28. On February 2, 2011, Patricia Leidl met with Jamila (a pseudonym) in Farah, Afghanistan. The following story is an account of their encounter, and all quotations are from that interview.

29. Physicians for Human Rights, *The Taliban's War on Women*.

30. From interviews by Leidl, November 10, 2009, with women who survived the Taliban era.

31. On July 20, 1997, for example, the Taliban forbade women from collecting the food aid doled out by international humanitarian agencies, prompting the World Food Programme to pull out altogether.

32. Physicians for Human Rights, *The Taliban's War on Women*.

33. G. W. Bush, "Remarks on Efforts to Globally Promote Women's Human Rights."

34. Mariam Mansury, telephone interview by Valerie M. Hudson, October 18, 2013.

35. "If We Betray Afghan Women, We Have Lost."

36. Nordland, "Top Afghans Tied to '90s Carnage."

37. See Jones, "The Forgotten War."

38. Nordland, "Top Afghans Tied to '90s Carnage."

39. Ibid.

40. See "Abdul Rashid Dostum."

41. These include such men as Abdul Rab Rassoul Sayyaf, who first brought bin Laden to Afghanistan, and Gul Aga Shirzai, a former governor and reported pederast. See Rosenberg and Nordland, "Afghan Presidential Hopefuls Are Told to Leave Guns at Home."

42. Christine Fair, interview by Valerie M. Hudson, October 14, 2013, Bloomington, Indiana.

43. International Crisis Group, *Women and Conflict in Afghanistan*, 7.

44. The actual system is more complicated than this, with two women per province for the lower house, and 16 percent plus one-half of presidential appointees in the upper house. All of this winds up being 25 percent in the end.

45. Crocker, interview, September 23, 2013.

46. See Haidari, "Afghan Women as a Measure of Progress."

47. Crocker, interview, September 23, 2013.

48. International Crisis Group, *Women and Conflict in Afghanistan*, 10.

49. Haidari, "Afghan Women as a Measure of Progress."

50. International Crisis Group, *Women and Conflict in Afghanistan*, 11.

51. Melanne Verveer, interview by Valerie M. Hudson, May 21, 2013, Washington, D.C.

52. See, for example, Taylor and Hamdard, "Taliban-Style Edict for Women Spreads Alarm in Afghan District."

53. Lough, "Guest Post: When Quotas Matter—Women on the Provincial Council."

54. Verveer, interview.

55. Babakarkhail and Crilly, "Helmand's Top Female Police Officer Shot Dead."

56. See Johnson and Faiez, "Afghan Students Protest Women's Rights Decree."

57. Nordberg, *The Underground Girls of Kabul*, 263.

58. Quoted in International Crisis Group, *Women and Conflict in Afghanistan*, 25.

59. See Starkey, "Law Will Let Afghan Husbands Starve Wives Who Withhold Sex."

60. Katzman, *Afghanistan*, 54.

61. Barr, "Women's Rights in Afghanistan Must Be Steadfastly Respected."
62. International Crisis Group, *Women and Conflict in Afghanistan*, 13.
63. See, for example, Babakarkhail and Crilly, "Helmand's Top Female Police Officer Shot Dead."
64. Ibid.
65. Ibid.
66. Zohra Rasekh, e-mail correspondence with Valerie M. Hudson, September 9, 2013.
67. That this finding contradicts more positive statistics mentioned earlier demonstrates that the way in which gains are measured makes all the difference. Outputs like enrollment may not translate into impacts like literacy. See Oates, "The Mother of All Problems."
68. International Crisis Group, *Women and Conflict in Afghanistan*, 15.
69. Ibid.
70. International Crisis Group, *Women and Conflict in Afghanistan*, 22.
71. Katzman, *Afghanistan: Politics, Elections, and Government Performance*, 54.
72. Mansury, interview.
73. On February 15, 2011, Patricia Leidl met with Fatima (no last name as is customary among poor people) in Farah, Afghanistan. The following story is an account of their encounter, and all quotations are from that interview.
74. Human Rights Watch, *"I Had to Run Away."*
75. Ibid.
76. Kelly, "Afghan Woman to Be Freed from Jail After Agreeing to Marry Rapist."
77. Kunduz Regional Office Press Unit, "Endless Pain Suffered by Sahar Gul Turned Into Scream."
78. Boone, "Afghan Child Bride Had Escaped Torturers but Was Sent Back."
79. Ibid.
80. Ibid.
81. Ibid.
82. Goldberg, "UN: Number of Afghan Women Targeted for Assassination Jumps Three Fold."
83. On October 21, 2011, Patricia Leidl met with Hosiy Sahibzada in Kandahar, Afghanistan. The following story is an account of their encounter, and all quotations are from that interview.
84. International Crisis Group, *Women and Conflict in Afghanistan*, 27.
85. Crocker, interview, September 23, 2013.
86. Fair, interview.
87. Crocker, "Women, War and Peace."
88. Chandrasekaran, "In Afghanistan, U.S. Shifts Strategy on Women's Rights as It Eyes Wider Priorities."
89. Jones, "Tomgram: Ann Jones, Can Women Make Peace?"
90. Crocker, interview, September 23, 2013.

91. International Crisis Group, *Women and Conflict in Afghanistan*, 36.

92. Mansury, interview.

93. For a full text of the address, see "Full Text: Malala Yousafzai Delivers Defiant Riposte to Taliban Militants with Speech to the UN General Assembly."

94. Lemmon, "Afghan Women Are Not 'Pet Rocks.'"

95. Crocker, "Women, War and Peace."

96. G. W. Bush, "State of the Union; President Bush's State of the Union Address to Congress and the Nation."

97. G. W. Bush, "Remarks by the President at Signing Ceremony for Afghan Women and Children Relief Act of 2001."

98. G. W. Bush, "For George W. Bush, Empowering Women in Afghanistan Lays a 'Foundation for a Lasting Peace.'"

99. Crocker, "Women, War and Peace."

100. Toosi, "'I Wasn't Tortured. But I Wasn't Free.'"

101. Mansury, interview.

102. K., interview conducted in confidentiality by Valerie M. Hudson, fall 2013.

103. Crocker, interview, September 23, 2013.

104. Mansury, interview.

105. Asia Foundation, "Executive Summary."

106. Crocker, interview, September 23, 2013.

107. K., interview.

108. Sanam Anderlini, telephone interview by Valerie M. Hudson, November 21, 2013.

109. Sima Samar, e-mail correspondence with Valerie M. Hudson, October 8, 2013.

110. Crocker, "Women, War and Peace."

111. Mansury, interview.

112. Abi-Habib, "Afghan Women Fear Rights Will Erode as U.S. Leaves."

113. As we have mentioned, PROMOTE should disburse at least $200 million, though it was planned as a $415 million multilateral program. Furthermore, it should be noted that there is a degree of Afghan discontent with PROMOTE. Zohra Rasekh said, "US and other international programs have ignored rural women and women in remote areas of the country for various reasons including lack of security issues in those areas. A recent USAID major program, PROMOTE, with over 200 million USD, for Afghan women, initiated by Secretary Hilary Clinton, has intentionally ignored the uneducated, rural and over 30 years of age females in Afghanistan. This major US funded program for Afghan women will have its [negative] consequences for Afghan women as soon as its inception, if not implemented in a culturally sensitive manner." Rasekh, e-mail correspondence.

114. Dobriansky and Verveer, "Don't Abandon the Women of Afghanistan."

115. Charlotte Ponticelli, interview by Valerie M. Hudson, June 28, 2013, Washington, D.C.

116. Crocker, interview, September 23, 2013.
117. Quoted in Lemmon, "Afghan Women Are Not 'Pet Rocks.'"
118. See, for example, Condon, "Obama Shuffles Cabinet but with No Female Nominees."
119. Anderlini, interview.
120. Crocker, "Women, War and Peace."
121. Quoted in Lemmon, "Afghan Women Are Not 'Pet Rocks.'"
122. Ann Jones, telephone interview by Valerie M. Hudson, July 8, 2013.
123. Crocker, interview, September 23, 2013.
124. Ibid.
125. L. Bush, "Afghan Women's Gains Are at Risk."
126. See "Sec. Kerry, Hillary Clinton, Laura Bush Advocate for Afghan Women's 'Hard-Fought Gains.'"
127. Quoted in "Sec. Kerry, Hillary Clinton, Laura Bush Advocate for Afghan Women's 'Hard-Fought Gains.'"
128. Crocker, interview, September 23, 2013.
129. Crocker, "Women, War and Peace."
130. Sethna, "Afghan Women's Rights Under Threat."
131. International Crisis Group, *Women and Conflict in Afghanistan*, 32.
132. Crocker, "Women, War and Peace."
133. Indeed, we are told that State Department efforts on the rule of law will see a remarkable increase in annual funding during the years of transition.
134. Oxfam, "Poverty and Unemployment Fuel the Conflict According to 70% of Afghans, New Oxfam Research Shows," press release, November 18, 2009, www.oxfam.org/pressroom/pressrelease/2009–11–18/poverty-unemployment-fuel-conflict-afghanistan.
135. Pande, "Activists Urge NATO to Protect Afghan Women's Rights."
136. Rasekh, e-mail correspondence.
137. Clinton, "Secretary Clinton's Speech at Afghanistan Conference."
138. "An Interview with Hillary Clinton."
139. See, for example, LaFranchi, "At NATO Summit on Afghanistan, Few Women's Voices Heard."
140. Quoted in Cordesman, "Afghanistan and the Tokyo Conference."
141. Ibid.
142. In addition to violence against women, EVAW also contains provisions against the sexual assault of children, which is all too frequent in a land of child marriages for girls and bacha bazi for boys. (See Wisniewski, "Kabul Urged to Protect Sexually Abused Children.") Indeed, we were struck by a comment made to us by Christine Fair, in light of what we have written about in chapter 2. She said, "The whole country is literally fucked: the first sexual experience for both boys and girls is to be raped by a grown man. We supported police chiefs who were boy rapists—our soldiers were forced to not say anything when they

witnessed the rapes of recruits in the Afghan army or police. We do so much to reinforce this evil. The 'strong men' we work with are horrible people, and now how could the 11 years of patronage they have built up be undone? They are not any better than the Taliban" (Fair, interview). Indeed, some say that the original impetus for the Taliban's rise to power was that they promised to ban bacha bazi, which catered to public outrage over the practice as perpetrated by the mujahideen (many of whom have become high-ranking officials in the Karzai government). In a sense, the United States backed the pro-pedophile side against the anti-pedophile side by invading Afghanistan, a very uncomfortable position for Americans. Patricia Leidl heard of these things when she was in the field as well: "When we began discussing Afghan attitudes towards women, 'Johansen' [a U.S. military officer] began shaking his head, at first slowly and then more violently. 'These guys are crazy,' he almost spluttered. 'They keep women locked up and the only relationships they have are with each other. They are *all* fucking each other. All of them. I swear.'" According to "Johansen," they had one police chief who got into serious trouble when U.S. police trainers discovered that he had beaten his wife so badly that he had almost killed her. Although married for two years, she could not get pregnant. The police chief had the brilliant idea that pummelling her to a pulp would surely persuade her recalcitrant womb to yield up the goods. "We took her to the hospital," said Johansen. "When our doctors examined her they discovered she was still a virgin. He had been having anal sex with her the entire time."

143. International Crisis Group, "Women and Conflict in Afghanistan."
144. Graham-Harrison and Amiri, "Taliban Peace Talk Plans Lead Afghan Women to Fear Loss of Rights."
145. Barsa, "Challenges to Securing Afghan Women's Gains in a Post-2014 Environment."
146. Fair, interview.
147. Mansury, interview.
148. See, for example, Afghan Women's Network, *Afghanistan: Monitoring Women's Security in Transition*.
149. Ferris-Rotman, "Leaning Out."
150. Rohde, "All Successful Democracies Need Freedom of Speech."
151. Suzanne Griffin, e-mail correspondence with Valerie M. Hudson, October 8, 2013.
152. CIA, *World Factbook: Afghanistan*.
153. Andrew Natsios, interview by Valerie M. Hudson, March 27, 2013, College Station, Texas.
154. Chandrasekaran, "In Afghanistan, US Shifts Strategy on Women's Rights as It Eyes Wider Priorities."
155. Roby and Tsongas, "Afghan Women Worry as the U.S. Departure Looms."
156. Crocker, interview with Hudson, October 22, 2013, College Station, Texas. The involvement of these lawmakers in this debate is not by happenstance.

The Bush Center notes, "To help focus congressional attention on the need to protect women's rights in Afghanistan, a bipartisan group of lawmakers led by Reps. Cathy McMorris Rodgers (R–Wash.) and Donna Edwards (D–Md.) recently launched the Afghan Women's Task Force." L. Bush, "Women's Rights Key to Afghan Success."

## 7. THE FUTURE OF THE HILLARY DOCTRINE: REALPOLITIK AND FEMPOLITIK

1. Hillary Clinton, "Remarks at the TEDWomen Conference" (speech at Ronald Reagan Building, Washington, D.C., December 8, 2010), http://www.state.gov /secretary/rm/2010/12/152670.htm.
2. Robin Morgan, interview with Valerie M. Hudson, New York City, May 14, 2013.
3. Garner, *Gender & Foreign Policy in the Clinton Administration*, 414.
4. B., interview conducted in confidentiality by Valerie M. Hudson, spring 2013.
5. Shelby Quast, telephone interview by Valerie M. Hudson, May 21, 2013.
6. Indeed, to prevent this, the Women, Peace, and Security Act of 2013 has been introduced to Congress. This legislation would codify the NAP and ensure its enforceability beyond the current administration. See Taylor, "Legislatively Speaking—Women at the Tables of Power Leads to More Sustainable Peace."
7. Rosa Brooks, telephone interview by Valerie M. Hudson, October 8, 2013.
8. Indeed, when we read this quote of Clinton's, we could not help wondering if it was a description of the Obama White House: "But as strong a case as we've made, too many otherwise thoughtful people continue to see the fortunes of women and girls as somehow separate from society at large. They nod, they smile and then relegate these issues once again to the sidelines. I have seen it over and over again, I have been kidded about it, I have been ribbed, I have been challenged in board rooms and official offices across the world. But fighting to give women and girls a fighting chance isn't a nice thing to do. It isn't some luxury that we get to when we have time on our hands to spend doing that. This is a core imperative for every human being and every society. If we do not complete a campaign for women's rights and opportunities, the world we want to live in, the country we all love and cherish will not be what it should be." See "Hillary Clinton: Helping Women Isn't Just A 'Nice' Thing to Do."
9. The British government has done even more than that: it has provided a gender expert to the U.N. negotiator's team (it had none), gender advisors to all sides of the negotiation, and organized civil society consultation procedures. Leimbach, "At Geneva II Talks in January, It is Not Enough to 'Add Women and Stir.'"
10. Caprioli, Nielsen, and Hudson, "Women and Post-Conflict Settings."
11. Chandrasekaran, "In Afghanistan, U.S. Shifts Strategy on Women's Rights as It Eyes Wider Priorities."

12. Dara Kay Cohen, interview by Valerie M. Hudson, April 4, 2013, San Francisco, California.

13. Brooks, interview.

14. Zenko, "City of Men."

15. Another area that needs attention, but is often overlooked, is that of translators in the field, where there is also a serious gender gap. Ann Jones points out that many of the programs she was involved with in Africa were undermined by the absence of female interpreters: males tend to translate what they thought women should hear, which was not necessarily empowerment. See Jones, *War Is Not Over When It's Over.*

16. B.2, interview conducted in confidentiality by Valerie M. Hudson, spring 2013.

17. Kerry, "Remarks at a Meeting of the Equal Futures Partnership."

18. S., interview conducted in confidentiality by Valerie M. Hudson, July 2013.

19. Caren Grown, interview by Valerie M. Hudson, May 20, 2013, Washington, D.C.

20. See, for example, Beaman et al., "Female Leadership Raises Aspirations and Educational Attainment for Girls."

21. Mariam Mansury, telephone interview by Valerie M. Hudson, October 18, 2013.

22. Brooks, interview.

23. Jen Klein, interview by Valerie M. Hudson, May 20, 2013, Washington, D.C.

24. Cybele Cochran, interview by Valerie M. Hudson, May 22, 2013, Washington, D.C.

25. Ibid.

26. Ibid.

27. Tobie Whitman, e-mail correspondence with Valerie M. Hudson, July 25, 2013.

28. Cochran, interview.

29. Lemmon, "Hillary Doctrine."

30. For example, we applaud David Cameron's decision to make sexual violence in war the key issue of discussion for the G-8 in 2013.

31. Anne-Marie Goetz, interview by Valerie M. Hudson, May 14, 2013, New York City.

32. Deborah Cavin, telephone interview by Valerie M. Hudson, March 19, 2013.

33. An example of this kind of polite pressure on allies is the Equal Futures Partnership initiative of the U.S. State Department under Clinton. For more information, see the Equal Futures Partnership fact sheet available at www.whitehouse.gov/the-press-office/2013/04/19/fact-sheet-equal-futures -partnership-promise-progress.

34. Swanee Hunt, telephone interview by Valerie M. Hudson, March 19, 2013.

35. Deen, "Security Council Vow on Women Lives Mostly on Paper."

36. The United Nations has established some hard targets. According to Anne-Marie Goetz of UNWomen, the United Nations has set a hard target that "15 percent of post-conflict spending has to target women's empowerment and gender equality. . . . And then there's other targets like when the UN finances emergency post-conflict employment, a minimum of 40 percent of those jobs have to be for women, or no more than 60 percent for either sex. And they're actually doing it. And you know, it's very hard to do that; you have to have childcare facilities and transportation. But they're doing it." Goetz, interview.

37. Olsson and Tejpar, *Operational Effectiveness and UN Resolution 1325—Practices and Lessons from Afghanistan*, 75.

38. Tobie Whitman, interview by Valerie M. Hudson, May 21, 2013, Washington, D.C.

39. June Shih, interview by Valerie M. Hudson, May 21, 2013, Washington, D.C.

40. The nine indicators are given in note 37 of chapter 5. See USAID, *Integrating Gender Equality and Female Empowerment in USAID's Program Cycle*.

41. B., interview.

42. Kristen Cordell, interview by Valerie M. Hudson, May 21, 2013, Washington, D.C.

43. Alexandra Tenny, interview by Valerie M. Hudson, April 26, 2013, Washington, D.C.

44. Rigoberta Menchú Tum, speech at Nobel Women's Initiative Conference, May 28, 2013, Belfast, Northern Ireland.

45. Tobie Whitman, e-mail correspondence with Valerie M. Hudson, July 25, 2013.

46. Kathleen Kuehnast, interview by Valerie M. Hudson, May 21, 2013, Washington, D.C.

47. Ibid.

48. Carter, *A Call to Action*.

49. Shirin Ebadi, speech at Nobel Women's Initiative Conference, May 27, 2013, Belfast, Northern Ireland.

50. Leymah Gbowee, speech at Nobel Women's Initiative Conference, May 27, 2013, Belfast, Northern Ireland.

51. Tavernise, "Broaching Birth Control with Afghan Mullahs."

52. We also really like Soraya Chemaly's International Feminist Networking Project, which offers an online map of feminist groups around the world, with contact information; see http://feministnetworkproject.wordpress.com.

53. Rebecca Chiao, e-mail correspondence with Valerie M. Hudson, August 9, 2013. All quotes by Chiao are from this e-mail correspondence.

54. See Gray, "Egyptians Patrol Tahrir Square for Mob Sex Assaults."

55. For more information on this project, visit the website at www.eyesondarfur.org/villages.html.

56. Visit Mobile For Development's website at www.gsma.com/mobilefordevelopment/lifestories/mwomen for more information on this initiative.

57. Scott Carpenter, presentation at the Futures Without Violence Open Square Summit, October 3, 2013, Washington, D.C. See also Pearlman, "How the Department of Defense Is Using Big Data to Combat Sex Trafficking."

58. Goetz, interview.

59. Jane Mosbacher Morris, telephone interview by Valerie M. Hudson, October 16, 2013.

60. Charlotte Ponticelli, interview by Valerie M. Hudson, June 28, 2013, Washington, D.C.

61. The 2013 figure is $1.9 billion.

62. Clinton, "Remarks on Evidence and Impact."

63. The database of the WomanStats Project is available at http://womanstats.org/index.htm.

64. See, for example, Hudson et al., *Sex and World Peace*.

65. Slaughter, "How to Halt the Butchery in Syria."

66. Goetz, interview.

67. Robin Morgan remembers that in the late 1970s, *Ms.* magazine had a special issue on how women would define security, which included pieces by Pat Derian, Bella Abzug, Gloria Steinem, herself, and others, which may represent the first time this definitional problematique was first explicitly addressed. Robin Morgan, interview by Valerie M. Hudson, May 14, 2013, New York City.

68. Moellendorf, "*Jus ex Bello* in Afghanistan," 161.

69. USAID, "Promoting Gender Equality in National Priority Programs (PROMOTE)."

70. Afghan Women's Network, *Afghanistan: Monitoring Women's Security in Transition*, 35.

71. Ryan Crocker, interview by Valerie M. Hudson, September 23, 2013, College Station, Texas.

72. K., interview conducted in confidentiality by Valerie M. Hudson, fall 2013.

73. Afghan Women's Network, *Afghanistan: Monitoring Women's Security in Transition*, 43.

74. "Community Radio in Afghanistan."

75. Quast, interview.

76. There have also been allegations that State Department personnel, including ambassadors, have engaged prostitutes, including child prostitutes, with impunity. See Fantz and Dougherty, "Prostitution, Drugs Alleged in State Department Memo."

77. Goetz, interview.

78. Hansen, "Sex and Drugs in Hell."

79. Adele Kibasumba, presentation at the Futures Without Violence Open Square Summit, October 3, 2012, Washington, D.C.

80. See, for example, McCleary-Sills and Mukasa, "External Evaluation of the Trust Fund for Victims Programmes in Northern Uganda and the Democratic Republic of Congo."
81. Tawakkul Karman, speech at Nobel Women's Initiative Conference, May 27, 2013, Belfast, Northern Ireland.
82. Kuehnast, interview.
83. Steven Steiner, interview by Valerie M. Hudson, May 21, 2013, Washington, D.C.
84. Joseph Vess, interview by Valerie M. Hudson, May 21, 2013, Washington, D.C.
85. Ibid.
86. "DRC-Uganda: Male Sexual Abuse Survivors Living on the Margins."
87. Couturier, "Rape of Men."
88. See, for example, Mitchell, "Domestic Violence Prevention Through the Constructing Violence-free Masculinities Programme."
89. "Engaging Men to Protect and Empower Women."
90. Palwasha Kakar, e-mail correspondence with Valerie M. Hudson, August 2, 2013.
91. Deborah Derrick, remarks at the Futures Without Violence Open Square Summit, October 3, 2013, Washington, D.C.
92. Sanam Anderlini, telephone interview by Valerie M. Hudson, November 21, 2013.
93. Louise Olsson, e-mail correspondence with Valerie M. Hudson, November 12, 2013. The U.S. NGO Futures Without Violence has created a similarly themed program called "Coaching Boys Into Men," which trains male athletic coaches to help their charges understand how to respectfully interact with women and girls.
94. Michele Flournoy, telephone interview by Valerie M. Hudson, December 18, 2013.
95. Yerman, "Women in the World Summit 2012."
96. See Office of the White House Press Secretary, "Fact Sheet: The Equal Futures Partnership—From Promise to Progress," press release, April 19, 2013, www.whitehouse.gov/the-press-office/2013/04/19/fact-sheet-equal-futures-partnership-promise-progress; Winter, "Air Force Academy to Get First Female Leader."
97. See USAID, *United States Strategy to Prevent and Respond to Gender-Based Violence Globally*.
98. Natsios, "Clash of the Counter-Bureaucracy and Development."
99. Ibid.
100. Natsios, "Clash of the Counter-Bureaucracy and Development."
101. See Beebe and Kaldor, *The Ultimate Weapon Is No Weapon*, 133.

102. Ibid.
103. Fair, interview.
104. Natsios, "The Foreign Aid Reform Agenda."
105. Alter, "Woman of the World."
106. Yasmeen Hassan, interview by Valerie M. Hudson, May 15, 2013, New York City.
107. Goetz, interview.
108. Michelle Barsa, interview by Valerie M. Hudson, May 21, 2013, Washington, D.C.
109. Kuehnast, interview.
110. As Clinton explained (with Julia Roberts), "Smoke from dirty stoves or open flames. Some 3 billion people live in homes where food is cooked on stoves or over fires burning fuels like wood, dung, charcoal, or agricultural waste. These fuels produce toxic fumes, and in poorly ventilated homes, the mix of chemicals can reach 200 times the level that the EPA considers safe to breathe. It can cause lung cancer, pneumonia, cataracts, low birth weight, even death. According to the World Health Organization, smoke from dirty stoves and fires kills almost 2 million people each year, most of them women and children. It kills more than twice as many people as malaria." See Clinton and Roberts, "'Clean Stoves' Would Save Lives, Cut Pollution."
111. Wheaton, "A Question of How Women's Issues Will Fare, in Washington and Overseas."
112. Crocker, interview.
113. See Lemmon, "Hillary Doctrine"; Clinton, "Remarks at the TEDWomen Conference."
114. Flournoy, interview.
115. Rothkopf, "Balance of Power."
116. Cindy McCain, presentation at the Futures Without Violence Open Square Summit, October 3, 2012, Washington, D.C.
117. Dee Dee Myers, presentation at the Futures Without Violence Open Square Summit, October 3, 2012, Washington, D.C.
118. Steele, *Walter Lippmann and the American Century*.
119. For example, one commentator asks "if [Clinton] is willing to stand up to the guys and take the risk of being branded a feminist rather than a 'realist.' That's a false dichotomy; she's clearly both. Clinton herself comments, 'In reality, I think we all need to be more of a hybrid, perhaps idealistic realists,' she said. 'Because leading effectively cannot be done without our values. And a great deal of what is happening today bears that out.'" Tax, "Can Afghan Women Count on Hillary Clinton?"; and " 'It Pains Me.'"
120. See Pinker, *The Better Angels of Our Nature*.
121. As noted by Farah Council of the Institute for Inclusive Security, this also implies that amorality, selfishness, and opportunism are not the foundation of a secure world—and thus not realist.

122. "Strengthening Women's Rights and Political Participation."

123. Donald Steinberg, telephone interview by Valerie M. Hudson, July 12, 2013.

124. Lauren Wolfe, interview by Valerie M. Hudson, May 14, 2013, New York City.

125. Over the past decade, a small "feminist hawk" movement did spring up within the United States and then by 2011 appeared to wither away. Though the feminist hawk stance would appear, theoretically, to be larger than the issue of "Islamofascist misogyny," this is the topic to which those on the Internet calling themselves feminist hawks were most devoted. See Richards, "Sexual Slavery and Jihadist Breeding Camps."; "NY Times Notices That 'Hawkish Sites' Have 'Taken Up Feminism'"; Heffernan, "Feminist Hawks."

126. Wendle, "The Aisha Bibi Case."

127. Soraya Chemaly, interview by Valerie M. Hudson, May 21, 2013, Washington, D.C.

128. Kasia Anderson, "Iraqi Women the Worse for War."

129. The next several paragraphs also appeared in Hudson et al., Sex and World Peace.

130. Anne-Marie Slaughter wants the record to be set straight: "The idea that the girls pushed the boys into war is ludicrous. We were dismissed for months as soft liberals concerned about 'peripheral' development issues like women and girls, and now we're Amazonian Valkyrie warmongers. Please." Alter, "Woman of the World."

131. Beebe and Kaldor, The Ultimate Weapon Is No Weapon, 93.

132. Anderlini, interview.

133. Goetz, interview. Indeed, Russia is the only member of the G-8 without a NAP, even though the G-8 declared sexual violence in war as its focus issue for 2013.

134. UNSCR 1889 specifies UNSCR 1325–pertinent country indicators that Member States will supposedly be required to report on for the first time in 2014.

135. Fall and Zhang, "Staff Recruitment in United Nations System Organizations."

136. These figures were calculated from U.N. gender statistics by mission for the month of September 2013. It is important to note that peacekeepers include both military experts and troops, and police figures include individual police and formed police units. For a detailed breakdown of gender statistics by mission, see United Nations Peacekeeping, "Gender Statistics."

137. European Parliament, Resolution 2011/2244, "Equality Between Women and Men in the European Union."

138. African Commission on Human and People's Rights, "Protocol to the African Charter on Human and People's Rights on the Rights of Women in Africa."

139. See, for example, Martinuzzi, "Davos Women Diminished as Male Discussion Skips Key Views"; Melissa J. Anderson, "Davos: Women and the Leadership Gap."

140. For a summary of the meeting, see "Deauville: The New Davos for Women in Business."

141. See, for example, Alvarez, "Sweden Faces Facts on Violence Against Women"; "Sharp Increase in Domestic Violence."
142. Valerie M. Hudson et al., *Sex and World Peace*.
143. Barsa, interview.
144. Steinberg, interview.
145. Whitman, e-mail correspondence.

# BIBLIOGRAPHY

★ ★ ★

"Abdul Rashid Dostum." *New Internationalist*, September 1, 2002. http://newint
.org/columns/worldbeaters/2002/09/01/abdul-rashid-dostum.

Abdullah, Abu Bakr. "Iran and Saudi Arabia Allegedly Funding Proxy War in
Yemen." *Al Monitor*, June 6, 2012. www.al-monitor.com/pulse/security/01/06
/war-between-the-houthis-and-sala.html.

Abi-Habib, Maria. "Afghan Women Fear Rights Will Erode as U.S. Leaves."
*Wall Street Journal*, November 13, 2013. http://online.wsj.com/news/articles
/SB10001424127887324439804578109492792633455.

Acharya, Arun K. "Tráfico de Mujeres Hacia la Zona Metropolitana de Monterrey:
Una Perspectiva Analítica." *Espacios Públicos* 12, no. 24 (2009): 146–60.

Afghan Women's Network. *Afghanistan: Monitoring Women's Security in Transition.*
Baseline Report, June 2013. www.cordaid.org/media/medialibrary/2013/10
/Transition_Monitor_Final_Draft_MWST_-_October_9_2013_2.pdf.

African Commission on Human and Peoples' Rights. "Protocol to the African Charter
on Human and Peoples' Rights on the Rights of Women in Africa, July 11, 2003.
www.achpr.org/files/instruments/women-protocol/achpr_instr_proto_women
_eng.pdf

Ahmed, Qanta. *In the Land of Invisible Women: A Female Doctor's Journey in the
Saudi Kingdom.* Naperville, Ill.: Sourcebooks, 2008.

Albright, Madeleine and Hillary Clinton. "Special Program in Honor of International Women's Day with Secretary of State Madeleine Albright and First Lady
Hillary Rodham Clinton." Speech at Department of State, Washington, D.C.,
March 12, 1997. http://usembassy-israel.org.il/publish/press/state/archive/1997
/march/sd30313.htm.

——. "Secretary of State Madeleine K. Albright and First Lady Hillary Rodham Clinton." Roundtable discussion, Washington, D.C., March 11, 1998. U.S. Department of State Archive. http://1997-2001.state.gov/www/statements/1998/980311 .html.

Alexander, Richard D. "Evolution, Culture, and Human Behavior: Some General Considerations." In *Natural Selection and Social Behavior: Recent Research and New Theory*, ed. Richard D. Alexander and Donald W. Tinkle, 509–20. New York: Chiron Press, 1981.

Al-Rasheed, Madawi. "Saudi Arabia Pleased with Morsi's Fall." *Al-Monitor*, July 4, 2013. www.al-monitor.com/pulse/originals/2013/07/saudi-arabia-glad -to-see-morsi-go.html.

Alter, Jonathan. "Woman of the World." *Vanity Fair*, June 2011.

Alterman, Eric. "'Blowback,' the Prequel." *Nation*, October 25, 2001. www.thenation .com/article/blowback-prequel#.

Alvarez, Lizette. "Sweden Faces Facts on Violence Against Women." *New York Times*, March 30, 2005. www.nytimes.com/2005/03/29/world/europe/29iht -letter-4909045.html.

Alwazir, Atiaf Zaid. "A Long Road Ahead for Yemeni Women." *Open Democracy*, December 3, 2012. www.opendemocracy.net/5050/atiaf-zaid-alwazir/long-road -ahead-for-yemeni-women.

Amnesty International. *Yemen's Dark Side: Discrimination and Violence Against Women and Girls*. Report for the U.N. Office of the High Commissioner for Human Rights, November 2009. www2.ohchr.org/english/bodies/hrc/docs/ngos /Yemen's%20darkside-discrimination_Yemen_HRC101.pdf.

Anderson, Kasia. "Iraqi Women the Worse for War." *AlterNet*, May 27, 2007. www.alternet.org/story/52103/iraqi_women_the_worse_for_war.

Anderson, Melissa J. "Davos: Women and the Leadership Gap." *Glass Hammer*, February 7, 2013. www.theglasshammer.com/news/2013/02/07/davos-women -and-the-leadership-gap.

"An Interview with Hillary Clinton." Lexington's Notebook (blog). *Economist*, March 22, 2012. www.economist.com/blogs/lexington/2012/03/foreign-policy.

Armstrong, Paul, "Japanese Politician Calls Wartime Sex Slaves 'Necessary.'" *CNN*, May 15, 2013. www.cnn.com/2013/05/14/world/asia/japan-hashimoto-comfort -women/index.html?hpt=hp_t3.

Asia Foundation. "Executive Summary." *Afghanistan in 2012: A Survey of the Afghan People*. 2012. http://asiafoundation.org/resources/pdfs/KeyFindingsandSummary .pdf.

Avakian, Paul N. "Guatemala's Praised Attorney General to Step Down Under Controversy." *Truthout*, March 2014. http://truth-out.org/news/item/22520 -guatemalas-praised-attorney-general-to-step-down-under-controversy.

Ayoob, Mohammed. "Political Islam: Image and Reality." *World Policy Journal* 11, no. 3 (2004): 1–14.

Babakarkhail, Zubair and Rob Crilly. "Helmand's Top Female Police Officer Shot Dead." *Telegraph*, July 4, 2013. www.telegraph.co.uk/news/worldnews/asia /afghanistan/10159122/Helmands-top-female-police-officer-shot-dead.html.

Baker, Aryn. "Afghan Women and the Return of the Taliban." *Time*, August 9, 2010. http://content.time.com/time/magazine/article/0,9171,2007407,00.html.

Barr, Heather. "Women's Rights in Afghanistan Must Be Steadfastly Respected." *Jurist*, March 20, 2014. www.hrw.org/news/2014/03/20/womens-rights-afghanistan -must-be-steadfastly-respected.

Barsa, Michelle. "Challenges to Securing Afghan Women's Gains in a Post-2014 Environment." *Inclusive Security*, October 29, 2013. http://docs.house .gov/meetings/AS/AS06/20131029/101427/HHRG-113-AS06-Bio -BarsaM-20131029.pdf.

Bathanti, Jacob. "Bishop Gerardi: A Life Devoted to Social Justice." Guatemala Human Rights Commission, n.d. www.ghrc-usa.org/AboutGuatemala /TimelineGerardiWebsite.pdf.

Beaman, Lori, Esther Duflo, Rohini Pande, and Petia Topalova. "Female Leadership Raises Aspirations and Educational Attainment for Girls: A Policy Experiment in India." *Science* 335, no. 6068 (2012): 582–86. doi: 10.1126 /science.1212382.

Beebe, Shannon D. and Mary Kaldor. *The Ultimate Weapon Is No Weapon: Human Security and the New Rules of War and Peace*. New York: Public Affairs, 2010.

Beevor, Antony. "'They Raped Every German Female from Eight to 80.'" *Guardian*, April 30, 2002. www.theguardian.com/books/2002/may/01/news .features11.

Begum, Sultana. "Still Waiting for Change in Yemen: Making the Political Transition Work for Women." *Oxfam*, September 24, 2012. www.oxfam.org/en/policy /still-waiting-change-yemen.

Benítez, Rohry, Adriana Candia, Patricia Cabrera, Guadalupe de la Mora, Josefina Martínez, Isabel Velázquez, and Ramona Ortiz. *El Silencio que la vos de todos quiebra: Mujeres y victimas de Ciudad Juarez*. Chihuahua: Editciones El Azar, 1999.

Benjamin, Medea. "Should Syria's Future Be Decided by Men with Guns?" *NationofChange*, January 20, 2014. www.nationofchange.org/should-syria-s-future-be -decided-men-guns-1390232021.

Benmehdi, Hassan. "Maghreb Women Fear Regression of Rights." *Magharebia*, June 27, 2013. http://magharebia.com/en_GB/articles/awi/features/2013/06/27 /feature-03.

Bernstein, Carl. *A Woman in Charge: The Life of Hillary Rodham Clinton*. New York: Alfred A. Knopf, 2007.

Biemann, Ursula. "Performing the Border: On Gender, Transnational Bodies, and Technology." In *Globalization on the Line: Culture, Capital, and Citizenship at*

*U.S. Borders*, ed. Claudia Sadowski-Smith, 99–120. Hampshire: Palgrave Macmillan, 2002.

Boone, Jon. "Afghan Child Bride Had Escaped Torturers but Was Sent Back." *Guardian*, January 2, 2012. www.theguardian.com/world/2012/jan/02/afghan -girl-escaped-torturers-sent-back.

"Bosnia-Herzegovina: Mass Rape, Forced Pregnancy, Genocide." *Equality Now*, June 1, 1993. www.equalitynow.org/node/97.

Bower, Eve. "New Protest Statement Builds in Iran—Men in Head Scarves." *CNN*, December 14, 2009. http://edition.cnn.com/2009/WORLD/meast/12/14/iran .headscarf.protest.

Boyd, Neil. *The Beast Within: Why Men Are Violent*. Vancouver, Canada: Greystone Books, 2000.

Breslaw, Anna. "Where Are India's 60 Million Missing Girls? The Tragic, Obvious Answer." *Jezebel*, August 10, 2013. http://jezebel.com/where-are-indias-60-million -missing-girls-the-tragic-1091500375.

Brightman, Robert. "The Sexual Division of Foraging Labor: Biology, Taboo, and Gender Politics." *Comparative Studies in Society and History* 38, no. 4 (1996): 687–729. doi: 10.1017/S0010417500020508.

Brown, Matthew H. "Nostalgia for Saddam Hussein's Rule." *Baltimore Sun*, December 28, 2008. http://articles.baltimoresun.com/2008-12-28/news/0812270092_1 _saddam-hussein-iraq-under-saddam-care-about-iraqis.

Brownmiller, Susan. *Against Our Will: Men, Women, and Rape*. New York: Fawcett Book, 1975.

Buchanan, Emily. "Women in Saudi Arabia to Vote and Run in Elections." *BBC*, September 25, 2011. www.bbc.co.uk/news/world-us-canada-15052030.

Burki, Talha K. "Yemen's Hunger Crisis." *Lancet* 380 (2012): 637–38.

Bush, George W. "Commencement Address at the United States Military Academy at West Point." *Presidential Rhetoric*, June 1, 2002. www.presidentialrhetoric. com/speeches/06.01.02.html.

——. "Commencement Address at the University of South Carolina in Columbia, South Carolina," May 9, 2003. The American Presidency Project. www.presidency .ucsb.edu/ws/?pid=407.

——. "For George W. Bush, Empowering Women in Afghanistan Lays a 'Foundation for a Lasting Peace.' " *Fox News*, discussion with Greta Van Susteren, March 31, 2011. www.foxnews.com/on-air/on-the-record/transcript/george-w -bush-empowering-women-afghanistan-lays-039foundation-lasting-peace039.

——. "Radio Address by Mrs. Bush," November 17, 2001. The American Presidency Project. www.presidency.ucsb.edu/ws/?pid=24992.

——. "Remarks by the President at Signing Ceremony for Afghan Women and Children Relief Act of 2001." Speech at National Women's Museum in the Arts, Washington, D.C., December 12, 2001. http://georgewbush-whitehouse .archives.gov/news/releases/2001/12/20011212-9.html.

———. "Remarks on Efforts to Globally Promote Women's Human Rights." Remarks at the White House, Washington, D.C., March 12, 2004. The American Presidency Project. www.presidency.ucsb.edu/ws/index.php?pid=64747&st=Human+Rights&st1=speech#axzz2j4z8NNDn.

———. "The State of the Union; President Bush's State of the Union Address to Congress and the Nation." *New York Times*, January 30, 2002. www.nytimes.com/2002/01/30/us/state-union-president-bush-s-state-union-address-congress-nation.html.

Bush, Laura W. "Afghan Women's Gains Are at Risk." *Washington Post*, November 14, 2013. www.washingtonpost.com/opinions/laura-bush-afghan-womens-gains-are-at-risk/2013/11/14/0c105688-4bed-11e3-9890-a1e0997fb0c0_story.html.

———. "Don't Abandon Afghan Women." *Washington Post*, May 18, 2012. www.washingtonpost.com/opinions/nato-should-not-abandon-afghanistans-women/2012/05/18/gIQAmDh9YU_story.html.

———. *Spoken from the Heart*. New York: Scribner, 2010.

———. "Women's Rights Key to Afghan Success" (blog), June 29, 2011. George W. Bush Institute, Dallas. www.bushcenter.org/blog/2012/09/13/womens-rights-key-afghan-success.

Camia, Catalina. "Clinton Warns of 'Extremists' Out to Control Women." *USA Today*, March 12, 2012. http://content.usatoday.com/communities/onpolitics/post/2012/03/hillary-clinton-extremists-control-women-/1#.UjaXdODAZZt.

Caprioli, Mary. "Gendered Conflict." *Journal of Peace Research* 37, no.1 (2000): 51–68. doi: 10.1177/0022343300037001003.

———. "Gender Equality and State Aggression: The Impact of Domestic Gender Equality on State First Use of Force." *International Interactions* 29, no. 3 (2003): 195–214. doi: 10.1080/ 03050620304595.

———. "Primed for Violence: The Role of Gender Inequality in Predicting Internal Conflict." *International Studies Quarterly* 49 (2005): 161–78. doi: 10.1111/j.0020-8833.2005.00340.x.

Caprioli, Mary and Mark A. Boyer. "Gender, Violence, and International Crisis." *Journal of Conflict Resolution* 45, no. 4 (2001): 503–18. doi: 10.1177/0022002701045004005.

Caprioli, Mary and Peter F. Trumbore. "Ethnic Discrimination and Interstate Violence: Testing the International Impact of Domestic Behavior." *Journal of Peace Research* 40, no. 1 (2003): 5–23.

———. "Hierarchies of Dominance: Identifying Rogue States and Testing Their Interstate Conflict Behavior." *European Journal of International Relations* 9, no. 3 (2003): 377–406.

———. "Human Rights Rogues in Interstate Disputes, 1980–2001." *Journal of Peace Research* 43, no. 2 (2006): 131–48.

Caprioli, Mary, Rebecca Nielsen, and Valerie M. Hudson. "Women and Post-Conflict Settings." In *Peace and Conflict 2010*, ed. J. Joseph Hewitt, Jonathan

Wilkenfeld, and Ted Robert Gurr, 91–102. Boulder, Colo.: Paradigm Publishers, 2010.

Caputi, Jane. "Goddess Murder and Gynocide in Ciudad Juárez." In *Making a Killing: Femicide, Free Trade and La Frontera*, ed. Alicia Gaspar de Alba and Georgina Guzman. 279. Austin: University of Texas Press, 2010.

Cardenas, Lourdes. "Juárez Opens Justice Center for Women." *El Paso Times*, March 29, 2012. www.elpasotimes.com/news/ci_20276981/ju-225-rez-opens -justice-center-women.

Carlsen, Laura. "Women Human Rights Defenders in Mexico Face Threats, Violence." *Americas Program*, December 14, 2011. www.cipamericas.org /archives/5818.

Carrasco, David. *City of Sacrifice: The Aztec Empire and the Role of Violence in Civilization*. Boston: Beacon Press, 1999.

Carter, Jimmy. *A Call to Action: Women, Religion, Violence, and Power.* New York: Simon and Schuster, 2014.

Castillo, Mariano. "Guatemala's Rios Montt Guilty of Genocide." *CNN*, May 13, 2013. www.cnn.com/2013/05/10/world/americas/guatemala-genocide-trial/index .html?hpt=hp_t2.

Center on Law & Globalization. "Voices from Rwanda: Rape and Mutilation During Genocide," n.d. http://clg.portalxm.com/library/keytext.cfm?keytext_id=134.

Central Intelligence Agency. *The World Factbook: Afghanistan*. Continually updated. www.cia.gov/library/publications/the-world-factbook/geos/af.html.

——. *The World Factbook: Guatemala*. Continually updated. www.cia.gov/library /publications/the-world-factbook/geos/gt.html.

——. *The World Factbook: Yemen*. Continually updated. www.cia.gov/library /publications/the-world-factbook/geos/ym.html.

Chandrasekaran, Rajiv. "In Afghanistan, U.S. Shifts Strategy on Women's Rights as It Eyes Wider Priorities." *Washington Post*, March 5, 2011. http://articles .washingtonpost.com/2011-03-05/world/35208059_1_afghan-women-afghan -government-land-rights.

Chelala, Cesar. "Rios Montt's Conviction Will Change Guatemala." *Japan Times*, May 17, 2013. www.japantimes.co.jp/opinion/2013/05/17/commentary/rios -montts-conviction-will-change-guatemala/#.Uj9UMCjAZZt.

"China's 1-Child Policy to Be Loosened: Labour Camps Closed." *CBC News World*, November 15, 2013. www.cbc.ca/news/world/china-s-1-child-policy-to-be -loosened-labour-camps-closed-1.2427684.

Chivers, C. J. "Seized Pirates in High-Seas Legal Limbo, with No Formula for Trials." *New York Times*, January 27, 2013. www.nytimes.com/2012/01/28/world /africa/seized-pirates-in-legal-limbo-with-no-formula-for-trials.html.

Chumley, Cheryl K. "Islamic Cleric Decrees It OK for Syrian Rebels to Rape Women." *Washington Times*, April 3, 2013. www.washingtontimes.com/news/2013/apr/3 /islamic-cleric-decrees-it-ok-syrian-rebels-rape-wo.

Clark, Mandy and Paul Nassar. "Analysis: Who's Backing Who as Syria's Civil War Threatens to Spread." *NBC News*, July 28, 2013. http://worldnews .nbcnews.com/_news/2013/07/28/19679903-analysis-whos-backing-who-as -syrias-civil-war-threatens-to-spread?lite.

"Claudia Paz y Paz Ousting Puts Spotlight on Guatemalan Justice System." *Guardian*, February 19, 2014. www.theguardian.com/global-development /poverty-matters/2014/feb/19/claudia-paz-y-paz-guatemala-justice-system.

Clinton, Hillary R. "Interview of Hillary Rodham Clinton By Joe Klein." Internal transcript, White House Office of the Press Secretary. February 6, 1993. www .clintonlibrary.gov/assets/storage/Research%20-%20Digital%20Library /FLOTUS-speeches/2011-0415-S/Box-001/2011-0415-S-flotus-press-office -interview-transcripts-volume-i-01-29-93-9-30-93-binder-02-06-93-klein-joe.pdf.

——. "Keynote Address by the First Lady at Scripps College." Speech at Claremont, Calif., April 26, 1994. www.clintonlibrary.gov/assets/storage/Research%20 -%20Digital%20Library/FLOTUS-speeches/2011-0415-S/Box-014/2011-0415 -S-flotus-statements-and-speeches-4-26-94-10-21-94-binder-4-26-94-scripps -college.pdf.

——. "Letter from Hillary Clinton to President George Bush on China's Human Rights Violations." *Life Site News*, November 16, 2005. www.lifesitenews.com /news/hillary-clinton-urges-president-bush-to-discuss-forced-abortion-on-china-tr.

——. *Living History*. New York: Scribner, 2004.

——. "New Hope for Afghanistan." *Time*, November 24, 2001. http://content.time .com/time/nation/article/0,8599,185643,00.html.

——. "Remarks at Female Heads of State and Foreign Ministers Luncheon." Speech at Waldorf-Astoria Hotel, New York, September 24, 2009. www.state .gov/secretary/rm/2009a/09/129598.htm.

——. "Remarks at the TEDWomen Conference." Speech at Ronald Reagan Building, Washington, D.C., December 8, 2010. www.state.gov/secretary /rm/2010/12/152670.htm.

——. "Remarks at the UN Commission on the Status of Women." Speech at U.N. Headquarters, New York City, March 12, 2010. www.state.gov/secretary /rm/2010/03/138320.htm.

——. "Remarks at the Women in the World Summit." Speech, New York City, March 10, 2012. www.state.gov/secretary/rm/2012/03/185604.htm.

——. "Remarks by the First Lady International Women's Day." Speech at Department of State, Washington, D.C., March 12, 1997. http://clinton4.nara.gov/WH /EOP/First_Lady/html/generalspeeches/1997/africa.html.

——. "Remarks of First Lady Hillary Rodham Clinton at a Special Event at the UN Social Summit." Speech at U.N. Department of Economic and Social Affairs, Copenhagen, Denmark, March 7, 1995. www.un.org/documents/ga/conf166/ gov/950307142511.htm.

——. "Remarks on Evidence and Impact: Closing the Gender Data Gap." Speech at Gallup Organization, Washington, D.C., July 19, 2012. www.state.gov/secretary /rm/2012/07/195244.htm.

——. "Remarks on the 15th Anniversary of the International Conference on Population and Development." Speech at Department of State, Washington, D.C., January 8, 2010. www.state.gov/secretary/rm/2010/01/135001.htm.

——. "Secretary Clinton's Speech at Afghanistan Conference." *Real Clear Politics*, January 28, 2010. www.realclearpolitics.com/articles/2010/01/28/secretary _clinton_speech_at_afghanistan_conference_100084.html.

Clinton, Hillary R. and Julia Roberts. "'Clean Stoves' Would Save Lives, Cut Pollution." *USA Today*, May 6, 2011. http://usatoday30.usatoday.com/news/opinion /forum/2011-05-06-Hillary-Clinton-Julia-Roberts-clean-stoves_n.htm.

"Clinton Addresses State Department First Day on Job." YouTube video, 8:40. From a speech by Hillary Clinton and televised by MSNBC, February 22, 2009. Posted by "taraisastar," January 23, 2009. http://youtu.be/QakfRGqXjEU.

"Clinton Pledges to Not Abandon Afghan Women." *Ms.*, May 14, 2010. www .msmagazine.com/news/uswirestory.asp?id=12399.

Cockburn, Cynthia. "The Gendered Dynamics of Armed Conflict and Political Violence." In *Victims, Perpetrators or Actors?: Gender, Armed Conflict and Political Violence*, ed. Caroline N.O. Moser and Fiona C. Clark, 13–29. New York: Zed Books, 2001.

Cohn, Carol. "Sex and Death in the Rational World of Defense Intellectuals." *Signs* 12, no. 4 (1987): 687–718. doi: 10.1080/10781910903206583.

Coleman, Isobel. "A Powerful Voice for Women Around the World." Op-ed, *New York Times*, May 12, 2013. www.nytimes.com/roomfordebate/2013/05/12 /judging-hillary-clinton-as-secretary-of-state/clinton-was-a-powerful-voice-for -women-around-the-world.

Combe, Rachael. "At the Pinnacle of Hillary Clinton's Career." *Elle*, April 5, 2012. www.elle.com/life-love/society-career/at-the-pinnacle-of-hillary-clintons -career-654140.

Commission for Historical Clarification (CEH; Guatemala). "Caso Ilustrativo No. 31: Masacre de Las Dos Erres." In *Guatemala: Memoria del Silencio*. Guatemala: CEH, 1999. www.prensalibre.com/noticias/justicia/Informe-casos-ilustrativos _PREFIL20120301_0002.pdf.

Committee of Agricultural, Commercial, Industrial, and Financial Associations (CACIF; Guatemala). "Saber Dejar Atrás el Pasado," n.d. http://cacif. org.gt/index.php?option=com_content&view=article&id=88&Itemid=464 &lang=es.

"Community Radio in Afghanistan." *New Media and Development Communication*, n.d. www.columbia.edu/itc/sipa/nelson/newmediadev/Afghan%20Radio%20Network .html.

Condon, Stephanie. "Obama Shuffles Cabinet but with No Female Nominees." *CBS*, January 10, 2013. www.cbsnews.com/8301-250_162-57563186.

Cooper, Helene and Steven L. Myers. "Obama Takes Hard Line with Libya After Shift by Clinton." *New York Times*, March 18, 2011. www.nytimes .com/2011/03/19/world/africa/19policy.html.

Cordesman, Anthony H. "Afghanistan and the Tokyo Conference: Hope, Fantasy, and Failure." *Center for Strategic and International Studies*, July 9, 2012. http://csis.org/publication/afghanistan-and-tokyo-conference-hope-fantasy-and -failure.

Couturier, Don. "The Rape of Men: Eschewing Myths of Sexual Violence in War." *On Politics* 6, no. 2 (2012): 1–14.

Crocker, Ryan. "Women, War, and Peace: Lessons from Afghanistan." Interview by Gayle T. Lemmon. *Council on Foreign Relations*, December 17, 2012. www.cfr .org/afghanistan/women-war-peace-lessons-afghanistan/p29684.

Crossette, Barbara. "U.S. to Help Girls in Poor Lands Stay in School." *New York Times*, March 8, 1995. www.nytimes.com/1995/03/08/world/us-to-help-girls-in -poor-lands-stay-in-school.html.

Crowe, Derrick. "TIME's Epic Distortion of the Plight of Women in Afghanistan." *Huffington Post*, July 31, 2010. www.huffingtonpost.com/derrick-crowe/times -epic-distortion-of_b_666097.html.

Cullather, Nicholas. *Secret History: The CIA's Classified Account of Its Operation in Guatemala, 1952–1954*. Stanford, Calif.: Stanford University Press, 1999.

Davis, Evan Grae, dir. "Trailer" for *It's A Girl*. Shadowline Films, 2012. 3:12. www .itsagirlmovie.com.

Davis, Patricia. "In Guatemala, A Mass Grave for the Truth." *Foreign Policy in Focus*, April 23, 2013. http://fpif.org/in_guatemala_a_mass_grave_for_the_truth.

Day, Tanis, Katherine McKenna, and Audra Bowlus. *The Economic Costs of Violence Against Women: An Evaluation of the Literature*. U.N. report compiled in preparation for secretary general's in-depth study on all forms of violence against women, 2005. www.un.org/womenwatch/daw//vaw/expert%20brief%20 costs.pdf.

de Alwis, Rangita de Silva. "Some Lessons from Other Post-Conflict Communities." In *Is the Arab Awakening Marginalizing Women?* Middle East Program Occasional Paper Series, Woodrow Wilson International Center for Scholars, 2012. www.wilsoncenter.org/sites/default/files/Arab%20Awakening%20Marginalizing %20Women_0.pdf.

"Deauville: The New Davos for Women in Business." *Euronews*, December 10, 2012. www.euronews.com/2012/10/12/deauville-the-new-davos-for-women-in -business.

Deen, Thalif. "Security Council Vow on Women Lives Mostly on Paper." *Inter Press Service*, November 23, 2012. www.ipsnews.

de Pablo, Ofelia and Javier Zurita. "The Invisible Genocide of Women." Vimeo video, 5:52. ca. 2012. Posted by de Pablo and Zurita. http://vimeo.com/36268697.

di Giovanni, Janine. "After the Arab Spring, Yemen's Women Are Left Behind." *Daily Beast*, December 10, 2012. www.thedailybeast.com/newsweek/2012/12/09 /after-the-arab-spring-yemen-s-women-are-left-behind.html.

Dilanian, Ken. "Short-Staffed USAID Tries to Keep Pace." *USA Today*, February 1, 2009. http://usatoday30.usatoday.com/news/washington/2009-02-01-aid-inside _N.htm.

"Discussion with Al-Dawsari: Tribal Governance and Stability in Yemen." *Yemeniaty*, August 31, 2012. http://yemeniaty.com/2012/08/discussion-with-al -dawsari-tribal.html.

Dobriansky, Paula J. and Melanne S. Verveer. "Don't Abandon the Women of Afghanistan." *CNN*, October 23, 2013. www.cnn.com/2013/10/23/opinion /dobriansky-verveer-afghanistan-women/index.html.

Doumato, Eleanor A. "Saudi Arabia." In *Women's Rights in the Middle East and North Africa: Progress amid Resistance*, ed. Sanja Kelly and Julia Breslin. New York: Freedom House, 2010. www.freedomhouse.org/sites/default/files/inline _images/Saudi%20Arabia.pdf.

Doyle, Kate and Carlos Osorio. *U.S. Policy in Guatemala, 1966–1996*. National Security Archive Electronic Briefing Book No. 11, George Washington University, n.d. www2.gwu.edu/~nsarchiv/NSAEBB/NSAEBB11/docs.

"DRC-Uganda: Male Sexual Abuse Survivors Living on the Margins." *IRIN News*, August 2, 2011. www.irinnews.org/report/93399/drc-uganda-male-sexual-abuse -survivors-living-on-the-margins.

Dreyfuss, Bob. "Obama's Women Advisers Pushed War Against Libya." *Nation*, March 19, 2011. www.thenation.com/blog/159346/obamas-women-advisers -pushed-war-against-libya#.

Dreze, Jean and Reetika Khera. "Crime, Gender, and Society in India: Insights from Homicide Data." *Population and Development Review* 26, no. 2 (2000): 335–52. www.jstor.org/stable/172520.

Eagly, Alice H., Mary C. Johannesen-Schmidt, and Marloes L. Van Engen. "Transformational, Transactional, and Laissez-Faire Leadership Styles: A Meta-Analysis Comparing Women and Men." *Psychological Bulletin* 129, no. 4 (2003): 569–91.

Easton, Nina, "Saudi Women Find a Way." *Foreign Affairs*, February 4, 2014. www .foreignaffairs.com/articles/140711/nina-easton/saudi-women-find-a-way.

Edlund, Lena. Hongbin Li, Junjian Yi, and Junsen Zhang. "Sex Ratios and Crime: Evidence from China." *Review of Economics and Statistics*. Accepted for publication, posted online April 2, 2013. doi:10.1162/REST_a_00356.

Ehrenfreund, Max. "Obama Cancels Meeting with Vladimir Putin: Criticizes Russian Anti-Gay Legislation." *Washington Post*, August 7, 2013. www.washingtonpost .com/world/obama-cancels-meeting-with-vladimir-putin-criticizes-russian

-anti-gay-legislation/2013/08/07/da43f24a-ff98-11e2-9711-3708310f6f4d_story.
html.

Elshtain, Jean Bethke. *Women and War*. Chicago: University of Chicago Press, 1995.

Eltahawy, Mona. "Why Do They Hate Us?: The Real War on Women Is in the Middle East." *Foreign Policy*, April 23, 2012. www.foreignpolicy.com /articles/2012/04/23/why_do_they_hate_us.

"Engaging Men to Protect and Empower Women." *Women for Women International*, n.d. www.womenforwomen.org/global-initiatives-helping-women /assets/files/MLP-fact-sheet.pdf.

Enloe, Cynthia. *Bananas, Beaches and Bases: Making Feminist Sense of International Politics*. Berkeley: University of California Press, 2001.

Erchak, Gerald M. "Family Violence." In *Research Frontiers in Anthropology*, Vol. 4, ed. Carol R. Ember and Melvin Ember, 3–18. Englewood Cliffs, N.J.: Prentice-Hall, 1994.

Erchak, Gerald M. and Richard Rosenfeld. "Societal Isolation, Violent Norms, and Gender Relations: A Re-Examination and Extension of Levinson's Model of Wife Beating." *Cross-Cultural Research* 28, no. 2 (1994): 111–33.

European Parliament. "Equality Between Women and Men in the European Union." Resolution 2011/2244, March 13, 2012. www.europarl.europa.eu/sides/getDoc .do?pubRef=-//EP//TEXT+TA+P7-TA-2012-0069+0+DOC+XML+V0//EN.

Fall, Papa L. and Yishan Zhang. "Staff Recruitment in United Nations System Organizations: A Comparative Analysis and Benchmarking Framework: Gender Balance and Geographical Distribution." Note prepared by the Joint Inspection Unit of the United Nations, 2012. www.unjiu.org/en/reports-notes/JIU%20 Products/JIU_NOTE_%202012%20_3_English.pdf.

Fantz, Ashley and Jill Dougherty. "Prostitution, Drugs Alleged in State Department Memo." *CNN*, June 12, 2013. www.cnn.com/2013/06/11/politics/state-department -allegations.

Ferraro, Geraldine A. "Human Rights for Women." *New York Times*, June 10, 1993. www.nytimes.com/1993/06/10/opinion/human-rights-for-women.html.

——. "Women's Rights, Human Rights." *New York Times*, August 22, 1995. www .nytimes.com/1995/08/22/opinion/women-s-rights-human-rights.html.

Ferris-Rotman, Annie. "Leaning Out." *Foreign Policy*, March 20, 2013. www .foreignpolicy.com/articles/2013/03/20/leaning_out_afghanistan_women _united_states.

"Fertility Rate, Total (Births per Woman)." *Index Mundi*, n.d. www.indexmundi. com/facts/indicators/SP.DYN.TFRT.IN.

Finklea, Kristin M. *Southwest Border Violence: Issues in Identifying and Measuring Spillover Violence*. CRS Report R41075. Washington, D.C.: Library of Congress Research Service, February 28, 2013.

Finlay, Barbara. *George W. Bush and the War on Women: Turning Back the Clock on Progress*. New York: Zed Books, 2006.

Fish, M. Steven. "Islam and Authoritarianism." *World Politics* 55, no. 1 (2002): 4–37. doi: 10.1353/wp.2003.0004.

Flaherty, Peter and Timothy Flaherty. *The First Lady: A Comprehensive View of Hillary Rodham Clinton*. Lafayette, La.: Vital Issues, 1995.

Florea, Natalie B., Mark A. Boyer, Scott W. Brown, Michael J. Butler, Magnolia Hernandez, Kimberly Weir, Lin Meng, Paula R. Johnson, Clarisse Lima, and Hayley J. Mayall. "Negotiating from Mars to Venus: Gender in Simulated International Negotiations." *Simulation & Gaming* 34, no. 2 (2003): 226–48. doi: 10.1177/1046878103034002005.

Fox, Edward. "How the Drug Trade Fuels Femicide in Central America." *In Sight Crime*, July 12, 2012. www.insightcrime.org/news-analysis/how-the-drug-trade -fuels-femicide-in-central-america.

Fukuyama, Francis. "Women and the Evolution of World Politics." *Foreign Affairs* 77, no. 5 (1998): 24–40.

"Full Text: Malala Yousafzai Delivers Defiant Riposte to Taliban Militants with Speech to the UN General Assembly." *Independent*, July 12, 2013. www .independent.co.uk/news/world/asia/the-full-text-malala-yousafzai-delivers -defiant-riposte-to-taliban-militants-with-speech-to-the-un-general-assembly -8706606.html.

Garner, Karen. *Gender & Foreign Policy in the Clinton Administration*. Boulder, Colo.: First Forum Press, 2013.

Gates, Robert M. *From the Shadows: The Ultimate Insider's Story of Five Presidents and How They Won the Cold War*. New York: Simon & Schuster Paperbacks, 2006.

Gbowee, Leymah. Speech at the Nobel Women's Initiative Conference, May 27, 2013, Belfast, Northern Ireland.

Geneva Declaration of Armed Violence and Development. *Global Burden of Armed Violence 2011*. 2011. www.genevadeclaration.org/en/measurability/global -burden-of-armed-violence/global-burden-of-armed-violence-2011.html.

"Genocide on Trial, Day 7: 'I Am Telling This to the Eyes and Ears of the World.'" NISGUA (blog), April 1, 2013. www.nisgua.blogspot.com/2013/04/genocide -on-trial-day-7-i-am-telling.html. NISGUA is the Network in Solidarity with the People of Guatemala.

Gettleman, Jeffrey. "Rape Epidemic Raises Trauma of Congo War." *New York Times,* October 7, 2007. www.nytimes.com/2007/10/07/world/africa/07congo .html.

Ghattas, Kim. *The Secretary: A Journey with Hillary Clinton from Beirut to the Heart of American Power*. New York: Times Books, 2013.

Giacaman, Viviana and Mariclaire Acosta. "Protecting Journalists and Human Rights Defenders in Mexico." Policy Brief. *Freedom House*, November 30, 2012. www.freedomhouse.org/article/protecting-journalists-and-human-rights -defenders-mexico.

Goldberg, Mark L. "UN: Number of Afghan Women Targeted for Assassination Jumps Three Fold." *UN Dispatch*, February 19, 2013. www.undispatch.com /un-number-of-afghan-women-targeted-for-assassination-jumps-three-fold.

Gonzalez, Laura. "Central America: Crisis Chews Women Up, Spits Them Out." *Inter Press Service News Agency*. November 21, 2014. www.ipsnews.net/2009/09 /central-america-crisis-chews-women-up-spits-them-out.

Graham-Harrison, Emma and Mokhtar Amiri. "Taliban Peace Talk Plans Lead Afghan Women to Fear Loss of Rights." *Guardian*, June 19, 2013. www.theguardian .com/world/2013/jun/19/afghanistan-women-rights-taliban-peace-talks.

Grant, Kate. "20 Minutes That Changed the World: Hillary Clinton in Beijing." *Huffington Post*, February 4, 2013. www.huffingtonpost.com/kate-grant/hillary -clinton_b_2603159.html.

Grant, Rebecca and Kathleen Newland. *Gender and International Relations*. Bloomington: Indiana University Press, 1991.

Gray, Jessica. "Egyptians Patrol Tahrir Square for Mob Sex Assaults." *WeNews*, January 25, 2013. http://womensenews.org/story/sexual-harassment/130124 /egyptians-patrol-tahrir-square-mob-sex-assaults#.UohYayjAZZs.

Greene, Jack P. and J. R. Pole, eds. *Colonial British America: Essays in the New History of the Early Modern Era*. Baltimore: Johns Hopkins University Press, 1983.

Guatemala Human Rights Commission/USA. Executive summary of *Guatemala's Femicide Law: Progress Against Impunity?* Report, May 2009. www.ghrc-usa .org/Programs/ForWomensRighttoLive/2009VAWReport_execsum.htm.

——. "Fact Sheet: Femicide and Feminicide." 2011. http://ghrc-usa.org/Publications /factsheet_femicide_2011.pdf.

Guatemalan Commission for Historical Clarification. *Guatemala: Memory of Silence*. Report presented to Guatemalan Government, Guatemalan National Revolutionary Unity, and U.N. Secretary General, February 25, 1999. www.usip .org/publications/truth-commission-guatemala.

"Guatemala: Outright Murder." *Time*, February 11, 1980. http://content.time.com /time/magazine/article/0,9171,950248,00.html.

Guzaro, Thomas and Terri J. McComb. *Escaping the Fire*. Austin: University of Texas Press, 2010.

Habboush, Mahmoud. "Child Bride in Yemen Dies of Internal Bleeding on Wedding Night: Activist." *Reuters*, September 10, 2013. www.reuters.com/article/2013/09/10 /us-yemen-childbride-idUSBRE98910N20130910.

Haidari, M. Ashraf. "Afghan Women as a Measure of Progress." *Foreign Policy*, March 18, 2013. http://afpak.foreignpolicy.com/posts/2013/03/18/afghan_women _as_a_measure_of_progress.

Hannagan, Rebecca J. and Holly Arrow. "Reengineering Gender Relations in Modern Militaries: An Evolutionary Perspective." *Journal of Trauma and Dissociation* 12, no. 3 (2011): 305–23. doi: 10.1080/15299732.2011.542611.

Hansen, Lene. *Security as Practice: Discourse Analysis and the Bosnian War*. New York: Routledge, 2006.

Hansen, Suzy. "Sex and Drugs in Hell." *Salon*. July 8, 2004. www.salon.com/2004/07/08/emergency_sex.

Hartman, Mary S. *The Household and the Making of History: A Subversive View of the Western Past*. Cambridge: Cambridge University Press, 2004.

Harvey, Frank P. and Michael Brecher, eds. *Critical Perspectives in International Studies*. Ann Arbor: University of Michigan Press, 2002.

Hastings, Deborah. "U.S. Soldiers Accepting Cash, Drugs for Mexican Drug Cartel Contract Hits." *New York Daily News*, September 13, 2013. www.nydailynews.com/news/national/drug-cartels-mexico-hire-u-s-soldiers-assassins-article-1.1454851.

Hausmann, Ricardo, Laura D. Tyson, and Saddia Zahidi. *The Global Gender Gap Report 2012*. Geneva: World Economic Forum, 2012.

Heffernan, Virginia. "The Feminist Hawks." *New York Times*, August 19, 2009. www.nytimes.com/2009/08/23/magazine/23FOB-medium-t.html.

"Hillary Clinton: Helping Women Isn't Just A 'Nice' Thing to Do." *Daily Beast*, April 5, 2013. www.thedailybeast.com/witw/articles/2013/04/05/hillary-clinton-helping-women-isn-t-just-a-nice-thing-to-do.html.

"Hillary Clinton U.N. Women's Conference Beijing, September 5, 1995." YouTube video, 2:57. Clinton Presidential Library. https://www.youtube.com/watch?v=xXM4E23Efvk.

"Hillary Sees Subjugation of Women as Threat to Security." *Dawn.com*, March 14, 2010. www.dawn.com/news/857688/hillary-sees-subjugation-of-women-as-threat-to-security.

Hirsch, Afua. "Domestic Violence 'Costs £5.8bn.' " *Guardian*, November 24, 2008. www.theguardian.com/lifeandstyle/2008/nov/25/gender-economy-domestic-violence-women.

Hudson, Natalie F. *Gender, Human Security and the United Nations: Security Language as a Political Framework for Women*. New York: Routledge, 2012.

Hudson, Valerie M., Bonnie Ballif-Spanvill, Mary Caprioli, and Chad F. Emmett. *Sex and World Peace*. New York: Columbia University Press, 2012.

Hudson, Valerie M., Bonnie Ballif-Spanvill, Mary Caprioli, Chad F. Emmett, and Rose McDermott. "The Heart of the Matter: The Security of Women and the Security of States." *International Security* 33, no. 3 (2009): 7–45. www.mitpressjournals.org/doi/pdf/10.1162/isec.2009.33.3.7.

Hudson, Valerie M., Donna L. Bowen, and Perpetua L. Nielson. "Clan Governance and State Stability: The Relationship Between Female Subordination and Political Order." Manuscript in preparation.

Hudson, Valerie M. and Andrea M. Den Boer. *Bare Branches: The Security Implications of Asia's Surplus Male Population*. Cambridge, Mass.: MIT Press, 2004.

Human Rights Watch. "Afghanistan: Escalating Setbacks for Women." July 16, 2013. www.hrw.org/news/2013/07/16/afghanistan-escalating-setbacks-women.

——. "Crisis of Impunity: The Role of Pakistan, Russia, and Iran in Fueling the Civil War." *Afghanistan* 13, no. 3. (July 2001). www.hrw.org/reports/2001/afghan2/Afghan0701.pdf.

——. "Egypt: Epidemic of Sexual Violence." July 3, 2013. www.hrw.org/news/2013/07/03/egypt-epidemic-sexual-violence.

——. *"I Had to Run Away:" The Imprisonment of Women and Girls for "Moral Crimes" in Afghanistan.* March 28, 2012. www.hrw.org/sites/default/files/reports/afghanistan0312webwcover_0.pdf.

——. *World Report 2013: Guatemala.* 2013. www.hrw.org/world-report/2013/country-chapters/guatemala.

Hunt, Swanee and Cristina Posa. "Iraq's Excluded Women." *Foreign Policy* 143 (2004): 40–45.

——. "Marshall and Clinton: A Shared Legacy." *Huffington Post*, January 30, 2013. www.huffingtonpost.com/swanee-hunt/george-marshall-hillary-clinton_b_2585790.html.

——. "Women Waging Peace." *Foreign Policy*, May 1, 2001. www.foreignpolicy.com/articles/2001/05/01/women_waging_peace.

Hyde, Jesse. "The 'Broken Windows' Theory Worked in Juarez." *Atlantic*, March 26, 2013. www.theatlantic.com/international/archive/2013/03/the-broken-windows-theory-worked-in-juarez/274379.

IDLO. "Afghanistan's Justice Training Transition Program," n.d. www.idlo.int/what-we-do/initiatives/afghanistans-justice-training-transition-program-jttp.

"If We Betray Afghan Women, We Have Lost." *Guardian*, August 14, 2010. www.theguardian.com/commentisfree/2010/aug/15/observer-editorial-afghanistan-womens-rights.

Indira, Rossie and Andre Vltchek. "Wahhabi War Waged on Indonesia's Shi'ites." *Asia Times*, December 7, 2012. www.atimes.com/atimes/Southeast_Asia/NL07Ae01.html.

Inglehart, Ronald and Pippa Norris. *Rising Tide: Gender Equality and Cultural Change Around the World.* New York: Cambridge University Press, 2003.

——. "The True Clash of Civilizations," *Foreign Policy* 135 (2003): 63–70. www.foreignpolicy.com/articles/2003/03/01/the_true_clash_of_civilizations.

International Crisis Group. *Women and Conflict in Afghanistan.* Asia Report No. 252, October 14, 2013. www.crisisgroup.org/~/media/Files/asia/south-asia/afghanistan/252-women-and-conflict-in-afghanistan.

Isaacs, Anita. "New Bad Old Times for Guatemala?" *New York Times*, May 14, 2014. www.nytimes.com/2014/05/15/opinion/new-bad-old-times-for-guatemala.html?hp&rref=opinion.

"'It Pains Me': Clinton Decries Plight of Women in Male-Dominated Countries." *World News*, December 7, 2012. http://worldnews.nbcnews.com

/_news/2012/12/07/15747187-it-pains-me-clinton-decries-plight-of-women-in
-male-dominated-countries.

Jamjoom, Mohammed. "Saudi Cleric Warns Driving Could Damage Women's Ovaries." *CNN*, September 29, 2013. www.cnn.com/2013/09/29/world/meast /saudi-arabia-women-driving-cleric/index.html.

"Jane Fonda Visits Guatemala to Put Spotlight on Murders of Women in Guatemala." *V-Day News Alert*, December 8, 2003. www.vday.org/node/1211# .UkDzrSjAZZs.

Jay, Nancy. *Throughout Your Generations Forever: Sacrifice, Religion and Paternity*. Chicago: University of Chicago Press, 1992.

Jha, Prabhat, Maya A. Kesler, Rajesh Kumar, Faujdar Ram, Usha Ram, Lukasz Aleksandrowicz, Diego G. Bassani, Shailaja Chandra, and Jayant K. Banthia. "Trends in Selective Abortions of Girls in India: Analysis of Nationally Representative Birth Histories from 1990 to 2005 and Census Data from 1991 to 2011." *Lancet* 377, no. 9781 (2011): 1921–28. doi:10.1016/S0140-6736(11)60649-1.

Johnson, Angella. "Freedom in Egypt? It Just Gave Men the Freedom to Rape Me in Tahrir Square: As Violence Erupts in Cairo, Woman Attacked by a Gang in Demonstration Recounts Her Ordeal." *Daily Mail*, July 6, 2013. www.dailymail. co.uk/news/article-2357633/Freedom-Egypt-It-just-gave-men-freedom-rape -Tahrir-Square.html#ixzz2ZFtDden6.

Johnson, Dominic D. P., Rose McDermott, Emily S. Barrett, Jonathan Crowden, Richard Wrangham, Matthew H. McIntyre, and Stephen P. Rosen. "Overconfidence in Wargames: Experimental Evidence on Expectations, Aggression, Gender, and Testosterone." *Proceedings of the Royal Society (Biology)* 273 (2006): 2513–20. doi: 10.1098/rspb.2006.3606.

Johnson, Kay and Rahim Faiez. "Afghan Students Protest Women's Rights Decree." *Associated Press*, May 22, 2013. http://bigstory.ap.org/article/afghan-students -protest-womens-rights-decree.

Jones, Ann. "The Forgotten War." *Nation of Change*, October 1, 2013. www.nation -ofchange.org/forgotten-war-1380640730.

——. *Kabul in Winter: Life Without Peace in Afghanistan*. New York: Picador, 2006.

——. "Remember the Women? *Nation*, November 9, 2009. www.thenation.com /article/remember-women.

——. "Can Women Make Peace?" *TomDispatch.com*, January 13, 2011. www.tom -dispatch.com/post/175340/tomgram:_ann_jones,_can_women_make_peace.

——. *War Is Not Over When It's Over: Women Speak Out from the Ruins of War*. New York: Metropolitan Books, 2010.

Jordan, Larry. "The Real Hillary Clinton." *Midwest Today*, June 1994. www.midtod. com/highlights/hillary.phtml.

Jordan, Mary. "'Hillary Effect' Cited for Increase in Female Ambassadors to U.S." *Washington Post*, January 11, 2010. www.washingtonpost.com/wp-dyn/content /article/2010/01/10/AR2010011002731.html.

"Karzai Lashes Out at the U.S. for Its Role and Focus in Afghanistan." *New York Times*, October 8, 2013. www.nytimes.com/2013/10/09/world/asia/karzai-lashes -out-at-united-states-for-its-role-in-afghanistan.html.

Katzman, Kenneth. *Afghanistan: Politics, Elections, and Government Performance.* CRS Report RS21922. Washington, D.C.: Library of Congress Research Service, August 14, 2013.

Kelly, Jeremy. "Afghan Woman to Be Freed from Jail After Agreeing to Marry Rapist." *Guardian*, December 1, 2011. www.theguardian.com/world/2011/dec/01 /afghan-woman-freed-marry-rapist.

Kerry, John. "Remarks at a Meeting of the Equal Futures Partnership." Speech at Waldorf Astoria Hotel, New York City, September 23, 2013. www.state.gov /secretary/remarks/2013/09/214573.htm.

Keyes, David. "Saudi Arabia's Religious Police Outlaw 'Tempting Eyes.'" *Daily Beast*, November 19, 2011. www.thedailybeast.com/articles/2011/11/19/saudi -arabia-s-religious-police-outlaw-tempting-eyes.html.

Khattab, Moushira. "For Women, the Arab Spring Has Yet to Arrive." *CBC Radio*, July 12, 2013. Audio file. www.cbc.ca/player/Radio/The+Sunday+Edition /Segments/ID/2396570393.

Khera, Reetika. "Crime, Gender, and Society in India: Insights from Homicide Data." *Population and Development Review* 26, no. 2 (2000): 335–52. www.jstor .org/stable/172520.

Knickmeyer, Ellen. "Activists Are Feeling Squeezed in Gulf Kingdoms." *Wall Street Journal*, July 26, 2013. http://online.wsj.com/article/SB10001424127887323971 2045786252191827826424.html.

Kunduz Regional Office Press Unit. "The Endless Pain Suffered by Sahar Gul Turned Into Scream." Afghanistan Independent Human Rights Commission. Updated January 8, 2012. www.aihrc.org.af/en/daily-reports/853/the-endless -pain-suffered-by-sahar-gul-turned-into-scream-.html.

LaFranchi, Howard. "At NATO Summit on Afghanistan, Few Women's Voices Heard." *Christian Science Monitor*, May 20, 2012. www.csmonitor.com/USA/Foreign -Policy/2012/0520/At-NATO-summit-on-Afghanistan-few-women-s-voices-heard.

Las Casas, Bartolomé de. *A Brief Account of the Destruction of the Indies.* 1542. Reprint, Baltimore: Johns Hopkins University Press, 1992.

Laura. *What War? Testimonies of Maya Survivors.* December 3, 2007. www.levinger .net/cualguerra/laura-2.

Lawrence, Regina G. and Melody Rose. *Hillary Clinton's Race for the White House: Gender Politics and the Media on the Campaign Trail.* Boulder, Colo.: Lynne Rienner, 2010.

Leatherman, Janie L. *Sexual Violence and Armed Conflict.* Cambridge: Polity Press, 2011.

Lee, Felicia R. "Battleground: Female Soldiers in the Line of Fire." *New York Times*, November 4, 2008. www.nytimes.com/2008/11/05/arts/television/05lion.html.

Leidl, Patricia. "Silent Spring: The Tragedy of India's Never-Born Girls." In *UNFPA State of World Population, 2005: The Promise of Equality: Gender Equity, Reproductive Health and the Millennium Development Goals*. United Nations Population Fund. 2005. www.unfpa.org/swp/2005/presskit/docs/india.doc.

Leimbach, Dulcie. "At Geneva II Talks in January, It Is Not Enough to 'Add Women and Stir.' " *PassBlue*, December 26, 2013. http://passblue.com/2013/12/26/at-geneva-ii-talks-in-january-it-is-not-enough-to-add-women-and-stir.

Lemmon, Gayle T. "Afghan Women Are Not 'Pet Rocks.'" *Foreign Policy*, November 21, 2011. http://afpak.foreignpolicy.com/posts/2011/11/21/afghan_women_are_not_pet_rocks.

——. "The Hillary Doctrine." *Newsweek*, March 6, 2011. http://mag.newsweek.com/2011/03/06/the-hillary-doctrine.html.

Levinson, David. *Family Violence in Cross-Cultural Perspective*. Thousand Oaks, Calif.: Sage, 1989.

"Libyan Men Now Allowed to Remarry without Consent of First Wife: Court Rule." *Al Arabiya*, February 7, 2013. http://english.alarabiya.net/articles/2013/02/07/264927.html.

Lindholm, Charles. *Generosity and Jealousy: The Swat Pukhtun of Northern Pakistan*. New York: Columbia University Press, 1982.

Lister, Tim. "Why We Should Care About Yemen." *CNN*, November 23, 2011. www.cnn.com/2011/WORLD/meast/06/03/yemen.matters/index.html.

Locke, Nany. "Valentine de Saint-Point and the Fascist Construction of Woman." In *Fascist Visions: Art and Ideology in France and Italy*, ed. Matthew Affron and Mark Antliff, 73–100. Princeton, N.J.: Princeton University Press, 1997.

Lorentzen, L. A. and J. Turpin. *The Women and War Reader*. New York: New York University Press, 1998.

Lough, Oliver. "Guest Post: When Quotas Matter—Women on the Provincial Council." *Sunny in Kabul* (blog), July 24, 2013. http://sunnyinkabul.com/2013/07/24/guest-post-when-quotas-matter-women-on-the-provincial-councils.

Lowen, Linda. "Hillary Rodham Clinton's Legacy—Making the Remarkable Unremarkable: Hillary's Campaign Mirrored the Choices We Make Throughout Their Lives." *About.com*, 2008. http://womensissues.about.com/od/commentaryon2008race/a/ChoosingHillary.htm.

Lu, Cheng. "Excess of Marriageable Males and Violent Crime in China and South Korea, 1970–2008." Unpublished manuscript, Nanjing University, 2010. http://paa2012.princeton.edu/abstracts/121243.

Macinnis, Laura and Amie Ferris-Rotman. "Insight: Afghan Women Fade from White House Focus as Exit Nears." *Reuters*, May 10, 2012. www.reuters.com/article/2012/05/10/us-nato-afghanistan-women-idUSBRE84919H20120510.

Mail Foreign Service. "Child Bride, 13, Dies of Internal Injuries Four Days After Arranged Marriage in Yemen." *Daily Mail*, April 9, 2010. www.dailymail.co.uk

/news/article-1264729/Child-bride-13-dies-internal-injuries-days-arranged-marriage-Yemen.html.

Marshall, Monty G. and Donna Ramsey. "Gender Empowerment and the Willingness of States to Use Force." Unpublished research paper, prepared for presentation at International Studies Association Annual Meeting, Washington, D.C., 1999.

Martin, Everett G. "The Right Way to Fight Anti-Guerilla Warfare." *Wall Street Journal*, July 30, 1981.

Martinuzzi, Elisa. "Davos Women Diminished as Male Discussion Skips Key Views." *Bloomberg*, January 28, 2013. www.bloomberg.com/news/2013-01-27/davos-women-diminished-as-male-discussion-skips-essential-views.html.

Marwan, Asma. "Virginity Tests for Indonesian School Girls?" *Bulletin of the Oppression of Women*, August 29, 2013. http://bulletinoftheoppressionofwomen.com/category/countries/indonesia.

Mattson, Corey, Marie Ayer, and Daniela M. Gerson. "The Maquilla in Guatemala: Facts and Trends." In *Beyond Borders: Thinking Critically About Global Issues*, ed. Paula S. Rothenberg, 481–87. New York: Worth Publishers, 2006.

Mayton, Joseph. "Egypt: Muslim Brotherhood and Women." *Ikhwanweb*, December 25, 2009. www.ikhwanweb.com/article.php?id=22307.

Mazurana, Dyan, Angela Raven-Roberts, and Jane Parpart, eds. *Gender, Conflict, and Peacekeeping*. New York: Rowman and Littlefield, 2005.

McCleary-Sills, Jennifer and Stella Mukasa. *External Evaluation of the Trust Fund for Victims Programmes in Northern Uganda and the Democratic Republic of Congo: Toward a Perspective for Upcoming Interventions*. International Center for Research on Women, 2013. www.icrw.org/files/publications/ICRW%20TFV%20%20Evaluation%20Report_0.pdf.

McCurry, Justin and Rebecca Allison. "40m Bachelors and No Women . . . The Birth of a New Problem for China." *Guardian*, March 8, 2004. www.theguardian.com/world/2004/mar/09/china.justinmccurry.

McDermott, Rose and Jonathan Cowden. "The Effects of Uncertainty and Sex in a Crisis Simulation Game." *International Interactions* 27, no. 4 (2002): 353–80.

McDonald, Mike. "Former Guatemalan Dictator Rios Montt Convicted of Genocide." *Reuters*, May 11, 2013. www.reuters.com/article/2013/05/11/us-guatemala-riosmontt-idUSBRE9490V420130511.

——. "Guatemala's Top Court Annuls Rios Montt Genocide Conviction." *Reuters*, May 21, 2013. www.reuters.com/article/2013/05/21/us-guatemala-riosmontt-idUSBRE94K04I20130521.

——. "Quiet Guatemalan Prosecutor Takes on Dictator, Drug Gangs." *Reuters*, May 29, 2012. www.reuters.com/article/2012/05/29/us-guatemala-prosecutor-idUSBRE84S0UW20120529.

McElhinny, Vincent. "Low Intensity Warfare, High Intensity Death: The Demographic Impact of the Wars in El Salvador and Nicaragua." *Canadian Journal of Latin American and Caribbean Studies* 21, no. 42 (1996): 211–41.

McKelvey, Tara. "Hillary Clinton, State Feminist?" *Nation*, March 4, 2013. www.thenation.com/article/172902/hillary-clinton-state-feminist#.

Mears, Bill and Ashley Killough. "Judge Blocks North Dakota's Restrictive Abortion Law." *CNN*, July 22, 2013. http://politicalticker.blogs.cnn.com/2013/07/22 /judge-blocks-north-dakotas-restrictive-abortion-law.

Melander, Erik. "Gender Equality and Interstate Armed Conflict." *International Studies Quarterly* 49, no. 4 (2005): 695–714.

Menchu, Rigoberta. *Crossing Borders*. New York: Verso, 1998.

——. *I, Rigoberta Menchu: An Indian Woman in Guatemala*. New York: Verso, 1984.

Mendez, Luz. "'I Don't Want to Die Without Seeing Justice': Sexual Slavery During Guatemala's Armed Conflict." *Americas Program* (blog), October 17, 2012. www.cipamericas.org/archives/8211.

Mesoamerican Initiative of Women Human Rights Defenders. *Femicide and Impunity in Mexico: A Context of Structural and Generalized Violence*. Report presented before the Committee on the Elimination of All Forms of Discrimination Against Women, CEDAW, 52nd sess., New York, July 17, 2012. http://cmdpdh .org/english/?p=1442.

Messmer, Marietta. "Transfrontera Crimes: Representations of the Juárez Femicides in Recent Fictional and Non-Fictional Accounts." *American Studies Journal* 57 (2012). www.asjournal.org/?p=466.

"Mexican Cartel Drug War Adding to Chicago Violence." YouTube video, 3:02. From a *CBS News* report. Posted by "CBSNewsOnline," August 23, 2012. www.youtube.com/watch?v=YdYitRcQp4E.

"Mexican Women Activists at Risk After Fleeing Death Threats." *Amnesty International*, March 17, 2011. www.amnesty.org/en/news-and-updates/mexican-women-activists-risk-after-fleeing-death-threats-2011-03-17.

Mill, John Stuart. *The Subjection of Women*. 1869. Reprint, Mineola, NY: Dover, 1997.

Miller, Barbara D, ed. *Sex and Gender Hierarchies*. Cambridge: Cambridge University Press, 1993.

Mills, Andrew. "Reforms to Women's Education Make Slow Progress in Saudi Arabia." *Chronicle of Higher Education*, August 3, 2009. http://chronicle.com /article/Saudi-Universities-Reach/47519.

Mitchell, Rhoda. "Domestic Violence Prevention Through the Constructing Violence-free Masculinities Programme: An Experience from Peru." *Gender & Development* 21, no. 1 (2013): 97–109. doi: 10.1080/13552074.2013.767516.

Moellendorf, Darrel. *Jus ex Bello* in Afghanistan." *Ethics and International Affairs* 25, no. 2 (2011): 155–64. doi: 10.1017/S0892679411000128.

Mokuwa, Esther, Maarten Voors, Erwin Bulte, and Paul Richards. "Peasant Grievance and Insurgency in Sierra Leone: Judicial Serfdom as a Driver of Conflict." *African Affairs* 110, no. 440 (2011): 339–66. doi:10.1093/afraf/adr019.

Molina, Marta. "In Guatemala, A Long Road to Justice." *World War 4 Report*, June 17, 2013. www.ww4report.com/node/12360.

Morena, Lydia C. H. "Affecting Violence: Narratives of Los Feminicidios and Their Ethical and Political Reception." PhD diss., University of Texas at Austin, 2012. http://repositories.lib.utexas.edu/bitstream/handle/2152/19473 /HUERTAMORENO-DISSERTATION-2012.pdf?sequence=1.

Morgan, Robin. *The Demon Lover: The Roots of Terrorism*. New York: Washington Square Press, 2001.

Morrow, John H., Jr. Review of *Taken by Force: Rape and American GIs in Europe During World War II*, by Robert Lilly. *Journal of Military History* 72, no. 4 (2008): 1324.http://muse.jhu.edu/journals/jmh/summary/v072/72.4.morrow .html.

Mukhashaf, Mohammed and Angus McDowall. "Yemeni Troops Advance; Donors Pledge $4 Bln Aid." *Reuters*, May 23, 2012. www.reuters.com/article/2012/05/23/ us-yemen-idUSBRE84M13020120523.

Murray, Christopher J. L. and Alan D. Lopez, eds. *The Global Burden of Disease: A Comprehensive Assessment of Mortality and Disability from Diseases, Injuries, and Risk Factors in 1990 and Projected to 2020*. Cambridge, Mass.: Harvard University Press, 1996.

Myers, Steven L. "Clinton Adds Her Voice in Support of Saudi Women." *New York Times*, June 21, 2011. www.nytimes.com/2011/06/22/world/middleeast/22clinton.html.

——. "Hillary Clinton's Last Tour as a Rock-Star Diplomat." *New York Times*, June 27, 2012. www.nytimes.com/2012/07/01/magazine/hillary-clintons-last-tour-as -a-rock-star-diplomat.html.

Nairn, Allan. "Ríos Montt Guilty of Genocide: Are Guatemalan President Pérez Molina, U.S. Officials Next?" Transcript and MPEG-4 video, 47:14. *Democracy Now*, May 13, 2013. www.democracynow.org/2013/5/13/ros_montt_guilty_of _genocide_are.

Natsios, Andrew. "The Clash of the Counter-Bureaucracy and Development." *Center for Global Development*, revised July 13, 2010, 1–49. www.cgdev.org /publication/clash-counter-bureaucracy-and-development.

——. "The Foreign Aid Reform Agenda." *Foreign Service Journal*, December 2008: 34–38.

——. "Time Lag and Sequencing Dilemmas of Postconflict Reconstruction." *Institute for National Strategic Studies* 1, no. 1 (2009): 63–76.

Nelson, Alyse. *Vital Voices: The Power of Women Leading Change Around the World*. San Francisco: Jossey-Bass, 2012.

Nobel Women's Initiative and Just Associates. *From Survivors to Defenders: Women Confronting Violence in Mexico, Honduras, and Guatemala*. NWI Delegation report, June 5, 2012. http://nobelwomensinitiative.org/2012/06/from-survivors -to-defenders-women-confronting-violence-in-mexico-honduras-and-guatemala.

Nordberg, Jenny. *The Underground Girls of Kabul*. New York: Crown Publishers, 2014.

Nordland, Rod. "Peace Effort with Taliban Is Excluding Women, Report Says." *New York Times*. November 24, 2014. http://www.nytimes.com/2014/11/25/world /asia/afghan-women-excluded-from-peace-overtures-to-taliban-oxfam-says.html.

——. "Top Afghans Tied to '90s Carnage, Researchers Say." *New York Times*, July 12, 2012. www.nytimes.com/2012/07/23/world/asia/key-afghans-tied-to -mass-killings-in-90s-civil-war.html.

North, Douglass C., John J Wallis, and Barry R. Weingast. *Violence and Social Orders: A Conceptual Framework for Interpreting Recorded Human History*. New York: Cambridge University Press, 2009.

"NY Times Notices That 'Hawkish Sites' Have 'Taken Up Feminism.'" *Jihad Watch*, August 25, 2009. www.jihadwatch.org/2009/08/ny-times-notices-that-hawkish -sites-have-taken-up-feminism.html.

Oates, Lauryn. "The Mother of All Problems: Female Literacy in Afghanistan." *Guardian*, June 21, 2013. www.theguardian.com/global-development -professionals-network/2013/jun/21/funding-education-in-afghanistan.

O'Kane, Maggie. "The Mistake of Being Muslim." *Guardian Weekly*, March 28, 1993.

Okin, Susan M. "Inequalities Between the Sexes in Different Cultural Contexts." In *Women, Culture, and Development: A Study of Human Capabilities*, ed. Martha Nussbaum and Jonathan Glover, 426–32. Oxford: Clarendon Press, 1995.

Olsson, Louise and Johen Tejpar, eds. *Operational Effectiveness and UN Resolution 1325—Practices and Lessons from Afghanistan*. Stockholm: Stockholm FOI, May 2009. www.peacewomen.org/assets/file/Resources/NGO/1325 _PracticeLessonsAfghanistan_SDRA_May2009.pdf.

Orlinsky, Katie. "Mexico's Female Vigilante Squads." *Daily Beast*, October 5, 2013. www.thedailybeast.com/witw/articles/2013/10/05/mexico-s-female-vigilantes -take-justice-and-safety-into-their-own-hands.html.

"Osama Bin Laden: A Chronology of His Political Life." *Frontline*, n.d. www.pbs .org/wgbh/pages/frontline/shows/binladen/etc/cron.html.

Oster, Emily. "Hepatitis B and the Case of the Missing Women." *Journal of Political Economy* 113, no. 6 (2005): 1163–1216.

"Oxfam in Yemen." *Oxfam*, n.d. www.oxfam.org.uk/what-we-do/countries-we-work -in/yemen.

Pande, Aru. "Activists Urge NATO to Protect Afghan Women's Rights." *Voice of America*, May 20, 2012. www.voanews.com/content/activists-urge-nato-to -protect-afghan-womens-rights/727483.html.

Paniagua, Daniela. "Ciudad Juárez: An Untold History of Femicide and Violence in the Western Hemisphere." *Examiner*, March 20, 2010. www.examiner.com /article/ciudad-ju-rez-an-untold-history-of-femicide-and-violence-the-western- hemisphere.

Papanek, Hanna. "To Each Less Than She Needs, From Each More Than She Can Do: Allocations, Entitlements, and Value." In *Persistent Inequalities: Women and World Development*, ed. Irene Tinker, 162–81. New York: Oxford University Press, 1994.

Pastrana, Daniela. "Mexican Women March for Rights, Mourn Slain Activists." *Inter Press Service*, April 12, 2011. www.ipsnews.net/2011/04/mexican-women -march-for-rights-mourn-slain-activists.

Paterson, Kent. "Femicide on the Rise in Latin America." *Global Politician*, March 10, 2006. www.globalpolitician.com/default.asp?21654-latin-america-feminism.

Pearlman, Alex. "How the Department of Defense Is Using Big Data to Combat Sex Trafficking. *Global Post*. November 19, 2014. www.globalpost.com /dispatches/globalpost-blogs/rights/dod-darpa-using-big-data-combat-sex -trafficking.

Pelosi, Nancy. Letter to the editor. *New York Times*, August 18, 1995. www.nytimes. com/1995/08/18/opinion/l-mrs-clinton-should-sit-out-beijing-meeting-975695 .html.

Perez D., Sonia. "Otto Perez Molina, Former General, Wins Guatemala Presidential Elections." *Huffington Post*, November 7, 2011. www.huffingtonpost .com/2011/11/07/otto-perez-molina-guatemala_n_1079366.html.

Perry, Elizabeth. *Rebels and Revolutionaries in North China, 1845–1945*. Stanford, Calif.: Stanford University Press, 1980.

Peterson, V. Spike. "Gendered National: Reproducing 'Us' Versus 'Them.' " In *The Women and War Reader*, ed. L.A. Lorentzen and J. Turpin, 41–49. New York: New York University Press, 1998.

——. *Gendered States: Feminist (Re)Visions of International Relations Theory*. Boulder, Colo.: Lynne Rienner, 1992.

Pettman, Jan J. *Worlding Women: A Feminist International Politics*. New York: Routledge, 1996.

Physicians for Human Rights. *The Taliban's War on Women: A Health and Human Rights Crisis in Afghanistan*. Boston: Physicians for Human Rights, 1998.

Pinker, Steven. *The Better Angels of Our Nature: Why Violence Has Declined*. New York: Viking Books, 2011.

"'Pipelines' and 'Burn Rates.'" *NGOConnect eNews*, March 2009. www. ngoconnect.net/documents/592341/749044/Financial+Management ++Pipelines+%26+Burn+Rates.

Poston, Dudley L., Jr., Eugenia Conde, and Bethany DeSalvo. "China's Unbalanced Sex Ratio at Birth, Millions of Excess Bachelors and Societal Implications." *Vulnerable Children and Youth Studies* 6, no. 4 (2011): 314–20.

Price, John. "The Kingdom of Saudi Arabia—Wahhabism and Oil Exports." *John Price: Former U.S. Ambassador* (blog), May 30, 2012. www.ambassadorjohnprice .com/the-kingdom-of-saudi-arabia-wahhabism-and-oil-exports/1925.

Proyecto Interdiocesano de Recuperación de la Memoria Histórica (REMHI). "Botín de Guerra." In *Guatemala: Nunca Mas*, chap. 5. Report published online by the Office of Human Rights of the Archbishop of Guatemala, April 24, 1998. www.odhag.org.gt/html/Default.htm.

Purdum, Todd S. "Hard Choice for White House on Hillary Clinton and China." *New York Times*, August 17, 1995. www.nytimes.com/1995/08/17/world/hard-choice-for-white-house-on-hillary-clinton-and-china.html.

——. "Hillary Clinton Discovers A New Role." *New York Times*, April 6, 1995. www.nytimes.com/1995/04/06/world/hillary-clinton-discovers-a-new-role.html.

——. "March 26–April 1; On the Road in Hillaryland." *New York Times*, April 2, 1995. www.nytimes.com/1995/04/02/weekinreview/march-26-april-1-on-the-road-in-hillaryland.html.

Quinn, Ben. "Ikea Apologises over Removal of Women from Saudi Arabia Catalogue." *Guardian*, October 1, 2012. www.theguardian.com/world/2012/oct/02/ikea-apologises-removing-women-saudi-arabia-catalogue.

Ramos, Joshua. "Demographics as Destiny: Globalization and the Resurgence of Religion Through Fertility." *Journal for Cultural and Religious Theory* 12, no. 3 (2013): 125–39.

Raymond, Gregory A. "International Norms: Normative Orders and Peace." In *What Do We Know About War*, ed. J.A. Vasquez, 281–97. New York: Rowman & Littlefield, 2000.

Reardon, Betty A. *Sexism and the War System*. New York: Teachers College Press, 1985.

Reynolds, Louisa. "Femicide Courts in Guatemala: A Beacon of Light in Fight Against Impunity." *UpsideDown World*, April 7, 2014. http://upsidedownworld.org/main/news-briefs-archives-68/4785-femicide-courts-in-guatemala-a-beacon-of-light-in-the-fight-against-impunity.

Rhem, Kathleen T. "Women's Rights a Priority; Humanitarian Aid Improves." *American Forces Press Services*, November 19, 2001. www.defense.gov/News/NewsArticle.aspx?ID=44432.

Richards, Lisa. "Sexual Slavery and Jihadist Breeding Camps: Women in the World of Bin Laden." *News Real Blog*, May 19, 2011. www.newsrealblog.com/category/feminism.

Richmond, Matt and Flavia Krause-Jackson. "Cows-for-Bride Inflation Spurs Cattle Theft Among Mundari in South Sudan." *Bloomberg*, July 25, 2011. www.bloomberg.com/news/2011-07-26/cows-for-bride-inflation-spurs-cattle-theft-among-mundari-in-south-sudan.html.

Riding, Alan. "Rights Forum Ends in Call for A Greater Role by U.N." *New York Times*, June 26, 1993. www.nytimes.com/1993/06/26/world/rights-forum-ends-in-call-for-a-greater-role-by-un.html.

Riley, Robin L., Chandra T. Mohanty, and Minni B. Pratt, eds. *Feminism and War: Confronting US Imperialism*. New York: Zed Books, 2008.

"Rios Montt, Guatemalan Dictator from Humble Start." *Agence France-Presse*, May 11, 2013. www.globalpost.com/dispatch/news/afp/130511/rios-montt-guatemalan -dictator-humble-start.

Robert F. Kennedy Center for Justice and Human Rights. "Guatemala: Rigoberta Menchú Tum," n.d. Biography and interview. http://rfkcenter.org/rigoberta-menchu-tum-2.

Robin, Corey. "Ronald Reagan: Effraín Ríos Montt Is 'Totally Dedicated to Democracy.'" *Crooked Timber*, May 11, 2013. http://crookedtimber.org/2013/05/11 /ronald-reagan-efrain-rios-montt-is-totally-dedicated-to-democracy.

Roby, Martha and Niki Tsongas. "Afghan Women Worry as the U.S. Departure Looms." *Wall Street Journal*, July 11, 2013. http://online.wsj.com/news/articles /SB10001424127887323336870457859637174808748.

Rohde, David. "All Successful Democracies Need Freedom of Speech: American Efforts to Create a Vibrant Free Press in Iraq and Afghanistan." Working Paper Series #2005-6, Joan Shorenstein Center on the Press, Politics, and Public Policy, spring 2005.

Rosenberg, Matthew and Rod Nordland. "Afghan Presidential Hopefuls Are Told to Leave Guns at Home." *New York Times*, October 6, 2013. www.nytimes. com/2013/10/07/world/asia/warning-to-aspiring-afghan-presidential-candidates -leave-the-guns-at-home.html.

Rosenthal, Elisabeth. "Women's Suicides Reveal Rural China's Bitter Roots." *New York Times*, January 24, 1999. www.nytimes.com/1999/01/24/world/women-s -suicides-reveal-rural-china-s-bitter-roots.html?pagewanted=all&src=pm.

Rothkopf, David. "The Balance of Power: Why Sexism Is Civilization's Greatest Shame." *Foreign Policy*, May/June 2013. www.foreignpolicy.com/articles/2013/04/29/the _balance_of_power.

Rubin, Michael. "Hillary Clinton's Legacy." *Commentary*, July 17, 2013. www.commentary -magazine.com/2012/07/17/hillary-clinton-legacy.

Ruddick, Sara. *Maternal Thinking: Toward a Politics of Peace*. Boston: Beacon Press, 1995.

Ruiz, Eduardo C. "Mexico's Cancer: Domestic Violence, A Virtual License to Kill." *Yucatan Times*, August 17, 2011. www.theyucatantimes.com/2011/08/mexicos -cancer-domestic-violence-a-virtual-license-to-kill.

Ruiz-Goiriena, Romina. "Rights Groups Fear Marines in Guatemala." *Marine Corps Times*, September 1, 2012. www.marinecorpstimes.com/article/20120901 /NEWS/209010305/Rights-groups-fear-Marines-Guatemala.

Salama, Vivian. "Abdullah Saleh: Yemen's Unsackable Leader." *Daily Beast*, February 25, 2013. www.thedailybeast.com/articles/2013/02/25/abdullah-saleh-yemen-s -unsackable-leader.html.

Sanford, Victoria. *Buried Secrets: Truth and Human Rights in Guatemala*. New York: Palgrave Macmillan, 2003.

——. "Victory in Guatemala? Not Yet." *New York Times*, May 13, 2013. www.nytimes .com/2013/05/14/opinion/its-too-soon-to-declare-victory-in-guatemalan-genocide .html.

Sanger, David E. "Wako Journal; History Scholar in Japan Exposes a Brutal Chapter." *New York Times*, January 27, 1992. www.nytimes.com/1992/01/27/world/wako-journal-history-scholar-in-japan-exposes-a-brutal-chapter.html.

"Saudi Arabia Eases Ban on Women Riding Bikes." *Al Jazeera*, last modified April 2, 2013. www.aljazeera.com/news/middleeast/2013/04/2013428030514192.html.

"Saudi Arabia Is 'World's Largest Women's Prison.'" *Siasat Daily*, May 29, 2011. www.siasat.com/english/news/saudi-arabia-world's-largest-women's-prison.

"Saudi Arabia (Majlis Ash-Shura): General Information About the Parliament." *Inter-Parliamentary Union*, last updated August 22, 2013. www.ipu.org/parline-e/reports/2373_A.htm.

"Saudi Arabia Must Decide on Women Drivers: Kerry." *Channel NewsAsia*, November 5, 2013. www.channelnewsasia.com/news/world/saudi-arabia-must-decide/874378.html.

"Saudi Police 'Stopped' Fire Rescue." *BBC*, March 15, 2002. http://news.bbc.co.uk/2/hi/1874471.stm.

Sauer, Jen. "Fighting Femicide in Guatemala." *Off Our Backs* 35, no. 3/4 (2005): 36.

Schonhardt, Sara. "Indonesian Women Told How to Ride Motorbikes." *New York Times*, January 14, 2013. www.nytimes.com/2013/01/15/world/asia/indonesian-city-plans-to-ban-women-from-straddling-motorbikes.html.

"Sec. Clinton Repeats Her Strong Opposition to Forced Abortion and Sterilization in China." YouTube video, 1:35. From a CSPAN recording of a 2009 hearing. Posted by "RH Reality Check RHRC," April 23, 2009. http://youtu.be/jDnpl6qo8vo.

"Sec. Kerry, Hillary Clinton, Laura Bush Advocate For Afghan Women's 'Hard-Fought Gains.'" Discussion at Georgetown Institute for Women, Peace and Security, Washington, D.C., November 15, 2013. www.georgetown.edu/news/afghan-women-symposium.html.

Seelke, Clare R. *Trafficking in Persons in Latin America and the Caribbean*. Congressional Research Service, July 15, 2013. www.fas.org/sgp/crs/row/RL33200.pdf.

Semlali, Amina. "Yemen's Women Make Their Voices Heard from Revolution to Constitution." *World Bank*, May 13, 2013. http://menablog.worldbank.org/yemens-women-make-their-voices-heard-revolution-constitution.

Sethna, Razeshta. "Afghan Women's Rights Under Threat." *Guardian*, June 20, 2013. www.theguardian.com/global-development/2013/jun/20/afghan-womens-rights-under-threat.

"Sharp Increase in Domestic Violence." *Stockholm News*, July 8, 2010. www.stockholm-news.com/more.aspx?NID=5609.

Sharp, Robert and Fahad Malaikah. "Yemen: A U.S. Strategic Partner?" *Small Wars Journal*, March 14, 2012. http://smallwarsjournal.com/jrnl/art/yemen-a-us-strategic-partner.

Shear, Michael D. "Obama Ends Overseas Trip with Award for Saudi." *New York Times*, March 29, 2014. www.nytimes.com/2014/03/30/world/middleeast/obama-saudi-arabia.html.

Sheehy, Gal. *Hillary's Choice*. New York: Random House, 1999.

Sheffer, Joe. "Yemen's Youngest Divorcee Says Father Has Squandered Cash from Her Book." *Guardian*. March 12, 2013. www.theguardian.com/world/2013/mar/12/child-bride-father-cash-spend.

"Shenzhen's Newborn Sex Ratio More Balanced." *People's Daily Online*, last updated April 15, 2005. http://english.people.com.cn/200504/15/eng20050415_181218.html.

Shoichet, Catherine E. "Mexico Reports More Than 26,000 Missing." *CNN*, February 27, 2013. www.cnn.com/2013/02/26/world/americas/mexico-disappeared/index.html.

Simons, Marlise. "U.N. Court, for First Time, Defines Rape as War Crime." *New York Times*, June 28, 1996. www.nytimes.com/1996/06/28/world/un-court-for-first-time-defines-rape-as-war-crime.html.

Simpson, Glenn R. "List of Early al Qaeda Donors Points to Saudi Elite, Charities." *Wall Street Journal*, March 18, 2013. www67.homepage.villanova.edu/andrew.gasperi/article%204.htm.

Slaughter, Anne-Marie. "How to Halt the Butchery in Syria." *New York Times*, February 23, 2013. www.nytimes.com/2012/02/24/opinion/how-to-halt-the-butchery-in-syria.html.

"Sleeping with the Devil: How U.S. and Saudi Backing of Al Qaeda Led to 9/11." *Washington's Blog* (blog), *Global Research*. September 5, 2012. www.global-research.ca/sleeping-with-the-devil-how-u-s-and-saudi-backing-of-al-qaeda-led-to-911/5303313.

Smuts, Barbara B. "The Evolutionary Origins of Patriarchy." *Human Nature* 6, no. 1 (1995): 1–35.

Sobek, David, M. Rodwan Abouhard, and Christopher G. Ingram. "The Human Rights Peace: How the Respect for Human Rights at Home Leads to Peace Abroad." *Journal of Politics* 68, no. 3 (2006): 519–29.

Special Inspector General for Afghanistan Reconstruction (SIGAR). *Quarterly Report to the United States Congress*, July 30, 2013. www.sigar.mil/pdf/quarterlyreports/2013-07-30qr.pdf.

Spillius, Alex. "WikiLeaks: Saudis 'Chief Funders of al-Qaeda.'" *Telegraph*, December 5, 2010. www.telegraph.co.uk/news/worldnews/wikileaks/8182847/Wikileaks-Saudis-chief-funders-of-al-Qaeda.html.

Stanford, Peter. "Women's Rights Campaigner Warns of Islamists Behind Yemen Uprising." *Daily Beast*, October 2, 2011. www.theguardian.com/world/2011/oct/02/womens-rights-islamist-yemen-uprising.

Starkey, Jerome. "Law Will Let Afghan Husbands Starve Wives Who Withhold Sex." *Independent*, July 10, 2009. www.independent.co.uk/news/world/asia/law-will-let-afghan-husbands-starve-wives-who-withhold-sex-1740229.html.

Steele, Ronald. *Walter Lippmann and the American Century*. New York: Vintage Books, 1980.

Steinberg, Donald. "USAID's Steinberg on Empowering Women Globally." Speech at USAID, Washington, D.C., January 28, 2013. http://iipdigital.usembassy.gov /st/english/texttrans/2013/01/20130123141334.html#ixzz2jDpFopnj.

Stephens, Joe and David B. Ottaway. "From USA, the ABC's of Jihad: Violent Soviet-Era Textbooks Complicate Afghan Education Efforts." *Washington Post*, March 23, 2002. A1.

Stojsavljevic, Jovanka. "Women, Conflict, and Culture in Former Yugoslavia." *Gender and Development* 3, no. 1 (1995): 36–41.

"Subjugation of Women Is Threat to US Security: Clinton." *Agence France-Presse*, March 12, 2010. www.google.com/hostednews/afp/article/ALeqM5ib71t2 -EuWmwDahxNKDaHxcEbfcYA.

Sylvester, Christina. *Feminist International Relations: An Unfinished Journey*. Cambridge: Cambridge University Press, 2001.

——. *Feminist Theory and International Relations in a Postmodern Era*. New York: Cambridge University Press, 1994.

——. "'Progress' as a Feminist International Relations." In *Critical Perspectives in International Studies*, ed. Frank P. Harvey and Michael Brecher, 178–88. Ann Arbor: University of Michigan Press, 2002.

Tavernise, Sobrina. "Broaching Birth Control with Afghan Mullahs." *New York Times*, November 14, 2009. www.nytimes.com/2009/11/15/world/asia/15mazar.html.

Taylor, Alan. "Rising Protests in China." *Atlantic*, February 17, 2012. www.theatlantic .com/infocus/2012/02/rising-protests-in-china/100247.

Taylor, Lena C. "Legislatively Speaking—Women at the Tables of Power Leads to More Sustainable Peace." *Milwaukee Courier*, October 12, 2013. http://milwaukee -courieronline.com/index.php/2013/10/12/legislatively-speaking-women-at-the -tables-of-power-leads-to-more-sustainable-peace.

Taylor, Rob and Folad Hamdard. "Taliban-Style Edict for Women Spreads Alarm in Afghan District." *Reuters*, July 20, 2013. www.reuters.com/article/2013/07/20 /us-afghanistan-edict-idUSBRE96J02220130720.

Tax, Meredith. "Can Afghan Women Count on Hillary Clinton?" *Guardian*, July 4, 2011. www.theguardian.com/commentisfree/cifamerica/2011/jul/04/women -afghanistan-taliban-clinton.

Tessler, Mark and Ina Warriner. "Gender, Feminism, and Attitudes Toward International Conflict: Exploring Relationships with Survey Data from the Middle East." *World Politics* 49, no. 2 (1997), 250–81.

Tétreault, Mary Ann. "Justice for All: Wartime Rape and Women's Human Rights." *Global Governance* 3, no. 2 (1997): 197–212. www.jstor.org/stable/27800163.

Thayer, Bradley. *Darwin and International Relations: On the Evolutionary Origins of War and Ethnic Conflict*. Lexington: University Press of Kentucky, 2004.

Thompson, Ginger and Gary Cohn. "Canada Moves to Expel Honduran Torture Figure." *Baltimore Sun*, July 12, 1995. http://articles.baltimoresun.com/1995 -07-12/news/1995193003_1_battalion-honduran-government-tortured.

Thomson, Marilyn. "Guatemala: Region's Highest Rate of Femicide." *Latin America Bureau*, March 27, 2013. http://lab.org.uk/guatemala-regions-highest -rate-of-murder-of-women.

Tickner, J. Ann. *Gender in International Relations*. New York: Columbia University Press, 1992.

——. *Gendering World Politics*. New York: Columbia University Press, 2001.

——. "Hans Morgenthau's Principles of Political Realism: A Feminist Reformulation." *Millennium: Journal of International Studies* 17, no. 3 (1998): 429–40. doi: 10.1177/03058298880170030801.

Toosi, Nahal. "'I Wasn't Tortured. But I Wasn't Free': Afghan Lawmaker Recounts Her Time in Taliban Captivity." *Associated Press*, September 21, 2013. www. freenewspos.com/news/article/d/140385/13%202013/i-wasn-t-tortured-but -i-wasn-t-free-afghan-lawmaker-recounts-her-time-in-captivity.

Tran, Mark. "Guatemala: One Woman's Campaign Against Violent Crime and Corruption." *Guardian*, October 8, 2013. www.theguardian.com/global-development/2013/oct/08/guatemala-violent-crime-claudia-paz-y-paz.

U.N. Children's Fund (UNICEF). *Behind Closed Doors: The Impact of Domestic Violence on Children*. Report prepared by Child Protection Section of UNICEF, 2006. www.unicef.org/protection/files/BehindClosedDoors.pdf.

——. "Yemen Statistics." Last updated February 24, 2003. www.unicef.org/infobycountry /yemen_statistics.html.

U.N. Development Programme. "Saudi Arabia." In *Human Development Report 2013: The Rise of the South: Human Progress in a Diverse World*. 2013. http://hdr.undp.org/sites/default/files/reports/14/hdr2013_en_complete.pdf.

U.N. Food and Agriculture Organization. *The State of Food and Agriculture 2010– 2011: Women in Agriculture: Closing the Gap for Development*. 2011. www.fao .org/docrep/013/i2050e/i2050e.pdf.

"U.N. High Commissioner for Human Rights Delivers 2013 Bram Fischer Lecture." The Rhodes Trust, Rhodes House, Oxford, February 14, 2013. www.rhodeshouse .ox.ac.uk/news/2013-bram-fischer-lecture.

U.N. Peacekeeping. "Gender Statistics." Last modified October 2013. www.un.org /en/peacekeeping/resources/statistics/gender.shtml.

U.N. Security Council. "Resolution 1325 (2000)." October 31, 2000. http://daccess -dds-ny.un.org/doc/UNDOC/GEN/N00/720/18/PDF/N0072018.pdf.

——. "Statement by President of the Security Council." Presidential Statement 2004/40, October 28, 2004. www.un.org/womenwatch/ods/S-PRST-2004-40-E.pdf.

——. "Statement by President of the Security Council." Presidential Statement 2005/52, October 27, 2005. www.un.org/womenwatch/ods/S-PRST-2005-52-E.pdf.

"U.N. Whistleblower Promoted." *Government Accountability Project*, March 25, 2005. www.whistleblower.org/press/press-release-archive/2005/1227-un-whistleblower -promoted.

U.S. Agency for International Development (USAID). *Gender Equality and Female Empowerment Policy*. Washington, D.C.: USAID, March 2012.

——. *Integrating Gender Equality and Female Empowerment in USAID's Program Cycle*. Washington, D.C.: USAID, July 2013. www.usaid.gov/sites/default/files /documents/1870/205.pdf.

——. "Promoting Gender Equality in National Priority Programs (PROMOTE)." www.fbo.gov/?s=opportunity&mode=form&id=17a9531dfa7d35ca6a30d6b303 c7433b&tab=core&_cview=0.

——. "Strengthening Women's Rights and Political Participation." Last updated August 13, 2012. www.usaid.gov/what-we-do/gender-equality-and-womens -empowerment/addressing-gender-programming/strengthening-womens.

——. *United States Strategy to Prevent and Respond to Gender-Based Violence Globally*. Washington, D.C.: USAID, August 2012.

"U.S. Army School of the Americas Frequently Asked Questions." April 28, 1999. http://web.archive.org/web/19990428095558/www.benning.army.mil/usarsa /FAQ/FAQ.htm.

U.S. Department of State. Bureau of Democracy, Human Rights, and Labor. "2011 Human Rights Reports: Guatemala." In *2011 Country Reports on Human Rights Practices*. May 24, 2012. www.state.gov/j/drl/rls/hrrpt/2011/wha/186518.htm#.

——. Bureau of Democracy, Human Rights, and Labor. *The Taliban's War Against Women*. November 17, 2001. www.state.gov/j/drl/rls/6185.htm.

——. Bureau of Diplomatic Security. *Guatemala 2012 Crime and Safety Report*. May 11, 2012. www.osac.gov/Pages/ContentReportDetails.aspx?cid=12153.

——. Bureau of International Narcotics and Law Enforcement. "Afghanistan Program Overview." www.state.gov/j/inl/narc/c27187.htm#women.

——. Bureau of International Organization Affairs and Bureau of International Information Programs. *Working for Women, Worldwide: The U.S. Commitment*. 2005. http://guangzhou.usembassy-china.org.cn/uploads/images /86Fbfpz9SZLHZ3v7tYdVBg/women.pdf.

——. Office of Global Women's Issues. "Fact Sheet: Promoting Gender Equality to Achieve Our National Security and Foreign Policy Objectives." March 27, 2012. www.state.gov/s/gwi/rls/other/2012/187001.htm.

U.S. Department of State and U.S. Agency for International Development. *Leading Through Civilian Power: The First Quadrennial Diplomacy and Development Review*. Washington, D.C.: U.S. Department of State, 2010. www.state .gov/documents/organization/153108.pdf.

"U.S. Secretary of State Hillary Clinton on Women's Issues." YouTube video, 2:04. From a CBC interview of Clinton by George Stroumboulopoulos. Posted by "TheHour," March 30, 2010. http://youtu.be/5oLgzHnzN5o.

Valdez, Diana W. and Aileen B. Flores. "Court Blasts Mexico for Juarez Women's Murders." *El Paso Times*, December 12, 2010. www.elpasotimes.com/news /ci_13981319.

Valencia, Nick and Arturo Chacon. "Juarez Shedding Violent Image, Statistics Show." *CNN*, January 5, 2013. www.cnn.com/2013/01/05/world/americas /mexico-juarez-killings-drop.

Valladares, Danilo. "Guatemala Heeds the Cries of Femicide Victims." *Inter Press Service*, January 21, 2012. www.ipsnews.net/2012/01/guatemala-heeds -the-cries-of-femicide-victims.

——. "Guatemala: Women-Only Buses Against Sexual Harassment." *Inter Press Service*, June 24, 2011. www.ipsnews.net/2011/06/guatemala-women-only -buses-against-sexual-harassment.

Van Auken, Bill. "Guatemalan High Court Upholds Overturning of Rios Montt Conviction." *World Socialist Web Site*, May 30, 2013. www.wsws.org/en /articles/2013/05/30/rios-m30.html.

Virk, Zakaria. "Why Old Saudi Men Are Marrying Syrian Teenage Refugee Girls." *Muslim Times*, March 24, 2013. /www.themuslimtimes.org/2013/03/countries /syria/why-old-saudi-men-buying-syrian-teenage-refugee-girls.

Weisfeld-Adams, Emma. "Factsheet: Women Farmers and Food Security." *Hunger Project*, September 21, 2008. www.thp.org/learn_more/speeches_reports /research/factsheet_on_women_farmers.

Wendle, John. "The Aisha Bibi Case: Her Father Wants to Petition the Taliban for Justice." *Time*. July 14, 2011. http://content.time.com/time/world/article /0,8599,2082912,00.html.

Wheaton, Sarah. "A Question of How Women's Issues Will Fare, in Washington and Overseas." *New York Times*, August 22, 2013. www.nytimes.com/2013/08/23/us /politics/a-question-of-how-womens-issues-will-fare-in-washington-and -overseas.html.

Whitworth, Sandra. *Men, Militarism, and UN Peacekeeping*. Boulder, Colo.: Lynne Rienner, 2004.

"Why Secretary Clinton Can't Mention Femicide in Juarez, Mexican Bordertowns." *BraveHeart Women* (blog), March 23, 2010. www.braveheartwomen.com /blog-entry/Ulyssas-Blog/Secretary-Clinton-Mention/13000046525.

Winsor, Curtin. "Saudi Arabia, Wahhabism, and the Spread of Sunni Theofascism." *Global Politician*, October 22, 2007. www.globalpolitician.com/print .asp?id=3661.

Winter, Michael. "Air Force Academy to Get First Female Leader." *USA Today*, March 1, 2013. www.usatoday.com/story/news/nation/2013/03/01/air-force -academy-first-woman-superintendent/1958107.

Wisniewski, Dan. "Kabul Urged to Protect Sexually Abused Children." *Radio Free Europe Radio Liberty*, February 11, 2013. www.rferl.org/content/afghanistan -boy-rape-victim/24899130.html.

WomanStats Project. "The High Rape-Scale in Saudi Arabia." *WomanStats Project Blog*, January 16, 2013. http://womanstats.wordpress.com/2013/01/16/the-high-rape-scale-in-saudi-arabia.

World Bank. *World Development Report 2012: Gender Equality and Development*. Washington, D.C.: World Bank, 2012. http://siteresources.worldbank.org/INTWDR2012/Resources/7778105-1299699968583/7786210-1315936222006/Complete-Report.pdf.

Wrangham, Richard and Dale Peterson. *Demonic Males: Apes and the Origins of Human Violence*. New York: Houghton Mifflin, 1996.

Yerman, Marcia G. "Women in the World Summit 2012." *Huffington Post*, March 16, 2012. www.huffingtonpost.com/marcia-g-yerman/women-in-the-world-summit_b_1349638.html.

Young, Iris M. "The Logic of Masculinist Protection: Reflections on the Current Security State." *Women and Citizenship* 29, no. 1 (2003). doi: http://dx.doi.org/10.1093/0195175344.003.0002.

Zabludovsky, Karla. "Doctor's Bath for Corpses Reinvigorates Cold Cases." *New York Times*, October 15, 2012. www.nytimes.com/2012/10/16/world/americas/mexican-doctors-bath-for-corpses-reinvigorates-cold-cases.html.

Zakaria, Fareed. "Zakaria: The Saudis Are Mad? Tough!" *Time*, November 11, 2013. http://content.time.com/time/magazine/article/0,9171,2156259,00.html.

Zalewski, Marysia and Jane Papart, eds. *The "Man" Question in International Relations*. Boulder, Colo.: Lynne Rienner, 1998.

Zarkov, Dubravka. *The Body of War: Media, Ethnicity, and Gender in the Break-Up of Yugoslavia*. Durham, N.C.: Duke University Press, 2007.

Zenko, Micah. "City of Men." *Foreign Policy*, July 14, 2011. www.foreignpolicy.com/articles/2011/07/14/city_of_men.

Zunes, Stephen. "Hillary Clinton on International Law." *Foreign Policy in Focus*, December 10, 2007. http://fpif.org/hillary_clinton_on_international_law.

# INDEX